Larson's New Book of Cults

D0972656

LARSON'S *New* BOOK OF CULTS

BOB LARSON

Tyndale House
Publishers, Inc.
Wheaton, Illinois

Unless otherwise indicated, Scripture quotations
are from the King James Version of the Bible.

Library of Congress Catalog Card Number 89-50922
ISBN 0-8423-2662-2, cloth
ISBN 0-8423-2860-2, paper
Copyright 1982 by Bob Larson
Revised edition copyright 1989 by Bob Larson
Printed in the United States of America

1 2 3 4 5 6 7 8 9 10 95 94 93 92 91 90 89

C O N T E N T S

PART ONE

AN

INTRODUCTION

TO

CULTS

· 1 ·

DRINKING

AT THE

FOUNTAIN

It was only five-thirty in the morning, but I had already been up over an hour. Most people rise early in Banaras, India, the Hindu "holy city." Each day more than one-half million spring from bed long before sunrise. Their trek to the shores of the river Ganges, the most sacred river in all Hinduism, must be completed before the tip of that glowing orb lifts above the eastern horizon.

Most of them carry buckets or vials — some kind of container — to ferry Ganges water back to their homes. The Ganges provides thousands of Banaras residents with their only source of water for drinking and bathing. Never mind that its putrid flow is spiked with human excrement and the carcasses of dead cattle. When its journey begins, high in the Himalayas, Ganges water may be pristine. But by the time it reaches the plains of Banaras, its translucent stream has turned into a murky green soup of sewage.

Vendors of various religious accessories vie for the attention of the devout Hindus hurrying toward the Ganges. They offer a wide assortment of pious wares. The most popular is a small garland of flowers costing more than these poor people can easily afford. But gaining the favor of the mother goddess of the Ganges is worth almost any price. To the non-Hindu it probably seems absurd. If that small string of petals were to festoon the buyer's neck or grace his home with fragrance, the expenditure might be considered a reasonable investment. But instead of hav-

9

ing some personal value, this small garland is taken to the Ganges and placed in its current to float downstream.

This wasn't the first time I had witnessed the daily Banaras ritual of sun worship. Ten years earlier the mist of the Ganges dawn had beckoned these curious eyes. At the same time, halfway across the Indian subcontinent, a musical group known as the Beatles had also traveled to this land of fables and fakirs. Their journey had taken them to Rishikesh where they chose to meditate at the feet of a bearded swami named Maharishi Mahesh Yogi.

In 1968 the Beatles proclaimed that Transcendental Meditation was the answer to all mankind's distress. Though the advice sounded strange to most Westerners, it wasn't the first time that the "virtues" of Hinduism had been exported beyond the shores of India. Long before the current invasion of mysticism took root in the philosophically sterile milieu of twentieth-century science and technology, the Eastern perspective was hailed as a superior worldview. In 1893 the Parliament of World Religions, held in Chicago, felt the first surge of what was to become a transcendental tidal wave. In praise of the Hinduistic concept of God, theosophists and swamis echoed the endorsement of nineteenth-century luminaries Emerson and Thoreau. (On the shores of Walden Pond, the latter had pored over pages of the *Bhagavad-Gita*.)

American Protestantism was jolted by the message of delegates to the Parliament who declared, "All is one. Man is divine. God is not out there; he is within every man." A seed had been planted, and the pluralism of republican democracy insured that it would grow wherever non-Christian thinking predominated. Mysticism flourished in the fifties beatnik culture of Jack Kerouac, Allen Ginsberg, Herman Hesse, and Alan Watts. With the advent of the flower-powered sixties, psychedelia fostered "religious" experiences that paralleled the introspection of Thoreau and the mystical vision in the *Tibetan Book of the Dead*.

The next step came in the late sixties. Young pop fans who had screamed their lungs breathless at the beguiling Fab Four in Shea Stadium now heard their music idols singing "I am he as you are he as you are me and we are all together" (from "The Walrus"). What did the Beatles mean? Alan Watts and crew smiled knowingly as the Liverpool Foursome went on to sing of "Instant Karma." It was left to George Harrison, after the group split, to erase all doubts about pop music's role in promoting Eastern religions when "My Sweet Lord" chanted praises to the Hindu pantheon.

As preparations were being made for a short boat trip down the Ganges,

I nostalgically surveyed how much Western culture had changed in those ten years. *Yoga, mantras,* and *gurus* had become as American as the proverbial apple pie. And it all began in Banaras. Here was the fountain of all Hinduism (and just up the road a few miles at Sarnath was the birth-place of Buddha and his "enlightenment"). As the boatman leaned against his oars to propel the rickety craft upstream, the first rays of the "sun-god" streaked above the earth's rim.

Devout Hindus streamed down the *ghats* (steps) leading to the water's edge. Small canopies sheltered stationary swamis who watched over the personal belongings of their devotional clients. Watches, exterior cloth-ing, and hand-carried items were placed at their feet for safekeeping while the devotees stripped to the bare essentials and launched out waist-deep into the waters. Worshipers clasped their hands in gestures of prayer as the ritual of dipping and bathing began. Some chanted mantras of praise to the Lord Sun. Others drank profusely from the river. On the banks the more energetic contorted their limbs in yogic postures. Those who arrived early were collecting their containers of Ganges water for the walk home.

Every few feet on the bank a *lingam* (a three-foot-high Hindu phallic symbol of fertility) rose above the *ghats.* The eye of a Westerner couldn't miss either this erotic symbol or the huge culvert pouring refuse into the stream near the spot where thousands performed their ceremonies. To remind these devotees that this outlet dispensed all the sewage of Banaras's 800,000 inhabitants would have been a futile warning. The Ganges is a god, and god is pure and "holy" no matter what the cholera statistics say to the contrary.

Farther upstream the boat passed near the burning *ghats,* the site where devout Hindus are cremated. Every orthodox Hindu wants to die in Banaras. Legend has it that doing so circumvents the endless cycle of reincarnation. Those whose bodies are burned in the "holy city" are freed from transmigrations and are absorbed directly into the Brahman Ab-solute. Only victims of smallpox and other contagious diseases are ex-empted. Fanatical Hindus fear that germs may be reincarnated ancestors; they thus avoid cremation the one time it would be medically advisable. In those cases, the bodies are thrown into the Ganges to pollute its waters in a deathly manner.

Having navigated the two-mile stretch of river rimmed with *ghats,* the oarsman steered toward the original point of departure. For me, the boat ride was a microcosmic reminder of how scenes so shocking a decade earlier were now familiar to the Western mind. What had changed?

Banaras appeared no different with its millennia-old religious rituals. What made Banaras seem less exotic was the extensive incursion such beliefs and practices had made on Western values and life-styles.

As the boat touched shore amidst a flotilla of garlands offered to appease the Ganges goddess, a wail of grief pierced the still morning air. Not far away, an Indian woman writhed in agony at the feet of a six-foot-tall stone idol—Hanuman, the monkey-god. Half human with a monkey's head, the lifeless statue was oblivious to the penitent's desperate pleas. Though her god failed to respond, she persisted in her cry for assistance, pressing herself against its cold limestone legs.

The cause of her desperation was indiscernible to one who couldn't speak Hindi. Even her fellow citizens paid little attention to her hysterical plight. Perhaps their subservience to the fatalistic philosophy of Hinduism dulled their ability to empathize. After all, whatever the source of her distress, the law of *karma* is immutable. If she were suffering, so be it. The will of the gods and the consequences of reaping have no ultimate remedy in this life, or the next. Even Hanuman surely knew that.

Though I couldn't understand her tongue, the grief of her spirit spoke a universal language. As with millions of Americans trapped in the bondage of cults, her petition for help went unheeded. Hinduism, the mother faith of many cults, had no spiritual nourishment to offer her pleading soul. In a word-picture this hungering Indian woman epitomized what the faith of the East has done to the hope of the West.

What struck me as most ironic was the date of this tragic April morning scene. As the pathetic woman sought the assistance of a mongrelized demigod to relieve her crushing burden, it just happened to be Easter Sunday. All around the world, millions of Christians were reaffirming the glorious news, "He is risen!" If this woman could have comprehended those three words in English, I would have rushed to her side with the message of hope in Christ. And if the reader had witnessed the same scene, your desire to share the message of Jesus would undoubtedly have been just as urgent.

Are we also aware that many others involved in cults languish in the same predicament? They kneel at the feet of Joseph Smith, Mary Baker Eddy, Charles and Myrtle Fillmore, Bhagwan Shree Rajneesh, Charles Taze Russell, L. Ron Hubbard, Herbert W. Armstrong, Meher Baba, and scores of others who claim (or claimed) to possess the answer to life's search for truth. Do the unheard and unanswered cries of today's cult adherents stir our spirits with compassion and love?

This book is the most exhausting, challenging, and compelling task

I have ever attempted. During long nights of burning midnight oil and consuming innumerable hours of intensive investigation, the plaintive wail of that Indian woman has been a haunting reminder of the urgency of this mission. It is for her, and for the sake of those who share her slavery, that this book has been carefully researched and prayerfully written.

· 2 ·

WHAT IS
A CULT?

An adequate definition of *cult* evades most people. *Webster's Ninth New Collegiate Dictionary* (1988) states that a cult represents a religious body that is "unorthodox or spurious." It also cites the wider perimeter of "devotion to a great person, idea, or thing," a frame of reference to which this book in part ascribes. Ronald Enroth points out that the origin of the word *cult* can be traced to the Latin *cultus,* which "connotes all that is involved in worship—ritual, emotion, liturgy, and attitude."

In Dr. Walter Martin's book *The Kingdom of the Cults,* Dr. Charles Braden is quoted as saying: "A cult . . . is any religious group which differs significantly in some one or more respects as to belief or practice from those religious groups which are regarded as the normative expression of religion in our total culture." Thus to designate any group as a cult obviously requires a subjective value judgment. Many respectable groups that are admired by society (e.g. Mormons, Baha'is) were considered repugnant and persecuted during their formation. Who is to say which of today's nontraditional eccentrics will be considered socially acceptable in years to come?

These are things that most cults share in common: (1) a centralized authority that tightly structures both philosophy and life-style; (2) a "we" versus "they" complex, pitting the supposed superior insights of the group against a hostile outside culture; (3) a commitment for each member to proselytize intensively the unconverted; and (4) an entrenched isolationism that divorces the devotee from the realities of the world at large.

14

Cultic philosophy is diverse, ranging from the rigidly ascetic to the sexually permissive. In the beginning many groups display sincere expressions of a humble desire to better society and follow God's will. At some point the founder's teachings are codified into an organized system of revelational authority. Allegiance to the founder's ideals becomes an absolute requirement. What may have been one man's honest opinion is then presented as having the weight of divine endorsement. If such a transformation takes place while the leader is still alive, he usually claims supernatural certifications for his beliefs. What then develops is a "type of institutional dogmatism and a pronounced intolerance for any position but their own," according to Dr. Walter Martin.

Though adherents may exhibit certain typical motivational characteristics, attitudes vary from selfish narcissism to abandonment of the ego for communal welfare. The person who seeks out a cult or is ensnared by cult propaganda also fits a composite psychological profile. Conventional solutions and institutions may have struck him as being sterile or unfulfilling. He is looking for an affirming community with which he can identify. Such a group will be all the more appealing if it offers a single, idealistic principle around which his entire life can revolve. In a society that is biblically illiterate, the deception of a cult is particularly enticing if it claims to have "restored" certain truths that have been lost or undiscovered.

Loneliness, indecision, despair, and disappointment are the emotional characteristics cult recruiters notice. They approach the unwary with an excessively friendly invitation to a lecture, free meal, weekend workshop, or other activity offering instant solutions to overwhelming problems. Surprisingly enough, few potential cultists bother to inquire about who is extending the offer, what is behind it, and what functions will take place. Vague answers are seldom challenged, leaving the recruiter an unassailable opportunity to obscure his intentions.

Cults generally attract prospects with an outpouring of attention and affection, the so-called "love-bombing" technique. Feeling, not doctrine, is the lure. In fact, the belief structure is seldom mentioned in the beginning. Cult leaders know that once an initiate has been reconditioned to accept their particular worldview, and as soon as he feels a sense of meaningful belonging, his mind will be ready to accept any teaching, including a belief that the leader represents God.

Approval, acceptance, belonging, authority—all those things that were missing are supplied by the cult. Motivation is generated by rewards for excessive zeal. Critical thinking is discouraged and corporate identification with some larger-than-life mission (as conveyed by the leader) causes the member to equate what is good for the cult as being good for him.

When the recruit's mind shifts into neutral, the period of intensive indoctrination begins. The effectiveness of this tactic is often enhanced by sensory deprivation, extreme amounts of physical activity coupled with fatigue, severance of all ties with family and friends, and the forsaking of all belongings and material possessions. In a short time, the initiate becomes emotionally and spiritually dependent on the cult for decisions, direction, and even the physical necessities of life. The outside world appears more and more threatening. Finally his mind "snaps," and "the sudden, drastic alteration of personality in all its many forms" takes place.

Young adult cult recruits are the least likely to consider thoughts of abandoning the group. Severing the cult-fostered dependency would mean having to cope with hardships and to fend for themselves in a hostile world. Any consideration of leaving immediately conjures guilt feelings of forsaking God's calling, falling into Satan's hands, or even worse, risking the wrath and judgment of God.

Even given the current anticult climate, few targets of the cults see their future as one of involuntary slavery and physical domination. Before joining any exotic sect, one should be aware of what could result: neurosis, psychosis, suicidal tendencies, guilt, identity confusion, paranoia, hallucinations, loss of free will, intellectual sterility, and diminished capacity of judgment. It will be much easier to avoid such consequences by identifying and recognizing the following psychological forms of "cult-coercion."

1. *Absolute loyalty.* Allegiance to the sect is demanded and enforced by actual or veiled threats to one's body or eternal spiritual condition.
2. *Altered diet.* Depriving one of essential nutrients and enforcing a low-protein diet can lead to disorientation and emotional susceptibility.
3. *Chanting and meditation.* Objective intellectual input is avoided by countering anticult questions with repetitious songs and chants.
4. *Conformity.* Dress, language, names, and interests take on a sameness that erodes individuality.
5. *Doctrinal confusion.* Incomprehensible "truths" are more read-

ily accepted when presented in a complex fashion that encourages rejection of logical thought.

6. *Exclusivity.* Those outside the cults are viewed as spiritually inferior, creating an exclusive and self-righteous "we" versus "they" attitude.

7. *Financial involvement.* All or part of one's personal assets may be donated to the cult, increasing a vested interest in sticking with it and lessening the chance of returning to a former vocation.

8. *Hypnotic states.* Inducing a highly susceptible state of mind may be accomplished by chanting, repetitive singing, or meditation.

9. *Isolation from outside.* Diminished perception of reality results when one is physically separated from friends, society, and the rational frame of reference in which one has previously functioned.

10. *Lack of privacy.* Reflective, critical thinking is impossible in a setting where cult members are seldom left unattended, and the ego's normal emotional defensive mechanisms can easily be stripped away by having the new member share personal secrets that can later be used for intimidation.

11. *Love-bombing.* Physical affection and constant contrived attention can give a false sense of camaraderie.

12. *Megacommunication.* Long, confusing lectures can be an effective tool if the inductee is bombarded with glib rhetoric and catch phrases.

13. *New relationships.* Marriage to another cult member and the destruction of past family relationships integrates one fully into the cult "family."

14. *Nonsensical activities.* Games and other activities with no apparent purpose leave one dependent upon a group or leader to give direction and order.

15. *Pavlovian control.* Behavior modification by alternating reward and punishment leads to confusion and dependency.

16. *Peer pressure.* By exploiting one's desire for acceptance, doubts about cult practices can be overcome by offering a sense of belonging to an affirming community.

17. *Sensory deprivation.* Fatigue coupled with prolonged activity can make one vulnerable to otherwise offensive beliefs and suggestions.

18. *Unquestioning submission.* Acceptance of cult practices is achieved by discouraging any questions or natural curiosity that may challenge what the leaders propagate.
19. *Value rejection.* As the recruit becomes more integrated into the cult, he is encouraged to denounce the values and beliefs of his former life.

The profiles and techniques presented in this chapter will not always be apparent with all cults or all adherents. One group may practice economic exploitation, while another allows its members to maintain a lifestyle that is financially independent from the cult. Certain cults entice members who are curious about their secret doctrines, while others openly evangelize by public propagation of their beliefs (though few cults qualify for this category). Most groups generally adhere to one or more of the characteristics that have been described.

· 3 ·
A CHRISTIAN
PERSPECTIVE
ON CULTS

Because Christians believe that each person has been created by God with intrinsic human worth, they oppose any form of social bondage that insults human integrity or violates the sovereignty of the will. This ideal alone places the church in opposition to most cults. But there are certain morally conscious cults with high ethical values, and these groups would oppose the dehumanizing practices of other groups. A cult may offend in one area without erring in another. For example, Mormonism maintains high ethical values while promoting tenets that are contrary to the Bible. Thus Mormonism is classified as a cult because of its teachings while a group such as The Children of God is considered cultic because both their doctrines and ethics are unscriptural. That's why it is so important for Christians to evaluate religious groups according to biblical criteria. As Dr. Walter Martin has observed, "A person can be morally good, but if he sets his face against Jesus, his fruit is corrupt." The term *cult* as used in this book is generally understood to have a negative connotation that indicates morally reprehensible practices or beliefs that significantly depart from historic Christianity.

Whether or not a particular religious group claims to be Christian is not a prime consideration. Its members may quote the Bible profusely and covet the endorsement of Christ for their efforts. But the premises of this book are based on two contingent factors that evaluate whether a group is cultic: (1) if it ignores or purposely omits central apostolic doctrines; or (2) if it holds to beliefs that are distinctly opposed to orthodox Christianity. Deviation from either criterion prohibits its inclusion in the Christian community. Whether a belief system conforms to Scripture or the extent to which it departs from biblical precepts is the ultimate gauge for truth and error. Thus, any group that intentionally manipulates its language to mimic evangelical beliefs must have its semantic distortions exposed. Any cult that places itself in opposition to historic Christianity should not be allowed to hide behind a cloak of religious good will or misleading terminology.

Many Christians are perplexed when cultists they confront seem to voice harmony with evangelical positions. They quote the Bible, profess devout reverence for Christ, and use the same familiar evangelical clichés. What the bewildered Christian fails to understand is that the cultists redefine orthodox terminology to suit their own belief systems. In such a case, the cult adherent should be forced to assume an intellectually honest stance with reference to indispensable Bible doctrines. Only then will their perfidy of language be revealed for its malicious intent. Such individuals need to be clearly warned they are "handling the word of God deceitfully" (2 Cor. 4:2), an act that insures their own destruction (2 Pet. 3:16).

Do false belief systems deserve credit for their good works? Many cults have made significant contributions to the social welfare of humanity. In some instances cult leaders are sincerely concerned about meeting the spiritual needs of seeking souls. Even though this book recognizes positive elements in certain cults, it must not be forgotten that the Bible requires reproof and rebuke of any teaching that exalts itself against the necessity of salvation through Christ (2 Tim. 4:2). According to scriptural criteria, any false teacher is a "deceitful Christ" (Phil. 3:18). Gratuitous words in recognition of positive values should not be mistaken for any endorsement of what the Bible calls "doctrines of devils" (1 Tim. 4:1).

The good works and apparent beneficial effects of a cult's belief system thus are inconsequential considerations. Healing, for example, cannot validate the biblical credibility of a cult's doctrine. The miracles of Pharaoh's magicians (as recorded in Exodus 7) illustrate that the supernatural is an arena where both godly and demonic powers operate. Only those with true scriptural discernment will be able to know whether good or evil should be credited as the source of any teaching. Jesus pointed out that apparent authority over evil spirits would not qualify one for entrance into heaven if the exorcist operated under a system of false doctrine (Matt. 7:21-23).

To evaluate a religious group according to biblical criteria, what areas of doctrine are vital for consideration? Just what are the scriptural perimeters beyond which no religious group may lay claim to biblical orthodoxy? While exclusivity, elitism, misplaced authority, and eschatological error are all cult characteristics, these distinctives are not germane to determining orthodoxy. The basic fault of cults is that they demote God, devalue Christ, deify man, deny sin, and denigrate Scripture. Therefore, correct theology regarding all of the following Bible doctrines is necessary to be in accordance with historic Christianity.

1. The attributes of God
2. The Person of Christ
3. The nature of man
4. The requirements of atonement
5. The source of revelation

These are the five basic areas of doctrine where truth may be distinguished from error. By delineating the position of historic Christianity regarding these five doctrines, we will lay a foundation on which we can evaluate individual cults. This is intended not as a weighty theological treatise but as a clear guide to combat the cult invasion, written not for the clergy alone but for the person in the pew. This does not mean that the author and publisher consider theology to be unimportant. In fact, the lack of sound biblical theology in our culture has resulted in a post-Christian era that enhances the myth of the cults.

There are three divisions to the analysis of each doctrine:

1. The historic Christian position. Although not comprehensive, this will provide a summary of the basic biblical belief.
2. Five Scriptures supporting the biblical doctrine. In most cases, dozens of biblical references could have been cited as corroborating evidence, but for the sake of brevity these five should suffice. Please note that all scriptural quotations are from the King James Version since this version is the one most frequently quoted (and misquoted) by cultists.
3. Examples of three specific cultic viewpoints on each doctrine. In some cases, there are many cultic variations but space limitations require condensing cult doctrines into these three categories. The cults listed as holding these teachings are representational examples only, not a complete catalogue of all cults adhering to such views.

21

GOD

Christian Theology. God is a personality who can speak and create and who possesses a mind and will (Gen. 1:1, 26; Jer. 29:11; Ezek. 18:30). God's character is eternal (1 Tim. 1:17), omnipotent (Rev. 19:6), omnipresent (Ps. 139:7-12), omniscient (Rom. 11:33), perfect (Deut. 32:4), and holy (1 Pet. 1:16). Both the Old and New Testaments proclaim the triune nature of God — Father, Son, and Holy Spirit. They are co-equal, co-existent, and co-eternal, three Persons of the same Substance (John 1:1-3; 14:26).

Supportive Scriptures

1. "There is but one God, the Father, of whom are all things" (1 Cor. 8:6).
2. "Before me there was no God formed, neither shall there be after me" (Isa. 43:10).
3. "And God said unto Moses, I AM THAT I AM" (Exod. 3:14).
4. "For there is one God" (1 Tim. 2:5).
5. "From everlasting to everlasting, thou art God" (Ps. 90:2).

Cult Doctrine

1. Impersonal, unknowable essence (Hinduism, Bahaism).
2. Divine idea, principle, or example (Christian Science, Unity).
3. Non-trinitarianism (Jehovah's Witnesses, The Way).

CHRIST

Christian Theology. The Apostles' Creed states: "Conceived by the Holy Ghost, born of the Virgin Mary, suffered under Pontius Pilate, was crucified, dead and was buried; He descended into Hell; the third day He arose from the dead; He ascended into Heaven and sitteth on the right hand of God the Father Almighty; from thence He shall come to judge the quick and the dead." Jesus Christ is the Second Person of the Trinity, the eternally Begotten Son of God who became flesh and is now our "great high priest, that is passed into the heavens . . . [who] was in all points tempted like as we are, yet without sin" (Heb. 4:14-15).

Supportive Scriptures

1. "In the beginning was the Word, and the Word was with God, and the Word was God. . . . All things were made by him; and without him was not any thing made" (John 1:1, 3).
2. "And the Word was made flesh and dwelt among us (and we be-

held his glory, the glory as of the only begotten of the Father)" (John 1:14).
3. "Every spirit that confesseth not that Jesus Christ is come in the flesh is not of God; and this is the spirit of antichrist" (1 John 4:3).
4. "Far above all principality, and power, and might, and dominion, and every name that is named" (Eph. 1:21).
5. "For in him dwelleth all the fullness of the Godhead bodily" (Col. 2:9).

Cult Doctrine
1. Merely a human being without divinity who attained "Christ Consciousness" (The Church Universal and Triumphant, The International Community of Christ).
2. Created being (Mormonism, Jehovah's Witnesses).
3. One of many *avatars* or revelations of God (Hinduism, Divine Light Mission).

MAN

Christian Theology. God created man in his own image (Gen. 1:26), perfect and without sin so that he could know and love God. Man is the highest distinction of God's creative genius, separate from him, made "a little lower than the angels" (Ps. 8:5) with dominion over all the earth (Gen. 1:28). In Eden, man fell by disobedience; henceforth all men are conceived in sin with a depraved nature destined for damnation unless they are spiritually reborn (John 3:3).

Supportive Scriptures
1. "The heart is deceitful above all things, and desperately wicked" (Jer. 17:9).
2. "By one man sin entered into the world, and death by sin; . . . all have sinned" (Rom. 5:12).
3. "For as by one man's disobedience many were made sinners" (Rom. 5:19).
4. "In sin did my mother conceive me" (Ps. 51:5).
5. "Their foolish heart was darkened" (Rom. 1:21).

Cult Doctrine
1. Divine, an emanation of the infinite Impersonal (Theosophy, Rosicrucianism).

23

2. Sinful but capable of attaining the same "Christ Consciousness" that Jesus did (Church Universal and Triumphant, Holy Order of MANS).
3. Destined to be a god (Mormonism, Worldwide Church of God).

ATONEMENT

Christian Theology. The Old Testament sacrifices foreshadowed the Lamb of God, "slain from the foundation of the world" (Rev. 13:8), whose shed blood would be the final sacrifice and cleansing for sin (1 John 1:7). Man, whose sinful rebellion has separated him from God, can now have "peace through the blood of his cross" (Col. 1:20) and be "reconciled" to God (2 Cor. 5:19) because of his vicarious, substitutionary death.

Supportive Scriptures
1. "Who his own self bare our sins in his own body on the tree" (1 Pet. 2:24).
2. "While we were yet sinners, Christ died for us" (Rom. 5:8).
3. "Neither is there salvation in any other: for there is none other name under heaven given among men, whereby we must be saved" (Acts 4:12).
4. "Without shedding of blood is no remission" (Heb. 9:22).
5. "If we confess our sins, he is faithful and just to forgive us our sins, and to cleanse us from all unrighteousness" (1 John 1:9).

Cult Doctrine
1. Good works and beneficent deeds will cause one to achieve at-one-ment with God (Unity, Bahaism).
2. Reincarnation will fulfill the law of karma (Scientology, Krishna Consciousness).
3. Universalism; all will eventually be saved (Mormonism, Christian Science).

REVELATION

Christian Theology. The Word of God in scriptural canon is inspired (God-breathed), inerrant, complete (Rev. 22:18, 19), and the only infallible rule of faith. It reveals the origin and destiny of all things; records God's dealings with mankind in the past, present, and future; and focuses on the person and work of Jesus Christ. The Bible inspires faith (Rom. 10:17) and will make men "wise unto salvation" (2 Tim. 3:15).

Supportive Scriptures

1. "All scripture is given by inspiration of God, and is profitable for doctrine, for reproof, for correction, for instruction in righteousness" (2 Tim. 3:16).
2. "Holy men of God spake as they were moved by the Holy Ghost" (2 Pet. 1:21).
3. "Thy word is a lamp unto my feet, and a light unto my path" (Ps. 119:105).
4. "The word of our God shall stand for ever" (Isa. 40:8).
5. "For the word of God is quick, and powerful, and sharper than any two-edged sword . . . and is a discerner of the thoughts and intents of the heart" (Heb. 4:12).

Cult Doctrine

1. The Bible needs additional subjective or written revelation for our age (Mormonism, The Walk).
2. The Word of God needs to be properly translated with accompanying explanations (Jehovah's Witnesses, The Way).
3. The Bible is one of many equally divine, sacred books (Unity, Bahaism).

This brief theological survey was not constructed to precipitate a quarrel with any particular cult. Satan, the source of all antichrist systems, is the Christian's real enemy. Those who expound erroneous doctrines may be sincere but misguided individuals. Our purpose is to determine the scriptural conformity of doctrines, not the motivational integrity of individuals.

· 4 ·

DISMANTLING
THE
MYTH

The swamis are coming from India, and they're taking away the flock. They're speaking of religion as dealing with the interior of life and not about dogmatic formulae and ritual requirements.
—Joseph Campbell, the late author of *The Masks of God* and former professor of literature at Sarah Lawrence College

Such is the way one writer described the current voguish interest in Eastern mysticism. Most Westerners don't seem to care that the Oriental system of faith is based on a tenuous, mystical foundation. The manner in which cults of the East present a veiled explanation of truth is apparently of no more concern to the modern mind than whether Joseph Smith (Mormonism's founder) really did discover golden plates buried in Palmyra, New York, or whether Victor Wierwille (founder of The Way) actually heard the voice of God. As a result, 20 million Americans involved in cults have placed their hope in belief structures with tenets based on mixtures of fact and fantasy.

It matters little to the mystic whether his system of worship is historically accurate. If Krishna's discourses with Arjuna in the *Bhagavad-Gita* are mere legends, pointing out this fact is dismissed with a shrug. Expediency is what counts. Consequently, Christianity's historical validation of a blood-stained cross and an empty tomb has little meaning to the mystic's mind. Whether Calvary and the Resurrection actually took place seems less important to the false religionist than what he sees as the allegorical grandeur of the story.

But truth *does* matter! When the legendary accounts that comprise the superstructure of mystical philosophy have collapsed, the child of God must be ready to offer the disillusioned an objectively valid response to the "whys" of life. When the myths have been shattered, the Bible-based Christian should be in a position to defend the claims of Jesus' divinity. "Be ready always to give an answer to every man that asketh a reason of the hope that is in you," the apostle Peter urged (1 Pet. 3:15). This book has been written to help provide that answer. The reader whose faith is experientially rooted in the living Logos will find on these pages a concrete intellectual rationale for pointing the cultist to the historical Christ.

American soil has been the foremost battleground in the war of the cults versus Christianity. It's ironic this struggle has occurred here. Both the devout and the deists who settled this land were committed to a transcendent faith that recognized a personal God based on the Judeo-Christian model. However, a careful study of America's past reveals that even those early years of settling and exploration were influenced by the breeze that became the tumultuous gale of twentieth-century cultism. The promise of free exercise of religion that originally lured people to this land also fostered utopian, communal, and apocalyptic dreams. The American vision has always been enamored with idealistic answers promising a simplistic and sacred explanation for life's purpose. This philosophy of "Manifest Destiny" has been most evident in times of cultural transition such as the Armageddon-crazed days of the industrial revolution. Today's cult invasion is the cultural extension of this uniquely American attitude.

Established religion, the legitimizer of the status quo, suffers today from the moral vacuum created in part by technology's triumph. In this setting, the myth of the cults helps to steady men's nerves and placate their fears. Exploring psychic inner space and conducting mythic ceremonies seem to reinforce each man's worth in the computer age. The ritualism and imagery of our twentieth-century cultic myths (whether they are a Mormon's proxy baptism or the promise of astral travel held forth by ECKANKAR advocates) awaken a sense of awe about man's relationship to the world around him. Most of all, the mythology of the cults reveals to the "faithful" where they belong in the scheme of the universe. From birth to death the cultist is guided by his myth with an assurance that each step fits into the divine order.

Souls for whom Christ shed his blood deserve a more spiritually fulfilling answer than that which is provided by modern myths. I bear a solemn obligation in writing this book. If Jehovah's Witnesses really do have inside information about the world's end, and if Scientology really can extinguish our hang-ups from past lives, you, the reader, have a right to know. If Moon is the Messiah or if Baha'u'llah was the Christ, then no personal prejudice should stand in the way of proclaiming these facts. But if these spiritual leaders and philosophers are in error, then every person whose life this book touches deserves to know the unvarnished truth.

The reader also has a right to know that the theological perspective of this volume is committed to an evangelical Christian stance. I have not been commissioned by any church or denomination. No official communion of any theological persuasion has given instructions to dismantle a particular philosophy held dear by any cult group or leader. Orthodox, Protestant, and Reformation presuppositions alone provide the frame of reference for the analysis of each cult. Two basic theological principles guide this study: (1) Jesus Christ is fully God, from eternity past to eternity future (Col. 2:10); and (2) obedience to the command that Christians are to "abhor that which is evil; cleave to that which is good" (Rom. 12:9).

This book is not intended to be a sociological or theological treatise. Its purpose is to aid and inform the average person whose friends or loved ones are involved in cult activities. *Larson's New Book of Cults* is also intended to prepare the layman who dreads the intrusion of the canvassing cultist knocking on his door. Each commentary is intended to be practical, embellished with my personal experiences confronting the cults. It also includes the insights gained from travels to over seventy countries (including many weeks of research in Indian and East Asian societies).

Why is the myth of the cults so attractive to modern man? Is the recent explosion of cult activity indicative of societal or spiritual factors? Has America's proclivity for "inventive" solutions caused her to turn Eastward? Is it the fault of science for heralding the advance of problemsolving by microprocessors? Can the innate spiritual hunger in man's heart be blamed for pursuing escapist solutions to desperate dilemmas? Or has mankind entered an age in which conflicting supernatural forces tug at his allegiance in one final bid for control of civilization before its last gasp?

The secular behaviorist would probably choose one or more of the above explanations while the evangelical Christian would, in all likelihood, check off all five. There are other causes one might add to this list. In his book *Those Curious New Cults,* William Petersen includes: (1) disillusionment with American political life; (2) dehumanization by science; (3) advent of the drug culture; (4) future fright (fear of nuclear or environmental cataclysms); (5) breakdown of the family; (6) popular culture (music and literature); (7) psychology and the occult (Jung to Joseph Rhine); (8) decline of the church; and (9) the ecology crisis.

Because of these and other reasons, an estimated 1,500 to 3,000 cult groups flourish in North American society. They range in size from groups of thousands of adherents to small bands of disciples numbering a few hundred or less. Membership is divided between established cults with reasonably respectable followings (e.g., Mormonism, Christian Science, Unity) and New Age cults. The latter believe that man's evolutionary spiritual ascent will reach fruition in a new-dawning era of utopian goals of spiritual brotherhood and peace. All cults have one thing in common. They consider the claims of Christ to be optional, not essential to salvation.

Idealistic young people whose quest for spiritual identity supersedes their desire for materialistic comfort are ripe for exploitation by cultic myths. The promise of psychic enhancement and raised consciousness has a powerful sway over the naive and unsuspecting. Adolescents who want to short-circuit intellectually the agonizing process of maturation can be easily victimized by a myth that offers a painless way of ignoring the discomfort of learning life's lessons the hard way. New Age cults are particularly adept at beckoning the lonely and confused to step over the threshold of an altered perception of reality. All the answers to mankind's great questions are dismissed by merging one's ego into the common good of the cult's vision for the future. The myth they offer is no passing fad. Their vision of remaking the world will endure even after the most optimistic predictions of a Reverend Moon have been proven false.

The mythology of cult teaching presents a formidable challenge to society. Secularists who once said, "It can't happen to my kids," have had their illusions shattered. Instead of reaching out to meet the needs of a searching generation, they have offered the solutions of governmental control or remedial deprogramming. Interference by the state in matters of religious convictions is a specter that could haunt religious freedom for years to come. Legislated regulations aimed at bizarre groups could one day be turned into edicts that would hinder legitimate alternative expressions of faith. Recent clashes between humanists and evangelicals illustrate all too succinctly that antireligionists would not hesitate to use any lawful power to thwart the concerns of born-again believers. "Today the Moonies, tomorrow the Pentecostals" may be a slogan of alarm worth heeding.

Those whose responsibility it would be to establish religious norms might well someday officially repudiate the Bible in favor of atheism. What then? Temporarily stemming the tide of cult brainwashing probably appeals to evangelicals, especially those whose children have become cult converts. But undermining First Amendment rights to achieve momentary suppression of an undesirable belief system might eventually invite suppression of biblically orthodox groups.

The plight of parents whose offspring have been unfairly captivated by mind-bending cults is a genuine concern of everyone, especially jurists. There is no way to calculate the emotional grief of a mother and father who suddenly find a family member undergoing a complete personality transformation. What is a parent to do when his own child sees him as an instrument of Satan and refuses to answer calls or letters? For some, deprogramming, forceable kidnapping, and "coercive dissuasion" seem to be their last hope.

For fees of more than $10,000 they enlist the services of a "professional" such as Ted Patrick ("Black Lightning"), who will abduct the cult adherent and sequester him in a motel room where his cult beliefs are persistently challenged. Patrick, whose activities have earned him frequent brushes with the law, claims to have deconverted more than 1,600 young people. Such conduct raises serious questions about violating the law to prevent so-called "greater injury" to one's mind and beliefs. It would appear that the First Amendment guarantees the right of any person to believe what he wishes. Patrick argues that certain cults have so perfected their recruitment techniques that their victims are effectively denied the privilege of free moral choice. Whether fighting fire with fire is justifiable, considering the circumstances, is a major question facing those concerned with protecting religious freedoms.

Most Christians would oppose violating an individual's will and integrity to free him from any kind of enslavement. They would argue that it is only the truth of Christ that makes any man free (John 8:32) and that violence should not answer violence. In analyzing this phenomenon, the Spiritual Counterfeit Project newsletter concluded, "We are convinced that the insidious infringements of personality which are involved in cultic manipulation of commitment should not remain totally beyond the reach of society and its sanctions. Since one of the key techniques of coercive persuasion is to isolate the prospective convert from any influence which might challenge or disrupt the belief-system, we believe that a person who has been subjected to such techniques should have an opportunity to evaluate his or her commitment and beliefs free from the self-reinforcing context of cult involvement with its propaganda, fear, guilt, and harassment." The S.C.P. recommends "reality testing" applied through the authority of the government "by means of conservatorship proceedings or some acceptable substitute."

Even if a morally and legally acceptable method to extract cult members is found, the fundamental issue of countering cult evangelism still needs to be addressed. The appalling number of cult devotees who have left evangelical ranks poses a crucial question. How well is the church training its members to understand the foundation of their beliefs? Countering the cult invasion requires that Christians be properly grounded in the biblical science of apologetics. Believers may need to be reminded that they have a sacred responsibility to "contend for the faith which was once delivered unto the saints" (Jude 3).

The prolific growth of the cults is not likely to recede anytime soon. As Dr. Walter Martin points out, Christians cannot sit back passively and assume that those teachers who are not of God will eventually fade away. Some who adopt this passive attitude cite Gamaliel's advice to the Jewish council (Acts 5:33-39) as their theological pretext. When Gamaliel advised his brethren not to oppose the apostles lest they also oppose God, his counsel was directed toward a consideration of anti-Christian persecution. Thus Gamaliel's proposition cannot be used to justify a failure to counter false doctrines. Adopting such an attitude would be to concede godly origin to the successes of major world religions that oppose Christian beliefs. To "just preach the gospel" and leave the cults to "hang themselves when they get enough rope" would be to confine the Great Commission to non-cult evangelism.

If Christians are to confidently challenge the cults, they must be spiritually prepared. "Judgment must begin at the house of God" (1 Pet. 4:17), and confronting the myth of the cults also means the church first has to purge its own ranks. Doing so requires facing some serious, introspective questions. What about the excessive authority conceded to Christian leaders who command large followings? How much attention is being paid to encouraging strong family units where young people find secure parental relationships that are too strong for cult authoritarianism to crack? Do laymen need carefully to weigh in light of Scripture the pronouncements of their respected leaders? (Even the apostle Paul acknowledged the necessity of such checks and balances in Acts 17:11.)

Should the church be reminded of the supernatural gifts and spiritual spontaneity that characterized its early growth and are now indicative of what sometimes attracts youth to cults? To dismiss the success of aberrant beliefs with the excuse that Satan has blinded the eyes of cultists could be a way of ignoring the fact that the true church is also at fault.

The apostle Paul's love for the church caused him to do more than merely issue a warning about "grievous wolves." His command to defend diligently the cause of Christ ushered forth day and night "with tears" (Acts 20:28-31). Paul's impassioned appeal, coupled with Christ's advance notice ("Behold, I have told you before," Matt. 24:25), leaves some churches in the embarrassing position of having abdicated the throne of dominion over men's souls to the more energetic cult groups.

Not everyone who reads this book will immediately become a missionary to counter the cults. But the knowledge on these pages will hopefully result in a prepared vessel whom the Lord can use when an appropriate opportunity presents itself. Some may choose to invade actively Satan's kingdom, being filled with the Spirit and determined to dismantle the myth that holds millions in spiritual servitude. Others will reach out with new love and empathy for those who sorrow because a family member has joined a cult. Still others may sense the need for rehabilitative follow-up programs that will minister to the emotional needs of those who have been ravaged by cult ideology. Any of these fruits will make this book worth its investment of time and energy. May God show you, the reader, what part you should play in helping to destroy the myth of the cults.

The major section of this book will give the reader a brief but comprehensive appraisal of those cults that are most threatening to the church of Jesus Christ. This book is primarily written for the nonprofessional who wants to know where a certain cult originated, how it developed historically, the nature of its main teachings, and its relationship to biblical truth. Though some cults exhibit an arrogant air of superiority, care has been taken not to counter this attitude with a spirit of antagonism. The unlimited grace of God that the apostle John so eloquently described (1 John 2:2) is extended to all who have not experienced salvation by grace, including the cultist. The cult adherent may wonder why the evangelical would dare to dispute his beliefs since they are presumed to be the "restored" or "revealed" truths of God. But such a response must be met with love that remembers that, except for God's intervention, the reader might also be ensnared in the same spiritual bondage.

Sound theology, doctrinal purity, and aggressive evangelistic techniques do not provide the whole answer to thwarting cultic expansion. Christians are not only known by their adherence to lofty ethics rooted in biblical theology. John 13:34-35 reminds believers that love is the mark of discipleship. And love for one's neighbor is the distinguishing characteristic of one's love for God. Such is the message of the Good Samaritan parable of Luke 10:30-35. A personal anecdote may emphasize this fact in a practical manner.

Just a few paragraphs prior to penning this very page, there was a knock at the door of my cabin. (Most of my writing is done at a mountain retreat where there are no phones or visitors to interfere.) It was pouring rain outside, and two drenched Japanese-American girls named Harriet and Ellen were seeking entrance. Once inside, they explained to my wife and me that the friends they were with had slid off a muddy road and wrecked their car. They asked for a ride to a nearby lodge where they could call a tow truck. No writer appreciates an interruption. However, there was no choice but to render them immediate assistance in their distress.

The two girls were soaking wet and covered with mud. Needless to say, my vehicle suffered the consequences! To make matters worse, on the way to the lodge the heater fan conked out and the knob to the defroster fell off. It was as if one irritation after another was being heaped upon me to exacerbate the situation. After phoning for a wrecker, the girls asked me for another ride to the place where they had joined their friends and left their car—a half hour's drive away. There was no question that these young ladies needed my help. What concerned me was that their plight had interfered with what appeared to be a more important spiritual responsibility—writing this book.

On the way to retrieve their automobile, the conversation centered on the weather and how the accident occurred. Finally, Ellen asked what I did for a living. That led to a lengthy explanation regarding my personal faith in Christ, something neither girl seemed to understand.

"Where do you attend church?" I asked.

"We're Buddhists," they replied.

Suddenly I knew why God had allowed this interruption. What I had considered an irritating infringement of my time was God's way of reminding me that this book was not as important as showing God's love and helping someone in need.

The devout Buddhist beliefs of Harriet and Ellen soon collided with my scriptural insistence that Christ is the only means of salvation. When we reached their car, Ellen's parting words climaxed the episode.

"Well, I guess we won't really know who's right until we're both dead," she concluded.

"But if Jesus was correct," I answered, "it will be a little too late for you to find out."

As I drove off, the Holy Spirit impressed upon me an important lesson. God loves mankind so much that he is willing to provide shelter and kindness even to those who reject his Son. My knowledge of the cults, particularly Buddhism, would probably have enabled me to argue effectively on an intellectual level with Harriet and Ellen. But God was more concerned about my extending a Samaritan act of love than my winning a theological debate in the defense of truth.

When I arrived back to the cabin, I was prepared to pursue this book with new resolve and enthusiasm. Most importantly, I felt the need to do something more than just issue a warning about the dangers of cults. Dismantling the myth is not only the work of biblical apologetics; it is also a labor of love.

PART TWO

AN

INTRODUCTION

TO

CULT

CONCEPTS

· 1 ·

UNDERSTANDING

CULT

CONCEPTS

It's a lyric from a Ray Charles song of the late fifties: "Tell me, what'd I say?" But it also expresses the sentiment of Western man in the late twentieth century who finds himself wondering about his own language. Every day millions of North Americans use words with a commonplace frequency that were unknown utterances scarcely two decades ago: *yoga, TM, karma, Zen, nirvana, mantra, guru,* to name just a few. In addition, words with ill-defined meanings are bantered about in casual conversation: *mysticism, transcendentalism, reincarnation, past lives, meditation, god-realization.*

What's going on? In brief, the way Westerners talk is being influenced by the way they live. The Judeo-Christian heritage may officially sanction society's institutions, but its concepts of God and reality rooted in objective revelation mean little to the average person. The worldview held by most is subtly embedded with a distinctly Eastern mode of interpreting man's relationship to God and the material universe. America's monetary system proclaims, "In God We Trust," but its spiritual consciousness bears the inscription, "Mystery Babylon." The whorish faith of Revelation's false religious system is no distant projection awaiting some distinctive prophetic fulfillment. Its ideology is already in our midst, merely awaiting the final unveiling of the Antichrist. Meanwhile, the words of man's mouth are preparing his mind for the domination of the Lawless One's totalitarian regime.

Words can do all that? Absolutely! Just think for a moment how often you hear someone calmly discuss his astrology sign or speak about yoga exercises and meditation. Cocktail conversations explore the merits of psychic power. "Human potential," "transpersonal," "holistic," "actualization," "higher consciousness," and many other terms of communication say more about what man really believes than any statistic about church attendance could reveal. And underlying all this are some basic presuppositions about the faith and hope that compels the man on the street.

Whether he wears a three-piece, pin-striped suit or a sweatshirt and sneakers, the modern religionist (whose thinking has been affected by Eastern cults) has much in common with his fellow citizens. His belief system may be summarized as follows: This material existence is not the Ultimate Reality. Spirit transcends the baser realm experienced by the objective senses, and enlightenment may only be realized intuitively. Feeling is more important than knowing. Being is of more value than doing. God is not a personal, transcendent deity before whom one is morally accountable. He'll not be found by looking out there. Inside of man dwells the divine essence, and introspection is the way to discover truth. Once one discovers the inner potential for spiritual power and knowledge, there is no longer any need to be bound by the outmoded ideas of heaven and hell, judgment, sin, and salvation. God is, after all, one's own cosmic consciousness, a Presence pervading all life. And communion with him is not the result of a reasoned search for hope in Someone. Subjectivism is the pathway to peace, and the solution to all problems is to deny they exist.

This categoric appraisal of the modern mind describes a majority of those who would nominally call themselves "Christians." These same individuals probably would hesitate if asked to supply a precise definition for words like *mysticism, self-deification,* and *pantheism.* Like a dry sponge, the Western mind, drained of spiritual moisture by the desert of scientific rationalism, now soaks up the "wisdom" of the East. As a result, many "Christians" pay lip service to the church of their choice while philosophically adhering to an occult/mystical/Hinduistic/Buddhist/Taoist/spiritualist concept of life.

The most elemental fact of man's existence is his search for God. *Theology,* which combines the Greek words *theos* (God) and *logos* (word), literally means "words describing the nature of God." Even the atheist, by this definition, has a theology. Though most people might feel inadequate to explain their personal beliefs, given the opportunity, they eventually articulate a belief system that is based on either the Good News of Jesus or the precepts of Mystery Babylon. When espousing the latter, they implicitly reject the orthodox ("correct belief") scriptural interpretations of historic Christianity.

Christianity is not based upon some relativistic impression of reality. It is rooted in the teachings of Jesus and the doctrines of the apostles, those who were privileged to sit at his feet and hear directly his words of life. Never once did they suggest that Christ had secretly given them access to divine mysteries that could only be discovered by a tedious search of esoteric truth. Peter, Paul, James, and John openly declared what they had received. Their message is based on the authority of the Old Testament and the apostolic office conferred upon them by the Lord. Not one of them claimed any private understanding of Jesus' teachings apart from the scrutiny of the other eleven.

The cults, no matter how diverse their origins, display a remarkable conformity of ideology. Considering that the source of cultic knowledge is the *gnosis* of Eden's serpent, the Bible-believing Christian is not surprised to observe such harmony. But all true believers, likewise, have a uniformity of doctrine that transcends all cultural and convictional barriers, such as the Bible's presentation of the origin and existence of life, and the eternal struggle between good and evil based on the perpetual conflict between God and Satan. Sin and rebellion began in the heart of Lucifer (Isa. 14; Ezek. 28), and their ultimate defeat (Gen. 3:14-15) and dissolution (Rev. 20) are a certainty. The conclusion of God's pronouncements have been settled (Ps. 119), and the source of a correct worldview must be based on the authority of Scripture (2 Tim. 3:16).

Christianity in the West may have felt it was impervious to any incursion of the devilish doctrines of the Eastern mindset. But during the last century "certain men crept in unawares . . . denying the only Lord God . . . Jesus Christ" (Jude 4). Very subtly, the language of the mystic has influenced the way in which contemporary man's theology perceives the goal of peace with God and eternal life. It would be impossible in a book of this scope to include every religious term that pervades our speech. This section will, however, analyze three of the most common words condensing the essence of today's spiritual outlook: *enlightenment, meditation,* and *reincarnation.*

· 2 ·

ENLIGHTENMENT

No matter what name it goes by, the goal is the same. It may be called "heightened awareness," *"nirvana," "satori,"* "transcendental bliss," "god-realization," "expanded consciousness," "altered perception of reality," or "cosmic consciousness." The discipline may be yoga, Zen, asceticism, or meditation. And the religious frame of reference may be Buddhism, Unity, Hinduism, Theosophy, or Scientology. When all of the semantic externals are stripped away, whatever remains is the nebulous goal of "enlightenment." How is it achieved, and what separates it from biblical Christianity?

The first step toward enlightenment, in the mystical sense of the word, is the negation of one's rational faculties. Man's mind is an obstacle on the pathway to a higher consciousness. Truth is not perceived to be an absolute of objective revelation. Its reality must be experienced pragmatically by psychic or suprarational input. Logic plays no part in finally determining that enlightenment has been achieved. I have debated many cultists who affirm the authority of their messianic leader. When pressed to explain how they decided to follow a man as god, the answer is the same: "I just know."

The subjectivized experience offered by many cult captains, whether it be the "knowledge" of Guru Maharaj Ji or the *shakipat* of Muktananda Paramahansa, forms its own proof. When no rational attempt is made to judge intuitional experiences by objective standards, the enlightened cult member fails to ask, "Is it right?" He only concludes, "It works, and that is enough."

Some mystics would even admit that their altered perception of reality might be fantasized or hallucinogenic. That probability doesn't matter to them. It's most frustrating, however, to debate a devotee of cosmic consciousness and try to proceed to a logical conclusion, only to have him roll his eyes back in his head and "trance out"! When he returns from his momentary trip, he dons a sweet smile declaring, "Try it, you'll like it," dismissing any further intelligent conversation. When thinking has been replaced by feeling, the sea of subjectivism swallows up any effort to distinguish between reality and illusion.

While Christians may share glowing testimonies of conversion experiences, Hebrews 11 clearly designates the believer's life as one of faith. This transforming confidence in God is based on the objective criteria of his promises as revealed in the written Word. Jesus Christ declared that the basis of eternal life is knowing God (John 17:3). Christians have a personal, conscious relationship with their Lord, one that combines the emotional dynamics of the new birth with the intellectual capacity to understand God's character by his creation (Rom. 1:10). Man's faith does not rely upon some empirical foundation of truth that is being psychically communicated. The "power of God" as revealed in the miracles of the historical Christ offers far more hope than the mythology of the mystic (1 Cor. 2:5).

After the rational mental processes have been negated, the mystic next pursues enlightenment by seeking to release his spirit from the limitations of the body. One intention of enlightenment is "to be at one with the universe." However, the "subtle" or "material" body clouds spiritual perception by its attachment to the world of senses, The mystic may release his spirit by yoga exercises or by astral projection. Once the shell of flesh is left behind, time and space have no boundaries, giving spiritual entities (demons) the opportunity to guide the "true self" as it searches for the essence of life out of the body.

The enlightenment resulting from shedding the bondage of the physical body is generally a perception of self-deification. This exaltation of the ego leads many to conclude that they are indwelt with a "Christ-consciousness," or even that they are God. In the monist view, such a conclusion is perfectly logical because the Creator and the created are all one of the same essence. When enlightenment has been experienced in this manner, God is reduced to an impersonal principle. Gone is any concept of judgment and moral accountability. One's own enlightened self becomes the arbiter of all actions and the gauge of all truth.

All procedures leading to enlightenment and all cultic systems achieving their own illumination must operate on these propositions: (1) the mind and the body inhibit the attainment of truth by their confining sensory capacity, (2) a universal unity of spirit pervades the universe, the essence of which includes the nature of God and the souls of men, and (3) time, space, and matter are all illusory, therefore ignorant of good, with sin being a figment of the mind and not a state of conduct.

Jesus was interrogated by the Jewish leaders of his day, (John 5), who demanded to know the authority by which he healed and forgave sins. Christ did not lure them down the road of speculative spiritual introspection. Instead, he offered himself and his words as the basis for determining the validity of his actions. Jesus did not dispel their skepticism by suggesting they sit by a riverbank and think deep thoughts about the cosmos. "He that heareth [exercises objective mental comprehension] my words [which contain guiding spiritual truth] and believeth [compelling the intellect by faith] on him that hath sent me, hath everlasting life," Jesus declared (John 5:24).

Instead of dispensing enlightenment, Jesus offers the light of his life. The Apostle John declared that Jesus is "the true light which lighteth every man." Why, then, do some men prefer the glimmer of a self-described state of higher consciousness to the penetrating glare of moral purity offered by the Lord? John tells us "that light is come into the world, and men loved darkness rather than light because their deeds were evil." At last, we see the real reason behind the mystic's search for spiritual illumination. It is not truly the radiance of God he seeks, but rather, shelter from the penetrating searchlight of God's Holy Spirit. And the enlightenment upon which he stumbles is the false glow of one whom the Bible depicts as a deceiving "angel of light" — the Devil (2 Cor. 11:14).

· 3 ·

R E I N C A R N A T I O N

"Say a prayer to your higher self and Almighty God. Your mental body will leave your physical body and come back down in this life having the answers to the questions you have posed."

This monologue was delivered by a psychiatrist who practices "past-lives therapy." His patient wanted to know why she was blind in one eye. Under a hypnotic state, she supposedly regressed in time and saw herself in New York. Her mental journey had taken her back to 1943 when she found herself in the body of another person hurling a bottle at her lover's face. As the psychiatrist moved her forward in time, she once again saw her boyfriend, this time with a patch over his eye. Now she was ready to return to her body. The answer was plain. She had committed a sin of violence in her last reincarnation, and in this life she had to be punished in order to work out her *karma*. What lesson had she learned? "My higher self says I must learn to control myself in this life," she replied to the psychiatrist.

This story is true. Whether the facts are accurate is open to question. The only certainty is that practitioners of past-lives therapy have their calendars full of appointments. It seems in our age of stress and tension, there are those who eschew any thought of assuming personal responsibility for the consequences of their conduct. It's much easier to blame everything on a former existence. Hindus have been doing it for centuries. Now, many Westerners are following the same karmic path of fatalism. Belief in reincarnation is on the rise, and the classic inquiry, "Who *am* I?" has been replaced by the puzzling question, "Who *was* I?"

With the shift away from ecclesiastical directives and moral absolutism, our society has a desperate need to explain the nature of its existence. Historically, the declension from faith to hedonism has not always resulted in atheism. Generally, man seeks something that will satisfy the spiritual vacuum left by the denial of God as a guiding force in his life. The growth of interest in occult phenomena illustrates that Western man has traded his unbelief for a new system of order and meaning. Astrology, psychic predictions, and parapsychological investigations are pillars of this new "religious" system, with reincarnation as a major part of its foundation.

Belief in reincarnation has reached a level of respectability. Those who talk about past lives are no longer considered odd. Films such as *The Reincarnation of Peter Proud* and *Heaven Can Wait* have focused attention on reincarnation, along with the best-seller *Jonathan Livingston Seagull*. Actress-author Shirley MacLaine's New Age manifestos consistently top the best-seller lists. In such books as *Dancing in the Light, Out on a Limb,* and the recent Number 1 best-seller *Going Within,* MacLaine discusses (among other odd subjects) her past lives. Back in the fifties, the book *The Search for Bridey Murphy* told the story of Virginia Tighe, a thirty-three-year-old housewife who under hypnosis assumed the personality of what was thought to be a nineteenth-century Irish woman. Virginia spoke with an Irish brogue and described in detail a land she supposedly had never seen. After millions had swallowed the tale, investigators discovered that Mrs. Tighe had a grandmother who spoke Gaelic and had given Virginia history books about Ireland to read as a child.

Virginia seems undaunted and professes to maintain her beliefs in reincarnation. Recently she was a guest on the set of the film *Audrey Rose,* adapted from the novel by Frank De Felitta. After hearing his six-year-old child play the piano as an accomplished musician, when, in fact, he had never taken lessons, De Felitta investigated Hindu texts on reincarnation and explored the writings of Edgar Cayce (discussed later in this book). The child explained that his fingers had moved spontaneously without any conscious effort. De Felitta took this to mean his son was the reincarnation of a great musician.

A variety of cults consider reincarnation to be an essential aspect of their teachings. Scientology proposes to remove the traumas of past lives by the use of a device called an E-meter. Almost all of the important Eastern cults base their quest for higher consciousness on the premise of reincarnation. Other groups espousing this belief include Rosicrucianism, Unity School of Christianity, Hare Krishna, Theosophy, and Urantia. But belief in reincarnation itself is not confined to exotic cults. More than 60 percent of Americans consider human events experienced in the past and passed on to future lives to be a reasonable probability.

The word *reincarnation* takes its root from the word *incarnation,* "*in carnis* (Latin), which means "in the flesh." Reincarnation refers to the cyclical evolution of each man's soul as it passes into another body after death. The process continues until the soul has reached a state of perfection and merges back with its source. In the theory of reincarnation, the soul can only inhabit another *human* body. Transmigration, the Hindu doctrine from which reincarnation originated, teaches that each successive cycle may result in the soul incorporating itself in organic or inorganic life, meaning anything from a chicken to a rock. The choice depends upon the karma accumulated by the soul in its previous reincarnations. Western advocates of "rebirthing" have generally emphasized reincarnation rather than transmigration, knowing that the principles of the latter might be rejected by the more educated adherent. The average American would not necessarily be offended by the possibility of reincarnating as a respectable human being, but the thought of coming back as a pig or a bug is hardly enticing.

The doctrine of karma has found surprisingly easy acceptance among Westerners. (Since the chapter on Hinduism deals extensively with this concept, it will not be thoroughly analyzed here.) In the earliest Hindu texts karma connoted an act of ritual significance. In later writings it was modified to illustrate how events in this life affect the quality of life in the next incarnation. Eventually, karma came to represent the immutable law of sowing and reaping, with pronounced punishment in future lives as a purification from evil in this life. It was hoped that this refining process would permit the soul to be worthy of reabsorption into the Universal Soul from which it came. In India, the teaching of karma justified the prejudices of the developing social strata, resulting in the infamous caste system. The Untouchable had no hope of bettering his lot. His miserable destiny had been predetermined by a former existence. Likewise, the priestly Brahmin class saw no need to extend acts of kindness to the less fortunate. To do so would interfere with the karma of those beneath them and bring disrespect upon the privileges of their class, a status that they deserved because of their conduct in previous reincarnations.

The Indian subcontinent is not entirely responsible for promoting the theory of reincarnation. Gnostic cults of the first century and early challengers to the new Christian faith flirted with the idea. They had taken their cue from the philosophy of Plato, who put forward the concept of dualism that had also been discussed by earlier Greek philosophers. Plato viewed the spirit as a positive entity encased in the evil "prison house" of the body. Therefore, man's spirit longs to be free from its captor and to return to its Source, fading into the nebulous consciousness of the Universal Soul.

Spiritualism's resurgence in the 1800s formally introduced reincarnation to Westerners. The foremost twentieth-century advocate was Edgar Cayce (discussed later in this book). Cayce, who had a church-oriented background, was at first hesitant to adopt the belief. However, his spiritual teacher, Arthur Lammers, convinced Cayce that reincarnation was an evolutionary process by which one could attain the perfection of Christ. Lammers insisted that Jesus taught reincarnation to his disciples, but the belief had been deliberately omitted as Bible translations passed from one language to another. Eventually Cayce came to believe that phrases refuting reincarnation such as "resurrection of the dead" and "last judgment day" were "meant to be understood symbolically rather than literally." In the end, Edgar Cayce ridiculed the idea that Christ was "offering a hit-or-miss, one-chance-only hope of survival."

Today's foremost secular "expert" on reincarnation (we cannot count Shirley MacLaine as an expert, though she is certainly the reincarnation "guru" for many people) is Dr. Ian Stevenson. A Montreal-born psychiatrist, Stevenson became interested in reincarnation while serving as chairman of the Department of Psychiatry at the University of Virginia School of Medicine. He has carefully documented 1,800 reported cases of reincarnation, each of which he has attempted to deduce with logical explanations. While most of these stories have been labeled as fraudulent or resulting from parapsychological phenomenon, Stevenson remains intrigued by those examples that appear to be legitimate. He theorizes that mental stress in this life could be alleviated if the traumas of previous existences could be identified. (He sounds very much like a Scientologist.) He even goes so far as to suggest that parents who believe in reincarnation have a head start on child-rearing. By accepting the fact that the baby had a history before conception, the child will be given greater respect as an individual, and that, he says, "could greatly reduce parental guilt."

Why have teachings about reincarnation been received so readily? On the surface, some of its claims do sound reasonable to those not grounded in biblical theology. First of all, since every man senses his own sinfulness outside of Christ, he must have a way to cope with the burden of unrighteousness. Reincarnation promises an eventual freedom from the confines of moral guilt. It also provides a future opportunity to finish every worthy goal in this life that remains uncompleted at death. The talented achiever may be convinced that any application of his skills will come to fruition in the next life, if not this one.

Above all, reincarnation seeks to provide the ultimate answer for understanding suffering and injustice. As Robert Morey points out in his book, *Reincarnation and Christianity,* "The ancient philosophers used the theory of karmic reincarnation to explain away such things as birth defects, physical handicaps, low IQs, retardation, personality traits, etc., because they had no knowledge of genetics or the DNA code. They assumed that all babies should normally be born in perfect health and that all birth defects had a mystical or religious explanation, thus giving a mystical quality to an obviously genetic problem."

Morey goes on to point out that since the "mentally and physically handicapped are receiving the karma they deserve, they have been left to suffer." What Morey so clearly illustrates is that the explanation of reincarnation only perpetuates the problem. Is it any wonder that health care and social services are seldom seen in the East, except where Christian missionaries have brought a healing hand? To be a Good Samaritan, according to reincarnation, would only interfere with the divine order of karmic punishment.

Apart from any appraisal of reincarnation in the light of scriptural scrutiny, mere logic dismisses most of its claims. If successive lives are designed to bring about moral refinement, then what good does it do to be punished for something you can't remember having done? Since a finite number of souls is assumed to exist as an extension of the Universal Soul, with some of them being purified and reabsorbed, then why is the world population increasing? The global birth rate obviously exceeds the death rate, so where do all those newly reincarnated souls come from? (Some reincarnationists tenuously argue that this discrepancy is made up by the addition of souls from other planets.) If the essence of karma is to rid humanity of its selfish desires, then shouldn't there be a noticeable improvement in human nature after all the millennia of reincarnations? If those such as the Marquis de Sade and Attila the Hun were on an evolutionary moral ascent, then why do we still have the Hitlers and Charles Mansons?

Above all, it seems obvious that belief in reincarnation virtually removes any incentive to excel morally, since there will always be a second chance. One needs only glimpse at the lands where karmic philosophy and theories of transmigration have held sway for centuries to see the subhuman view of life fostered by these teachings. If suffering is the result of sin in other peoples' lives, then what recompense is there for the pain endured by malformed children whose broken limbs were deliberately twisted to make them more useful to professional begging syndicates? Why lift a man from the gutter to clean his sores and feed his belly if some impersonal, unforgiving law of retribution is perpetuating his hunger? What eventual economic and social price will the West pay someday when it reaps the whirlwind of its fascination with the essence of karmic thought in reincarnation? Will we, too, create a generation callously indifferent to human misery because all concepts of ultimate accountability have been swept from our culture and replaced by the philosophy "I'll do better the next time around"?

Unexplainable cases of cognition and other phenomena that seem to support reincarnation continue to baffle those who seek to determine scientifically the validity of claims regarding past lives. In the strictest sense, there is no objective way to verify or deny such occurrences. Some tales of former existences are obviously fraudulent. People with low self-esteem have been known to invent marvelous stories in which they were persons of power, beauty, and nobility in another age. But what about those cases where an individual recounts in precise detail a number of verified facts concerning another place or time about which he presumably knew nothing?

Intuitive recall ("déjà vu," as it is commonly known) is the experience of having done something or having been somewhere before. Could this explain the phenomenon of reincarnation? It should be noted that the human subconscious mind contains an incalculable record of sights and sounds, most of which have long since been forgotten. Movies, TV programs, photographs, songs, and literature may provide bits and pieces from which the mind composes the image of a person or place, creating the feeling that it all happened in precisely the same way at some other time in the past. Even though the person or place may not be consciously recalled, the mind may have been imprinted with the memory of an instance with striking similarity. Some psychologists have also speculated that cases of déjà vu result when the experiential and memory functions of the brain go slightly out of phase. In this case, one really *has* been there before—a split second earlier.

Spontaneous recall, the memory a child may have concerning a previous life, is often intriguing but seldom verifiable. Most cases reported by researchers such as Dr. Stevenson (mentioned earlier) involve children raised in cultures with a predisposition to belief in reincarnation. Considering the vivid imagination of most youngsters, it would take little parental encouragement to spin a tale of fascinating proportions. The resulting doting attention would enable even a child's mind to construct a very believable scenario.

What about the girl's case at the beginning of this discussion? Did hypnotism actually regress her to another life in New York circa 1943? Hypnosis is an unreliable technique to judge qualitatively. Deeply imbedded memories may surface that seem to validate reincarnation. A good novel or an impressive film, long since forgotten, may set the stage for a compelling story the hypnotist accepts as a first-person account. Under hypnosis, the subject has a tendency to be suggestively guided by the hypnotist, who may bring forth information that he in part has unwittingly planted. In summary, hypnosis is hardly a reliable investigative tool to probe the proofs of reincarnation.

The greatest danger in using hypnosis to verify reincarnation is the subject's spiritually vulnerable condition, in which a trance state could be manipulated by demonic forces. The information about another life being impressed upon the mind may come from an alien spiritual source. Since these beings have existed far back beyond the span of recorded history, they could easily construct a verifiable time, person, and place, because they were there! Such a case would indeed seem legitimate, since the demon could supernaturally provide any data necessary apparently to confirm a previous existence. And the individual in question could honestly claim to have had no means of secretly or unwittingly obtaining such information. People may be led to assume that since the facts are correct, the phenomenon verifies reincarnation. But confirming a particular circumstance does not automatically verify that it actually took place. If the source of the information is evil, and if the application is unbiblical, nothing is proved except that Satan is able supernaturally to manipulate one's consciousness. The spiritual source of reincarnation episodes needs to be tested (1 John 4:1), and the accuracy of the facts in question must be verified.

In spite of reincarnation's unconcealable ethical and spiritual inconsistencies, advocates seek to buttress their claims by quoting Scripture. While acknowledging that the Bible does not explicitly endorse reincarnation, they do cite a few verses that appear to support their theories.

These references are listed below, along with the orthodox perspective on each passage.

1. Matt. 14:2 – His critics may have suggested that Jesus was a reincarnation of John the Baptist, but the Bible doesn't endorse their claim. Even by the tenets of reincarnation such a proposition would not have been possible, since Jesus was a grown adult when John was beheaded.

2. John 8:58 – If Jesus had actually suggested he was a reincarnation of Abraham, the Jews would have dismissed him as a lunatic. They tried to kill Christ because they knew that his claim to be the "I Am" before Abraham was an assertion of his eternally preexistent deity.

3. Heb. 7:1-4 – Melchizedek is merely presented as a type of Christ, whose priesthood is a point of comparison with that of Jesus. Even if one accepts Melchizedek as a theophany (Old Testament appearance of Christ), which I do not, such a conclusion would still not endorse a belief in reincarnation.

4. Matt. 11:14 – To say that John the Baptist was a reincarnation of Elijah is to ignore his own answer to those who raised this possibility. "I am not," he emphatically declared (1 John 1:21). Luke plainly records that it was in the "spirit and power," the *style* of Elijah's ministry, that John came (Luke 1:17).

5. John 3:1-8 – Jesus clearly indicates in this passage that he is speaking of a spiritual, not natural birth. The emphasis is upon God's requirement for entrance into his kingdom, not a succession of cyclic rebirths on a journey to nirvana.

In contrast to the attempt made by reincarnationists to justify their beliefs by quoting certain Scriptures, the Bible is filled with proof texts that deal a fatal blow to any hopes of an evolving soul. Here are some passages that may be cited to refute reincarnation:

1. Phil. 1:21 – "For me to live is Christ and to die is gain." The "gain" by death of which the Apostle Paul speaks expresses his longing to be immediately "with Christ."

2. 2 Cor. 5:8 – "We are confident and willing rather to be absent from the body, and to be present with the Lord." To leave this body is to be instantly in the presence of Jesus, not floating

around the realms of the spirit world waiting in line for another body to inhabit.

3. Acts 7:59—"And they stoned Stephen, calling upon God, and saying, Lord Jesus, receive my spirit." While being stoned, Stephen beheld Christ awaiting him in glory upon the moment of his death, without having to perfect his karma through any further lives.

4. Luke 23:43—"Jesus said, Verily I say unto thee, To day shalt thou be with me in paradise." The thief on the cross received the promise of paradise that very day, instead of a lecture on how he'd be punished in the next life for the sins leading to his crucifixion.

5. Acts 17:31—"Because he hath appointed a day, in which he will judge the world in righteousness. . . ." How could the certainty of God's judgment be specified by an appointed day if varying numbers of reincarnations would be necessary for each person before all mankind could be perfected?

6. Eccles. 12:7—"Then shall the dust return to earth as it was: and the spirit shall return unto God who gave it." Solomon in his wisdom declared that the destination of man's spirit is not another body, but an appearance before God to be judged.

7. 1 John 3:2—"But we know that, when he shall appear, we shall be like him; for we shall see him as he is." The expectation of every Christian is to be like Christ in the resurrection, instead of acquiring multiple identities through a series of reincarnations.

8. Rev. 3:21—"To him that overcometh will I grant to sit with me in my throne. . . ." The redeemed of Christ look forward at death to being joined with Christ, reigning with him instead of being indistinguishable, absorbed into an impersonal essence.

9. John 9:1-3—"And as Jesus passed by, he saw a man which was blind from his birth. And his disciples asked him, saying, Master, who did sin, this man, or his parents, that he was born blind? Jesus answered, Neither hath this man sinned, nor his parents: but that the works of God should be made manifest in him." When the disciples echoed a popular notion similar to the principles of karma, Jesus succinctly stated that the child's blindness since birth was in no way associated with either his moral conduct or that of his parents.

These Scriptures indicate that reincarnation and the Bible are mutually exclusive. No false claim of countless opportunities of reformation can stand alongside the finished work of Christ's redemption. The sacrifice of Christ on the cross and the shedding of his blood cannot be compatible with a system of belief that denies his atonement. The law of karma inhibits any choice of the will to determine a life of obedience to God's plan. It is a selfish concept that sees no merit in sacrifice for the welfare of others, and only despair and resignation, not hope, are its result. Reincarnation offers no loving God, no forgiving grace, and robs the Almighty of his attribute of mercy.

The Apostle Paul told Timothy (1 Tim. 4:1) to avoid any doctrine that comes of demonic inspiration. Reincarnation surely qualifies in this regard, for it seeks to replace the hope of the Christian faith—the Resurrection. Paul's great treatise on the resurrection found in 1 Corinthians 15 states without compromise, "If Christ be not raised, your faith is in vain" (v. 17). It is no wonder that a fatalistic gloom permeates any religious system that upholds reincarnation. As Paul put it, "If in this life only we have faith in Christ, we are of all men most miserable" (v. 19). It is the promise of eternal life with Jesus immediately beyond the grave that brings worth and meaning to serving Christ in this life.

Daniel foreshadowed the hope of Christ's victory over death (Dan. 12:2) by reminding the reader that either shame or everlasting life await all who die. Jesus affirmed the same alternatives in John 3:36, and offered the proof of his own body to substantiate his promise. He invited Thomas to place a hand in his side (John 20:27) and challenged his disciples to touch him, to feel his flesh and bones (Luke 24:39). Such infallible proofs were witnessed by hundreds of his followers over a period of forty days, removing any doubts that he had conquered man's last enemy. Instead of directing them to prepare for successive reincarnations, Jesus instructed them to prepare for the day when they too would be raised from the dead to be with him forever (1 Thess. 4:17)!

· 4 ·

MEDITATION

Meditation is one of the most misunderstood words in the vocabulary of cults. The average noncultist is put off by shaven heads, secret ceremonies, and mind control. But meditation has such a harmless ring to it. After all, the Bible encourages meditation. So, whatever other practices of cults may raise eyebrows, meditation is seen as possibly beneficial and certainly not dangerous. Such a conclusion is erroneous. In fact, of all the techniques facilitating the goals of cult philosophy, meditation probably ends up being the one practice that is the most spiritually devastating. Meditation isn't a neutral indulgence. Its benefits or damage depend on why and how one meditates.

Though the Western world has rediscovered the phenomenon of a contemplative life, meditation is as old as the Hindu Vedic scriptures and the Book of Joshua. "This book of the law shall not depart out of thy mouth; but thou shalt meditate therein day and night," the Word of God declares (Joshua 1:8). Since the words "meditate" or "meditation" appear twenty times in the Old and New Testaments, it is unquestionable that the lost art of biblical meditation is strongly endorsed in Scripture. What, then, makes it different from the procedures recommended by TM and other Eastern cults?

The "how" of mystical meditation involves a process of shutting down the mind. While the Bible emphasizes the importance of knowledge as a key to communion with God, the mystic wishes to pacify the will and ego until they no longer function actively. Christianity teaches that the channel of the mind represents one avenue by which God reveals his laws and love. The Creator has gifted man with the capacity of reason, which plays an important role in discerning the will and ways of the Lord. Eastern mysticism considers the mind to be an enemy of the spirit. Therefore, it must be set aside by techniques that cause it to cease functioning.

This assault on the mind may involve a physical or verbal means of stilling its processes. Fasting, posturing positions, long periods of silence, and repetitive *mantras* are just a few of the techniques employed. The mantra is the most popular and frequently used method. By repeatedly chanting a word or syllable over and over, the neurosensory faculties of the body become fatigued and shut down. This psychophysiological phenomenon can be illustrated by noticing, when entering a room with a foul odor, that the smell gradually becomes indistinguishable. In a similar manner, repeating a word over and over causes the meditator to lose touch with the objective meaning of the word. For example, saying the word "chair" in a repetitious fashion for fifteen minutes may actually render the mind incapable of consciously comprehending the relationship between what becomes a nonsensical sound and a material object on which one sits, a "chair." If the mantra is based on the name of a pagan deity or spiritual principle, an even more powerful and dangerous effect takes place that may actually induce a tranced-out state of altered consciousness.

The "why" of mystical meditation is predicated on the goal of god-realization and the merging of one's consciousness with the Universal Mind. Once the mind has been emptied of any awareness regarding the objective, external world, the meditator becomes conscious of what appears to be a unifying oneness of reality. In such a condition, mystical meditators often report a state of joy, peace, and indescribable bliss. If the meditator has previously been coached in a system of religious philosophy by which he can interpret the experience, he readily identifies it as achieving union with Ultimate Reality.

What really happens? The intensity of the experience may trigger biological responses similar to the effect drugs have when creating illusionary experiences. It might be that demonic beings seize upon the opportunity of an emptied, unguarded, and defenseless mind to create spiritistic hallucinations. On the other hand, the dormant powers of the human spirit may suddenly be unleashed. Whatever triggers the reaction, this much is certain. The mystical meditator should not be deceived into thinking that he has communed with the Lord. At best, he has only come face to face with his own alter ego, which the Bible declares to be "desperately wicked" (Jer. 17:9-10). At worst, he could have left his mind and body to an evil invasion by spirit beings associated with the particular discipline employed.

Is there any place for meditation in the life of a Christian? Yes, if the hows and whys conform to biblical standards. The child of God has no need to twist his limbs or to sit in any particular position in order to properly meditate. There is no virtue in slowing one's pulse, closing one's eyes, or being certain that unrestrictive clothing allows one to relax properly. The Christian meditator is not trying to empty his mind. Instead, he seeks to fill it with the knowledge of God. Psalm 119 speaks of meditation "all the day" with "understanding" (vv. 97-99). There is no suggestion here of any rigidly ascetic discipline, but rather a natural flow of constant concentration on the things of the Lord throughout the waking hours—working, walking, driving, eating, and talking.

Christians approach meditation differently from the mystics because they believe that the intellect was ordained of God to be a recipient of his truth. God, who is infinite and beyond our complete understanding, has graciously condescended to express himself through the human communicative skill of language. The Living Word became the written Word that we might comprehend enough of his ways to appropriate salvation through his Son. Our relationship to God is based on the experience of his presence and the understanding of his Word by which we properly evaluate the subjective dimensions of conversion.

The root word of *meditation* implies a ruminating process of slowly digesting God's truths. It involves concentrative, directive thought that ponders the laws, works, precepts, word, and person of God. "Meditate on him" is the message of Scripture. The meditation of man's soul is to be "acceptable in the sight of the Lord," not predicated on some glassy-eyed encounter with an overactive ego. In short, meditation is prayer and communication with the Lord of the Universe, not the worked-up state of hyperventilation found in some cults.

Biblical meditation is not formless and aimless. It is the natural process of being constantly absorbed by God's life and love. And it means setting aside the mundane things of this world to concentrate on the kingdom of God. Mystical meditation worships the self as a divine inner manifestation of God. Biblical meditation reaches outward to a transcendent God who lifts us above our sinful inner nature to fellowship with him through the blood of his Son. The Christian who meditates according to the scriptural pattern finds his mind "renewed" (Rom. 12:2). Unlike the mystic whose deepest thoughts lead to darkness, the believer who actively thinks upon those things that are of a "good report" (Phil. 4:8) finds comfort and direction for the activities of life.

PART THREE

CULTIC

ROOTS

IN

WORLD

RELIGIONS

· 1 ·
PROLOGUE

The superstructure of modern cultism is built upon the foundation of past religious speculations. As Solomon expressed it, "There is no new thing under the sun. . . . Is there any thing whereof it may be said, See, this is new? It hath been already of old time, which was before us" (Eccles. 1:9-10). While each cult claims to have newly revealed truth, most are syncretistic coalescences of beliefs borrowed from the religious systems that have superseded them.

Modern cults often borrow bits and pieces from each other (est from Mind Dynamics and Lifespring from est). Others trace their lineage directly to the classic religions of man (Hare Krishna to Hinduism, and Black Muslims to Islam). Even when a cult may not have an obvious link with a major religious system, the inherent nature of its teachings indicates roots in a faith of the past. When the Christian Scientist denies the existence of matter, he owes a debt of gratitude to the Hindu philosophers who expounded the concept of *maya* (referring to the illusory nature of the material world). The karate student may only be interested in perfecting physical prowess, but the martial art he practices could not have existed without the enlightenment of Buddha and the *satori* of certain Zen masters. Each guru imported to our shores, from Yogi Bhajan to Muktananda Paramahansa, only echoes the variation of a theme developed millennia ago.

For these reasons, it is important to understand the current proliferation of cults in the perspective of their spiritual heritage. Only by understanding a doctrine in its original form are we able to distinguish the subtleties of its contemporary variations. And by observing how much knowledge today's cultists have borrowed from ancient teachers and sages, we can determine more easily the commonality of cultic inspiration. Understanding the eclectic inclinations of cult systems may lead one to conclude that some kind of masterminded conspiracy is underfoot.

Why is it so many cults deny the existence of evil, the personality of God, and the necessity of an atoning Savior? Why do they gravitate so often to reincarnation, astrology, and other occult practices? Why is there such reverence for the *man* Jesus, but no recognition of his sinless deity? And why is the Bible quoted so often, but at the same time denied the importance of its validity? Is there something or someone behind it all?

The evangelical Christian answers a resounding, "Yes!" He has not forgotten Lucifer's first rebellious challenge to the Lord, "I will be like the Most High!" Since Satan is by nature a destroyer and not a creator, he is handicapped by his own evil attributes. That's why there is so little originality in false teachings. The devil can only mimic God by taking what is true and twisting it just enough to produce an erroneous facsimile of reality. By studying the major religions of the world we uncover the essence of this diabolical error. As we enter the center of the spider's web, we can then trace from this focal point the vast network of "new" spiritual disciplines mushrooming into existence.

· 2 ·

HINDUISM

"Truth is one. They call him by different names," proclaim the *Vedas*, most sacred of all Hindu texts. In a nutshell, that is the essence of Hinduism, the most absorptive, assimilative, and perhaps oldest false religion of mankind. In fact, the revered sage Mahatma ("Great Soul") Gandhi once wrote: "A man may not believe in God and still call himself a Hindu."

To know Hinduism, one must first understand the Indian culture and history. Unlike most religions that have an ecclesiastical order and hierarchical governing body, Hinduism might be viewed as religious anarchy in action. But what would be viewed as a weakness by other devotional structures is seen as a source of durability by the Hindu. Time is on his side. Since the Aryan Indo-Europeans stormed into the subcontinent from the north in 1500 B.C., Hinduism has grown in zeal and numbers. Even though its rituals and beliefs are inextricably interwoven with the Indian social fabric, its amalgamating tentacles have reached out beyond 680 million Indian devotees to the shores of North America.

The term *Hinduism* is derived from the Sanskrit word *Sindhu* or *Indus* (ocean or river), a geographical instead of theological designation first used by the Persian invaders. This origin underscores the importance of understanding Indian history, which is divided into four periods. The first is called pre-Vedic and dates back beyond three millennia. Known as Dravidians, the earliest settlers of the Indian Peninsula were animis-

61

tic. Local deities were worshiped in a fashion resembling witchcraft. The Aryan conquerors brought their own gods, such as Soma, deity of the hallucinogenic soma plant. The *Vedas* ("wise sayings" or "knowledge") dominated the religious philosophy of this second period. Originally these texts were orally preserved, but by 1000 B.C. they were collected into written form (such as the ten-volume set of 1,028 hymns and prayers known as the *Rig Veda*). The extreme polytheistic nature of Hinduism developed during this time. (Hinduism proverbially has 33 million gods, although the number is a metaphorical allusion to the seemingly infinite array of deities and is not intended to be a definitive numerical designation.)

It was during this second historical period that the caste system began developing. Castes were originally an outgrowth of vocational classifications: *Brahmins* were priests and scholars; *Kshatriyas* the rulers and soldiers; *Vaishyas* the merchants and farmers; *Sudras* the peasants and servants. In later centuries, this class division was presumed to be a justification for the doctrines of karma and reincarnation (earlier discussed). One's caste became fixed at birth and was so immutable that a Brahmin dying of thirst would not take water from a Sudra lest he be polluted.

Eventually, a social mosaic of 3,000 subcastes developed with those known as Untouchables at the bottom of the list. Untouchables were seen as virtually inhuman and good only to clean dirt, excrement, and blood. Though Gandhi and other reformers persuaded the Indian Parliament to outlaw Untouchability in its 1949 Constitution, it remains a hallowed tradition in the villages where most Indians live. There, endogamy, marriage only within one's caste, is a socially enforced practice. While other castes may not share the degradation of the Untouchables, they are intimidated with the knowledge that they were created from the feet of Brahma while the Brahmins sprang from Brahma's face.

About 600 B.C. the third (Upanishadic) period dawned on India. The *Upanishads* transformed the dominant religious outlook from a positive view of fulfillment to an escapist outlook seeking release from life. In the *Rig Veda* the old Vedic gods were merely finite superhumans who indulged in licentiousness and debauchery. The *Artharvaveda* emphasized themes of exorcism and spellcasting in its 6,000 verses. In contrast, the 108 poems of the *Upanishads* (which means "sitting at the feet of" and conjures images of sages instructing disciples) synthesized what would become the basic doctrines of Hinduism.

Hinduism had always been a grassroots religion of the masses, but the

Upanishads developed it into a monistic, philosophic faith. Life was seen as an endless cycle of the soul's transmigration (*samsara*). Escaping the retributive law of karma and achieving liberation (*moksha/mukti*) from the wheel of life would occur only when the *atman* (individual soul) would be identified with and absorbed by the Universal Soul (Brahman). This establishment of a religious worldview known as Brahmanism was the beginning of modern Hinduism as it is known today. Its two basic theological premises are rooted in pantheism (the belief that God is at one with and pervasive in all created matter) and monism (the idea that "all is one," the universe exists as a unitary principle).

The final period of Hinduism's development occurred after the beginning of the Christian era when the Vedantic literature became the dominant scriptures. Under the leadership of the philosopher Shankara, who expounded the theory of *maya* (all matter and reality is illusory), Hinduism enjoyed a revival from the corrupt and sterile forms that had developed. Self-renunciation and moral duty (*dharma*) became a pathway to freedom from the self and inclusion in the impersonal One (*nirvana*, a heavenly state).

Maya, in all its ramifications, is the explanation the Westerner is given when he sees the suffering and poverty of India. I have walked the streets of Indian cities where millions sleep on sidewalks and naked children bathe in gutters. Even as a writer, words seem inadequate to describe the sight of lepers and the congenitally deformed banging on the taxi window to beg for *buckshesh* (handouts) and wretched waifs with crippled bodies rummaging through garbage for morsels of food.

The Hindu has inoculated himself against any empathy for his fellow man. All of the universe is *lila*, God's cosmic game. And pain and pleasure are not absolutes but an illusion. The suffering one sees is not real, it is *maya* and therefore unworthy of any efforts to alleviate. Furthermore, to extend kindness to those who are less fortunate would be to disobey the law of karma. That poor creature is suffering because of his sins in a past life, and lending any assistance to his state would violate the sacred principle of divine vengeance.

It might appear to the reader as though Hinduism is a religion too complex to explain in terms of basic presuppositions. As one writer stated, "It rejects nothing. It is all comprehensive, all tolerant, all compliant." Still, there are some common denominators in Hinduism's past and present.

All Hindus do share the same basic scriptural foundation. Granted, certain sects may emphasize one school of literature over another, but the *Vedas* and *Upanishads* remain supreme. (Other revered scriptures include the *Mahabharata, Sutras, Ramayana, Aranyakas,* and the *Brahma-Sutra.*) The most popular Hindu writing is the portion of the Indian epic, the *Mahabharata,* known as the *Bhagavad-Gita,* "Song of the Lord." It might well be called the bible of India. (This volume will be discussed in more detail in the analysis of Hare Krishna later in the book.) The *Gita's* message centers on developing indifference to desire, pleasure, and pain. Its message of "salvation" is found in Krishna's words, "Whoever surrenders to me is not destroyed." Hindus also share a similar view of God, man, and their relationship to each other. At the heart of Hinduism is a monotheistic conundrum that views reality as being of one essence, but also insists that it has many forms or expressions (polytheism). The human soul *(atman)* is divine and yearns for union with Brahma. This Brahma-atman unity produces an illuminating, mystical experience. In this state, the self or ego is dissolved, extinguished by the oneness of God. Since man is ultimately God, and sin is merely an illusion, moral guilt and final judgment for one's conduct are moot concepts.

The divisions of Hinduism are more devotional than theological. One's favorite deity tends to classify the school of thought and form of ritual to which one ascribes. Brahma is the Creator (*Brahma* is the masculine form of *Brahman,* which is neuter), *Vishnu* is the Preserver, and *Shiva* (sometimes spelled *Siva*) is the Destroyer. These three comprise the Hindu Trinity. Though there are hundreds of deities with whom the Hindu is usually familiar, it is Vishnu and Shiva who elicit the most devotion. Followers of these gods are divided into Vaishnavites and Shaivites. Vaishnavites generally concentrate their attention on one of Vishnu's ten incarnations (i.e. *Rama, Krishna, Buddha,* and *Kalkin* who is yet to appear). As the Vedic sun god, Vishnu's popularity was based on his power to reincarnate. The Symbionese Liberation Army, associated with the Patty Hearst kidnapping and the sixties' radicalism in the U.S., chose as its symbol a seven-headed cobra, a manifestation of Vishnu as *Sesha* the serpent king. Shiva, however, attracts the most attention and devotion. The multiplicity of characters he assumes in Indian folklore has enhanced his popularity. A study of his disguises and forms says much about the essence of Hinduism. Here are some examples: *Bhairava* — the patricidal god of terror using his father's skull for a bowl; *Ardhanarisvara* — an androgynous, hermaphroditic sexual image; *Nataraja* — lord of the dance with four arms. Shiva wanders naked about the countryside on his white bull *Nandi,* overindulging in drugs and encouraging starvation and self-mutilation. The innermost sanctuaries of Shiva temples always feature a *lingam,* the stylized erect phallus that symbolizes his rampant sexuality.

On a moral scale, his female consorts assume no better role. *Shakti,* for example, encourages orgies, temple prostitution, and annual sacrifices. She is also credited with originating *sutee,* the sacrifice of widows throwing themselves into the fire of their husband's funeral pyre. (This practise was opposed by the nineteenth-century reformer Rammohun Roy, but continues today in remote areas.) But it is Shakti's manifestation as *Kali* that presents her most sinister and bloodthirsty image.

Idols of Kali show her standing on a beheaded body, wearing a necklace of human skulls. I have personally witnessed animal sacrifices at Kali temples. When priests were questioned as to the bloody overtones of a god trampling corpses, they replied that the image of Kali portrays a "dualistic perspective of illusion and reality." Philosophy aside, even today there are a reported 100 human sacrifice murders every year in India, all in honor of Kali.

To comprehend fully the philosophical structure of Hinduism, one must first understand the concepts of karma, reincarnation, and the doctrine of *avatars.*

Karma is "an inexorable law of retributive justice . . . an internal law of nature independent of . . . the gods." Unlike the sowing and reaping law of Galatians 6:7, karma has no final judgment. Its consequences are felt in this life, and the next, and so on. Every act in this life influences the fate of the immortal soul's next incarnation. The wealthy and healthy are viewed as having accumulated good karma in a previous life, while the less fortunate are seen as getting their just reward for past sins. In other words, sin and punishment are mathematically adjusted on a divine scale.

In the system of karma, there is no forgiving Savior to redeem the consequences of one's deeds. The action of karma keeps moving onward, adding good or evil to its credit in a merciless manner. Though all Hindus seek *moksha,* liberation from the bondage of karma, most resign themselves to the fact that they may need to be reborn millions of times to accomplish the feat. Evangelical Christians may find karma a difficult belief to understand since they are accustomed to the idea that, although each man is accountable to God, he can also become a new, forgiven creation in this life (2 Cor. 5:17). (John 9:1-3 is the most direct biblical account refuting karma: Jesus pointed out that a certain man's blindness did not result from sins in a previous existence.)

The doctrine of reincarnation, which influences so many New Age cults, is an integral belief of Hinduism. Though an earlier chapter covered the subject exhaustively, a few comments are in order at this point. Whereas the Christian anticipates a resurrection of his body, the Hindu views his physical nature as the source of his soul's bondage. Even animals are subject to the cycles of rebirth known as *samsara*. The Bible teaches that each human maintains his personal identity throughout all eternity. In Hindusim, the consciousness of each individual is irrelevant since he might come back after death as a monkey or goat or even a plant (in extreme Hinduistic views).

In spite of attempts to cite biblical pretexts supporting reincarnation (i.e., the Transfiguration in Matthew 17 and Jesus' statement in John 8:58 – "before Abraham was, I am"), Hebrews 9:27 explicitly states that all men die once. In contrast to reincarnation's uncertain game of chance with life, in John 5:28-29 Jesus indicated but two destinations for living souls: "the resurrection of life" and "the resurrection of judgment." The basis for the theory of reincarnation is that man can eventually work out his own salvation, contrary to the Christian doctrine of grace. In addition, it marks a fundamental difference in the view of creation. Hinduism sees each soul as but a portion of the First Cause with only legendary explanations as to how each being came into its original state of existence. This is a sharp contrast to the Genesis account of man's origin as occurring from a divine act of creation by a purposeful God possessing a moral will.

Since the doctrines of karma and reincarnation leave man in a somewhat hopeless state, victimized by the forces of cosmic chance, the Hindu philosophers needed to inject some ray of hope. The impact of Christianity forced Hinduism to come up with some method of illustrating the personality of an impersonal god and thus show the way to avoid endless transmigrations. The theistic branch of Hinduism made the Unknowable God more approachable by suggesting that he would occasionally incarnate in some illusory form visible to man. Such a god-man is called an *avatar*. This event is not a constant occurrence, but only takes place once for each age when man is in desperate need of such assistance.

Krishnaites cite the *Bhagavad-Gita* as the best example of God incarnating in flesh, though twenty-one other examples are also mentioned in the epic. Unlike Christ who came to earth to be an eternal Savior by dying once for the sins of men (Heb. 10:10-12), the Hindu avatar must return again and again to show men the way to God. The god Vishnu, whose job it is to sustain the universe, takes human birth in the form of *Narayana,* the seed of all avatars. Of this belief the *Srimad Bhagavata* states, "As countless rivers are born from an ocean that never goes dry, so countless are the descents of the lord."

Below the rank of major incarnations (Krishna, Rama, et al.) there are "minor rays from the supreme radiance," partial or lesser avatars. *Swamis* are learned, usually celibate, monks who follow the ascetic road to God. *Sadhus* are the less educated "holy men" who seek spiritual merit by meandering restlessly (and often naked with cow dung in their hair) across India. A step up the Hinduistic ladder is the guru, a religious teacher who has mastered the path of yoga. He may be a Perfect Master, a *satguru* capable of transmitting instantaneous enlightenment and thus leading disciples directly to god-realization.

The avatar, on the other hand, is a human object of veneration and worship. He is supposed to possess supernatural powers (*siddhis*) and is said to be totally merged with God. His incarnation is seen as an act of love since he is totally enlightened. Thus, he has no karmic unfinished business to settle on earth, which would require his return. An avatar may show human emotion, since he is in a body, but his spiritual perception is supposed to be beyond the *maya* of time and space.

Hinduism has no single system of salvation. Instead, the philosophy of *yoga* ("union with God") offers four different pathways to God, depending on the disposition of the seeker. *Bhakti Yoga* ("the way of devotion") is the most popular god-road in India. Love toward god is expressed by devotion to a guru who is the embodiment of divine grace. This way may also involve the recitation of god-name mantras. *Karma Yoga* ("the way of service") generally appeals to more active individuals who are willing to perform ceremonies diligently, make pilgrimages, and carry out actions of good work. *Jnana Yoga* ("the way of knowledge") requires that one seek out sadhus and gurus and also explore the sacred Hindu scriptures. By knowledge the seeker comes to realize the divine nature of his atman. *Raja Yoga* ("the way of contemplation") inculcates meditation techniques that are known as the "royal road." The devotee must learn to discipline his body and mind to achieve *samadhi,* union with the Absolute.

On a practical level of daily life, these disciplines involve an endless array of idolatrous ceremonies and rituals. Deities kept in the home must be "awakened," "fed," "washed," and "put to sleep" each night. These acts of *puja* ("worship") are followed with exacting detail. There are temples to visit, offerings (money, flowers, fruit) to deposit, and pilgrimages to make. Every devout Hindu hopes at least once in his life to visit the "holy city" of Banaras, or the sacred source of the Ganges at Gaumukh, high in the Himalayas. He may settle for some major festival like the famous Car Festival of Jugannath in Puri, where devotees suicidally throw themselves in front of a huge chariot bearing a deity's image. Despite the lofty philosophical ideals of Hinduism, its effect can be seen in the more bizarre outgrowths inherent in this ancient faith.

In some villages, temples care for and feed sacred rats at a cost of $4,000 a year. Such vermin dispose of 15 percent of India's grain. The cobra, which is also worshiped, kills 20,000 Indians each year. Females, which Hindu legends relegate to a decidedly inferior state, are so despised that some Indian mothers deliberately strangle their girl babies. Sadhus, in the name of religious devotion, have been known to sit on a bed of nails and not speak for years, grow their hair into seven-foot braids, stand on a leg like a stork for months, or hold an arm outstretched until it has atrophied.

But sacred cows get the most publicity—all 159 million of them, which is 20 percent of the world's total. (Since the cow is believed to be the mother-goddess of life, its urine is drunk to purify the soul.) They freely roam the streets of urban centers like Bombay and Calcutta, depositing dung everywhere. Aged holy cows are even provided with rest homes called *gosadans*. I once observed two Indian women fighting over a pile of warm fresh cow manure. A swami nearby explained their zeal by declaring, "Since the cow is a god, the cow is holy. Therefore, whatever comes out of the cow is also holy."

These and other less desirable aspects of Hinduism have sparked momentarily effective reform movements. The most successful was that of Buddha, who developed the Hindu ideal of *ahimsa* (nonviolence to all living things) into a social creed. (Buddhism will be discussed in more detail in the next chapter.) The Jains, led by the sixth-century ascetic Mahavira, enforce the command against killing to such an extent that present-day followers of this sect still avoid even swatting a fly.

Jains strain the water they drink, sweep the path in front of them lest they step on an ant, and sometimes go on death-defying fasts as the ultimate way to avoid destroying any life-form. Mahavira proclaimed that spiritual truth could be found in the "three jewels" of Right Faith, Right Knowledge, and Right Living. In pursuit of these goals, Jain monks never bathe, brush their teeth, or sleep on a bed. With such a rigidly ascetic view of life it is little wonder that Mahavira's disciples today number little more than a million worldwide.

The other major reform movement in Hinduism's history was the fifteenth-century upheaval of Sikhism brought about by the guru Nanak. Disavowing castes and idolatry, he grafted Islamic ideals onto a Hinduistic system of salvation-by-works, to which he added the grace of god (whom he called Sat Nam, "True Name"). The *Granth,* a collection of poems and prayers from the first four Sikh gurus, is Sikhdom's bible and is literally worshiped as a symbolic guru. Sikhism eventually turned into a militant brotherhood marked by five "Ks": *kes,* long hair; *kangha,* comb; *kacha,* short pants; *kara,* iron bracelet; *kirpan,* sword. It is said that if a Sikh ever unleashes his sword, its blade must draw blood, even if it is his own. Sikhism remains a vital faith for eight million Indians and more than 200,000 Americans (to be discussed later in reference to Yogi Bhajan).

The final reform movement that needs consideration is the Vedanta movement organized in the 1800s by Swami Vivekananda. India's conquest by England created a Hindu renaissance in response to the incursion of an alien culture and religion. Vivekananda, a disciple of Sri Ramakrishna, insisted that man's greatest good was to express his humanity. In 1893 he created a sensation by addressing the Parliament of Religions in Chicago. His emphasis was on the unity of all religions with special importance placed on promoting Vedantic Hinduism with missionary fervor.

With nearly 100,000 spiritually curious young Americans flocking to India's shores each year, the exportation of Hinduistic variants will likely continue. Hinduism apparently has little about which to worry. Governmental policies in India render it a virtual state religion, thwarting Christian missionary efforts. As the West embarks upon a post-Christian pilgrimage, Hinduism may continue to look ever more attractive in spite of its inconsistencies and abject failures to alleviate human misery in its own motherland. Certainly the popularity of such award-winning films as *Gandhi* and *A Passage to India* show that the West is more and more favorably inclined to India and its spiritual essence. Kipling's dictum suggesting that East and West were diametric opposites that would never meet may prove to be a hollow prophecy that could not have predicted spiritually bankrupt Occidentals looking for hope in the ancient Indus valley.

Founder: No founder or exact date of origin is known. The precepts of Hinduism go back at least 4,000 years and have evolved over the millennia without a codified form.

Text: Hindu scriptures: *Vedas, Upanishads* and other *Sruti* (canonical revealed scriptures) plus the *Smriti* (traditional, semicanonical writings).

Symbol: What has become known in the twentieth century as the Nazi swastika. In the Sanskrit it was known as *svastika,* meaning "conducive to well-being." Originally it denoted the duality of the universe and implied good luck.

Appeal: Most religious systems (excepting Christianity) may promote an inclusive viewpoint but ultimately require adherence to specific beliefs that set them apart from other devotional structures. Hinduism is an all-encompassing faith that strives to adopt other doctrines into its own interpretation and frame of reference. In the words of Radha Krishna, "While fixed intellectual beliefs mark off one religion from another, Hinduism sets itself no such limits." Its doctrines of karma and reincarnation insure even the most evil men that there will be a second chance to progress upward spiritually.

Purpose: Each soul is an immortal part of the Universal Soul from which it came. Reemergence into the Impersonal Absolute is the goal of each living creature. One must therefore choose the system of god-realization that will most expediently avoid the cycles of rebirth (reincarnation) and permit him to achieve oneness with God.

Errors: The polytheistic and idolatrous practices of Hinduism are pagan forms of worship that constitute collusion with demonic forces. Karma's system of salvation-by-conduct is contrary to the biblical doctrine of salvation by the sole grace of God. The Hindu cannot acknowledge his need of a Savior without repudiating his entire belief system. As Vivekananda said, "It is a sin to call a person a sinner." The Hindu strives to attain purity by becoming a god, instead of having his sins washed away by the imputed righteousness of a transcendent, personal God. Christ cannot be accepted as an incarnation of Vishnu or Krishna. (In the *Bhagavad-Gita,* chapter 10, Krishna declares, "I am the prince of demons.") Romans 1 denounces those who worship the creation rather than the Creator. In this respect, consider this quote from the *Vedas:* "Worship, O Cow, to thy tail-hair, and to thy hooves, and to thy form."

Background Sources: *Great Religions of the World* (Washington, D.C.: National Geographic Society, 1971), 34-76; John Garabedian and Orde Coombs, *Eastern Religions in the Electric Age* (New York:Tempo Books, 1969); *Religions of the World* (New York: Barnes & Noble, 1965); Kenneth Boa, *Cults, World Religions and You* (Wheaton, Ill.: Victor, 1980); J. Gordon Melton, *The Encyclopedia of American Religions* (Wilmington, N.C.: McGrath, 1978); *Time,* 11 March 1974, 6; Ibid., 16 March 1981; *Newsweek,* 1 April 1979, 68; Ibid., 4 May 1981, 89; Ibid., 4 June 1979, 50; *East West Journal,* February 1978; Ibid., July 1978, 49; *Hamilton Spectator,* 6 March 1980.

Address/Location: The entire nation of India and smaller representations in Asia and the West.

· 3 ·

B U D D H I S M

Theravada, Mahayana,
Tibetan, Zen

If consumer laws of full disclosure were applied to the "sale" of religions, Buddhism would probably be left on the shelf. Many Westerners who reject the complexities and sophistication of modern life have investigated the ancient faith of India and Asia. They wrongly assume that the mystical road laid out by Gautama Buddha is a simplified path to truth. In fact, Buddhism is perhaps the most complex and paradoxical of all Eastern religions. Buddha's Eightfold Path to *nirvana* is an intricate system of rules and regulations that can require a lifetime to master.

Buddha was born in 563 B.C. in the small town of Lumbini near Nepal's border with India. The accounts given of his life are filled with facts and fables that are impossible to verify historically. As a result, the reader should be aware that the following information obtained from Buddhist tradition is partly legendary. Maya, Buddha's mother, was the wife of a ruler from the Kshatriya caste. One night she dreamed that a white elephant had a sexual relationship with her. Shortly thereafter, she found herself pregnant and bore a son whom she named Siddhartha, who was to become Gautama Buddha. Gautama was Buddha's family name. The name Buddha means "enlightened one." He is also known as Shakyamuni, referring to the Kingdom of Shakya in which he was born. Sometimes, devotees call him *Tathagata* (Truth-Winner) or *Bhagara* (Lord).

Buddha was born a prince, and during his formative years he knew only the confines of palace pleasures. When he needed cheering, his father, Suddhodana, would summon 40,000 dancing girls. At the age of sixteen Buddha married the princess Yasodharma, who bore him a son named Rahula. Everything in his aristocratic surroundings went smoothly until his early twenties. Though forbidden to roam the countryside, he left the palace grounds one day and was abruptly confronted with the realities of life.

Buddha witnessed a scene that shattered the illusions of his princely perception. A gnarled and bent old man was soliciting alms. This was Buddha's first encounter with poverty and the frailty of human existence. On other journeys beyond the palace walls he was confronted with death and disease. But the day he met a shaven, ascetic monk had the most effect upon him. The religious devotion of this monk was a sharp contrast to the leisure and wealth he had known. From that point onward, Buddha found his life unfulfilling. Finally, on his twenty-ninth birthday, he left his wife and child behind to seek the peace of nirvana and discover the cause of all suffering.

Buddha began his search by studying with two yoga masters. Unsatisfied with this approach, he turned to extreme asceticism. Sometimes he would stand without sitting for weeks. At times his diet consisted of a single grain of rice each day. In desperation he even tried eating his own excrement. One night, on his thirty-fifth birthday, as a full moon shone above, he sat down under a pipal tree in a forest near Buddha Gaya. Buddha declared, "Until I have attained understanding, I will not rise from here." That night he entered a trance state and, according to legend, remembered his previous incarnations. His "divine eye" was quickened, and he was able at last to extinguish all his ignorance and desires.

When he arose from the foot of the *Bodhi* ("wisdom") tree, Siddhartha had become Buddha. Life's problems were no longer an enigma to him. In a sermon at the nearby deer park he revealed his "truth" to five disciples. "Birth is sorrow, age is sorrow, and death is sorrow," he told them. Suffering, he explained, is the result of man's desire to seek pleasure in the existence of this life. Grief can only be excluded when a man ends all his cravings. Buddha's discovery may be summarized in these three premises: (1) existence is suffering; (2) desire causes suffering; and (3) ridding all desire ends suffering. These precepts led to a fourth conclusion: desire can be eradicated by following what Buddha called the Eightfold Path. Buddha's spiritual insights became known as the Four Noble Truths, a so-called Middle Way between asceticism and hedonism.

During Buddha's time, Northeast India was embroiled in religious and political ferment. The parochial philosophy of the Brahmanistic Hindu leaders had disenchanted the masses. In this spiritual vacuum, religious sects and charismatic leaders abounded. But Buddha was different. He dared to question the authority of the *Vedic* scriptures and advocated abolishing both the caste system and the priesthood. He also wanted to do away with prayers and ritual. Buddha even suggested that the concept of God be abolished. For the next forty-five years of his life (he died at eighty of dysentery), Buddha traveled, begging for food and setting up communities to further his teachings. With missionary zeal he commissioned his followers: "Go ye now out of compassion for the world and preach the doctrine which is glorious." Buddha's *dharma* ("way" or "doctrine" or literally "work"—*dhamma* in the Pali language that he spoke) was aimed at ending the cycle of suffering in successive transmigrations. (He borrowed Hinduism's concepts of *karma* and reincarnation.) Escape from the sorrow of existence would be possible by reaching nirvana, a condition of infinite bliss likened to an extinguished flame. Nirvana, meaning "blow out," would be the result of reaching a state where all desire is eradicated. Though local deities could be petitioned for immediate benefits, no god could facilitate the search for nirvana's enlightenment. Only the Eightfold Path would lead to this exalted spiritual realm.

The eight steps to salvation in Buddha's system are as follows: (1) Right Belief—correctly understanding the Four Noble Truths free of illusion and superstition; (2) Right Resolve—maintaining pure motives; (3) Right Speech—speaking truthfully; (4) Right Conduct—living peacefully and honestly; (5) Right Livelihood—choosing an occupation that harms no one; (6) Right Effort—seeking knowledge with self-control; (7) Right Thought—keeping an active self-critical mind; and (8) Right Concentration—practicing meditation and Raja Yoga with earnest zeal.

Such high ideals were intended to dissolve the illusion of self and free one from the wheel of existence. Buddha taught that self-effort is the key to understanding the truth. According to a pamphlet published by the Buddhist Church of America, patience and perseverance matter more than "the blood of crucifixion, [God] sacrificing his own being" on the cross. God "is not a Creator . . . does not judge or punish . . . is not transcendent" and is not a deity of "fear and mercy."

Buddha was indifferent to the question of man's origin and refused to recognize any supernatural authority in the cosmos. Man is the center of the Buddhist universe, and only what he does matters. Heaven or hell are *conditions* of feeling and emotion, not loci. No eschatalogical scheme is speculated, and no reason is offered for the reality of death and sin. Self-control, not the remission of sin, is its central doctrine. In Buddha's own words, "Seek in the impersonal for the eternal man, and having sought him out, look inward—thou art Buddha."

Buddhism appears to be a simple system of belief. In fact, it is one of the most complex of all Oriental faiths. In addition to the Four Noble Truths and the Eightfold Path, the following practices and doctrines are considered essential to attaining Buddhahood: 1. The state of *Arahatship* (being worthy) contains thirty-seven precepts to be followed by the devout Buddhist. Twenty-nine of these are in addition to the requirements of the Eightfold Path. 2. Five obstacles hinder one's approach to enlightenment—sloth, pride, malice, lust, and doubt. 3. Three refuges must be affirmed by all who belong to the *Sangha* (brotherhood of monks): refuge in Buddha, the dharma, and the Sangha. They also must adhere to 227 regulations that, among other things, forbid them to touch a woman (even their mother) or drink unstrained water (lest they kill any living thing). 4. Man has no soul but rather exists in Five Conditions: body, feeling, ideas, will, and pure consciousness. 5. Ten Commandments are propagated, the last five of which apply only to the Sangha. These "shalt nots" include: killing, stealing, adultery, lying, drinking intoxicating liquors, eating after midday, being present at any dramatic or musical performance, applying personal adornment or perfume, sleeping on a comfortable bed, and owning silver or gold. 6. Three Principles guide the Buddhist in his search for nirvana. The First Principle designates thirty-one planes of existence, from Higher Spiritual Beings on down through humans and lower Beings-in-Torment (who endure an existence similar to purgatory). The Second Principle teaches that one's karma determines his spiritual plane, though progression and retrogression are constant throughout successive transmigrations. Finally, the Third Principle promises "complete awareness" by practicing contemplation. The one who achieves this state is supposed to become immune to all feeling and emotion, including hate and love. Four progressive stages of awareness await the seeker: *Sotapatti Magga, Sakadagami Magga, Anagami Magga,* and *Arahatta Magga.* Some Buddhists believe that an individual who attains *Sotapatti Magga* can no longer "kill, seduce . . . utter falsehood, take drugs . . . make evil utterances or have bad thoughts."

For generations after his death, Buddha's teachings were orally communicated. In 245 B.C., a council of monks was held to decree the sacred teachings in written form. They drew up a three-part document in the Pali language that became known as the *Tripitaka* ("Three Baskets of Law"). Kasyapa, an original disciple of Buddha, was credited as the source of the *Abidharma Pitaka*, a basic interpretation of Buddha's message. The *Vinaya Pitaka*, containing rules for the monastic life and the Ten Commandments mentioned above was the work of another disciple named Upali. The Third "basket," or *Sutta Pitaka*, expounds Buddha's sermons and parables.

During the so-called "Indian Empire" of the ruler Asoka, Buddhism spread rapidly throughout India and Asia. After Asoka's death, Buddhism split into two main schools, one liberal and the other conservative. The latter became known as *Theravada* ("The Way of the Elder" – also sometimes called *Hinayana*, "The Lesser Vehicle"), based on the writings of an early disciple of Buddha named Sariputta. Theravada Buddhism emphasized monastic life as the pathway to nirvana and became entrenched in Burma, Sri Lanka, Cambodia, and Thailand. The canon of the *Tripitaka* became its main source of doctrine. Hinduism, which had become an abstract faith for many Indians, experienced a revival during the first century A.D. Gupta dynasty. It was at this time that *Mahayana* ("The Greater Vehicle") Buddhism emerged. Its more liberal school is prevalent in China, Korea, Japan, Tibet, Indonesia, Nepal, and Vietnam. Mahayana Buddhism is more of a cult religion utilizing incense, magic, and occult rituals. Buddha figures are objects of deified worship. (Standing, Buddha symbolizes compassion. Sitting, he signifies serenity.) The Mahayana Buddhist does not strive to become a saint *(arhat)*. More than anything he desires to be a *bodhisattva* – one who attains the supreme perfection of Buddhahood but denies his entry into nirvana to return and help mortals on their spiritual pilgrimage in this life.

Theravada (the way of the few) and Mahayana (the way of the many) are so distinct in their beliefs and practices that they almost represent two entirely different religions. The godless, virtually atheistic system of Theravada is worlds apart from the Mahayana school with its polytheistic legends of gods and goddesses. The essence of Mahayana is faith in the divinity of Buddha (and a line of *bodhisattva*). Theravada pursues the more theologically abstract goal of nirvana. A minor variant, *tantric* Buddhism, borrowed the Hindu belief in *Shakti* sexual power and developed a cult devoted to idols and magic. The union of the individual with the divine is accomplished by ritual sexual intercourse. Coitus is said to combine the opposite forces of the universe (positive masculine and negative feminine) resulting in the cohabitant's ability to perform supernatural acts.

With a quarter-billion adherents, Buddhism is the world's fourth largest major religion (behind Christianity, Islam, and Hinduism). Its numbers in North America, estimated between 100,000-200,000 (excluding Nichiren Shoshu, discussed later in the book) are growing rapidly. The image of saffron robes and begging bowls may be foreign to the Western mind, but the concept of joining a cosmic flow to abolish the ego goes down well in an age that has turned inward. Those who look Eastward for spiritual answers may find Christianity's promise of heaven less attractive than Buddhism's mystical, impenetrable "truths." To a drug-saturated generation, problem-solving by constructive action appears less desirable than the subjective quest for nirvana.

Archaeologists recently recovered a huge sandstone casket in the ruins of an ancient city near Kapilvastu, India. The inscription on the coffin indicates that the contents are the mortal remains of Buddha. "Be a lamp unto yourself," the sage declared before his death. This instruction sharply contrasts with the biblical claim to such guidance (Ps. 119:105). Buddha's wisdom, backed by the evidence of his own decayed body, seems far less credible than the Word of God, which bears the authority of Christ's empty tomb. Whether the Good News of Jesus will prevail over the introspective appeal of Buddha is a fundamental choice that may well determine the spiritual direction of Western culture.

TIBETAN BUDDHISM

Padina Sambhava, a famed pagan exorcist, introduced Buddhism to Tibet in A.D. 747. His reputation so impressed the king that the entire land soon was following his blend of Hindu/Buddhist beliefs mingled with spells and secretive *tantric* ceremonies. Devotees preceded acts of sexual union with the ritualistic consumption of wine, meat, fish, and parched grains. They instituted a priesthood of *lamas* ("superior ones") and designed prayer wheels with inscribed litanies.

Mantras and *mandalas*, mystic diagrams, were also adopted. The former (to be discussed in more detail in the analysis of TM) was believed to possess a sound able to induce transcendent experiences. *Mandalas,* circular cosmograms of the universe, were also used as an aid in worship. (The center of the *mandala* was thought to be a focal point of the universe.) Adherents of Tibetan Buddhism were taught that merely glimpsing a *mandala* could start one on the road to nirvana. They also developed the legend of *Shambhala,* an imaginary kingdom of enlightened citizens. This central Asian civilization was said to be the spiritual inspiration of the entire world. Their "warriors" were people of compassion and awareness who still serve as models of Tibetan Buddhist aspirations.

In 1951 Chinese Communist soldiers invaded the mountaintop kingdom of Tibet. At that time, the Dalai Lama (his Buddhist name is Tenzin Gyatso, meaning "radiant oceans of wisdom") was worshiped by his 6 million fellow Buddhist citizens as a god-king. Tibetans bowed before the sight of his portrait and prostrated themselves outside his 1,300-year-old Jokka Temple. The Dalai Lama finally fled the Communists in 1959, taking 110,000 refugees with him. He settled in Dharamsala, India, vowing he'd return someday to his native land. Today the Dalai Lama heads a government in exile, visiting world capitals and disciples in preparation for his awaited return as the spiritual and political leader of Tibet.

The advent of Buddhism in Tibet was so successful that by the time of the Communist invasion, as many as 10,000 monks studied at one monastery. Neighboring kingdoms in Nepal, Sikkim, and Bhutan also felt the Buddhist influence. Because of Tibet's isolation and inaccessibility, some Buddhist scholars believe it has preserved the purest form of Buddhism. Devout Tibetan Buddhists insist they are custodians of the correct traditions and esoteric teachings of the Indian saints and sages.

A major Tibetan Buddhist text, *The Tibetan Book of the Dead* (or *Bardo Thodal*) has had great influence among America's youth. The volume is an occult guide to aid one's traverse through the existence of *bardo*, the dreamlike realm between death and reincarnation. In the sixties, some who experimented with LSD reported hallucinogenic visions paralleling experiences in *The Book of the Dead,* stirring Western interest in this exotic faith. Tibetan Buddhists believe that the demons, spirits, and powers of witchcraft encountered in *The Book of the Dead* are real forces to be avoided and appeased.

The theory of reincarnated lamas (*bodhisattvas*) came to prominence in the fifteenth century. According to this doctrine, the soul of a dead lama passes to a newborn boy. The current Dalai Lama, the fourteenth incarnation in Tibetan Buddhism's line of spiritual succession, was chosen at age two after oracles were consulted. Marks found on his shoulders (said to be remnants of a deity's two extra arms) established the proof required to designate his office. The young lad also had to identify correctly the crown of his predecessor from among five examples.

The Dalai Lama has toured the West, has had glowing praise from the press and gratuitous plaudits from ecumenical religious leaders. He disarms reporters by insisting, "I'm just a humble monk." However, he did consent to perform the *Kalachakra* ceremony on a recent trip to the U.S. Participants were promised instant enlightenment and Buddhahood after completing only seven future rebirths. The essence of Tibetan Buddhist philosophy is expressed in the Dalai Lama's view of life: "If the situation can be fixed, there is nothing to worry about. If it can't be fixed, there is nothing to worry about. After all, things are due to past karma."

Such views are of crucial concern to American evangelicals who lament Buddhism's growing foothold in North America. The first Western Buddhist university has been established in Boulder, Colorado. Started by Chogyam Trungpa Rinpoche, a forty-two-year-old Tibetan exile, the Naropa Institute has effectively introduced *tantric* teachings in the West. The institution boasts thousands of summer students and a distinguished faculty including poet Allen Ginsberg and theologian Harvey Cox. Rinpoche, who was believed to be an incarnation of a revered monk, developed an enticing curriculum that includes an array of mystical and spiritualistic disciplines.

I had the opportunity to witness a Naropa-sponsored ceremony held on the University of Colorado campus. Fifteen hundred students (many of them having graduate status) paid eight dollars each to witness the Tibetan Buddhist Vajra Crown Ceremony. His Holiness, Gyalwa Karmapa, was introduced as an incarnation in a lineage of *bodhisattvas*. As one having attained Buddhahood, he claimed the ability to transmit spontaneous spiritual insight. He was ushered to a ten-foot-high throne that had been constructed for the occasion. The ritual he performed consisted of his holding a black hat over his head for two minutes and forty-eight seconds! Nearly everyone in the highly educated audience was overwhelmed at the sight of such a "holy" and "enlightened" man.

Former Christian missionaries to Tibet report that Tibetan Buddhism is the most openly occult of all non-Christian world religions. Even the monks themselves make no pretense about their consorting with demonic demigods. This acknowledgment emphasizes the irony that this sect of Buddhism should gain such a powerful influence in a Christianized land. Devotees in the homeland of the Dalai Lama have kept his bedroom untouched since the day he fled, awaiting his return. Perhaps the demonic forces behind Tibetan Buddhism have deliberately prolonged his exile as a means of exporting this ancient, shamanistic faith.

ZEN BUDDHISM

"What is the sound of one hand clapping?" Most people would easily recognize this riddle without knowing either its purpose or source. This conundrum and 1,700 others like it are known as *koans*, paradoxical questions concerning imponderable thoughts. The perplexity posed by the *koan* is designed to lead the mind toward intuitive truth. In the world of Zen, logic and reason are taboo. As one Zen practitioner put it, "Be nothing, think nothing." Zen may be defined as concentration with an empty mind.

The ancient sage, Bodhidharma, who is generally credited as being the founder of Zen practices, studied Buddhism in India for over forty years. He returned to China and encouraged the ruling Emperor Wu to adopt the technique he had developed known as "wall meditation." To prove his diligence at Zen, Bodhidharma sat in a cave while staring at a wall for nine years. He eventually lost the use of his legs through atrophy and even had to cut off his eyelids so he could sustain open-eye meditation.

Nearly seven centuries later, two Japanese Buddhists developed what were to become the two prominent schools of Zen: Eisai originated the *Rinzai* sect in 1191, and Dogen initiated the *Soto* sect in 1227. Both disciplines strived to achieve the same goal of enlightenment, though Soto claimed it must be gradually attained while Rinzai insisted it could come as a flash of insight.

The *koan* is but one of several terms distinctive to the nomenclature of Zen. *Bodhi, satori, mondo* and *zazen* are other words describing Zen concepts. *Bodhi* refers to the "awakening" of introspective truth. Buddhism has traditionally held that *bodhi* could only be possible after many lives. Zen purports to offer *bodhi* here and now, perhaps today or at least in several years. Experiencing the immediate perception of truth is known as *satori*, a condition in which the meditator realizes all reality as one (pantheism). In such a state, there is no such thing as right or wrong, only subjective reality pervades the consciousness. Alan Watts, the late writer and mystic, described the state of *satori* this way: "At this moment [the universe] is so completely right as to need no explanation or justification beyond what it simply is."

Though Zen offers enlightenment more quickly than traditional Buddhism, achieving *satori* is no easy task. Zen is an arduous training of the mind with *koans* and *zazen* (seated meditation). The *roshi* (Zen master) invites the initiate to enter a *zendo* (meditation hall) where an altar and idol of Buddha are the focal points. Practicing *zazen* in the proper manner may require at least two three-hour periods each day. Hallucinogenic visions and demonic apparitions are common occurrences to persistent

Zen meditators. A thick pillow is the only comfort provided, and correct physical posture is crucial. The back must be kept perfectly erect to be certain the ears, shoulders, and navel are in proper alignment. The teeth are to be firmly closed, and the eyes have to be left open at all times. During *zazen,* the meditator is instructed to free his mind of all earthly attachments and think of "neither good, nor evil."

A pool, a rock, a flower—any object can be used to focus one's attention. The *roshi* may verbally assault the student with *mondos,* a series of rapid questions. Chief of these is the *koan* (discussed earlier). Abstract paradoxes are presented to boggle the meditator's mind. Contradictory and confused statements are posed so that he delves more deeply inward to fathom truth. If he dozes, the master may subject him to shouts and painful blows from a *keisaku* ("warning stick"). Such rigorous self-discipline accompanied by unanswerable questions is intended to trigger a newly conditioned view of reality. Ironically, in the words of Dr. T. Susuki, a foremost Western Zen master, "Zen teaches nothing."

While the precepts of Zen may not be based on specific theological doctrines, the inherent Buddhist worldview that results from *zazen* causes the meditator to see himself as an integrated part of the Whole. Buddhism presupposes that only one essence exists and that we are all somehow part of this one essence (monism). This teaching is contrary to the Christian assertion that the Eternal One (God) created the world and man out of nothing. Thus, no part of this material existence is part of God. There is an eternal distinction between the Creator and the created. The inherent contradictory nature of the anecdotal *koan* conditions the devotee to reject reason and logic and instead rely on mystical experience to test truth. Zen is ultimately an egocentric search for subjective authority while inherently denying any objective authority for morality.

Since Zen has no God, even the priests have no role of intercession for sin. There is no speculation on the nature of creation or the future of an afterlife, since everything considered important is embodied in the experience of the moment. Zen adherents consider their practices to be the quintessential essence of Buddhism, liberating the devotee from all life's miseries. Christians may see *satori* as a false perception of spiritual insight. But many young Americans who have experimented with its rigorous spiritual disciplines are obviously fascinated with the idea of Zen's narcissistic non-answers.

Founder: Siddhartha Gautama, born 563 B.C., Lumbini, Nepal. Died 483 B.C., Kapilvastu, India.

Text: *Tripitaka* Canon divided into the *Abidharma Pitaka,* the *Vinaya Pitaka,* and the *Sutta Pitaka.*

Symbols: Figure of Buddha standing with one arm raised, seated in a lotus position, or reclining.

Appeal: Truth is said to have a subjective quality that can only be experienced, not objectively communicated. Buddhism is attractive to those who find objective belief systems to be sterile and devoid of spontaneous reality. Concepts of moral accountability in an afterlife are replaced with a passive approach to traditional religious issues. Enlightenment promises a state of bliss beyond human comprehension.

Purpose: The Eightfold Path promises to rid followers of mankind's four basic evils—sensuality, the desire to perpetuate one's own existence, wrong belief, and ignorance. Those who attain Buddhahood will entertain only pure thoughts and be indifferent to wealth, pain, and pleasure. In brief, the goal is maximum well-being with a minimum of active effort.

Errors: The original ethical ideals of Buddha degenerated into a system of theological dogmas with Buddha as god and nirvana as a postmortem heaven. Idolatrous sects that advocate demonic ceremonialism and the propitiation of spirits constitute a form of witchcraft that is scripturally forbidden (Deut. 18). The greatest commandment of Jesus to love one's neighbor unselfishly (Matt. 22:35-39) contrasts sharply with the introspective egocentricity of Buddhism that has produced social indifference in the lands it has dominated. Scripture presents an orderly universe under the control of a sovereign God. Buddhists see karmic chance as life's only guiding force and make no attempt to explain the nature and origin of sin.

Background Sources: Wilson and Wildon, *Occult Shock and Psychic Forces* (San Diego: Master Books, 1980); Walter Martin, *The Kingdom of the Cults* (Minneapolis: Bethany Fellowship, 1977); John Garabedian and Orde Coombs, *Eastern Religions in the Electric Age* (New York: Tempo Books, 1969); *Great Religions of the World* (Washington: National Geographic Society, 1971); J. Gordon Melton, *The Encyclopedia of American Religions* (Wilmington, N.C.: McGrath Publishing Co., 1978); Pat Means, *The Mystical Maze* (San Bernardino, Calif.: Campus Crusade for Christ, 1976); *Religions of the World* (New York: Barnes and Noble, 1965); Kenneth Boa, *Cults, World Religions and You* (Wheaton, Ill.: Victor, 1980); Naropa Institute promotional literature; *To The Point International,* 1 November 1976, 46; Ibid., 7 March 1977, 10; *Newsweek,* 18 August 1980, 52; *Time,* 14 February 1977, 86; Ibid., 27 July 1981, 71; *The Denver Post,* 11 March 1972, 8; Ibid., 18 October 1974, 6BB; Ibid., 8 August 1975; Ibid., 11 June 1976: 7BB; Ibid., 16 July 1976, 7BB; Ibid., 20 August 1976, 5BB; Ibid., 3 September 1976, 2BB; Ibid., 14 August 1981, 26; "Is There a God?" (pamphlet of the Buddhist Church of America).

Address/Location: Buddhism is the dominant religion in many Asian countries. In the U.S. there are Buddhist churches and meditation centers in most large cities. One of them is the Naropa Institute, 1111 Pearl St., Boulder, CO 80302.

· 4 ·

TAOISM

What do acupuncture and the martial arts have in common? Both practices view the body as a microcosmic organism that needs to be balanced with the macrocosm of the universe in order to achieve physical well-being. Both are also rooted in an Oriental philosophy that teaches a duality of equilibrium known as *yin* and *yang*. Taoism, the root of this theory, has been the victim of official governmental persecution in its homeland of China. But while the Communist rulers seek to stamp out this ancient faith, Westerners increasingly look to it as an antidote in a neurotic, materialistic age. Taoism (pronounced dow-ism) is not a major world religion. But its teachings influence so many modern cults that a brief survey of its precepts is essential.

Lao-tse was born in southern China in 604 B.C. His name, meaning "wise old child," was derived from the legend that he was born an old man. He was an archivist who wearied of political life and dropped out of society. For decades he lived in a hut on the slope of a mountain. It was there, at eighty years of age, he wrote the bible of Taoism, *Tao Te Ching*. The 5,000-word volume discussed the nature of life in relationship to its harmony with the universe. *Tao* means "way" and *Te* denotes "virtue." Thus, the book came to be known as "the way of virtue," or simply the Tao ("the way").

Chuang Tzu, a third-century B.C. Chinese philosopher, spread the teachings of Lao-tse. Chuang believed the *Tao Te Ching* was the source of all wisdom and the solution to all life's problems. Though Taoism origi-

84

nally ignored a Creator-God, the principle of the Tao eventually was equated with a God-concept. "Before the Heaven and Earth existed, there was something nebulous . . . I do not know its name and I address it as Tao," Lao-tse wrote.

The Tao is considered to be eternal and all-pervasive. Taoism teaches that when events and things are allowed to exist in natural harmony with the macrocosmic force, peace will result. The wise man is supposed to order his life according to the Tao, living passively in tune with the universe. The basic doctrines of Taoism are summarized in practical form as the so-called Three Jewels: compassion, moderation, and humility. Goodness, simplicity, gentleness, and purity are also virtues Taoism seeks to inculcate.

The most important aspect of Taoistic philosophy to consider when discussing modern cults is the dualistic view of opposites known as *yin* and *yang*. These two essences are said to symbolize the complementary nature of all forces in the universe that seem to be diametric. Yang is the positive force of good, light, life, and masculinity. Yin is the negative essence of evil, death, and femininity. All matter is said to contain both yin and yang, and orderly affairs are possible only when these two qualities exist in a state of proper equilibrium. When they are unbalanced, the rhythm of nature is disturbed with strife, resulting in conflict. Like water molds itself to a container, man must learn to balance his yin and yang to live in harmony with the Tao, returning good for evil and overcoming strength with weakness.

In time, the doctrines of Taoism were transmuted into a ritualistic superstitious system with the *Tao Te Ching* as a source of magical incantations. Lao-tse was deified and worshiped with offerings of sacrifices. His disciples claimed power over nature and became soothsayers and exorcists. The idealism of early Taoistic speculation evolved into a folk religion emphasized by placating demons with gifts in order to insure a safe passage on earth.

Taoism has some similarities with Buddhism. Like the teachings of Siddhartha, classical Taoism insisted that the intellect could not comprehend the unknowable. Understanding is not derived from knowledge or theory but by comprehending what is obvious. The belief in an impersonal principle that sustains life is not unlike Buddhism's atheistic approach to morality. In fact, Japanese Zen has been strongly influenced by Taoism. Many New Age cults are founded on a philosophy combining the principles of Buddhism and Taoism in a syncretistic manner.

Books and university courses based on the "Tao of physics" suggest that the principles of Taoism are scientifically verifiable. As researchers delve more deeply into subatomic physics, they discover phenomena appearing to suggest a certain kind of duality (e.g., protons and electrons, matter and antimatter). Most scientists would contend that such findings are coincidental and bear no relationship to the wider philosophical speculation of the yin/yang theory.

The very fact that an integration of the pure science of physics and the essentially occult hypotheses of Taoism would actually be considered by the intelligentsia is an interesting commentary on the Western mind. Historically, scientific research has been of prime concern to Occidental nations because their religious traditions have been founded on Christian beliefs. Explorers, inventors, and scientists concluded that since God is an orderly, sovereign Creator, his cosmos is also fashioned in a precise manner that invites systematic investigation. The scientific method of inquiry that brought mankind such marvelous technological advances would not likely have evolved in a Taoist setting. Objective verification has been the foundation of Western science, while subjective experience and mysticism have been the cornerstones of Eastern philosophy. During the last several decades Eastern thought has turned to objective verification of subjective mystical experience while Western thought has become increasingly more subjective and mystical. If it becomes acceptable for the West to combine science and subjectivism, then testing for truth will become meaningless, and the door will be opened for unrestrained occult experiences, all supposedly condoned by the "objective" judgment of science.

The "Star Wars" movie epics, including *The Empire Strikes Back,* have been profoundly influenced by Taoistic philosophy. In conceptualizing "The Force," producer George Lucas borrowed heavily from the hypothesis of a primordial, universal energy flow that is neither good nor evil. Since the motive of the individual determines the moral nature of the force (e.g., Luke Skywalker uses "The Force" for good and Darth Vader uses it for evil), it thus possesses a duality whose positive and negative components are equivalent.

This is, of course, not compatible with biblical theology that sees God as the omnipotent source of all that is good. Satan, the Scriptures declare, was created by God and therefore has limitations on both his authority and power. As the source of all evil, the devil opposes the work of God, but he is not an equalizing, harmonizing opposite.

The idea of "The Force" is from a concept found in Chinese philosophy that envisions *ch'i* (or *ki*) as a basic flow of energy sustaining all life.

Chʾi (pronounced key) embodies the characteristics of the Tao, possessing a dual nature of yin and yang. In the martial arts, one's equilibrium with the Tao is established when *chʾi* flows through the body and is extended to disable one's opponent. Acupuncture views physiological health as an evidence of properly balanced yin and yang. If either essence is out of equilibrium, disease and illness result. Restoring health necessitates a disruption of the flow of yin and yang by applying a "counter-irritant" (an acupuncture needle). Once the equilibrium has been re-established, the Tao of *chʾi* can flow freely through one's body bringing healing. Even yoga has incorporated the Taoistic premise of *chʾi,* the force, as a sustainer of life and physical prowess. The *chakras* of yoga must be carefully aligned so that the body resides harmoniously with the Tao (though this term is not generally referred to by yogis).

This brief survey could not possibly explore all the ramifications of Taoist philosophy as it affects modern thought. Yoga and the martial arts will be discussed later in the book, and the reader will then see how the principles of Taoism are so crucial to the undergirding philosophy of these practices.

Evangelicals may conclude that Lao-tse might have stumbled upon a basic non-Christian perception of reality that to one degree or another has found its way into all false Eastern religious systems. Taoism's insistence upon having discovered "the way" certainly collides with the contention of Jesus in John 14:6 that he is the Way. As the Western world gradually shifts its footing from the objective knowledge of revealed truth to the subjective interpretation of perceived truth, the reader should note carefully the results of this shift in science, religion, and culture. Bodhidharma's years in that cave and Lao-tse's hermitage in his hut may portend a Western trend toward reflective isolation that will bring about a retreat from societal and scientific progress.

Founder: Lao-tse, a contemporary of Confucius, born 604 B.C., in southern China and died in 517 B.C., though accounts report he was never seen again after departing from his mountain hut. Some scholars insist he was a legendary figure and doubt he ever existed.

Text: *Tao Te Ching,* a 5,000-word book written in seclusion by Lao-tse.

Symbol: The Tao. See chapter on the Martial Arts for a detailed description.

Appeal: Ecological concern about the despoiling of Earth's environment makes Taoism's appeal to abide peacefully with nature, very attractive to the young. Technology has alienated man from nature and, in contrast, Taoism promotes a veneration of primordial life-giving forces.

Purpose: "The Great Tao flows everywhere," wrote Lao-tse. One should not attempt to decipher its origin or nature but merely adapt to its flow. The *Tao Te Ching* states, "To yield is to be preserved whole. To be bent is to become straight." Taoism is an anti-intellectual faith that elevates contemplative thought on abiding with nature's apparent laws, rather than inquiring to comprehend the structure of these principles. "Abide by the effect, and do not seek to discover the nature of the cause," might be the Taoist's creed.

Errors: Pure, classical Taoism is atheistic and borders on being pantheistic. Modern Taoism is polytheistic and idolatrous and involves consultation with familiar spirits. It falls under the indictment of Romans 1:25 by worshiping the supposed creation principle of the Tao more than the personal Creator God of Scripture. The contemplative life of virtue and gentleness may appear ethically valid, but it fails to deal with the sin-nature of man (1 John 1:8) and offers no remedy to restore man's fellowship with God. Respecting the laws of nature should be an outgrowth of man's stewardship of dominion over Earth, not a form of religious devotion.

Background Sources: Kenneth Boa, *Cults, World Religions, and You* (Wheaton, Ill.: Victor, 1980); John Garabedian and Orde Coombs, *Eastern Religions in the Electric Age* (New York: Tempo Books, 1969); *Religions of the World* (New York: Barnes and Noble, 1965); Ernest H. J. Steed, *Two Be One* (Plainfield, N.J.: Logos International, 1978).

Address/Location: Before the Communist takeover, one out of every eleven Chinese was a Taoist, primarily of the polytheistic/animistic variety. Its practice has diminished in China but continues fervently in Chinese societies of Southeast Asia. Taoism is not an organized religion in the U.S., but its philosophical principles are found in many Eastern-oriented cults.

· 5 ·

I S L A M

Including Sufism and
Black Muslims

"There is no god but God, and Muhammad is the Messenger of God."
Those thirteen words comprise the Muslim (or Moslem—"one who sub-
mits") *Shahada* (confession of faith). Five times a day the devout, from
sheiks to camel drivers, respond to the *muezzins* (callers to prayer) and
bow toward Mecca. Some Muslims display a round spot on their foreheads, an indelible souvenir memorializing the thousands of times they
have touched the ground in respect to the Prophet's command.

The Christian is taught to thank God for his blessings and to petition
him for divine favor. Not so with the Muslim. His passive fatalism will
not permit him to seek spiritual merit or to desire material provisions.
Islam means "submission," and that definition is the sum of a Muslim's
faith. *Inshallah*—"if God wills"—is the byword of Arabic conversation.
In *umma* (the world community of Islam), faithful Muslims view every
event, the fortuitous and accidental, as an expression of Allah's divine
will.

Separating Islam from its Arabic cultural heritage is impossible. More
than a religion, it is an all-encompassing way of life with its own jurisprudence system and traditional honor code. It is an intolerant faith that has
impeded progress and repressed women. Perhaps this is because the
Muslim tends to see the world in black and white. There are only two
classes of people: *Dar ul-Islam,* those who have submitted, and *Dar ul-
harb,* those who resist. The latter are fair game for missionary efforts,

89

financial pressure (e.g., the oil embargo), the "sword of Allah" in a *jihad* ("holy war"), or whatever measures are necessary to bring them under the authority of Islam.

Today, the crescent and star of Islam fly on the flag over a half-dozen nations. Adopting the evangelism techniques of Christianity, Muslims have broken out of their mud huts and desert terrain to confront the world with the message of Muhammad. Saudi Arabia has even financed a communications satellite to beam the Koran's precepts. Since October 1973 when Egyptian soldiers stormed the Suez and the oil embargo brought the West to its knees, the cry "Allahu Akbar!" ("God is great") has been heard with new fervor.

Islam began with the mystic visions of a nondescript camel driver named Ubu'l-Kassim (who became known as Muhammad). For six months he had been in solitary meditation in a cave at the foot of Mount Hira near Mecca. Had he not married a widow named Khadijah, fifteen years his senior, he might have spent his life on caravan journeys. Khadijah's wealth gave Ubu'l-Kassim the time he needed for ascetic reflection.

Muhammad was born in A.D. 570 in Mecca. He was yet a baby when his father died, and his mother passed away when he was six. Abu-Talib, an uncle, raised the young lad and took him on lengthy trips to Egypt and throughout the Near East. During these travels Muhammad engaged in lively conversations with Jews and Christians. From these encounters he learned the theological concepts that were later to influence his teachings.

In Muhammad's time, the Arabian peninsula was populated by wandering tribes that practiced various forms of polytheistic idolatry. The pantheon of deities they worshiped included angels, demons (*djinn*), and a supreme god known as Allah. Ubu'l-Kassim seemed an unlikely challenger to confront such a firmly entrenched animistic religious system. He was afflicted by a strange disorder that caused him to foam at the mouth and fall into unconscious trances. Christians might well wonder in retrospect whether such phenomena reflect the symptoms of demonic possession as represented in the Bible. Muhammad himself questioned whether the seizures were divine or devilish, but his wife encouraged him to ignore any such considerations.

According to Islamic tradition, at forty years of age he entered the Hira cave and was confronted by a being who identified himself as the angel Gabriel. "Proclaim!" Gabriel declared, choking Muhammad into submission. "Proclaim in the name of the Lord the Creator who created man from a clot of blood." During periodic return visits to Hira, the frequency of revelations increased. What he saw and heard was summarized in what became Islam's sacred book, the Koran (*Qur'an*, "recitation"). Over a twenty-two-year period, Muhammad memorized all 78,000 words of the Koran's 114 chapters and transmitted its teachings orally (he was illiterate).

Its message encountered stiff resistance from the pagan populace. Wealth and material gain were their "gods," and Muhammad (which means "the Praised One") insisted they share their wealth with the poor in exchange for the promise of a glorious afterlife. The God about whom he preached was a transcendent being who was both lawgiver and divine arbiter. Muhammad's theology proclaimed a Day of Judgment with severe punishment for the unbeliever. This harsh warning of accountability was contrasted with a sensual heaven where green meadows, rivers of wine, and beautiful virgins awaited the faithful.

Few converts accepted this message in the beginning because his denunciation of idol worship threatened the livelihood of Meccan businessmen. Those who followed Muhammad were stoned and beaten. In A.D. 622, he received a vision warning of mortal danger. His escape toward the oasis of Yathrib, 250 miles away, became known as the *Hegira* ("migration" or "flight"). This event marks the beginning of the Moslem era. Later, the name Yathrib was changed to Madinat al-Nabi (Medina), the "city of the prophet," second only to Mecca as a Muslim spiritual center.

To raise funds for his spiritual quest, Muhammad sanctioned plundering expeditions that raided caravans. Even during his native land's traditional month of peace, his followers mercilessly attacked innocent citizens. During this time when Muhammad ruled as a king and prophet, he forged the Islamic concept of the *jihad* ("exertion"), the "holy war" that advocates military ventures in God's name. Those who died in battle were promised immediate transition into Paradise. In 628, Muhammad led a force of 10,000 men toward Mecca and in a bloodless coup gained control of the city. Within ten years of his Hegira, all Arabia was under his control.

In 632, not long after his triumphal entry into Mecca, Muhammad died. One of his early disciples, Abu Bakr, was chosen as a successor, establishing the system of religious leaders known as *caliphs*. Filled with religious zeal, Muslim armies spread the message of Islam to India, across North Africa, and into Spain. Had it not been for the Battle of Tours in 732, all Europe might have succumbed to the message of the Koran. A capital was established in Baghdad, and the *caliph* who ruled from there was the most powerful man on earth and headed a regime spanning three continents.

The Islamic empire was to last for a thousand years. Arabs developed the concept of algebra, and their skills in architecture helped them devise the pointed arch that was to grace Europe's lofty cathedrals. Sugar, paper, apricots, and rice were introduced to the West. Constantinople became the headquarters of the Ottoman Empire in 1453, which endured until Arab power diminished in the twentieth century.

What is the key to Islam's current and past successes? The simplicity and directness of the Koran has left no room for compromise. Its history, fables, regulations, and threatening description of hell compel believers into single-minded devotion. Jews are damned by Allah, and Christians are told that faith in Christ as God incarnate is "blasphemy . . . whoever joins other gods with God—God will forbid him the Garden, and the Fire will be his abode." (The doctrine of *shirk* forbids associating anyone or anything with God's divinity.)

Islam does accept the virgin birth of Christ and even the scriptural account of his miracles. However, the Muslim's interpretation of how these events occurred is not compatible with biblical theology. The Bible is seen as a corrupt rule of faith inferior to Muhammad's message. Twenty-eight prophets are mentioned in the Koran, but none compares with the last and greatest of all—Muhammad. Though he took ten wives and encouraged military savagery, his tomb draws millions of disciples who pay their respect with solemn admiration. He improved the condition of slaves, and although his ruling that a man could have four wives seems inconsistent with spiritual ideals, it was an improvement over the conditions of his day because he insisted that each spouse had to be treated equally and kindly.

The *surahs* (chapters) of the Koran are augmented by the *Hadith,* which contains traditions recounting the deeds of Muhammad. As a supplement it serves a role similar to that of the Jewish Talmud. But the Koran is considered to be more than just another Islamic holy book. Muslims believe that every word was literally dictated by God and that its substance is eternal and uncreated. As a result, the Islamic Five Pillars of Faith are binding rules of conduct. These Pillars are:

1. Reciting the *Shahada.* Every day the Muslim must publicly affirm the monotheism of God and the prophetic status of Muhammad.
2. Daily prayer toward Mecca. Morning, noon, late afternoon, sunset, and before bedtime, all Muslims must say their prayers while kneeling

with their foreheads touching the ground. Most Muslims go through the procedure in a mechanistic manner, but such constant repetition serves to reinforce the piety of their faith.

3. Almsgiving (*zakat*). Charity was originally a voluntary act to aid the poor and purify one's remaining material possessions. Today, the principle of donating one-fortieth of one's income has become an institutionalized tax in most Muslim countries, averaging 2.5 percent annually.

4. Fasting during the month of Ramadan. Between sunrise and sunset, no eating or drinking is permitted. This occasion is determined by the lunar calendar and commemorates the month Gabriel supposedly delivered the Koran to Muhammad.

5. The *Hajj* (pilgrimage to Mecca). Every Muslim must attempt to make this journey once in a lifetime as a deed of merit facilitating his salvation. Once there, he walks seven times around the *kaaba* (a cubical building housing a black stone). If the jostling crowd permits, he must also kiss the rock (probably a meteorite), which Muslims believe was carried to earth by Gabriel. The *kaaba* is said to have been originally built by Ishmael and Abraham on the spot where Adam uttered his first prayers to God. Other holy sites in the area are visited, and a ritual sacrifice of goats, sheep, or camels may be performed. Pilgrims may also throw stones at the sacred pillar to "stone Satan," reenacting the stones Ishmael heaved at the devil when the Evil One attempted to dissuade Abraham's son from submitting to his father's plans to offer him as a sacrifice. (The Koran says it was Ishmael, not Isaac, whom Abraham laid upon the altar of Mt. Moriah.)

Other beliefs and practices associated with Islam are: using a ninety-nine bead rosary to recount the unmentionable names of Allah (the camel is the only creature said to know the 100th); holding mass-type services for the dead; forbidding statues and music in mosques; insisting on circumcision; veiling women's faces with the *purdah* and draping their bodies in the ankle-length *chador;* permitting polygamy; abstaining from drinking alcohol, eating pork, and gambling; meeting for congregational worship at noon on Fridays; building *minarets* (towers from which to broadcast the call to prayer); abolishing a priesthood and having the *Imam* serve as spokesman for the faith; believing that Christ did not die but was taken up to heaven; teaching that Jesus will return in the last days to convert the entire world to Islam; and enforcing the "law of apostasy," whereby converts to other faiths (especially Christianity) may be imprisoned or lose their jobs and possibly their lives. It should be noted that

Islam is a complex faith, spanning many cultures and countries; there-fore, the list in this paragraph should not be considered as categorical. The beliefs and practices of various Muslim sects are as diverse as those found in Christian denominations.

The code of ethics known as the *Shari'a* ("the path to follow") enforces the morals and doctrines of the Koran. In the face of what the Muslim perceives to be encroaching decadent Western values, the Shari'a's stern application of "an eye for an eye" system of penal justice seems a reason-able deterrent to crime and immorality. Today, from Bangladesh and Pak-istan to Iran and Saudi Arabia, flogging and stoning is again meted out to thieves and adulterers. Beheadings and amputations may seem grue-somely harsh, but to the Muslim the Shari'a represents 1,400 years of accumulative ethical standards that impose discipline for turbulent times. Fortunately, such brutal punishment is rare, since exacting standards of proof are required. (Even usury is forbidden by the Shari'a, forcing some Middle-Eastern banks to come up with novel schemes to charge interest under another name.)

Not all Muslims regard the Shari'as with equal esteem. Like all reli-gious movements, Islam is a fragmented faith with numerous sects. The three most prevalent are listed below:

1. *Wahhabi*. This group tends to be the most strict and puritanical. Mo-hammed Ibn Abd al-Wahhab founded the sect in the eighteenth century by preaching strict adherence to the Koran. Saudi Arabia's moralistic, authoritarian rule is an example of Wahhabi devotion.

2. *Shiites* (from *shi'ah* meaning "partisans"). They believe that only descendants of Muhammad's family are the rightful heirs to spiritual leadership. Since Muhammad bore no son who survived him, his cousin and son-in-law, Ali (who married his daughter Fatima), are considered to be in the line of the Prophet's succession. Found mainly in Iran, Yemen, Algeria, and Iraq, Shiites tend to revere the Shari'a (though not as fer-vently as the Wahhabi). About 10 percent of all Muslims belong to this branch of Islam. Their leaders, Imams, wield dogmatic spiritual authority, as in the case of the late Ayatollah Khomeini of Iran. Some Shiites believe that a twelfth Imam who disappeared in 882 will return someday as a messiah, the *Madhi* ("guided one"), to establish a king-dom on earth. In Kashmir once a year young Shiahs parade through the streets of Srinagar, scourging their bodies with knives and chains. This self-mutilation ritual laments the martyrdom of Hussain, Ali's son and

the Prophet's grandson, who was massacred in an attempt to restore the seat of Islam to Medina. A powerful Islamic leader named Muawiya had refused to recognize the succession of Ali, taking the title of *caliph* himself and moving the headquarters of Islam to Damascus. This event lead to perpetual enmity between the Shiites and the *Sunnites* (discussed below), who followed Muawiya. Subsects such as the *Ismailis* believe that an Imam of sinless perfection with power to perform miracles always dwells on earth. During the twelfth century a group of *Ismailis* known as the *hashshashin* (hashish eaters) killed Muslim leaders while in a crazed, drugged state. (From this we get the word "assassin.") They are firmly entrenched today as a merchant class in India and East Africa. The Aga Khan is their Imam.

3. *Sunnites* (from *sunnah,* "the tradition of the Prophet"). Ninety percent of all Muslims consider themselves adherents of this orthodox sect. Since Muhammad left no clear instructions concerning his successor, Sunnites decided their Islamic leader should be nominated by representatives of the community. The *ulama,* Sunnite religious scholars, have less authority than the Imam and are considered to be teachers and wise sages. Sunnites accept the line of succession as passing on through four *caliphs:* Abu Bakr, Omar, Othman, and Ali.

The diversity of Islam is one of its greatest assets. On the steppes of Central Asia, devout Muslims fill mosques every Friday under the watchful eye of the ruling Soviet Russian authorities. Iran's Imams have assumed dictatorial control to oust the Shah from his Peacock Throne. Across the vast Sahara, black Africans gather beside oases to study the Koran, a book written by an Arab whose descendants loaded their ancestors on slave ships to the New World. And in faraway Indonesia (with the world's largest Muslim population), students memorize the Koran while their elders mix entrenched local deities with Islam's fervently monotheistic system.

America's 4,644,000 Muslims maintain a much lower profile. Evangelicals tend to approach them warily, remembering the massacres of Christians (5 million in Turkish Armenia) and persecution of missionaries for which Muslims are infamously known. Of all major religious bodies, the conversion rate of Muslims turning to Christianity is probably the lowest because Islam pervades all areas of a native Muslim's life. For him to turn to Christ is almost the same as committing suicide. Few Islamic countries enjoy freedom of religion, and even where such freedom is sanctioned by the state it is rejected by the culture. When a Muslim decides to place his faith in Christ, for all practical purposes he loses his family, his culture, his history, his economic stability, and his social life. One who leaves Allah for Jesus Christ walks from the life of the Islamic community to the death of being a social outcast. Perhaps evangelicals should not resent the seeming arrogance displayed by the present Arabic spiritual descendents of Muhammad. God did promise to make of Ishmael's offspring a great nation (Gen 16:9-11; 17:20; 21:13,18; 25:12-18). Their ascent to world influence might well be viewed as a fulfillment of biblical prophecsy.

Founder: Muhammad the Prophet, born Ubu'l-Kassim in Mecca, 570. Died in Medina, 632 in the arms of his favorite wife, Aisha.

Text: The Koran, containing prayers, rules of etiquette, and calls to wage "holy wars." It is supplemented by the traditions of the *Hadith*. In addition, Muslims also revere the *Tauret* (Pentateuch) of Moses, the *Zabur* (Psalms) of David, and the *Injil* (Evangel) of Jesus.

Symbols: Crescent moon and star.

Appeal: The simplicity of Islam's message is its chief attraction: one God, a rigidly defined method of worship, and a clearly explained destination of man's soul. Its system of salvation by good deeds and ardent devotion offers solace for those who conform to the outward display of piety without having to experience a spiritual rebirth of their inner nature.

Purpose: All other religions are seen as satanic expressions of polytheism. Allah alone is to be praised and worshiped. Muhammad originally prayed facing Jerusalem and gave the Jews an opportunity to submit to his spiritual authority. When they refused, he persecuted them severely. Christians must also be opposed, violently if necessary. In the eyes of a Muslim, if Jesus were God, it would have been unjust for God to have punished his own nature. All Muslims have a sacred mission: by force of persuasion to bring the entire world under Allah's dominion.

Errors: Though Allah is omniscient, merciful, and compassionate, the Muslim holds him in such transcendent awe that he is virtually unapproachable. The message of John 3:16 that "God so loved the world" is an alien concept to Islam. God is to be feared and strictly obeyed, but his attributes cannot be personally experienced in man's heart. Allah demands a codified system of submission, but he offers no immediate forgiveness of sin in return. The certainty of salvation known by the Christian (John 3:36; 5:24) is but a vague hope to the Muslim who awaits the Day of Judgment when works, not grace, will determine his destination in the next life. Christians cannot accept the authority of the Koran because it seeks to supplant the Bible.

Background Sources: "America's Facing Toward Mecca," no author cited, *TIME* 23 May 1988, 49. *Great Religions of the World* (Washington: National Geographic Society, 1971); *Religions of the World* (New York: Barnes and Noble, 1965); Kenneth Boa, *Cults, World Religions and You* (Wheaton, Ill.: Victor, 1980); *Christianity Today,* 21 March 1980, 24-27; *Newsweek,* 26 February 1979, 38-41; *Christian Life,* September 1977, 22-67.

Address/Location: Since one-sixth of the world's population follows Islam, its disciples are found everywhere. Islamic strongholds are concentrated primarily in the Middle East, Indonesia, and North Africa, where more than 90 percent of the population is Muslim.

SUFISM
The most exotic variant of Islam proposes to reach God not through the Five Pillars but by entering trance states induced by dancing. The *Sufis* (their name comes from the wool *[suf]* of their undergarments) are a mystical Islamic branch rooted in the ascetic pietism of Muhammad's followers. Al-Hasan of Basra (643-728) was an early advocate of Sufism, as was Melvana Celaleddin Rumi, a Turkish mystic who lived in the thirteenth century.

Sufism's emphasis is on union with God through meditation and ritual rather than koranic obedience. Combining Islamic doctrines with Christian and Gnostic beliefs, they have developed a pantheistic theology with a spiritual hierarchy of *awliya* ("saints"). Chief of these is *Qutb,* the Pole of the World. Sufi leaders known as *shaikhs* are held to be saints, and many of them have practiced celibacy, though it is not a requirement of their office.

While the average Muslim is content in submitting to the will of Allah, the Sufi wants an immediate, ecstatic experience of oneness with God. The means to accomplish this is a once-secret rite of twirling dance maneuvers. It was Rumi who adapted Asian shamanistic practices and formed a ritualistic approach to Islam. His disciples became known as "whirling dervishes" (dervish means "beggar" in Turkish). Until recently, dervishes were illegal in their native Turkey, a ban imposed by Kemal Ataturk, who considered their beliefs an impediment to his modernization schemes.

Rumi watched a goldsmith at work one day and as a result was brought into a state of whirling ecstasy. He developed a special dance routine requiring a twirling motion. To master this choreographed movement 1,001 hours of training are required. Dervishes turn for an hour or more at a time without any sign of fatigue, repeating the name of Allah in prayer to the accompaniment of a musical beat. Eventually they enter an unconscious trance state and fall on the floor, an act that is supposed to represent an "awakening from indifference."

Until recently, this esoteric "metaphysics of ecstasy" was a path available only to initiates. Now, Sufis are performing in public, and their beliefs and practices are being openly explained. The dervish ritual is presented as a way for the teacher to expel from the pupil "gross energy," which would otherwise hinder his spiritual progress. The costume worn is a white skirt that represents a shroud and a high felt hat symbolizing a tombstone.

Among the eight Sufi precepts are: a concentrated breathing technique, returning to God from the material world, and being aware of the Divine Presence. "When you turn," says a foremost Sufi devotee, "you do not turn for yourself but for God . . . so the light of God may descend upon the earth."

Though traditional Islam has had little impact on the counterculture of youth in America, Sufism has attracted more than 6,000 adherents. The Sufi goal of higher consciousness through chants and meditative dancing blends well into the mystical landscape of contemporary religious cults.

Founder: Melvana Celaleddin Rumi, who established the tradition in Konya, Turkey, in 1273. Pir Vilavat Inavat Khan is the current director and president of the Sufi Order.

Text: Islamic scriptures and Gnostic texts.

Symbol: The *Samazen* (pupil) posing with the circular skirt preparing for circumambulations (walking meditation).

Appeal: Sufism is a way to experience ecstatically oneness with God, if one assumes that the mystical trance state achieved by dervishes is a form of communion with God. The counterculture fascination with consciousness-expanding modes of religion provides a fertile environment of curiosity among the young, which has led some to experiment with Sufism.

Purpose: Sufi literature declares, "The greatest principle of Sufism is *Isha Allah Ma'bud Allah*, God is love, lover, and beloved." Harmony with all the world's religions and peoples is said to be accomplished by each individual contemplating the immanence of God.

Errors: Sufism virtually ignores the question of sin and redemption. Its lack of fixed doctrinal structure means that belief resides in a subjective, mystical interpretation of truth. The *awliya* could be classified as familiar spirits (demons), with *Qutd* a personification of Lucifer. Dervish trance states exhibit the characteristics of biblically defined demonic possession.

Background Sources: J. Gordon Melton, *The Encyclopedia of American Religions* (Wilmington, N.C.: McGrath, 1978); Sufi advertisements in occult journals; *Time*, 16 April 1979, 52; *The Denver Post*, 29 August 1975, 3BB; Ibid., 14 May 1976, B-9; Ibid., 14 January 1977, 5BB; Ibid., 25 February 1977, 5BB.

Address/Location: Sufi Order, c/o Shahnawaz Jamil, 408 Precita Ave., San Francisco, CA 94110.

BLACK MUSLIMS

Mention Black Muslims to the average person and he immediately thinks of incendiary hate rhetoric directed toward the "blue-eyed devil" white man. On second thought, he may recall the day that a spunky boxer named Cassius Clay insisted he henceforth be referred to as Muhammad Ali. True sports fans would also remember the name of Kareem Abdul-Jabbar, formerly known as the seven-foot-tall basketball wizard Lew Alcindor.

In 1913, a North Carolina black man named Timothy Drew arrived in Newark, New Jersey, under the name Noble Drew Ali. He founded the Moorish-American Science Temples on the doctrine that Negroes were of Moroccan (Moorish) origin and that Jesus was a black man killed by white Romans. Many of his teachings were taken from *The Aquarian Gospel,* an occult book written by Levi Dowling.

When Ali died, Wallace Fard, a door-to-door salesman from Detroit, suddenly appeared on the scene claiming to be Ali's reincarnation. He asserted that he was born in Mecca and had been sent to America to redeem the black man from the "Caucasian devil." One of Fard's spokesmen, Elijah Muhammad (formerly Robert Poole) helped him to found the Nation of Islam. Muhammad insisted that Fard was an incarnation of Allah. By the time Fard mysteriously disappeared from sight in 1935, Muhammad had assumed leadership of the organization.

While incarcerated as a conscientious objector during World War II, Elijah Muhammad, the Messenger of Allah, effectively recruited black prisoners for his cause. His message to them was simple: Wallace Fard was God—the Messiah predicted by Christians and the *Mahdi* proclaimed by Muslims: the white beast (created by a mad black scientist) has been allowed to reign for 6,000 years, and that period ended in 1914; the time is ripe for the Nation of Islam and the divine black godmen guided by Allah to arise and claim control over the world.

Malcolm X was the mouthpiece of Elijah Muhammad and was an eloquent evangelist until he was murdered by one of Muhammad's rivals on February 21, 1965. Membership blossomed in the turbulent, racially tense sixties. Dozens of temples were opened in ghetto neighborhoods, usually by acquiring the abandoned churches of white congregations who fled to the suburbs. A half-million circulation newspaper, *Muhammad Speaks* (now called *Bilalian News*), was hawked by well-dressed, militantly organized youth.

Black Muslims bought thousands of acres of farmland to promote self-help enterprises. They opened businesses and projected an image of discipline, cleanliness, and morality. Though their racial intolerance separated them from the world community of Islam, they did practice some Muslim precepts. Eating pork, gambling, smoking, and drinking liquor were forbidden. Members prayed five times a day facing Mecca. Women were admonished to respect their husbands and were required to have their heads covered. The Koran was deemed to be the holy scripture of God's prophet, although they also entertained fanciful speculation about the black man having originated on the moon 65 trillion years ago.

Though most critics labeled their theology as "racial hatred," Black

Muslims preferred to call their views "social separation." They wanted no part of integration. Why should they? The white man's day of destruction was coming, and blacks should avoid sharing in his judgment. Heaven and hell were considered irrelevant concepts because the black man in America had already gone through the hell of slavery.

Upon the death of Elijah Muhammad in 1965, his son Wallace took over the movement. His initial lackluster leadership left some doubting whether he could adequately fill his father's shoes. His most important accomplishment has been to drop the strident racial invectives that had aroused the fear and dread of whites. This new image has enabled the Black Muslims to gain official recognition as an orthodox Islamic body under the name Community of Islam in the West. Followers are now referred to as *Bilalians* (Bilal was supposedly the first black convert of the Prophet Muhammad). Estimated members of adherents in the Community now range from 50,000 to 150,000. Just how serious they are about establishing a black separatist nation remains to be seen.

Founder: Timothy Drew, born 1886 in North Carolina. The modern success of Black Muslims is due to leadership of Wallace Fard, Elijah Muhammad, and Malcolm X.

Text: The Koran. The Bible is also considered a source of truth so long as it is reinterpreted without the white man's lies.

Symbols: Crescent and star of Islam.

Appeal: Ghetto black youth who feel exploited by the predominantly white society are promised the vision of a black-ruled nation. The call to nationalistic supremacy promotes self-respect based on a strict moral code that produces individual prosperity.

Purpose: Since God is black and the black man is a god, recognizing these "facts" will help blacks to shed the "white man's religion." Black Muslims promote a self-sufficient black economy and demand to have seven or eight states ceded to them in order to establish a black nation. Their stern rules and moral conduct aid them in the rehabilitation of society rejects.

Errors: The Black Muslim god is Wallace Fard, believed to be Allah incarnate, the savior of mankind. This is, of course, incompatible with the unique claim to divinity established by Jesus Christ (Acts 4:12). Peter's vision in Acts 10 leaves no room for any practice of racial superiority. The Bible teaches that all men are sinners (Rom. 3:23; 6:23) and in need of God's saving grace, no matter what the color of one's skin.

Background Sources: William J. Petersen, *Those Curious New Cults* (New Canaan, Conn.: Keats Publishing, 1975); J. Gordon Melton, *The Encyclopedia of American Religions* (Wilmington, N.C.: McGrath, 1978); Walter Martin, *The Kingdom of the Cults* (Minneapolis: Bethany Fellowship, 1977); "Black Muslims and the Baptist Witness" (Atlanta, Ga: Home Mission Board, SBC); *Time,* 10 March 1975, 83; *Christianity Today,* 12 May 1980, 29.

Address/Location: Temples found in the urban areas of major U.S. cities.

PART FOUR

AN

ENCYCLOPEDIA

OF

CULTS

AETHERIUS
SOCIETY

The Aetherius Society is one of the best-known UFO groups. Founded in 1954 by Londoner Dr. George King, the Society encourages members to be willing channels of communication with extraterrestrial beings. King's involvement in Spiritualism and various forms of occultism has well suited him for leadership of this strange cult. The Society was formed when King supposedly received a message from the "cosmic brotherhood" of "space masters"–their chief spokesman being Master Aetherius of Venus. King was chosen to be the "primary terrestrial channel" for the communications these creatures desired to transmit. The purpose of this activity (which includes messages from Master Jesus and Aetherius himself) is to enlist terrestrials on the side of the "space masters" in their war against certain "black magicians" living on earth.

The Aetherius Society has U.S. centers in Detroit and Los Angeles and publishes a periodical, *Cosmic Voice.* Society members are encouraged to maintain contact with orbiting spaceships and assist the occupants of these circling saucers, whose mission it is to direct their "energy" through the minds and bodies of King's followers.

Background Sources: J. Gordon Melton, *Encyclopedia of American Religions,* vol. 2 (Wilmington, N.C.: McGrath, 1978); Ronald Enroth, *The Lure of the Cults* (Chappaqua, N.Y.: Christian Herald Books, 1979).

See also UFOs.

AMERICAN

INDIAN

RELIGIONS

The young, mostly white members of the Peyote Way Church of God worship by trekking into the desert, chewing peyote buttons, and waiting for visions. Peyote is a hallucinogenic cactus and can be used legally for religious purposes by American Indians. It is widely used as a sacrament in the Native American church.

The Peyote Way Church of God was founded by Immanuel Trujillo, a half-Apache who once objected, ironically, to the use of peyote by whites. Today his group claims to have a legitimate religious connection with peyote to get around the provisions of anti-drug laws. Both the Peyote Way Church of God and the Native American Church use the age-old worship methods of the North American Indians.

Freedom of religion has only recently been granted to Native Americans. In a 1983 landmark legal decision, the Forest Service was prevented from building a road along the Siskiyou Mountains. This area had been used for centuries by the Karok, Tolowa, and Yurok tribes for religious purposes. Federal trial and appellate courts determined that Native American use of the wilderness for religious purposes warranted protection under the First Amendment.

A federal judge in New Mexico ruled in 1986 that use of peyote by Indians was sacramental. A restaurant supply firm was found guilty of religious discrimination for refusing to hire a Navajo man who admitted he used peyote during religious ceremonies.

Peyote, similar to LSD and mescaline in both chemistry and effects, originally was little known outside its natural growing range in northeastern Mexico and the Rio Grande valley. Sixteenth-century Spanish explorers noted the use of the drug among the Aztecs. One commented that "those who eat of it see visions either frightful or laughable. . . . [It] gives them courage to fight and not feel fear nor hunger nor thirst; and they say it protects them from danger."

After the decline of the Aztec civilization, peyote use continued among the Mexican desert tribes, notably the Huichol and Yaqui. It was carried north after the Civil War by Comanche and Kiowa raiding parties and eventually spread to more than 50 tribes. Peyote use was added to the Christianity the tribes had learned from Catholic and Protestant missionaries. John Wilson, the Caddo-Delaware Indian who founded the Ghost Dance movement in the late nineteenth century, told of his peyote-inspired vision. Wilson said he saw the road "which Christ had taken in his ascent [leading] from Christ's grave to the Moon in the Sky" and was told to walk in this path for the rest of his life.

In 1918, Indian peyote-users claiming to be Christians formed the Native American Church at the suggestion of white anthropologist James Mooney. In 1960, an Arizona judge ruled that peyote use by Indians was sacramental. In 1968 the Federal Drug Act limited use of mescaline and peyote to persons at least one-quarter Indian-blooded.

Peyotism and Indian philosophy were popularized in the 1960s and 1970s by Carlos Castaneda's *The Teachings of Don Juan.* More recently, Lynn Andrews's books and lectures sparked a resurgent interest in Native American religion, this time with a New Age flavor. Though her approach is feminist and does not advocate use of drugs to obtain self-knowledge, she shares with Castaneda an emphasis on totem spirits and shamanism.

The shaman—medicine man—was respected by nearly all North American Indians. The primary religious figure of most tribes, the shaman fulfilled the functions of priest, soothsayer, and doctor. Shamans were generally male, though some Great Basin tribes allowed women to hold the office. Eskimo shamans were said to cure sickness by undertaking out-of-the-body journeys in search of a patient's missing soul, which was then restored to the ailing body.

Shamanistic ability was sought in dreams or visions, usually through totem animals or "power beings," who taught the seeker how to use the magic healing and knowledge bestowed upon him. Shamans sometimes used their powers for less honorable reasons and consequently were feared. In some regions, witchcraft and magic were commonplace, as were sorcerers who supposedly could change themselves into animals or birds.

Among some Southeastern tribes, elaborate funerary practices supported a belief in ghosts and an afterlife. Each tribe had its own view of the universe, but most believed in a bewildering variety of spirits. Each plant and animal had a guardian spirit that looked after its kind, and many tribes observed strict hunting and fishing rituals to avoid offending the deer or salmon. Some tribes believed in a single creator, the Great Spirit. Others revered pantheons of minor deities and legendary trickster figures. The Hopi believed in a cyclical series of creations and worlds, while other tribes refuted a Creation altogether, declaring that the world had always existed.

Vision quests, solitary journeys into the wilderness to encounter spirit guides, were a popular form of maturity rite among many tribes, most notably the Plains Indians. They did not always require the use of drugs. Sometimes a vision was induced by fasting and forced sleeplessness in a secluded spot.

Rituals of endurance in the name of religion were common among many tribes. The Plains Indians still perform the sacred Sun Dance, in which men dance four days without food, water, or sleep. Among the Sioux and some other groups, self-torture was practiced during the Sun Dance. Dancers strained to pull themselves free from ropes tied to wooden skewers piercing their chests and backs. Such old rituals are being practiced with renewed fervor by young adherents of Native American religions to recapture the shamanistic mysteries of ancient tribal ceremonies. Christians know such rituals are unnecessary, for God does not expect man to suffer to prove his worthiness.

In these complex technological times, the simpler faiths and life-styles of the Native American peoples are attractive to spiritually disenchanted individuals. But such nostalgia about that primitive life-style is misdirected. The truth is, most Indians spent their days concerned with the harsh basics of survival. They fed themselves through hunting, gathering, or crop-growing and had to deal with vagaries of natural phenomena that often interfered with the successful hunt or good harvest. Their religions reflected this, and they established rites to propitiate spirits who might be benevolent one moment and cruel the next. In contrast, the Bible teaches true salvation comes from God, not through peyote-inspired visions or spirits in animal forms.

Founder: Most American Indian religions have traditional indigenous origins. The Native American Church for Christian Indians, who use sacramental peyote in worship ceremonies, was founded in 1918 by tribal peyotists at the suggestion of James Mooney.

Text: American Indian religions have an oral tradition of original myths and folklore tales about cultural heroes and trickster animals. Some of these have been translated and written down by anthropologists, but many remain unknown to outsiders.

Symbols: Cultural symbols vary from tribe to tribe. Examples are animals, birds, plants, natural phenomena, supernatural beings, cultural heroes and heroines, masks, totems, ceremonial costumes, sand paintings, kachinas, songs, and dances.

Appeal: Modern man may sense a primitive wisdom in the religion of Native Americans and be attracted to the concept of harmony between man and nature.

Purpose: Traditional American Indian religions served primarily to interpret life, making little distinction between the secular and the religious aspects of day-to-day living.

Errors: Few American Indian religions acknowledge the Christian doctrine of sin and redemption, seeing man as a part of the whole of nature and not in need of being redeemed by a messiah or savior. Emphasis is placed on spiritism and pantheism. Spiritual visions are deliberately induced by ingesting peyote and other drugs. A belief in totem animals may lead to occult experiences with demons. Shamanism includes magic and witchcraft-like practices.

Background Sources: *The Anchorage Times,* 29 January 1978, B4; *Christianity Today,* 26 June 1981, 37; *Dallas Times Herald,* 14 December 80, 6, 8-9, 13-14, 31; *Denver Post,* 2 August 1974, 3HH; *East West Journal,* May 1977, 55; Ibid., June 1984, 30, 36; *Encyclopedia Britannica,* 15th edition, 1986, vol. 13, 322, 326, 329, 332, 335, 339, 343, 347, 351-352; Ibid., vol. 26, 1033-1034; *Liberty,* May-June 1986, 6; *New Age Journal,* June 1984, 46; *Rocky Mountain News,* 4 April 1986, 45.

ANANDA

MARGA

YOGA

SOCIETY

What Hindu-oriented group would dare consider its founder a *Maha-Guru (avatar* — incarnation of God), even after he had been sentenced to life imprisonment for murder? The Ananda Marga Yoga Society claims that distinction, though its leader, Shrii Shrii Anandamurti (also known as Prabhat Ranjan Sarkav), was later found innocent in a new trial. Still, the Indian government frowns on the organization, insisting it is fascist and teaches ritual murder. In the United States this group's public image is quite different. It has attracted an estimated 3,000 to 4,000 members who pursue the way of Ananda Marga ("joy"). One of its strongest followings is located in Australia.

The path of joy and bliss is laden with yogic principles and practices, including initiation by a guru and daily mantric meditation. Special emphasis is placed upon *Kiirtan* dancing, a swaying routine with raised arms. This motion is accompanied by a chant known as *Baba Nam Kevalam,* which means, "The cosmic father is everywhere." These choreographed steps are designed to increase spiritual vibrations and help one realize that "all of creation is a manifestation of the Lord." In addition to the *kundalini* yogic techniques employed, charitable service to society is encouraged as a way to "break down the ego-bound mind."

Background Sources: Pat Means, *The Mystical Maze* (San Bernardino, Calif.: Campus Crusade for Christ, 1976); *The Denver Post,* 15 August 1975, 4BB.

ANTHROPOSOPHICAL
SOCIETY

By reason of their inherent pragmatism and staunch Lutheran heritage, generations of Germans have given rise to few exotic and esoteric organized religious movements. Rudolph Steiner's Anthroposophical Society is a notable exception. Steiner, born in Austria in 1861, became a Theosophist and headed the German division of the Theosophical Society, which was chartered in 1902. After publishing his *Spiritual Hierarchies* in 1909, Steiner split with Theosophy over its growing emphasis on Eastern religious philosophy. His philosophy then became Anthroposophy ("the wisdom of man," from *anthropos*, "man," plus *sophia*, "wisdom"). This "spiritual science," a form of "true Christianity," was also called "Christian Occultism."

Borrowing heavily from a variety of mystical traditions, Steiner theorized that man and earth are embarked on a progressive evolutionary journey overseen by certain beings of the "supersensible" spirit world. Reincarnation, *karma*, *chakras*, and meditation are all concepts of his system, which proposes that human perfection comes through a succession of embodiments. Even the earth goes through evolutionary cycles, the current stage being its fourth reincarnation. From his writings in more than one hundred books, Steiner imaginatively developed a complex history of mankind, including the mythology of Atlantis.

Christ, who was human until receiving the Christ-Essence at his Jordan River baptism, is the only being to undergo one incarnation. His spiritual, "phantom" (not bodily) resurrection was clairvoyantly perceived by the disciples. Through Steiner's techniques of meditation, all who follow Anthroposophy may also receive the Christ within them. Though Anthroposophists consider the Bible to be a valuable document of secret knowledge, their main focus of attention is in Steiner's works, which assume an authority above and beyond Scripture. By meditating on Steiner's words, the acolyte becomes capable of mediumistically communicating with initiates and departed beings of the spirit world.

Other concepts of Anthroposophy include: *Eurythmy,* a form of rhythmic movement; the founding of Waldorf Schools, institutions dedicated to awakening spiritual consciousness in children; and a "fall" of humanity that has reduced man to a baser consciousness, rendering him incapable of knowing his true origin and destiny.

Dornach (near Basel), Switzerland, is the current world headquarters of Anthroposophy, coming to North America by way of German immigrants whose successors now claim 30 centers and 13 Waldorf Schools. A sacramental branch of the Anthroposophical Society offers a liturgical form of "Christianized" Anthroposophy called the Christian Community. With its priests and ministers looking after the flock, the Christian Community maintains a separate identity with no formal ties to Anthroposophy, though it has no accommodation with orthodox Christianity. Though Steiner taught that a form of mystical Christianity replaced the outdated Eastern religions, his syncretistic result was an occult system more attuned to Spiritualism than the Good News. Rudolph Steiner was unquestionably an intelligent, articulate man whose perception of Christ as the "Lord of Karma" was clouded by his own subjective interpretation of occult phenomena.

Background Sources: *Spiritual Counterfeits Project Newsletter,* vol. 3, no. 1, (February 1977), 4-7; J. Gordon Melton, *The Encyclopedia of American Religions,* vol. 2 (Wilmington, N.C.: McGrath, 1978).

See also Theosophy.

ARICA

INSTITUTE,

INC.

What more could one ask for than "body vitality . . . mental clarity . . . a permanent higher level of awareness" and a "perfect society?" Such are the promises of the Arica Institute. Arica in Quechua (the language of many Andes Indians) means "open door." Arica is also the name of a Chilean town to which 54 Americans were lured in 1971. They had been invited by a Bolivian philosophy teacher and mystic, Oscar Ichazo.

Ichazo offered to take these seekers of truth beyond the inhibitions of their egos to "the Permanent 24," a secret name describing the mysterious state of "unity with emptiness." That original small group has now grown to an estimated 25,000 adherents (by Arica estimates), who have undergone Ichazo's training, plus some 2,500 new candidates, who each year shell out $995 apiece for induction into Arica. Arica instructors practice what they call "scientific mysticism," claiming it will uncover *TOHAM KUM RAH*, "the mystical name of the radiant being," inside each person.

Arica draws from the religious philosophies of Hinduism, Zen, and Tibetan Lamaism (though Arica literature proclaims it is "not a religion") in order to develop psychocalisthenics, a series of 23 movement-breathing exercises designed to awaken vital energy. One such exercise, the *Audicon Plantar,* teaches students to lie on the floor and absorb sound with their feet. In addition to breathing techniques, African dances, Egyptian gymnastics, Hindu mantras and incantations, the seekers engage in "mentations." This odd practice requires the student to concentrate on a separate section of his body for specified time periods:

8 minutes 40 seconds for the colon and kidneys, 10 minutes 45 seconds for the liver, etc.

In its offer to restore the essence of man's perfection, Arica attracts many who are emotionally disturbed or disenchanted with other self-improvement therapies, such as Esalen (discussed in a separate section). Ironically, Oscar Ichazo blames the ills of humanity on society's failure to adopt his ideas wholeheartedly. Consequently, he now offers 40-day courses (the original training took three months) for universities and retirement communities.

Background Sources: *Time,* 29 May 1972, 88; Ibid., 9 November 1981, 20; *East-West Journal,* June 1976; Arica promotional advertisement, copyrighted 1973.

See also Human Potential Movement.

ASATRU FREE ASSEMBLY

(Norse Neopaganism)

Former Roman Catholic Steve McNallen traded Christianity for paganism. His search for a different faith started when he was a senior at Midwestern University in Wichita Falls, Texas. McNallen spent ten years researching Norse religions and compiling a collection of pagan prayers before establishing Asatru Free Assembly in Breckenridge, Texas, in 1971. Resembling Thor, the macho deity he adulates, the red-bearded McNallen claims to gain strength and wisdom through examples of ancient Norse gods and goddesses and believes man harmonizes more closely with nature by observing changes in the moon and stars.

McNallen and his wife, Madeline Hutter, also a former Catholic, set up an office in their home to publish *Runestone,* a newspaper with 500 subscribers. Asatru claims 1,000 followers in the United States. Their Assembly is the tip of a Norse neopagan iceberg that represents thousands who believe ancient Scandinavian mythology. Steve McNallen says such groups as the Odinist Fellowship, the Odinist Committee in England, Asatrufolks in Iceland, and Asatru Free Assembly were created within months of each other and without knowledge of each other's existence. Steve McNallen and his wife worship such Norse gods and goddesses as Thor, Odin, Freya (foremost goddess-representative of the Vanir, a race of fertility gods), and Frigg, who is the one-eyed Odin's wife. Odin ranks highest among the gods, but mighty Thor is more popular. Thor is Odin's son and god of the sky, thunder, and fertility. He also is responsible for law and order in Midgard, the World of Men. Steve

McNallen says, "Everybody knows Thor. He's the good ol' boy among gods and . . . would be the patron god of Texas."

McNallen and his wife were remarried at a ritualistic festival called an *Althing,* where, after a celebratory feast, a huge hammer was burned as an offering to Thor. Visitors came from several states to participate in Viking games, to hear lectures, and to attend *blots* (pronounced "bloats"), ceremonies to worship the gods. To that end, they poured wine upon the ground, chanting, "Hail to you, Freya! Smile on us!"

Wearing long red tunics and silver replicas of Thor's hammer around their necks, McNallen and Madeline honor gods and goddesses by chanting in Old Norse with closed eyes and drinking wine from an animal horn as part of their religious celebration. Traditionally the honey wine called mead is drunk at such ceremonies, but other liquids are acceptable.

Vikings once ruled northern Europe all the way to the Mediterranean. They worshiped the Aesir, a pantheon of twelve gods, who ruled the heavens and earth under Odin, variously called the Terrible One, Father of Battle, and All-father. Odin supposedly rides an eight-legged horse and shares his rule with a plethora of other gods and goddesses, a pre-Christian polytheistic belief. In about A.D. 1000 Norse mythology succumbed when Scandinavia fell to Roman religious rule.

In Old Norse, Asatru means "belief in the gods." Also known as Odinism, Asatru makes little distinction between Norse deities and mortal man. Followers believe their gods live close to earth and indulge in the experiences of everyday life, like glorified human beings. Asatru stresses that its deities are personifications of the forces of nature. Thor, Odin, and others are friends, never masters. Followers assume positions of equality with their gods, who are revered for qualities of defiance and will power.

Each Norse deity is responsible for different aspects of the universe. Odin is respected for wisdom, poetry, and magic. Thor, also called the Thunder God and the Charioteer, is the farmer's friend, a warrior and toiler. Balder epitomizes courage and goodness. The Asatru Free Assembly states, "A religion without a goddess is halfway to atheism." Frigga is respected as mother of the gods, and Nerthus is worshiped as Mother Earth, whose wounds man is obligated to heal. Frigga is accorded special honor as the mother of gods. Freya, the "eternal feminine," is respected as the creator of life. For the courageous, direct contact with the gods and goddesses is promised, while the less brave can expect less potent contact.

Followers of Asatru believe man is master of his own soul, that man, not Jesus Christ, is his own salvation. After death, the worthy go to the realm of the gods called Asgard, while sinners are relegated to eternal gloom, cold, and fog. The Asatru Free Assembly also advocates reincarnation, and faithful followers deplore the conversion of Germanic peoples to Christianity. Forces of nature—the moon, solstices, cycles of the year—are celebrated. Displays of courage, speaking out against bureaucracy, hospitality to guests, and preserving the environment are considered religious acts. Loyalty and brotherhood are supreme virtues.

Followers believe they control their destinies by heroic action, that mankind's fate can be molded by taking risks, defending one's rights, and by not compromising one's beliefs. Its code of conduct stresses courage as a primary virtue, also the necessity of honoring the religion of their ancestors—ancient Norse gods and goddesses, who control all facets of human existence.

Sex is viewed as a vital part of nature to be enjoyed without guilt. In stark contrast to the tenets of Christianity, neopagans feel society is best served when each individual develops his full potential by creating a satisfying sex life. Pagans view sex as a clean, wholesome activity that needn't include matrimony.

Asatru followers accept various forms of worship, avoiding hierarchically determined structures. Members are free to worship whatever god they wish in whatever manner. They believe the only proper expression of self is to experience what they call the rhythm of nature. They do not bow to their gods and goddesses, stressing that equal spiritual footing be shared by the deity and worshiping mortal. Societal skills and human characteristics are revered, rather than Christ's sacrifice on the cross.

Some Asatru Free Assembly adherents worship daily, using various symbols—cakes, spears, swords, and horns. Steve McNallen says, "I realized . . . we could choose what deities to follow." He also claims the Asatru Free Assembly performs no animal sacrifices. But in Iceland, where paganism is resurging, such sacrifices can be approved by the health department and conducted at authorized slaughterhouses.

Asatru is more widespread than its small membership indicates. While public pagan worship was outlawed in Iceland 900 years ago, Nordic paganism was officially recognized in 1972 as a legal religion. People in Iceland recently demanded that plans for a new road be altered to avoid crossing a hill frequented by fairies. Their appeal was honored, the road's course shifted.

Odinists have been accused of being closet neo-Nazis, though publicly they lament that Nazi Germany used old Norse symbols during its infamous regime. The swastika, principal emblem of Nazism, originally represented both Thor's hammer and the wheel of the sun. Such negative connotations attached to Asatru are aggravated by heavy emphasis on genetic superiority in Odinist literature. Several articles in *Runestone* observed that "[Psychologist Carl] Jung's original idea was that . . . archetypes were not culturally transmitted but inherited genetically." A member of the Asatru Free Assembly was quoted as saying, "We are not racists, but we are racially aware."

Though Asatru Free Assembly activities were officially discontinued in November 1987, its beliefs continue to be practiced among various self-styled Norse neopagan groups.

Founder: Steven McNallen, a former Catholic, established Asatru Free Assembly in 1971 in Breckenridge, Texas.

Text: Norse myths teaching that man can learn wisdom and qualities of strength, courage, honor, joy, and freedom from ancient Norse gods, who share equal status with humans.

Symbols: Ancient Norse amulets and objects of war, including swastikas, runes, helmets, swords, animal horns, red wooden shields, Viking axes, wooden sculptures of gods and goddesses.

Appeal: Asatru is an individualistic religion based on the arbitrary choice of lenient gods, who are like friends one honors and respects. Norse gods make no objectified moral demands of followers, instead promising self-indulgent rewards through a loosely structured belief system.

Purpose: The forces of nature are celebrated with feasts. Gods and goddesses of Norse mythology are invited to intervene in life, providing wisdom, strength, courage, and energy.

Errors: Asatru's religious system is constructed upon mythology rather than historical fact or biblical truth. It supports reincarnation and proposes that man is master of his soul. Witches and druids are accepted as legitimate representatives of Asatru, and many gods are esteemed as models to be imitated. Racist overtones refute Christ's promise that all those who believe in him will earn eternal salvation. Occult overtones introduce the idea of a hidden, divine energy beyond human understanding, an essence that is interdependent with man.

Background Sources: *Fort Worth Star Telegram,* 16 December 1985, 13A,18A; Margot Adler, *Drawing Down the Moon,* rev. ed. (Boston: Beacon Press, 1986); *Oregon Journal,* 22 February 1979, 4; Kevin Crossley, *The Norse Myths* (Holland, New York: Pantheon, 1980); *The Denver Post,* 23 May 1975, 3BB.

Address/Location: Asatru Free Assembly, P. O. Box 1754, Breckenridge, TX 76024.

ASCENDED MASTERS

In Yugoslavia, manifestations of the Madonna allegedly appear to school-children. Throughout the United States, crosses of light are reportedly seen in the sky. At a remote faith-healing center in the slums of Nairobi, Kenya, Sister Mary Akatsa welcomes a guest speaker into her fold. His name, she claims, is Jesus Christ.

Across the nation and around the world, followers of Ascended Masters are proclaiming that the appearances of superior spiritual beings portend the Second Coming. At least one promoter asserts the Maitreya, the metaphysical Lord of the Second Advent (also known as Jesus), will announce his return by appearing on television. Benjamin Creme declares the exact day Christ as Maitreya arrived on earth was July 19, 1977. Alive and well in London's Pakistani community, Maitreya is apparently in no hurry to reveal to the world his identity as an Ascended Master.

G. W. Ballard is credited with founding the Ascended Masters ideology. In 1930, while at Mount Shasta, California, Ballard said he was visited by St. Germain, a spiritual being who, during his time on earth, had attained "Christhood." Following this meeting, Ballard used the pen name Godfre Ray King and published his first two books, *Unveiled Mysteries* and *The Magic Presence*.

Ballard's St. Germain series proclaimed to the world the "I AM," or individualized God Presence within us. It also declared the existence of a cosmic government, whose hierarchy consisted of former earthly residents. Believers in Ascended Masters claim that, as members of the earth's governing body, these discarnate entities provide necessary instruction on purifying, energizing, and harmonizing human thought. Through correct ideas, Ascended Masters' teachings profess that anyone can obtain perfection, stop all suffering, and become divine.

Ensconced within Eastern mysticism and metaphysics, followers of the Ascended Masters embrace such concepts as astral projection, trance channeling, and reincarnation. Sananda, a member of the Council of Seven, or highest ruling body of the solar system, reportedly had previous earth incarnations, including Jesus of Nazareth, the biblical figures Melchizedek, Elijah, and Moses, plus Gautama Buddha and Socrates.

In Ascended Masters' theology, God is defined as a "creative force that has a negative and positive polarity, as each atom in creation has its negative and positive poles." He is comprised of seven major groupings: will and power; intelligence and wisdom; personal love and feeling; crystallization; unity, integration, healing, and balance; transmutation, cleansing, and purification; divine love, peace, and rest. The Son is the product of God's duality of Father-Mother.

Life is under the tutelage of guardian angels. Strife enters our lives via negative thoughts. Criticism, condemnation, and judgment cause all suffering, including disease. Death supposedly occurs when the body is not purified, and the Guardian Angel's life ray is withdrawn. Once dead, the spirit takes on new dimension and remains in this form until it receives additional cosmic instruction.

Twenty-six years after G. W. Ballard's introductory encounter with St. Germain, the Ascended Masters initiated contact with confirmed atheist Pauline Sharpe. Born in Brooklyn, New York, in 1925 of Jewish parents, Sharpe was told to prepare for the second coming of Jesus the Christ. Chronological excerpts of her channeled communication with the Ascended Masters from 1958 to 1970 are compiled in her 1974 book *MAPP to Aquarius.*

Claiming to have been anointed by her master teacher, Sananda/Jesus, Sharpe is known as Nada Yolanda to followers of the Ascended Masters. The name Nada, taken from her past incarnation as a high priestess of the Sun Temple, represents her "reborn" self-identity, while Yolanda is her soul aspect.

Together with Charles Boyd Gentzel, "reborn" as Mark Age, Yolanda developed the Mark-Age of Ascended Masters, a partnership that spanned 21 years. In death, the former Boyd Gentzel channels to Yolanda as El Morya, Chohan, or Director of the First Ray of Will and Power.

The cosmic aspects of the Ascended Masters bear a striking resemblance to the science fiction movies of the 1930s and 1940s. Sprinkled with additional heresies, such as Gnosticism and Pelagianism (the belief in saving oneself through moral effort), followers of the Ascended Masters claim control over their spiritual and worldly destinies. They discount the importance of Jesus Christ and assert that increased consciousness leads the way to a new interplanetary dimension. Their belief that man's fall from grace occurred following the Second Golden Age 2.5 million years ago contradicts Scripture.

Founder: G. W. Ballard

Text: The Bible; G. W. Ballard (pen name Godfre Ray King), *Unveiled Mysteries* and *The Magic Presence; The Ascended Master Discourses* by "Various Ascended Masters"; *The "I AM" Discourses* by "The Great Divine Director"; *I AM* magazine, which the Ballards published in the late 1930s and early 1940s.

Symbols: A winged flame, reading from left to right, *A I M,* with the *I* twice as high as its flanking letters. Also, seven rays representing life. Rays of varying colors represent various aspects of the "I AM" belief.

Appeal: The promise of interplanetary alliance and peace. Promises control over one's spiritual and physical being.

Purpose: According to Ascended Masters' literature, "To give help from their octave of life," which mankind must have at this time to stand against the onrush of world destruction, because no outer activity in the world today can solve the world's problems or stop the destruction that human beings are releasing against each other.

Errors: Christ is placed on the same level as other religious teachers. Like many metaphysical approaches to reality, there are Eastern influences of metaphysics and mysticism, along with Gnosticism, pantheism, Pelagianism, and syncretism.

Background Sources: Mrs. G. W. Ballard and Donald Ballard, *The Purpose of the Ascended Masters "I AM" Activity* (Santa Fe, N.M.: St. Germain Press, 1942).

Address/Location: St. Germain Press, Chicago, Illinois. Western branch: Sante Fe, New Mexico.

See also Church Universal and Triumphant.

ASSEMBLIES

OF

YAHWEH

In 1979, the U.S. Supreme Court declined to review a Colorado suit brought against the state Motor Vehicle Division by two members of the Assembly of Yhwh-Hoshua. David Johnson and Anthony Virgil had been denied drivers' licenses for refusing on religious grounds to have their photographs taken. They claimed their faith forbade making graven images. The Colorado State Supreme Court ruled that compelling reasons exist for requiring photographs on drivers' licenses and that "no alternative less restrictive of religious freedoms" is acceptable. Unimpressed, members of the sect near Pueblo, Colorado, promised to continue driving, with or without licenses. An aversion to photography is only one trait of the fundamentalist Assembly of Yhwh-Hoshua, whose members also oppose hospitals, doctors, medication, Social Security, banks, Medicare, and unemployment insurance.

The Assembly of Yhwh-Hoshua was founded in the 1970s by Laycher Gonzales, who said he first learned of the Name of God from a hitchhiking prospector named O. K. Skidmore. A year after the lawsuit over the drivers' licenses, Gonzales was accused by a former member of using mind-control techniques on his followers.

Believing that the Hebrew words *YHWH* (Yahweh without the vowels) and *Hoshua* (Joshua) are the only true names for God and Jesus, they blot out from their books all other names of God. The common names for the months and weekdays are not used, since they have pagan origins. Children are educated in church schools with Mennonite textbooks.

Science is considered unnecessary and is ignored. A modest dress code requires wearing loose robes over street clothes at all times. Alcohol, tobacco, drugs, jewelry, dancing, dating, cologne, and haircuts are forbidden. Secular and religious artwork are considered blasphemous. Christmas and Easter are not observed as holidays.

Another offbeat organization with more mystical overtones was Dr. Henry Clifford Kinley's Institute of Divine Metaphysical Research, founded in 1931 after the doctor supposedly had a face-to-face conversation with God (who Kinley called Yahweh-Elohim). This divine revelation led to Kinley's lifelong preaching of the universal calamity that would mark the end of the modern age.

Divine Metaphysical Research and the Assembly of Yhwh-Hoshua are only two of many splinter groups derived from the 1930s Sacred Name Movement. Today the most common name for the faith is the Assemblies of Yahweh, though various spellings of the name are used.

Headquarters of the oldest group, the Assemblies of Yahweh, founded in 1939 by C. O. Dodd, are in Holt, Michigan. Originally known as the Assembly of Yhwh, it now uses the more easily pronounced spelling of God's name. The group publishes *The Faith* magazine and distributes literature through the Faith Bible and Tract Society. The loosely organized assembly has congregations around the country and proposes to restore the true names for God (Yahweh and Elohim) and Jesus (Yahshua).

The Pennsylvania-based Assemblies of Yahweh had its origins in the Sacred Name Broadcast, begun in 1966 by Jacob O. Meyer. It publishes *The Sacred Name Broadcaster* and offers free literature from its headquarters at Bethel, Pennsylvania.

The Assemblies of Yahweh believes in keeping the Old Testament commandments to the Israelites. Members observe Saturday instead of Sunday as their day of devotion and celebrate Passover, Hanukkah, and other Jewish festivals. Because the Assembly of Yahweh is based on the Old Testament faith, members closely follow the ancient Israelites' religious laws, which include observance of food restrictions and tithing. Apostolic practices borrowed from the New Testament include baptism by immersion, footwashing, anointing, and a belief in divine healing. Salvation comes through accepting the "revealed, personal Name of our Heavenly Father, YAHWEH, and the Name of His Son, our Savior, YAHSHUA the Messiah."

Both the Michigan and Pennsylvania assemblies reject the teaching about the Trinity. According to the Bethel group's Statement of Doctrine, such a belief has no basis in the Scriptures. The Holy Spirit is defined as "the mighty power from the Heavenly Father and the Messiah dwelling within us so that we may . . . bring our lives into a state of perfection." This power is imparted by Assemblies of Yahweh elders through laying on of hands after baptism. Members do not ingest addicting or illegal drugs, believing the Holy Spirit will leave impure, unsanctified bodies.

The Bethel Assembly's doctrine also rejects the traditional Christian concept of an eternal hell. They believe the wicked will be completely destroyed in a lake of fire known as Gehenna. They do recognize a personified Devil and believe he will be destroyed at the end of the Millennium.

The Bethel Assembly also stresses nonviolence. Members are advised to refrain from all military duty. The Assembly recommends conscientious objection, with alternate service in other fields approved by the U.S. government.

The Bethel Assembly patterns its church government after that of the early Christians. Individual assemblies are led by a pastor, who is assisted by a teaching elder and a deacon. Doctrinal matters are decided by bishops and ordained ministers, who preside over the appointed body of male elders. Appointments are lifelong, though faithless elders can be removed for transgressions. Women are forbidden to preach. Assembly of Yahweh tithes feed into a general fund at Bethel, from which local assemblies take allowances.

Members do not take each other to court over legal matters. Family life is important, and divorce is discouraged. Parents teach their children religion, since the Assembly of Yahweh believes there is no scriptural basis for Sunday schools. Women are required to cover their heads during services. Evangelism and conversion of others is the overall aim of the Assemblies of Yahweh, and each member is encouraged to witness to nonbelievers.

Assemblies of Yahweh literature liberally cites chapter and verse of both the Old and New Testaments, drawing upon biblical support for all tenets and practices. In reality, they have made the Old Testament more important than the New. Assemblies of Yahweh proponents write lengthy articles about their faith, carefully deleting when possible the vowels from the words God, Lord, and Christ. This approach to theology places more emphasis on how to spell Christ's name than how to live by his Word.

Founder: The Assembly of Yahweh faith derived in the 1930s from the Sacred Name Movement among some Church of God (Seventh-Day) ministers. Some of the individual Assemblies and their founders are: Institute of Divine Metaphysical Research—Dr. Henry Clifford Kinley, 1931; Assemblies of Yahweh (Holt, Michigan)—C. O. Dodd, 1939; Scripture Research Association—A. B. Traina, 1940s; Assembly of Yahvah—L. D. Snow and E. B. Adam, 1949; Assemblies of Yahweh (Bethel, Pennsylvania)—Jacob O. Meyer, from The Sacred Name Broadcast, 1966; Assembly of YHWHHOSHUA—Laycher Gonzales, 1970s.

Text: Several Assemblies of Yahweh groups have issued their own translations of the Bible. Among these are *The Restoration of Original Sacred Name Bible,* Missionary Dispensary Bible Research; *The Sacred Name Bible,* translated by A. B. Traina; *The Sacred Scriptures* (Bethel Edition), Assemblies of Yahweh, Bethel, Pennsylvania.

Symbols: The Assemblies of Yahweh (Bethel, Pennsylvania) display Hebrew lettering on the cover of their Bible, *The Sacred Scriptures.* They also partake of unleavened bread and grape juice as symbols of the Savior's body and blood during their Passover observance.

Appeal: Many are attracted by the strict morality of the Assemblies of Yahweh faith. Some join out of a sincere desire to change their life-styles by obeying God's commandments.

Purpose: Assembly of Yahweh members believe the commonly used names of God and Jesus are human inventions. Their purpose is to replace these words with the "true" and "divinely revealed" Sacred Names.

Errors: They deny the Holy Trinity, the orthodox concept of hell as a place of eternal punishment, and reject Christian holidays in favor of Jewish ones. They believe the only Christians to be saved will be those that use the Sacred Names and that obedience to the Old Testament religious laws can win spiritual salvation.

Background Sources: *The Denver Post,* 10 October 1979, 1-2; J. Gordon Melton, *Encyclopedia of American Religions,* vol. 1 (Wilmington, N.C.: McGrath, 1978), 476-479; Dr. Henry Clifford Kinley, *Infallible, Biblical and Scientific Proof of How, When, and for What Purpose the*

Universe Was Created (Hollywood, Calif.: Institute of Divine Metaphysical Research, 1969); *Pueblo Chieftain and Star-Journal,* 13 December 1980, 1, 6A; *The Rocky Mountain News,* 2 October 1979, 10, 42; *The Sacred Name Broadcaster,* April 1983, 2-5; *The Sacred Scriptures* (Bethel, Penn.: Assemblies of Yahweh, n.d.), 1-2; *Statement of Doctrine* (Bethel, Penn.: Assemblies of Yahweh, 1981), 2-10.

Address/Location: The Assemblies of Yahweh, Bethel, PA 19507.

ASSOCIATION

FOR

RESEARCH AND

ENLIGHTENMENT

(Edgar Cayce)

"All healing comes from God," declared the prim, pleasant-looking lady lecturing to a group of curious tourists. The statement seemed suspect in view of her earlier complimentary remarks about American psychic Edgar Cayce. She had already pointed out that in Cayce's theology "sin" is separation from that which is correct, such as wrong diet or negative thoughts. For an example, she explained that Cayce once declared constipation to be a "sin" since it disrupted the body's normal functions. With that in mind, I wasn't going to let her comment on healing go unchallenged. After all, this was the headquarters building of the Edgar Cayce organization, and she was their official representative to address visitors. If anyone was authorized to speak on behalf of Cayce's beliefs, she certainly ought to be the one.

"Who is God?" was the question it seemed logical to pose.

"God is whatever you perceive him to be," was the reply. "The One Source, the Creator, the First Cause, That from which all emanates."

Such ambiguity certainly contrasted with the personal Deity revealed in the Holy Scriptures. Perhaps that should have come as no surprise. Cayce, the "sleeping prophet" who as a child aspired to be a missionary and claimed to have read the Bible completely through each year of his life, eventually departed from orthodoxy. His theology mixed metaphysics with mysticism, flavored by strong doses of teaching on reincarnation.

Cayce's life was replete with strange phenomena. One story claims that as a baby he cried for the entire first month of his life until an old black woman suggested pricking the nipples of his breasts with a pin. When that was done, milk came out. From that point on, young Edgar rarely ever cried. Later in life he recalled that during childhood he was constantly surrounded by what he called "play folk." They disappeared when others were around, although his mother saw them occasionally. As Edgar grew older and increased in size, these "play folk" also seemed to increase in stature. One day they simply failed to show up, and that was the end of their communication with Cayce.

A turning point in his life occurred at age 13. The presence of a woman appeared and offered to grant him any request. Edgar responded that he wanted to help others when they were sick. No sooner had his petition been stated than the apparition vanished.

He was not the first in his family to exhibit psychic tendencies. His father had a strange power over snakes, and his grandfather had a widespread reputation as a water-witcher. The elder Cayce could also make tables move and brooms dance. But Edgar's supernatural powers were even more strange. For one thing, he discovered at an early age that he could sleep with a book under his pillow and awake the next morning with its entire contents indelibly fixed in his mind.

When evangelist Dwight L. Moody was passing through town, Edgar shared with him his story of visions and voices. Moody warned him that evil spirits could create such things. According to Cayce's official biography, *There Is a River,* the evangelist also left open the possibility that Edgar might be a prophet as described in Numbers 12:6.

Edgar Cayce's psychic meanderings came to a crossroads at the age of 24 when he lost his voice. Doctors failed to offer a cure, so hypnotists were consulted. After being subjected to a deep trance state, Cayce's voice returned, and his throat was instantly healed.

Shortly after this, Cayce's technique of hypnotic self-cure was expanded to diagnose the ills of others. A. C. Layne, the hypnotist who had facilitated Cayce's voice restoration, suggested that Edgar self-induce a sleep-trance condition and attempt to see what was wrong in another person's body. Cayce did just that and described in detail Layne's physical condition. Physiological, biological, and pharmacological terms were uttered from Cayce's mouth although he had only a grammar school education. Even Cayce admitted the voice was not his own.

Layne enlisted Cayce as an assistant to his lucrative practice of suggestive therapeutics and osteopathy. Layne told Cayce he had a clairvoyant gift and called his diagnoses "readings." Cayce started out with altruistic motives and refused to accept any money for his cures. As his fame spread, he became convinced that all this success was the fulfillment of the request granted him by the woman who had appeared to him many years before.

Cayce continued teaching Sunday school and rationalizing his psychic experimentation by claiming it was a God-given calling. He remained reasonably orthodox in his doctrines until 1923. That's when he met Arthur Lammers, a student of Theosophy and occultism. Lammers encouraged Cayce to go beyond his physical readings of ills to cultivate the practice of life readings. These revelations contained analyses of spiritual and philosophical matters. From then on, Cayce departed sharply from biblical truth.

During his lifetime, Edgar Cayce gave in excess of 16,000 readings. Of that total, 14,246 were stenographically recorded and are indexed and filed in the locked, fireproof vaults of the headquarters building of the Association for Research and Enlightenment (ARE). The ARE was founded in 1932 to research and preserve his readings. Virginia Beach, Virginia, was chosen as a location because Cayce had prophesied it would be a haven safe from future cataclysms (earthquakes, floods, etc.) that would befall America. The ARE is now under the leadership of Cayce's son, Hugh Lynn Cayce.

The physical readings of Cayce were the main source of his attraction. Over a period of 43 years, he gave 8,985 readings proposing cures for the body and mind. In his state of altered consciousness, he expounded on diet, eating habits, and diagnoses for patients who sometimes were miles away. His homespun remedies often had remarkable curative effects; however, some of his prescriptive suggestions were a little farfetched. He told cancer victims they need never worry if they ate three almonds a day. (ARE literature points out that almonds contain laetrile, the now discredited cancer cure.) Patients who smoked moderately (six to eight cigarettes a day) were informed that their habit was harmless, a position not supported by modern research.

Some of Cayce's physical readings were undoubtedly beneficial for their practical, medicinal effect. Natural remedies for natural maladies should not be seen as being indicative of miraculous cures. And the success of such therapy should not validate the source of its information. The authenticity of Cayce's readings rests on whether his comments on scriptural matters are biblically sound. It's faulty logic to suggest that religious pronouncements can be trusted if the voice uttering them is also correct when analyzing ills. Psychic success is not a sufficient gauge for spiritual validity.

To trust Edgar Cayce because he was a sincere, devout man who read the Bible and taught Sunday school is dangerous reasoning. His charitable platitudes can't be used to judge the veracity of his readings, even when some of them seem to square with the Bible. Ardent altruism is no substitute for total harmony with the revelational truth of Scripture. By this measure Cayce's lofty sentiments fall far short of biblical standards. Much of what Cayce taught is extrabiblical. When questioned as to why he placed so much emphasis on the Essenes (a monastic sect not mentioned in Scripture), he replied, "We have received it [this information] psychically." Psychic revelation was also the source of information for his contention that Jesus was initiated into secret societies in India and Egypt. Cayce also rambled on about souls descending from apes and expounded theories concerning advanced civilizations in the lost lands of Atlantis and Lemuria. He encouraged nearly every form of occultism from astrology to auras, from astral projection to ancient Egyptian mysteries.

Reincarnation was a key part of his belief system. Cayce admitted that reincarnation is not taught in the Bible but blamed the omission on third-century translators whom he claimed deliberately excised it from canon. Reincarnation is even used to justify sexual perversion. In the official ARE publication *Many Mansions*, a homosexual's conduct is excused as resulting from a psychological imprint from a former incarnation.

According to Cayce, God created all souls in the beginning, and they enter the material, earthly plane by choice to work out their faults and thus achieve atonement with God. Jesus Christ of Nazareth was appearing in his thirtieth incarnation, having been on earth before as Adam, Enoch, and Melchizedek, among others. In Cayce's view, Christ has now worked out his karmic debt and become a Christ-soul. Cayce referred to Jesus as the "Master," and "our Elder Brother." The latter term probably came from the influence of a Mormon lady who lived in the Cayce home during Edgar's childhood. She claimed to have been a wife of Brigham Young.

ARE literature calls Cayce's readings the "most impressive record of psychic perceptions ever to emanate from a single individual." That may be true, but even his proponents admit his prophecies have proved to be only 90 percent accurate. Critics place his rate of accuracy even lower. He failed by underestimating Hitler's inclination for evil and struck out again by declaring that New York would be dumped into the sea in the seventies. People are still looking for the elusive Atlantis he prophesied would arise in the twentieth century.

How much of Cayce's readings came from his subconscious mind, influenced by outside sources, cannot be determined. Those familiar with demonic phenomena find in Cayce's readings a curious consistency with the kind of utterances associated with spiritism. One thing is certain: Though the extrabiblical aspect of Cayce's interests cannot objectively be evaluated, his claim to be a prophet is clearly without a scriptural base. One hundred percent accuracy (Deut. 18:20-22) is the requirement for those who speak on behalf of God, whether awake or asleep.

Founder: Edgar Cayce, born March 18, 1877, on a farm near Hopkinsville, Kentucky. Died January 3, 1945, in Virginia Beach, Virginia.

Text: Numbers 12:6, "If there be a prophet among you, I the Lord will make myself known unto him in a vision, and will speak unto him in a dream."

Symbols: Dove and cross or letters ARE.

Appeal: Those suffering painful and incurable illnesses may turn to Cayce's physical readings when medical science cannot help. If their suffering is alleviated, they consider his life readings a source of truth explaining the nature of their cure.

Purpose: The ARE exists to index and catalog Cayce's readings for those seeking help for physical maladies. Inquirers may be referred to one of 400 physicians who are ARE members and utilize Cayce's approach to health. Publications and lectures disseminate further information regarding Cayce's life readings on religion. The headquarters building houses a large occult/metaphysical library for research.

Errors: Cayce's undocumented revelations of historical events, erroneous prophecies of geologic alterations, and unsubstantiated tales of lost empires should cause serious students of history and the Bible to question his credibility. If Jesus was once incarnated as Adam, then he is not a sinless Redeemer. Cayce's solution for sin is not forgiveness in this life but the promise of many future lives to make ourselves acceptable to God.

Background Sources: Various ARE-approved publications, including *Many Mansions, There Is a River, The Edgar Cayce Reader, The Sleeping Prophet,* ARE membership solicitation letters.

Address/Location: Association for Research and Enlightenment Inc., Box 595, Atlantic Ave. at 68th St., Virginia Beach, VA 23451.

ASTARA

"It is possible that I may have erred in receiving them [messages from the teachers of the spirit world]. Therefore if errors are brought forth in the lessons, it is I who am to blame. I alone must be held fully responsible," says Earlyne Chaney, as quoted in *Astara's Book of Life,* First Degree Lesson 1.

Mrs. Chaney's admission of fallibility is rare among spiritualists. But lest anyone should think she approaches the teachings of Astara with ambivalence, she confidently declares (in the same booklet from which the above quote was taken): "It [Astara] guides the disciple toward the inner mysteries of life, death, God, man—and the ultimate initiation: immortality." Critics of Astara may wonder if the journey into such knowledge is really advisable. After all, it is hardly credible to claim supernatural spiritual inspiration while at the same time acknowledging that such inspiration may contain error.

Astara means "a place of light" and is taken from the name of the Greek goddess of divine justice, Astraea. The teachings form an eclectic cult that encompasses spiritualism, Theosophy, yoga, Christianity, mystery schools, Rosicrucianism, and various occult orders and disciplines. For those who ask, "Why then follow Astara?" Mrs. Chaney answers, "Astara has come forth as a Light Bearer in the latter part of this century." (Evangelical Bible students will find that comment noteworthy, since "light bearer" is the meaning of *Lucifer,* the name of the devil.)

Astara certainly promises a lot. Among its claims are soul progression, the solving of life's enigmas, the developing of "inner faculties," the healing of illnesses, spiritual brotherhood, expansion of consciousness, self-unfoldment, and God-realization. Membership in Astara is said to be like a "Cosmic Bank Account" where you earn interest in peace of mind and enlightenment. Members are told that when death comes they will "fade from consciousness and go to the Valley of Rewards" where they will "find again all they have deposited in the Cosmic Bank."

When she was 28 years of age, Earlyne Chaney's world was shattered by the death of her fiancé. The event had been prophesied by a spirit-being named Kut-Hu-Mi, with whom she had communicated clairvoyantly since she was a child. (Kut-Hu-Mi taught her to develop psychic powers, including a methodology called *The Great Work of the Pentralia,* which contains a secret yoga system called *Lhama Yoga.*) Two years after this tragedy, she met and married Robert Chaney, a spiritualist who had his own spirit guide named Ram. Earlyne then left the acting profession, and in 1951 she and Robert moved to California where they formed the Astara Foundation.

Though regular services are held at the organization's headquarters in Upland, California, most of the teaching is carried on through correspondence courses. Astarians are led through four degrees containing at least 20 lessons each. The first few instructions explore elementary occult-mystical practices. As the studies progress, the initiate is gradually introduced to Secret Documents revealing the Astarian sign, word, and handgrip. At this point the techniques of Lhama Yoga are taught. Almost every kind of psychic phenomena is pursued, with the exception of Ouija boards and automatic handwriting. Chaney acknowledges the demonic nature of such practices by warning members against the "disastrous consequences of those who indulge in them."

Healing plays a central role in Astarian philosophy. The *Voice of Astara,* the Foundation's monthly publication, abounds with testimonies from those who have experienced supposedly miraculous cures. Members are encouraged to send their healing petitions to the headquarter's shrine where a group of four Astarians, known as the Circle of the Secret Seven, will intercede on their behalf. Neophyte Astarians are told that these individuals are "dedicated ones who touch and influence the cosmic powers of etheric realms for cosmic assistance."

The Chaneys draw from Masonic, Rosicrucian, and Theosophical beliefs. But their central doctrines are rooted in the teachings of Hermes Trismegistus, the ancient Egyptian magician who is believed to be the organizer of the original Mystery School from which all others were derived. Another Egyptian named *Zoser* is the Chaneys' current spiritual guide. His god-name is *Neterkeht,* which literally means "God in flesh," and Astarians are told to call on his name if in need of healing. Members have been known to see materializations of Zoser, whom it is said gives of his efforts exclusively to Astara.

Despite these pagan overtones, Astara still endeavors to hide itself behind a veneer of Christian beliefs. While accepting the tradition of *avatars,* including Buddha, Astarians insist that God was most completely revealed in Christ, whom the Chaneys profess to revere as "the Light of the World." This "Cosmic Christ" is said to be "the Lord of our planet, begotten before the beginning of our time and age." The Astarian denial of Christ as Creator God, eternal and the Only Begotten of the Father, is consistent with the minor role he actually plays in Astara. Issues of the *Voice* abound with messages from Kut-Hu-Mi, but few biblical references are cited. The lessons do quote certain scriptural passages, but only out of context to support occult principles.

The whole system of Astara is highly complex and includes phenomena such as Arcane Biorhythms, *prana* breath techniques, ethereal bodies, astral projection, polarity, and laws of vibrations and correspondence. The secret word, sign, and handgrip are apparently taught during trance states. Members are told that the "Divine Hierarchy of Great Beings who once brought wisdom and knowledge to man" have come again from the "Universal Brotherhood" to reveal life's mysteries through Astara. Considering the possibility that these Great Beings may be familiar spirits, there is little comfort in Earlyne Chaney's admonition that "the presence of Astarian Masters overshadows your life."

Founders: Robert and Earlyne Chaney.

Text: Genesis 1:1-3 is paraphrased without any indication that the Chaneys' version is extrabiblical: "And God said, 'Let there be Light in the minds of men.' And God created channels through which the Light might come. And one of them was Astara. And God looked upon Astara and He saw that it was good."

Symbol: Seven-pointed "Star of the West," merging inside with the "Lotus of the East."

Appeal: Those with an interest in occult and psychic phenomena find what appears to be a historical basis for discovering hidden truths. Its secret ceremonies and promises of miraculous healing are also an attraction. Recruitment flyers offer to send information on topics such as the superconscious mind, self-realization, Oversoul, the Dead Sea Scrolls, astral projection, and achieving spiritual selfhood.

Purpose: To blend Eastern religious philosophy and ancient mystery schools (especially Egyptian) with Christianity.

Errors: Astarians decree verbally, "I am perfect," denying man's sinful nature. Without historical evidence, Astara claims Christ traveled to Egypt, Tibet, and India and was initiated there at mystery schools. The Bible is said to have hidden truth that requires special interpretation to be "rightly understood." The exclusive nature of Christ's salvation is denied by Astara's teaching that many paths lead to the Infinite Being. The founders of Christianity are said to have "brought forth the doctrine of the resurrection of the physical body at the Judgment Day. A blind, believing humanity accepted the doctrine, and some still do." The Bible's warning against familiar spirits (Isa. 8:19-20) is ignored, and spirit guides (demons) are revered and elevated above Christ.

Background Sources: Miscellaneous Astara literature: "Astara's Book of Life," "You and Astara," *Voice of Astara* (various issues); J. Gordon Melton, *The Encyclopedia of American Religions* (Wilmington, N.C.: McGrath, 1978), 183-184; Robert Chaney, Pamphlet/flyer from Astara, 24 March 1987.

Address/Location: 800 West Arrow Highway, P. O. Box 5003, Upland, CA 91785.

See also Spiritualism.

A S T R O L O G Y

It's there in your newspaper every day. You don't really believe in it, but the horoscope is fun to read. Most of the time it's just good for a laugh. You don't take it seriously like some people. What harm is there in just casually checking to see what's in store for your sign of the zodiac? Sure it's an occult practice, but you don't look at it that way. On the other hand, there was that one day the prediction for your sign did come true. You wonder . . . . Astrology, along with palmistry, witchcraft, numerology, and other forms of the occult, has always interested a few, but today this fad has turned into a phenomenon. George Gallup says that 32 million (one in five adult Americans) believe in astrology, and that eight of ten can name the sign under which they were born. Right now there are three times as many astrologers as there are clergymen in the Roman Catholic church. Nearly 2,000 newspapers carry a daily horoscope. And (to show that astrologers are as media-conscious as anyone else) some cable TV stations carry horoscopes. (Interestingly, *TV Guide* magazine, which has as its main purpose keeping readers abreast of TV trends and programming, has an astrology page in each issue.) Many sensitive people were aghast at the discovery in 1988 that President Reagan's wife Nancy had consulted an astrologer, apparently with a view to influencing her husband's political decisions. What seemed so remarkable was not that Nancy had been involved with astrology but that the American public as a whole reacted with a yawn.

Not too long ago, 186 distinguished scientists issued a no-nonsense statement savagely attacking astrology. Their declaration pointed out, "The time has come to challenge directly and forcefully the pretentious claims of astrological charlatans. It's simply a mistake to imagine that the forces exerted by stars and planets at the moment of birth can in any way shape our future." In spite of such a scathing condemnation, belief in the effect celestial bodies can exert over human affairs continues unabated. This has been helped, no doubt, by the fact that some renowned people — notably the late psychologist Carl Jung, for example — believed in astrology.

Does astrology work? Is it a harmless pastime? Is there anything wrong with casually consulting one's daily horoscope? What does the Bible say about astrology?

Fifty centuries ago the Chaldeans of the Babylonian Empire observed the influence of the sun upon the earth and the moon upon the seas. They concluded that the planets were gods and, therefore, certain conjunctions of their movements would have an effect upon wars, governments, and the destinies of men. Other methods of fortune-telling, such as surveying the entrails of animals, often proved unpredictable. The positions of the stars were dependable.

The ancients, as well as current astrologers, computed their predictions with a geocentric view of the universe. Imagine a spoked wheel. The center where the spokes meet indicates the location of the earth, and the outer rim signifies the path the sun takes through the heavens each day as it revolves about the earth. According to the astrologers, the area indicated by the outer rim is about 16 degrees wide and represents the zones of the zodiac. What concerns zodiac consultants are certain star constellations that appear within the pathway of the sun as it travels through the heavens. This band is divided into 12 equal sections representing the 12 divisions, or "houses," of the astrological zodiac.

During the course of a year, the 12 constellations, or signs of the zodiac, move through each of the 12 houses. In addition, each of the nine planets as well as the moon and sun move through each house every 24 hours. Just why the ancients did not take the many other constellations besides these 12 into account is uncertain. It may be that they reasoned the sun's rays would have to shine through the constellations to affect the people on the earth below, keeping in mind that the earth is at the center of the model of the universe to which we're referring.

To determine one's horoscope, the exact geographical spot of birth is coordinated with the date and hour of delivery. The conjunctions and relative positions of all heavenly bodies are considered by the angles they form with relationship to each other. From this information the horoscope is eventually computed.

As reasonable as this simplified illustration sounds, it is based on a faulty premise. Astrology originated in the pre-Copernican age when the earth was thought to be the center of the universe. Now, scientists assure us that the sun does not circle the earth but vice versa. Because astrology is based upon this erroneous concept, its suppositions and conclusions have no scientific basis.

Astrology also has other factual discrepancies. The earth has an uneven wobble as it spins on its axis. As a result, the zodiac has shifted. Today, the sun's rays actually enter each of the constellations about one month earlier than they did centuries ago when the present astrological charts were finalized. This means that current horoscope readings are inaccurate by a factor of 30 days. Even if the predictions of astrology were true, the characteristics of each sign would not apply to the months they have been assigned.

A new book by an astrologer entitled *Astrology Fourteen* asserts that there are actually 14 constellations in the zodiac. If the predictions of astrology were to be scientifically correct, these two extra constellations would have to be included when casting a horoscope. And what about the billions of other celestial bodies outside our own galaxy? Why aren't their influences considered? The answer is that the heavens were not fully explored when the practice of astrology was developed.

Some people are born without a horoscope. What about those who live north of the Arctic Circle? No planet assigned to the zodiac is visible there for several weeks out of the year. Does this mean that Eskimos and some Norwegians have no celestial influences upon their lives and no astral destinies to guide their behavior?

Astrology is a universal practice in pagan religions. But no two false religions agree on the same attributes for each sign. If you were to have your horoscope computed by a Hindu in India, it would read much differently from that of a Buddhist in Bangkok. The arbitrary characteristics assigned to constellations seem inconsistent. One horoscope may say Aquarians are practical and patient while another designates them as restless and skillful. The only constancy appears to be a suitable ambiguity designed to apply to almost any personality.

The predictions of horoscopes are not only capricious, but these prophecies are also prone to a high degree of error. If most astrologers had their forecasts periodically reviewed for accuracy, their reputations would fade quickly. Carroll Righter, whose syndicated column is read by millions, once predicted that Spain's Franco would remain healthy (he died) and that J. Edgar Hoover would have an improved physical condition (he, too, expired less than five months later). Jeanne Dixon, who credits the Almighty with her foreknowledge, once declared that Jackie Kennedy would not remarry. Apparently her zodiac charts never bothered to consult a Greek shipowner by the name of Aristotle Onassis. Those who say their astrological talent is a "gift from God" need to be reminded that the Lord's qualifications for a prophet leave no room for error (Deut. 18:22).

Astrologers depend heavily upon the accuracy of determining the exact moment of birth in relationship to the position of heavenly bodies. But who determines when a child is born? Mother Nature? Often the doctor decides the hour of birth for the convenience of his schedule as well as the mother's welfare. Would it then be possible for a physician to thwart one's astrological destiny by using drugs to manipulate the moment when the baby emerges? Also, since life begins at conception, wouldn't that moment more accurately reflect the choice of one's astrological sign?

Astronomers, those who engage in the true science of stargazing, completely reject astrology, relegating it to the ranks of superstition. Yet millions of people waste hours and dollars studying the signs of the zodiac. In the end, they usually learn nothing about themselves except what they read into their horoscope (which generally is of a complimentary nature).

The first Bible reference to astrology is probably in Genesis 11. Here we find the story of the building of the tower of Babel. Archaeologists have now discovered that this structure and similar towers were actually *ziggurats,* which the early Chaldeans erected to survey the heavens. Some ziggurats have been unearthed that give evidence of zodiac signs actually inscribed on the circumference at the top. The Bible says the purpose of the tower of Babel was to "reach unto heaven." This biblical metaphor could more accurately be paraphrased, "a tower whose top may be used to reach out unto the heavens." The Chaldeans were not simple and ignorant but a highly advanced civilization. They had sense enough to know it was not literally possible to build a tower that would actually extend that far into the atmosphere. There is little doubt its real purpose was to survey the stars for astrological purposes. Because these men sought to discover their destiny in the stars rather than communicate with God, judgment was brought upon them.

The Bible explicitly denounces astrology in many other passages. In Jeremiah 10:2 we read, "Learn not the way of the heathen, and be not dismayed at the signs of heaven; for the heathen are dismayed at them."

The prophet goes on to equate astrology with idolatry and describes the vain way in which the heathen seek to please and follow their astrological gods.

The clearest command against astrology is found in Deuteronomy 18, beginning with verse 9. As the children of Israel were about to enter the Promised Land, God issued severe warnings against the practices of the heathen in that territory. One such warning is against any Israelite becoming an "observer of times," which is an astrologer. This practice, God declares, is "an abomination unto the Lord." The penalty for its practice was death by stoning. Consulting one's horoscope, whether seriously or casually, is an act defying one of the most solemn warnings of Scripture.

The futility of trying to use astrology to interpret God's dealings with man is portrayed in Daniel 2:27-28 and 4:4-17. In the former instance, Nebuchadnezzar's dream confounded the wisest of the court astrologers. Even though they were pagans, these seers were quick to recognize that true perception of the unknown is an attribute of "a God in heaven that revealeth secrets." Many years later, Belshazzar was reminded of the dilemma his father Nebuchadnezzar faced when he, too, was confronted by a mystery that his most trusted soothsayers could not unfold. Once again the Lord's servant, Daniel, was called upon because his wisdom excelled that of Satan's prognosticators.

Those who consult astrology are displaying an anxious and fretful attitude. Jesus said in Matthew 6:25 that we should "take no thought" for what might happen in the future. He declared that the necessities of life would be provided by our heavenly Father if we would seek him first. Man does not need to know what lies ahead if he faces tomorrow with the help of God. The Christian may not know the future, but he does know the One who holds the future in his hands.

Psalm 19:1 says: "The heavens declare the glory of God; and the firmament showeth his handiwork." The emphasis of astrology is upon nature rather than the God of nature. This Psalm points out that the purpose of the heavens is to declare the glory of God, not the affairs of men.

The underlying philosophy of astrology declares that one's destiny can be found in the stars. In contrast, Christianity teaches that the events of life are determined by a combination of God's sovereign will and man's personal moral choices. Astrology, on the other hand, attempts to destroy man's accountability to God. Horoscope devotees may think they can fall back on blaming the stars for their actions. But the Bible teaches that someday all mankind will stand before God to be judged (Rom.

14:12). Man is responsible for his conduct, and the Lord will not take into consideration the lame excuse that certain stars and planets were in the wrong conjunction.

Christians are to trust the Holy Spirit to guide their lives, knowing that "the steps of a good man are ordered by the Lord" (Ps. 37:23). The guesswork predictions of astrology should hold no interest for believers who follow "a more sure word of prophecy" (2 Pet. 1:10). God in his mercy has veiled the future from man's eyes (except for those events detailed in eschatological biblical references). If it were possible to know the events of tomorrow in detail, most people would not place their confidence in God's wisdom to look lovingly after our future. Satan, who according to Isaiah 14:14 wanted equality with the Lord, still desires to be man's substitute god. Astrology is a tool the Devil uses to entice men to replace trust in God with a faithless dependence upon the whimsical uncertainties of the horoscope.

Founders: Chaldeans of the ancient Babylonian Empire.

Text: Various occult volumes and oral traditions. Some Bible passages are taken out of context to condone astrology.

Symbols: Twelve zodiac signs.

Appeal: In an age of uncertainty, people look for something to bring structure to their lives. Political, economic, and social turmoil create fear and uncertainty that some feel could be assuaged by knowing the future. Astrology becomes a faith system, with the horoscope its liturgy. Those who have abandoned the church find solace in astrology's tenets.

Purpose: Astrology postulates that human lives are influenced (and in some cases predetermined) by the fixed position of certain heavenly bodies at the moment of birth. Earthly events are also affected by the relative positions of the planets and stars. Important decisions and momentous occasions should be considered with respect to their relationship regarding the horoscope.

Errors: The scientific discrepancies are well documented and acknowledged by the majority of scientists and astronomers. Numerous Scriptures denounce astrology for its erroneous prophecies and its false worship of the creation rather than the Creator (Rom. 1). The eternal destiny of each soul is determined by man's volitional choice, not a fatalistic conjunction of heavenly bodies.

Background Sources: *The Toronto Star,* 16 April 1977, A3; *Hell on Earth* (Carol Stream, Ill.: Creation House, 1974); Charles Strohmer, *What Your Horoscope Doesn't Tell You* (Wheaton, Ill.: Tyndale, 1988).

Address/Location: None applicable.

B A H A I S M

"We may never pass this way again." This song has wafted over the air-waves of a thousand radio stations, along with songs like "Year of Sunday." The lyrics of the latter implore, "People, return to the tree of oneness." Both tunes were composed and performed by Jimmy Seals and Dash Crofts, two of modern music's more successful minstrels. Both songs contain an explicit endorsement of the religious faith Seals and Crofts have in common—Bahaism.

Bahaism promotes noble and altruistic goals. Above all, it desires to unify mankind into one religious kingdom. This attempt to be a watershed for all faiths in the oneness of God is laudable but impossible to achieve. The doctrines taught by the religions of this proposed union are in many instances quite contradictory. Thus any effort to accomplish a global, religious synthesis is a futile task. Still, Bahaism continues to pursue its goal of reconciling religious opposites. Such idealism has attracted nearly 5 million followers in more than 160 countries, including about 110,000 in America.

The Baha'i concept of religious unity, international government, and planetary interdependence began in Persia over a century ago. A 25-year-old businessman, known as Mirza Ali Muhammad (1819-1850), announced in 1844 that he was the Bab ("Gate") who would be the forerunner of the "Promised One" who would be a manifestation of God. Six years later he was killed. One of his followers, a Persian nobleman named Mirza Husayn Ali, known today as Baha'u'llah ("the glory of God"), came to believe he was the one prophesied by Mirza Ali Muhammad. Baha'u'l-lah spent most of his life in prison for plotting against the Shah. In 1863, in Baghdad, he declared that he was the promised *Madhi* (Messiah), a progressive revelation of God onward from Abraham, Moses, Krishna, Buddha, Zoroaster, Jesus, and Muhammad.

As the Comforter of John 14:6, the "second coming of Christ," Baha'u'llah had a big task to fulfill. His divine claims were cut short in 1892 when he died at the age of 75. His son, Abdu'l-Baha, brought the message of Bahaism to the United States in 1912. He spent eight months spreading the faith to Americans and laid the cornerstone at the attractive $2.5 million Baha'i Temple in Wilmette, Illinois. Upon Abdu'l-Baha's death, the mantle of Baha'i leadership was passed to his grandson, Shoghi Effendi, who expired in 1953. Since then, the rulership of Baha'ism has been in the hands of a National Spiritual Assembly.

Baha'i belief has been summed up in the dictum, "The earth is but one country and mankind its citizens." Underlying this statement of faith are twelve principles: the independent search for truth, the oneness of the human race, the unity of all religions, the elimination of all prejudice, the harmony of science and religion, the equality of men and women, universal education, a universal language, abolition of extreme wealth and poverty, world court, work as worship, and justice with universal peace. As Baha'is see it, mankind is currently headed toward a socioeconomic cataclysm. Out of this tragedy a "golden age" will dawn, and Baha'is will be the only ones prepared to rule in this new world order. "War shall cease," said Baha'u'llah, "and all men shall live as brothers." Unlike more passive cults, Baha'is evangelize vigorously to help fulfill their founder's prophecy.

The religious practices of Bahaism are similar to Islam (with a modified Western twist), though the two faiths are entirely separate religious systems. In fact, the Baha'i faith seriously offends orthodox Muslims in its belief that the line of prophets does not end with Muhammad but includes Baha'u'llah and prophets yet to come. In Iran, members of the Baha'i faith are severely persecuted and often sentenced to death for "heresy." A mob destroyed the House of the Bab in Shiraz, the Baha'is' holiest shrine. One apparent goal of the late Ayatollah Khomeini was to eliminate Bahaism in the land from which it originated. Tens of thousands of Baha'is fled Iran after the Islamic Revolution in 1979 until the Khomeini regime stopped issuing them exit visas. Many of the refugees settled in America, which granted them refugee status as victims of religious persecution. About a thousand refugees a year escape over the Iranian border into Pakistan and from there settle into communities around the world.

Central to every Baha'i community is an elected nine-member spiritual assembly. Baha'is hold weekly gatherings, an annual fast, and follow a special calendar with New Year's Day occurring on March 21. There is no professional clergy, and leaders are forbidden to reveal exact membership figures to the public. The estimate of more than 17,000 "localities" is based on the assumption that even one member living in an area constitutes a locality. In a manner similar to Muslims, Baha'is are expected to pray at certain times during the day; they are also encouraged to make at least one pilgrimage to their Mecca—the temple in the city of Ak'ka (near Haifa, Israel) where Baha'u'llah died and where Mirza Ali Muhammad was buried (on nearby Mount Carmel).

As with most religious systems that emphasize their inclusiveness, the inherent result of Baha'i teachings is exclusiveness. Bahaism claims to be the ultimate fulfillment of Judaism, Buddhism, Islam, Zoroastrianism, Hinduism, and Christianity. While proclaiming the merits of all world religions, Bahaism also insists that these faiths must now concede to the supremacy of God's fulfilled revelation in Baha'u'llah. However, disagreements between the disciples of Krishna, Muhammad, and Buddha are sufficient to preclude any hope of their uniting. The suggestion that they could also mute their differences with Bahaism is equally unlikely.

It is impossible for biblical Christianity to unite with Bahaism. Those who believe that "all the fulness of the Godhead bodily" dwells in Christ (Col. 2:9) would be unwilling to demote their Savior, accepting him as only one of nine manifestations of God. Acceptance of Bahaism means that one must deny the substitutionary atonement of Jesus Christ and ignore the distinctions of other world religions. Baha'is teach that all major religions hold to essentially the same truths. If this is the case, why are the tenets of Bahaism and Christianity mutually exclusive? The conclusion of this question cannot be ignored no matter how loving, kind, and considerate the followers of Baha'u'llah may be.

Founder: Mirza Husayn Ali (1817-1892), known as Baha'u'llah. He proclaimed in 1863 that he was the manifestation of God for this current age.

Text: The writings of Shoghi Effendi and Baha'u'llah (especially the *Tablets,* which are considered as authoritative as the Bible). Their teachings may be summed up in the saying, "Oneness of humanity, oneness of religion, oneness of God."

Symbols: The number nine, a sacred designation dictating the structure of their temples (nine sides) and the size of local organizations (a minimum of nine members).

Appeal: Those who long for world peace and elimination of religious divisions over peripheral differences see Bahaism as a gracious faith with high ideals.

Purpose: Since all religions are presumed to have some merit and essential agreement, Baha'is hope to unite all faiths to prepare man for spiritual advancement in this life as well as in the next.

Errors: Baha'is teach that man cannot know God directly, but only through his messengers. Baha'is rob Christ of his incarnate deity by placing him on the same level as other religious teachers. He is also accorded a position inferior to that granted to Baha'u'llah. Baha'is do not believe in the bodily resurrection of Christ, the inerrancy of the Bible, eternal punishment, a literal hell, or the blood atonement of the cross. In place of these doctrines is a syncretistic religious system with Baha'u'llah as the central figure and fountain of all truth. The paradox of differences in the nature of God as he is viewed by various world religions is ignored in favor of the oneness theme of Bahaism.

Background Sources: Walter Martin, *The Kingdom of Cults* (Minneapolis: Bethany, 1965), 252-258; *The Denver Post,* 18 October 1974, 7BB; Ibid., 20 June 1975, 2BB; *East/West Journal,* December 1977, 80-83; *Newsweek,* 24 March 1980, 61; "The World Center of the Baha'i Faith," informational brochure handed to visitors of the Shrine of the Bab in Haifa, Israel; Kenneth L. Woodward, with Janet Huck, "Iran's Holy War on Baha'is," *Newsweek,* 25 January 1982, 73; Ruhiyyih Jahanpour, "Refusal to Give Up Her Faith Led to Imprisonment, Torture and Exile for an Iranian Baha'i," *People,* 9 September 1985, n.p.; Fergus M. Bordewich, "Iran, Holy Terror," *The Atlantic,* April 1987, 28, 30; Pamphlet, National Spiritual Assembly of the Baha'is of Canada, "Do You Know in What Day You Are Living?"; Pamphlet, National Spiritual Assembly of the Baha'is of the United States, "A New Way to Bring People Together: The Baha'i Faith"; W. Kenneth Christian, *Basic Facts of the Baha'i Faith* (Wilmette, Ill.: Baha'i Publishing Trust, n.d.).

Address/Location: Baha'i World Center, Haifa, Israel, is the international headquarters. U.S. headquarters is Baha'i National Center, Wilmette, IL 60091. Main U.S. temple is in Wilmette. Centers and teaching groups in most major world cities.

See also Unity School of Christianity.

BLACK
MAGIC

When a 21-year-old man was arrested in Miami for murder, the homicide sergeant called it a "black magic thing." Miguel Cardenas shot and killed his victim because he was convinced the man had put a curse on his grandfather. The grandfather had recently died, and Miguel attributed his death to a black magic spell. He decided to put a violent, deadly end to the source of sorcery. Black magic made Miguel a murderer.

Black magic has also inspired numerous money-making schemes. In Denver, a woman known only as Sister Yolanda Martinez performed seances and black magic rituals for fascinated customers. She convinced women that their jewelry and money were cursed and instructed her victims to bring in their valuables so she could remove evil forces from them. She then made off with the jewels and money. Sister Yolanda bilked naive victims out of $22,000.

Black magic advocates are known to carry fetish bags containing potions and animal bones, as well as an occasional human finger. Some black magicians poke pins into voodoo dolls to inflict pain or misfortune upon those who have angered them. Still others cast black magic curses on career opponents to frighten or intimidate them into resigning their positions. With the help of hexes, black magicians hope to advance in a world of professional rivalry.

Black magic was first introduced to the New World by slaves from West Africa. These African captives had a strong religious system of magical and supernatural beliefs and practices. In Africa, religion and magic were not separated as they were in Europe and America, and black magic religion was deeply entwined in every phase of their lives. They believed the sun to be omnipotent, and they worshiped river and thunder spirits. Among African slaves, black magic worship was primarily an individual practice, informal and ritualistic. The custom began during slavery when slaves were forbidden to gather in groups. Often a slave would steal into the woods at night to hold his own religious service. As in West Africa, he worshiped a multitude of spirits and gods, praising in particular gods associated with natural objects. In addition to their polytheistic belief system, West Africans worshiped their ancestors and believed a person's powers did not end with death. Dead people simply moved to another plane of existence from which they watched over their descendants. If something went wrong in their lives, these spirits could intervene and protect their families.

Today black magic is practiced by people of all races and ages for numerous reasons, ranging from rivalry to revenge. Ancient theory holds that demons dwell within every person and can be malevolently manipulated through black magic. These spirits are reached with the use of necromancy, spells, tarot cards, Ouija boards, astrology, and witchcraft.

The recent revival in astrology and belief in the supernatural has contributed to an increased popularity in black magic. For many, black magic seems to satisfy the need for order and discipline in a world of chaos. The occult leads people to believe that spirits can be contacted and used for one's own benefit. Examples of malevolent black magic can be found in such cults as voodoo and Santeria. (See the separate section on voodoo/Santeria.)

Sorcery is considered to be magic that aims to harm other people, that is, "black" magic. In contrast, magic used for beneficent ends is "white" magic. Practically speaking, every shade of gray magic exists between black and white magic. Most black magic advocates believe that through the use of charms, spells, and potions, spiritual powers can be manipulated for one's own advantage. Thus, people selfishly practice all types of magic to achieve their own ends, seldom distinguishing between black and white versions.

Caucasian practitioners of black magic are more formal, seeking magical assistance during defined times, usually during meetings or services. They generally don't express their religious beliefs to any great extent in daily routines. Among Afro-Americans involved in black magic, however, the occult has historically been part of their everyday existence, deeply etched into their lives. This tradition has been carried on by their ancestors. Consequently, they are more likely to discuss it openly. For both Caucasians and Afro-Americans occult magic provides its advocates with a system by which gods and spirits can be contacted. Satanic black magicians like Anton LaVey evoke the idea that the power of the Devil can be summoned and used toward evil ends. Known as America's black pope, LaVey and thousands of Satanists employ black magic to manipulate spirits and supernatural powers to frighten or hurt others.

Black magicians concentrate on violence and devastation and believe man's savage nature is a counterpart of the universe and its nature. They believe man's turbulence and triumphs parallel the universe on a smaller scale. Human emotions such as pity, lust, love, and hate exist on both the universal and the mortal levels. These dynamic universal energies are named after gods and planets. The lifeblood of the world is the sun, since its light and warmth are necessary for life on earth. Mars, the Roman war god, is the name bestowed upon the ferociously destructive force of the universe.

Black magicians inflict disease, physical danger, and unfortunate circumstances on victims. Many people are tempted to use black magic to get even with enemies or get ahead in life. Charms and spells can eliminate an enemy or protect against someone else's black magic. Fetishes supposedly make one person love another or cause him to follow someone else's wishes. They can also be used to persuade someone toward benevolence or to change a bad fate to a good destiny.

Christians recognize the destructiveness of dabbling in the Devil's territory. Black magic dealings with occult powers conflict with the Christian ethic of turning the other cheek. Christians believe in the personal power of God and his Son, Jesus Christ. The worship of nature or any other gods is considered blasphemous. Emotions such as pride, lust, and hate are deemed wicked and self-defeating. Christians instead choose to concentrate on love, forgiveness, and unselfishness. Choosing to place their faith in God, Christians reject black magic as a cult in direct conflict with the gospel.

Some would argue that black magic is not always evil, that black magic medicine men usually practice "good" magic. Witch doctors do sometimes attempt to use their knowledge and powers for beneficial purposes. These magicians create healing potions from plants, herbs, and minerals and also extend advice to those ask it. Frequently they counsel fellow cultists on how to protect against evil forces, as well as how to prosper or gain good fortune.

West African black magic beliefs included witches, ghosts, and vampires as a part of their system, concepts that constitute the closest similarity between African and European magic. According to European black magic tenets, a witch's greatest desire was to eat people by sucking their blood. Many of today's witches carry on this malevolent heritage of their ancestors and use their powers for evil purposes.

Even white witches acknowledge the danger of dabbling in black magic. They guard against these evil spirits by drawing magic circles around themselves. When witches call up a spirit, they know the summoned entity is powerful and dangerous. Since witches frequently use such drugs as belladonna, aconite, and hemlock, their minds and personalities are often vulnerable to evil spirits. Mediums and witches who consort with spirits tell tales of others in their "craft" who became insane or committed suicide under the influence of evil spirits.

Christians recognize that dabbling in black magic will lead to spiritual enslavement by demons. In the New Testament, black magic (witchcraft) is considered a "work of the flesh" in Galatians 5:20. Christians should refuse to be lured into the fascination of witchcraft and black magic. Instead, they should arm themselves with God's Word and allow the Lord to guide their lives. Brewing up an evil spell is dealing with the Devil and can only lead to spiritual death.

Founders: West African slaves who brought their system of religion and superstition to the New World. Their beliefs incorporated supernatural and magical beliefs and practices.

Text: Orally transmitted traditions and esoteric ceremonies self-devised by evil inspiration.

Symbols: Several, including a gate that represents "Ogu," the god of fire; a primitive head of a three-horned beast, which represents "Bossli," the god of the sea; a simple heart, which represents "Erzulie," the god of love.

Appeal: Black magic attracts those who lust for power and want to dabble in the unknown, especially those seeking fame and wealth without working for it. For some, black magic supplies simple cosmic answers to frustrations in a world of nuclear threat, starvation, pollution, and political strife. Through black magic rituals, people find order and comfort in universal truths. Also, people are greatly fascinated by secretive things, which contributes to the macabre appeal of black magic and other occult activities.

Purpose: People use black magic to control the future and other people's lives. Magicians practice their trade to get revenge on enemies or to protect themselves from bad spells. Black magic rituals are also used to intimidate or harm fellow employees, so the black magician can be promoted or achieve more authority over others.

Errors: Necromancers attempt to foresee the future by contacting spirits of the dead. Scripture admonishes that the entities magical mediums consult are not really dead but are instead the same demons encountered in other methods of fortune-telling. Black magicians believe they are in control, but they are actually slaves to the demons guiding the activities. Black magic tends toward evil and selfish indulgence without moral restraint. Deuteronomy 18 lists the occult practices of black magic that the Lord has forbidden; 2 Corinthians 6:14-15 warns against any collusion with such secret works of darkness.

Background Sources: *Rocky Mountain News,* 16 August 1988, 8; *Miami Sun,* 7 May 1983; *Faith for the Family,* November 1977, 3-5; *The Dallas Morning News,* 13 April 1984, 22A; *Newsweek,* 24 February 1986, 64; *Witchcraft, Mysticism, and Magic in the Black World,* 1974, 13, 16-19, 26; *Encyclopedia Britannica,* 1986, 88; *Faith,* November 1977, 5.

Address/Location: Originally Africa. Prevalent in Central and South America, also in urban centers in the United States.

See also Crowleyism, Macumba, Voodoo/Santeria, Witchcraft.

BRANHAMISM

When a drunken driver killed William Branham in 1965, most people assumed that the fame of this itinerant "Jesus only" (nontrinitarian) preacher would fade into obscurity. But Branham was not just another evangelist. He claimed to be *the* prophet for this dispensation (presumed to be the Laodicean Age), the voice of Revelation's seventh messenger. Today, Branhamites can still be found from the backwoods of Appalachia to the prairies of Saskatchewan. They gather in small groups to study the few books he wrote and listen to primitively recorded tapes of his sermons. To such zealots, there is one born among men greater than John the Baptist, and that man is William Branham.

Branham was born in 1909 in the hills of Kentucky, the son of a bootlegger. At seven years of age, he experienced the first of several visions that were destined to guide his life. On May 7, 1946, he spent a night in a cave where an angel supposedly appeared to him and explained his past and future. The angel also revealed how God would enable him to heal people. Many of his contemporaries were concerned about the spiritualistic overtones exhibited by Branham's gift of healing. The presence of a disease would set off vibrations, causing his hand to swell. Sometimes he would see a fiery ball dance about the room and then hover over those upon whom he would pronounce healing. (I was present during a 1965 Branham meeting when the ball of fire supposedly appeared. No visible phenomenon was evident to the audience, but many of those present accepted Branham's explanation without question.) But despite persistent warnings from fellow ministers that his visions might be demonic, Branham was undeterred.

Branham traveled widely overseas and achieved a wide measure of acceptance among some mainline Pentecostal groups. But his small congregation in Jeffersonville, Indiana, provided the primary channel for his teachings. Branham told his parishioners that God spoke to him out of a pillar of fire and revealed the mysteries of Revelation 5–8. This led him to predict future events, including Hitler's rise to power (correct), and the destruction of America by an explosion in 1977 (incorrect). In fact, the book that contains this later prophecy, *The Seven Church Ages,* also designated 1977 as the first year of the Millennium.

During the forties, Branham held large healing campaigns during which thousands experienced miraculous cures. Those who knew Branham intimately claimed he was a humble, self-effacing, withdrawn man who, in spite of an unlearned background, had a remarkable sense of spiritual understanding. Was he a person who started out sincerely but later succumbed to doctrinal error because he lacked adequate theological training? Were his visions and angelic visitations of godly origin, or was he cleverly deceived by Satan?

Retrospective analysis cannot conclusively answer these questions. But it is possible to decipher Branham's theology and weigh its inconsistencies against orthodox Christian doctrine. Even Branham's most devout followers would have to admit that his unscriptural views generate some measure of skepticism regarding his claim to be a prophet for the end times.

Branham was nontrinitarian, claiming that Jesus was created and not the eternal Son of God. He also believed that Cain and Abel were born from separate impregnations, the former by the serpent's seduction and the latter by Adam. Though he accepted the existence of a literal lake of fire, he contended that it would be destroyed eventually. Some of his prophetic statements were fulfilled, while others contain glaring errors.

Analyzing the credibility of living cult leaders is relatively easy. But those vanguards who have passed away can only be judged by the written documents they left. Without question, Branham sincerely believed he was a servant of God whose revelations were from the Lord. To question his theology is not to suggest his conversion was false or that all he did was in error. But even if God did confer spiritual gifts upon the life of William Branham, his current followers seem to have forgotten Paul's warning of 1 Corinthians 3. Christians are not to carnally adulate men, no matter how dynamic or charismatic they may be. God alone deserves total devotion.

Founder: William M. Branham, born 1909, died 1965.

Text: Malachi 4:5 (Branham claimed to be the fulfillment of this prophecy, the "Elijah" of the so-called Laodicean Age).

Symbol: None.

Appeal: To those who feel the organized church world is apostate and in need of divine revelation by a prophet from God.

Purpose: To perpetuate Branham's teachings by tract distribution and listening to his tape-recorded messages in small groups.

Errors: Branham denied the Trinity and eternal punishment; inaccurate foretelling of future events; wrong interpretation of Eve's fall; possible satanic deception by supernatural occurrences.

Background Sources: Western Tract Mission, Saskatoon, Saskatchewan, Canada; "William Branham" (pamphlet), Cal Beisner, Christian Research Institute; "God's Word Came to the Prophet William Marion Branham," tract by Spoken Word Publications; *William Branham, A Man Sent from God,* Gordon Lindsay, published and copyrighted 1950 by William Branham; *An Exposition on the Seven Church Ages,* William Branham.

Address/Location: Rural areas of central Canada, Appalachia, and midwestern USA.

C H I L D R E N

O F

G O D

(Family of Love)

"They went out from us, but they were not of us." The Apostle John's appraisal of first-century heretics (1 John 2:19) might well describe how early Jesus Movement pioneers felt about the Children of God. (In the early 1980s the name *Children of God* was changed to *Family of Love* to avoid identification with the bad publicity attached to the COG image.) In 1981 the far-flung clan of David "Moses" Berg spanned 72 countries and claimed an estimated membership of 10,000. Today Berg's "Royal Family" empire is in shambles.

David Berg was the son of a devout Christian and Missionary Alliance couple. His father, Hjalmer, pastored and taught at a Christian college. Virginia, his mother, was a radio evangelist. David married Jane Berg in 1944 and entered Christian service as an evangelist. He gradually soured on organized religion and began to associate with fringe religionist O. L. Jaguers and TV evangelist Fred Jordan. During the earlier years of the West Coast Jesus revolution, Berg joined his mother in directing a Teen Challenge coffeehouse. It was there that his radicalized, antiestablishment gospel took root among religiously zealous hippies, resulting in a group originally called Teens for Christ.

In August 1968 Berg's public declaration, "The War on the System," was printed in the Huntington Beach newspaper. In it he declared his "war on the system—the educational system, the church system, the parental system . . ."

In 1969 Berg left the coffeehouse and with about 50 followers headed on a trek to Arizona, which he later described as a time analogous to Israel's wanderings in the wilderness. The ragtag group took organized form with members assuming new biblical names. Twelve groups were formed, named, and patterned after Israel's twelve tribes. Maria, a Tucson church secretary, joined the movement and later was elevated to the status of Berg's mistress. Jane was nicknamed "Mother Eve" and was allowed certain sleeping "rights" with David. (Eventually she left the cult.)

They couldn't go back to California because Berg had twice "prophesied" the exact date the entire wicked state would slide into the ocean. Their meandering ended when Fred Jordan invited them to settle on his Texas Soul Clinic Missionary Ranch.

When the first wave of controversy hit the COG with charges of kidnapping and brainwashing, Fred Jordan kicked them out. By this time, the COG numbered at least 2,000 and had the strength to survive alone. A subsidiary called THANK COG (consisting of favorably disposed parents of COG members) was activated to counter the charges of FREE COG parents who claimed their offspring were unfairly controlled by Berg. Communal organizations were divided into colonies. To communicate with his increasingly fragmented followers, Berg hit upon the concept of circulating periodic newsletters that came to be called "MO Letters," which he continued after he withdrew from the daily operation of the group in the early 1970s. The rambling and grammatically shabby content of Berg's epistles evolved into what were considered divinely commissioned pronouncements. MO letters were said to be God's inspired word for today, far superior to what was written in the Bible thousands of years ago. Letters were categorized according to the ranks of insiders who had access to them.

Though no official systematic theology was promulgated, a philosophical and methodological structure did emerge. A pyramidal system of leadership (with Berg at the apex) placed "babes" (new converts) at the bottom and ensured that Berg's "Royal Family" (members of his immediate family and a few select others) remained in total control. As an autocratic messiah, he claimed to have direct communication with God—the Lord's "Moses" for today. His word was unquestioned, and even "murmuring" against his views was considered a mortal sin.

The practices of the COG stir volatile reactions wherever they go. Commune members languish in often unsanitary quarters, are sometimes refused medical treatment, and are kept on a subsistence diet of food "procured" from local supermarkets. The "Revolutionary Contract" they sign turns over all possessions to the COG, and most contacts with past friends and family are abruptly severed unless such individuals are considered sources of revenue for the group. No member is ever left alone. Parents are to be hated and despised along with the corrupt political system of the United States. (At one point Berg prophesied that the comet Kahoutek would collide with earth and destroy America.)

Daily hours that are not spent pouring over MO letters are dedicated to "litnessing"—evangelizing by literature distribution. Litnessing is also a primary source of cult income, with strict quotas set as a barometer of fervency for the cause. The other basic source of income is through what amounts to religious prostitution, called "FFing" ("flirty fishing") in COG parlance. Female members are encouraged to offer their bodies as an inducement for men to join the organization, though the "fish" are expected to pay for such favors. Children conceived through FFing are called "Jesus Babes." (Unwed mothers are euphemistically referred to as "widows.") Husbands are admonished to offer their wives as a symbol of their devotion to the cause. If venereal disease is contracted, it is seen as a willingness to suffer for the cause of Christ. Berg admits he himself is afflicted. In fact, Berg asserts that Jesus practiced sexual intercourse with Mary and Martha and deliberately contracted venereal disease to illustrate his identification with human infirmities.

Considering Berg's sexual preoccupation, it is understandably wise of him to restrict certain MO letters to his immediate intimates. Sex is a central theme of the salacious MO letters. Nothing is forbidden. Even homosexuality and sodomy, once considered taboo, have been legitimized "within the limits of the love of God." Topless bathing is promoted, girls are admonished not to wear undergarments, and most go braless. According to David Berg's daughter Deborah, the COG "perpetuates all forms of adultery, fornication, deception, sodomy, homosexuality and lesbianism, child sex, adult/child relations, and teaches as doctrine incest."

A marriage relationship (approved of first by colony leaders) consists of simply going to live with the chosen partner—legal civil ceremonies are seen as part of "Babylon's" corrupt system. Lesbianism and incest are considered particularly desirable.

Berg's system of sexual philosophy also includes the following: wife-swapping—justified by the "all things in common" passage of Acts 2:44; punishing female members by requiring them to masturbate before male observers; fondling children and sleeping with them in the nude; and the belief that God had intercourse with Mary to procreate Jesus! "God is in the business of breaking up families . . . salvation sets us free from the curse of clothing and the shame of nakedness," Berg writes. "God is a pimp," he blasphemously declares. "Experience a spiritual orgasm by being filled with the Spirit." When questioned about his personal sexual excesses, Berg argues that he is God's King David and that, like his namesake, his own promiscuity has been condoned by the Almighty.

The most startling aspect of Berg's sexual obsession is his claim to indulge in succubus relationships—sexual intercourse with spirit beings whom he calls "goddesses." In fact, Berg has a long history of flirtation with the occult. He contends that "spiritual counselors" visit him regularly and even enter his body to speak through his mouth. One of them, Abrahim, is supposedly a gypsy king who has been dead for over a thousand years. Berg has also been involved in palmistry, fortune-telling, and astrology. "Spiritualistic churches are not so bad after all," he concludes.

In Berg's eyes, the COG are the 144,000 of Revelation 7 and 14, the restored Israel. After the United States falls to Communism, the Antichrist will briefly reign until Satan takes over. The majority of professing Christians will take the mark of the beast, but the COG will remain the Lord's faithful.

In spite of his unimpressive record of past prophecies (the comet Kahoutek failed to destroy America), the end, according to Berg, will come in 1993. Non-COG members need not fear, however, since Berg's universalist theology leaves room for a second chance; few will be left to inhabit hell. In fact, those living can even now pray people out of hell.

Due to their unfavorable reputation in the U.S., the COG moved its international headquarters to Zurich, Switzerland. Currently Berg's whereabouts remain unknown. According to rumor, Berg has gone into hiding somewhere in Switzerland.

Though Berg once applied for Israeli citizenship, he eventually turned violently anti-Semitic. He courted the favor of Libya's Qaddafi and said about Jews, "Devils incarnate . . . if I had a gun I'd shoot them myself!" One bulletin published by a parents' organization reported that Berg, sheltered by Qaddafi, had organized an international call girl ring. The bulletin also stated that many COG members live as vagabonds in West Germany. In Britain, officials investigated the COG solicitations for money, finding leaflets that amounted to "instruction in prostitution" for COG girls "working in 'escort' agencies in London." Called "Heaven's Magic" in the Philippines, COG members are making their presence felt in that country.

Over the years, Berg's coarse language (MO letters are spiced with four-letter expletives) and immoral philosophy may have finally taken their toll. Defectors abound, including members of his immediate family and even Barbara Cane ("Queen Rachel"), who was Berg's heir apparent.

Berg's own wife and children left the cult. His son Paul leapt to his death in the Swiss Alps in 1973, no longer able to cope with the bizarre teachings and abusive authority of his father. Berg's daughter Deborah Berg Davis eventually left with her husband, Bill. In 1972 her father gave her the title of Queen, but when she refused his sexual advances she was denounced and her sister, Faithy, succeeded her. Deborah left in 1978 after her husband was excommunicated. In 1984 Deborah, who now professes orthodox Christianity, published a book exposing the COG's secret cult practices. Her husband, Bill, stated that the COG "preached the gospel of rebellion. . . . We would teach them . . . how to tell your parents you hate them, how to rebel against the government, how to fight the 'System.' "

Even the most effectively brainwashed followers of cult leaders cannot permanently overlook their leader's delusions of grandeur and his claims of divine endorsement. As Carole Hausmann and Gretchen Passantino put it in *The New Cults,* "The Holy Spirit is not some love potion. The Father is not some oversexed god. The Son is not a promiscuous bachelor with VD." That conclusion has also apparently been reached by more than one former COG member.

Founder: David Brandt Berg, born February 18, 1919. The COG coalesced into a viable organization circa 1970.

Text: The Bible, but more prominently the periodic MO letters, rambling discourses by which Berg communicates with his followers. Most letters have strong sexual overtones and artwork and go by titles like "Sex Works!" and "Come on, Ma! Burn Your Bra!" Other letters discuss matters of doctrine and rail against the "Systemites" — anyone not in agreement with COG ideals.

Symbols: None known, except the ubiquitous 8 1/2-by-11-inch folded MO letters handed out to passing motorists or pedestrians.

Appeal: COG recruiters concentrate on lonely young people who may be disenchanted with the establishment's economic or religious institutions. Bible verses are quoted out of context along with a positive image of happiness and brotherhood to suggest the COG are truly dedicated Christians. The recruit is bombarded with guilt that he is part of a condemned satanic system and will never again have a chance to faithfully serve God.

Purpose: "Pull down, destroy, and throw out the old order," Berg implores with revolutionary fervor. Mankind is in the last generation, and the United States is the "great prostitute that sits on many waters" and the "Babylon" of Revelation. Only the COG will remain true to God and escape the world's impending doom. They eventually will rule the earth as an elitist group through whom God's promises will be fulfilled.

Errors: At times Berg denies the Trinity ("I don't believe in the Trinity."). But on other occasions he promotes a Father, Mother, and Son conglomerate. The Holy Spirit, "Holy Queen of Love," is portrayed as a half-naked woman. Christ is declared to be a created being, in a misinterpretation of Revelation 3:14. Scriptural injunctions against consulting familiar spirits are ignored (Deut. 18:9-14; Jer. 14:14) by communicating with what Berg calls "God's Witches." He also denies God's promises of blessings to the Jews (Acts 3:18-26; Rom. 9:4-5) by cursing: "May God damn the God-damned Jews." By encouraging fornication, polygamy, incest, and adultery, Berg stands in opposition to the biblical view of sex in marriage as expressed by Paul in Hebrews 13 and Ephesians 5. In his rebellion against the historic church, Berg has, in the words of anticult researcher Jack Sparks, "managed to transform a gigantic personal temper tantrum against authority into a worldwide movement."

Background Sources: *Christianity Today,* 28 February 1977, 19-23; Ibid., 25 February 1980, 40-41; Jack Sparks, *The Mindbenders* (Nashville: Thomas Nelson, 1977); Ronald Enroth, *Youth Brainwashing and the Extremist Cults* (Grand Rapids: Zondervan, 1977); Walter Martin, *The New Cults* (Santa Ana, Calif.: Vision House, 1980); Eric Pement, "Children of God Still Active," *Cornerstone,* n.d., 30; Eric Pement, "Built on a Lie," *Cornerstone,* n.d., 4; "Ex-Children of God 'Queen' Tells Story," *Eternity,* January 1983, 10; "Children of Children of God," *Eternity,* July-August 1984, 24; Interview in *Fundamentalist Journal,* October 1985, 22; "Family of Love," *Encyclopedia Britannica,* 1986, 674;

Bob Larson, *Strange Cults in America* (Wheaton, Ill.: Tyndale, 1986), 70-71.

Address/Location: Last known headquarters in Zurich, Switzerland.

CHRISTIAN
SCIENCE

Doug and Rita Swan had watched their 16-month-old baby convulse and scream with pain for twelve days. When they finally rushed him to the hospital, it was too late. Little Matthew died six days later. As devout Christian Scientists, Doug and Rita had tried to follow their faith. Their church "practitioner" had told them to stop praying, tell no one, and ignore Matthew's anguished condition. Rita Swan, who now runs CHILD (Child Health Care Is a Legal Duty) says she was threatened by the practitioner when she began to doubt. After all, "Mother" Mary Baker Eddy had declared that sin, illness, and disease are all illusions of the mind to be corrected by right thinking.

The tragic story of Matthew Swan is only one of many. Fortunately for Christian Scientists, most states (44 at the publication of this book) in the U.S. have passed laws that protect them from prosecution for negligence if they shun medical assistance for a family member. However, courts are now raising serious questions about the neglect of children in such instances. Several cases are being tried, and recently Christian Science parents in Sarasota, Florida, were found guilty of murder in the negligent death of their seven-year-old child.

Christian Science has historically rejected chiropractic treatments, vitamins, nutrition, and drugs, as well as immunizations. When pain or sickness strikes, Scientists are admonished to deny "material sense testimony"—what their five senses tell them. Even a mother's protective instinct is derided as a "false, mortal belief." Church members may

166

have broken bones set, but they aren't permitted to entertain any medical diagnosis because Mrs. Eddy taught that consulting a physician breaks the First Commandment.

How can such an unenlightened belief hold authoritarian sway over people? Christian Science has so insulated itself from interaction with other religious groups that members feel a sense of isolation. They are reluctant to talk with outsiders and are forbidden to read any critical literature. They have reason to be impressed with their church. Mrs. Eddy had declared, "There is one way to heaven . . . divine science shows us this way. The second appearing of Jesus is unquestionably the spiritual advent of the advancing idea of God, as in Christian Science." Worship is carried on in expensive, beautiful buildings. Reading rooms are well appointed and cheerfully staffed at highly visible locations. The *Christian Science Monitor,* their daily newspaper with a circulation of over 100,000, is a highly respected journalistic organ with several Pulitzer prizes to its credit.

Mary Baker Eddy was certainly not modest in her claims, and most church members admire her as an infallible mother. She proclaimed that her teachings were God's "final revelation." Mrs. Eddy also asserted divine inspiration for her book *Science and Health with Key to the Scriptures.* The very choice of the word *key* in its title was based on her belief that she was the woman of Revelation 12. Many of her early followers accorded her a status of equality with Christ, a belief she did nothing to dissuade. Unfortunately for Christian Scientists, the historical record of her life gives one a decidedly different impression.

Mary Ann Morse Baker was the daughter of New Hampshire Congregationalists. Her childhood was characterized by emotional disturbances and frequent illnesses. At the age of 22 she married George Glover, who died seven months later. Her second marriage to a dentist, Dr. Daniel Patterson, ended in divorce. In 1877 she married Asa Eddy, her first disciple and the first Christian Science practitioner.

It was while she was married to Dr. Patterson that her life changed abruptly. Seeking relief from a spinal illness in 1862, she visited a spiritual healer by the name of Phineas Parkhurst Quimby. He practiced a form of mind-over-matter healing that he called Christian Science. While the depth of Quimby's influence on her is questionable, he stimulated her development of the religious teachings she eventually called Christian Science. Research has shown that Mrs. Eddy plagiarized heavily from a dissertation written by Francis Lieber, a German-American philosopher.

In 1866 Mrs. Eddy (Patterson) fell and injured herself. She later claimed that the fall left her with only three days to live (though her physician denied such a diagnosis). On the third day she reported that after reading Matthew 9:2 she experienced a miraculous cure. From then on, she felt her mission was to spread this "new" discovery of Christian Science. In 1875 she published *Science and Health,* offering healing to those afflicted with any number of maladies. The Church of Christ, Scientist, was incorporated in 1879.

Many people are favorably disposed toward Christian Science in spite of its bad publicity regarding cases when medical treatment was withheld. Some have heard glowing testimonials of healing from church members. Others note the conservative, well-educated, upper socioeconomic types who attend Christian Science meetings. They certainly seem well-intentioned, and few would condemn their effective ministry to those plagued with emotional ills and psychosomatic afflictions. But the evaluation of any cult must be based on substance, not image. The source of its authority and power, as well as the biblical validity of its views, are essential criteria to judge its worth. Such a critical analysis leaves Christian Science lacking in many areas.

Attending a Christian Science service immediately impresses one with its departure from mainstream Christian practices. There is no clergy, only lay readers and designated full-time practitioners who administer the church's healing techniques. No ordinances are recognized, and the service is ended with a reading of the Lord's Prayer (the verses interspersed with Mrs. Eddy's interpretations). Membership is restricted to only those who sever relationships with any other church or religious organization. *Science and Health* is read alternately with Bible quotations, giving the distinct connotation that the Word of God is useless without Mary Baker Eddy's illumination.

The government of the church is outlined in the *Manual of The Mother Church,* published in 1895. Mrs. Eddy continually revised this manual, intending that it would remain the authority in her church after she was gone. She entrusted the execution of the provisions of the manual to a self-perpetuating, five-member board of directors, who oversee the basically democratic framework of the branch churches.

The doctrines of Christian Science are not overtly evident to the casual observer. Much of Eddy's terminology sounds good until the surface is scratched to reveal her semantic frame of reference underneath. Influenced by the New Thought fad of her day, she underpins all her doctrines with the Hindu concept of an evil, illusory, material world. In this system, that which is spirit is the only true reality. This notion flavors her concepts of God, sin, and salvation. Here is a sampling of her teachings: man did not fall; death is an illusion; angels are God's thoughts; God is divine Mind; Genesis 2 is a "lie"; the Virgin Birth was a spiritual idea; the Trinity is pagan; evil and sin are imaginary; disease can be removed by right thinking; Jesus was not God; heaven is a state of mind; hell is nonexistent; prayer to forgive sin is pointless; Christ did not die; his resurrection was spiritual and not physical; and the shed blood of Christ is ineffectual for sin.

The core of Christian Science teaching is the doctrine of healing. Nothing else the church propagates draws more potential members. Mrs. Eddy was constantly challenged by the medical leaders of her day to produce evidence of one bona fide healing of a medically diagnosed case of organic disease. She did not and could not. In the end, even she turned to physicians and was treated with the painkiller morphine. Still, Christian Science maintains her belief that Jesus revealed to people their illusion of illness and thus cured them. Christian Scientists propose to go and do likewise.

Undeniably, there are some cases of Christian Science healing that deserve acknowledgment. Those who believe they have been healed are quick to embrace the entire scope of church teachings.

What really happens in these cases? Since medical verification before or after the fact is not allowed, no one knows how many cures were induced by alleviating the psychosomatic root of the problem. Emotional illnesses may have been removed by the psychologically soothing effect of the practitioner's therapy. Some ex-members argue that in Christian Science healing only the symptoms are ignored, a decision that may later result in suffering that could have been alleviated with proper medical treatment. In addition, the encounter of Moses with Pharaoh's magicians in Exodus 7 illustrates Satan's ability to precipitate apparent miracles. In fact, supernatural healing is a trademark of many demonic cults, including Satanism and Spiritualism. When a healing occurs, it should not necessarily be construed as an indication of divine approval of what the healer believes.

With rumored declines in membership rocking the foundation of the Mother Church in Boston, the future of Christian Science is uncertain. There are far fewer members today than the nearly 300,000 estimated in 1936 by the U.S. Census Bureau. The number of practitioners listed in *The Christian Science Journal* has dropped from about 12,000 in the 1950s to about 3,000. (Interestingly, membership has increased in Third

World countries.) Mrs. Eddy prophesied that "in fifty years or less, Christian Science will be the dominant religious belief of the world." That prediction seems as misguided as her contention that "man is incapable of sin, sickness, and death." Auschwitz and Mrs. Eddy's own decayed body seem sufficient proof to question this optimistic evaluation as well as her many other claims.

Founder: Mary Baker Eddy, born 1821 as Mary Ann Morse Baker. *Science and Health* published in 1875 and Church of Christ, Scientist, incorporated in 1879. She died in 1910.

Text: Matthew 9:2, supposedly an affirmation of Mrs. Eddy's own healing, which led her to formulate Christian Science beliefs.

Symbols: The seal of a cross ringed by a crown.

Appeal: The healing and health promised by Christian Science meets man's emotional need to overcome fear of pain and suffering. Eddy's teachings appeal to those seeking a philosophical basis for ignoring man's unregenerate nature and necessity of repentance. The reality of evil can be excused as an apparition of the mind.

Purpose: The "myths" of traditional Christian belief must be eradicated. Man is perfect and should strive for the same Divine Mind that Jesus attained. Sickness can be eradicated once a person sees that pure thoughts will dispel the illusion of disease. As the one true church, members are encouraged to affirm that God is good and therefore good is God. In such a system, evil cannot exist since matter (evil) does not exist.

Errors: Few orthodox Christian doctrines are left unassaulted. Christian Science is biblically not Christian, and it is manifestly not scientific. Its theology is universalistic. Jesus was said to be hiding in the sepulcher (he didn't die), so his resurrection holds no hope for believers, contradicting Paul's exposition of 1 Corinthians 15.

Background Sources: *Newsweek,* 21 June 1976, 87; *Christianity Today,* 10 October 1975, 6-11; M. Thomas Starkes, *Christian Scientists and the Baptist Witness* (Home Missions Board, S.C., n.d.); *People,* 31 March 1981, 30-32; Kenneth Boa, *Cults, World Religions and You* (Wheaton, Ill.: Victor, 1980); *Encyclopedia Britannica,* 1986 ed., s.v. "Christian

Science"; Walter Martin, *The Kingdom of the Cults* (Minneapolis: Bethany Fellowship, 1977); Kenneth Woodward, "The Graying of a Church," *Newsweek*, 3 August 1987, 60; "A Mild Matron Goes Modern," *Time*, 26 September 1988; William Dunn, "Conviction for Beliefs Ominous," *USA Today*, 70 April 1989, 3A; John Larrabee, "States Take on Power of Prayer," *USA Today*, 2 May 1988, 2A.

Address/Location: Mother Church in Boston, Massachusetts. Local churches in most U.S. cities of reasonable size. About a third of its nearly 3,000 congregations are located in 56 countries outside the U.S.

CHURCH

OF

ARMAGEDDON

(Love Family)

Meekness, patience, and courage sound like admirable biblical qualities. But in the Church of Armageddon (sometimes called the Love Family), these virtues represent the newly adopted names of cult members. Since the Love Family considers all Christians to be descendants of the Israelites, Israel is added as a surname. Presiding over the clan is Love Israel, a former salesman named Paul Erdmann, who formed the Seattle-based cult in the 1960s by gathering followers to whom he expounded his visions and revelations.

Taking his cue from Revelation 16:16, in which Armageddon is mentioned, Erdmann (Love Israel) teaches his disciples that they are the true family of God. New members turn over all of their possessions to the church, cut off all communication with the outside world (including their parents and relatives unless such contacts result in donations of money and materials), and devote themselves to the goals and person of Love Israel. The disciples are also taught to adhere to some strange and unusual beliefs. Eating is considered to be a sacrament; the consumption of marijuana, hashish, and mushrooms are also sacraments; children are severely disciplined; marriage is replaced by "bonding" under Love Israel's authority; yoga is exercised; outside medical assistance is forbidden, and toluene (a solvent) vapors are inhaled as a religious rite. (After two members died from this practice, it has apparently been discontinued.)

Though Love Israel undoubtedly "transformed" his followers from insecure outcasts to self-confident zealots, they paid a great price in sacrificing personal freedom. A mass defection in the early 1980s nearly destroyed the cult; departing members charged Love Israel with conning them into accepting his total control over their lives and income, while he lived in luxury and they struggled with necessities. In the mid 1980s, after a brief period in Los Angeles during which he reexperienced an awakening to the world's troubles, he returned to Washington state to regain control of the Love Family. He is now working to rebuild the commune.

Fortunately, the growth of the group has never surpassed a few hundred members, a statistic of small consolation to anyone who has a loved one captivated by this cult. With Love Israel as the focus of attention, the Love Family seems to be more an extension of his own personal ego rather than a "fulfilled" New Testament organ of Christ's body.

Background Sources: J. Gordon Melton, *The Encyclopedia of American Religions,* vol. 2 (Wilmington, N.C.: McGrath, 1978); Ronald Enroth, *Youth, Brainwashing and the Extremist Cults* (Grand Rapids, Mich.: Zondervan, 1977).

THE CHURCH OF BIBLE UNDERSTANDING

(Forever Family)

His usual appearance has been associated with a shaggy beard, stringy hair circling a bald forehead, military fatigues, Converse All-Star yellow sneakers, a chain of brown leather pouches, a dozen colored felt-tip pens in his breast pocket, and a large round pin proclaiming, "Get Smart, Get Saved." This is hardly the image one would envision for a revered spiritual leader who likens himself to Elijah and hints that he may know the exact hour of the Lord's return. But then Stewart Traill, ex-atheist and former secondhand vacuum cleaner salesman, is not a typical Messianic cult leader.

After an apparent religious conversion in Allentown, Pennsylvania, in the early seventies, Traill began teaching Bible studies and collecting a following. With his wife and new converts in tow, he formed the Forever Family in 1971. Concerned that the name lacked respectability, in 1976 it was changed to the Church of Bible Understanding (COBU). He continued to prosper until he headed a far-flung fellowship estimated to be 10,000 strong (only a few hundred remain), and he amassed a fortune, including a $2 million-a-year rug-cleaning business and four airplanes, one of them a $300,000 turboprop.

In the wake of the Jonestown debacle, Traill's prospects soured. The location of his headquarters was shifted until the present Philadelphia site was selected. Although membership has dwindled, it appears to have stabilized. Ex-members complained of being encouraged to work for a pittance (all earnings are turned over to church leaders) and being housed

174

in rat-infested lofts. The IRS put the rug-cleaning operation out of business, and the truth of his divorce and remarriage surfaced. Traill, 46, and his wife had exchanged accusations of adultery in a messy divorce proceeding, after which he married his COBU secretary—half his age—only six weeks later.

An exact picture of COBU doctrine is sketchy, since few definitive statements have been published. Its communal life-style is regimented into categories known as "guardians" (active members who are leaders), "sheep" (advanced believers), and "lambs" (new converts). Those who have left the commune report having been intimidated by suggestions that "backsliders" may meet a tragic end. The remaining COBU members devoutly believe that they have (via Traill) the one true access to "Bible understanding." Traill contends that God deliberately secret-coded the Scriptures and that only his "figure system" and "color-coding" scheme hold the keys to the true interpretation of the Word of God.

Though the basic appeal of COBU is directed toward a "personal acceptance of Christ" with "old-time religion" terminology, Traill's denial of the Trinity and his unsubstantiated berating of detractors ("CCs"—short for "Contentious Christians") hardly endears him to mainstream evangelicals. In addition, Traill challenges his converts to break off all familial relationships on the premise that those over 30 (excepting Traill) are too spiritually hopeless. He keeps his flock in line with a mixture of constant emotional abuse mingled with fatherly praise and kindness.

In spite of his attempts to improve his personal appearance as well as COBU's image, the prognosis for any substantial growth of the cult seems doubtful. The question of whether or not most COBU members are "genuinely saved" is open to speculation, but their coercive and rigidly methodical methods of "witnessing" are unlikely to garner many adherents.

Background Sources: Eric Pement, "Shepherd without Compassion: Stewart Traill and the Church of Bible Understanding," *Cornerstone*, vol. 11, no. 60, n.d., 32-33; Joseph Duffy, *Contemporary Christianity*, vol. 6, no. 3 (March-April 1977); *Today Magazine (Philadelphia Inquirer)*, 24 June 1979; *Alternatives*, vol. 4, no. 6 (April-May 1977); *The Sunday Record*, 25 September 1977.

THE
CHURCH
OF THE
LIVING WORD

John Robert Stevens, the founder of The Church of the Living Word, commonly called "The Walk," was a classic example of what happens when one is raised in a Christian environment and departs into error. Stevens used evangelical terminology to justify his private revelations. Consequently, the truth of Scripture was altered slightly enough to be detected, but not sufficiently to be overtly obvious. "The Walk" members use colloquial Christian catch-phrases that they have redefined. For example, when Stevens said he was "speaking the Word of the Lord" he actually referred to a mediumistic revelation of his Christ-attained perfection. Those not familiar with his cult would assume that he was merely talking about preaching. Such a twist in logic and language is consistent with his whole approach to scriptural truth.

Stevens was reared in a preacher's home, though he later departed from Foursquare and Assemblies of God groups after a dramatic vision in 1954. He claimed this experience was similar to Paul's encounter on the road to Damascus. In a bitter breakaway from the church of the same name founded 50 years earlier by his father, W. J. "Dad" Stevens, Stevens began the movement that now claims 100 churches, with headquarters in Iowa and California.

The father-son rift culminated in a lawsuit by John against his father. The younger Stevens accused his father and associates of mishandling large sums of church money, bilking worshipers, and abusing their leadership. "Dad" Stevens countersued, charging the John Stevens organization with conspiring to "take over the church . . . real and personal property" belonging to the elder Stevens and his associates. J. R. Stevens died of cancer amid the legal battle, at which time his church claimed holdings that included ownership of a 1,100-acre farm in Brazil, a 300-acre commune (Shiloh) near Kalona, Iowa, and a 150-acre retreat near Fresno, California.

In Stevens's scheme of teachings, the Bible was considered outdated and thus needed to be supplemented (and eventually replaced) by impromptu, spoken prophecies. During frequent, lengthy, emotion-charged services, members were encouraged to deny reason and yield to extemporaneous utterances that represent "the living word." The one who spoke was more than a mere channel of Christ. He was said literally to become Christ, a self-deification doctrine that was central to the church's beliefs.

Such individualistic revelations were important but always subject to the ones expounded by Stevens, who claimed apostolic authority. Members were taught that Scripture would confuse them unless they followed Stevens's interpretation. This authoritarian manner of control also extended to the personal affairs of members. Day-to-day decisions had to be subjected to church supervision, since "The Walk" is assumed to be the only true church capable of guiding one's life.

As the church evolved, occult and psychic phenomena became more evident. Since a central doctrine having to do with perfectionism states that Christians become a part of God in a manner bordering on deification, their divine natures become willing recipients of mystical experiences. This merging of one's nature with God negates the sense of personal identity, further opening up one's spirit to experience transcendent levels of consciousness. At some church services, participants are encouraged to raise the level of their vibrations, a practice bordering on the spiritualistic manner of inducing altered states of mind.

Many "Walk" members (there are about 5,000 members worldwide) are born-again refugees from sterile churches. They have been attracted by a sense of belonging due to the group dynamics and claims of supernatural gifts of tongues, prophecy, and healing. These well-meaning people might overlook the occult nature of references to auras and "transference" of spiritual power. But their sincerity is no excuse for claiming superiority over all other churches and denominations. Such an exclusive attitude is not in harmony with 1 Corinthians 12, which emphasizes the unity of Christ's body in spite of its diversity.

Since the death of Stevens, Shiloh is no longer affiliated with the California or Iowa factions. The vast wealth of the church is a source of contention between divisions of The Walk, some siding with John Robert's second wife, and others aligning with contingents of the California church.

Founder: John Robert Stevens, born August 7, 1919, Washington, Iowa. Died of cancer June 4, 1983.

Text: Acts 9:3-4 (Stevens legitimatizes his apostolic authority by equating his visionary experience with Paul's Damascus road encounter); John 16:13 is interpreted to assume that subjective revelation should supplant and augment objective biblical truths.

Symbols: None known.

Appeal: Disaffected Christians from nominal church backgrounds may find in "The Walk" a more spontaneous encounter with spiritual reality. Those familiar with Eastern religions and occult phenomena will easily recognize the similarities between these practices and Stevens's teachings.

Purpose: Members are taught that all other churches belong to a false Babylonian system and that The Church of the Living Word is restoring the active presence of God's truth by the use of supernatural gifts and revelation.

Errors: Stevens's teachings rob Christ of his personhood by claiming that he is now embodied in the Church and that Christians can be a deified extension of Christ. "Be robed with deity itself—God's very nature being reproduced in you," Stevens implores. A conclusion of this belief is that The Church of the Living Word essentially represents the Second Coming of Christ, replacing the literal return of the person of Christ in the clouds (Acts 1:11). First John 2:2 admonishes that Christians can and do sin. They are to repent and ask forgiveness (1 John 1:8-9), not strive for a sanctified state of self-deification.

Background Sources: "John Robert Stevens and The Church of the Living Word," *Spiritual Counterfeits Project Newsletter,* September 1976, vol. 2, no. 7; Walter Martin, *The New Cults,* (Santa Ana, Calif.: Vision House, 1980,), 269-296; miscellaneous writings by John Robert Stevens, including *To Every Man That Asketh,* etc.

Address/Location: Last known headquarters in Los Angeles, CA.

CHURCH
UNIVERSAL
AND
TRIUMPHANT

"I am that I am," says Elizabeth Clare Prophet as she conveys her blessing on the audience who has just heard her discourse. Guru Ma, as she is known to her followers, has not only plagiarized God's reply to Moses (Exod. 3:14), but she also makes some other phenomenal claims. She purports to be a reincarnation of the biblical Martha, stating that in a former life Jesus spoke directly to her one day while she was kneading bread with her sister, Mary. Christ commanded her to keep incarnating until God's Spirit would be poured out at the dawning of the Aquarian Age. Elizabeth Clare Prophet believes that hour has come, and she is the only present-day medium of truth endorsed by the Ascended Masters (beings who have passed on to an elevated spirit plane). Those who follow her teachings, as received from the Great White Brotherhood (a community of Ascended Masters said to be sages of hidden wisdom and knowledge), will have their souls purified by the Violet Consuming Flame so that they may achieve Christ-consciousness.

To the uninitiated, such ideas may seem a little confusing. But to indoctrinated followers of the Church Universal and Triumphant, it's all part of an effort to transcend the laws of karma and acknowledge one's inner divinity. Some cult groups can be explained in fairly simple terms. But the Church Universal has concepts and nomenclature that need defining before any analysis of church belief is possible.

During the early twentieth century, occultists and Theosophists such as Guy and Edna Ballard developed a system of religious philosophy around the concept of Ascended Masters. The theory is similar to a gnostic belief that God, who is impersonal and unknowable, must be approached by deified, human intermediaries. These Masters are the messengers whom God uses to reveal his truth. They have passed beyond the cycles of reincarnation to merge their consciousness with God. Now, these "elder brothers and sisters who have gone before" divulge the hidden mysteries of truth by discourses transmitted through selected human messengers. Elizabeth Clare Prophet claims to be their sole channel of communication for this hour. Foremost among these Ascended Masters is Saint Germain, a French eighteenth-century occultist. His associates in this spirit realm include Jesus the Christ, Mary, his mother, Master Kuthumi, Master Godfre, and El Morya (the main source for Prophet's message). This fraternity is known as The Great White Brotherhood.

Building on the spiritualistic concepts of the Ballards and other Theosophists/occultists, Mark L. Prophet founded the Church Universal and Triumphant (known then as Summit Lighthouse) in 1958. Prophet told his followers he was the second coming of the legendary Sir Lancelot. He also said that while driving a railroad spike one day in Minnesota he'd had a vision of El Morya, an Ascended Master. While serving as a medium, Mark met Elizabeth Clare Wulf at a meeting in 1961. After leaving their spouses, two years later they were married.

The union seemed logical, since Elizabeth claims her first encounter with spirits occurred at about four years of age when she was surrounded by "angelic hosts." While she attended college, voices directed her to books about St. Germain. Through the years, a variety of spirit beings communicated with Elizabeth. But it was not until she met Mark that she felt her calling in life was fulfilled. Mark Prophet, 20 years her senior, died of a stroke in 1973. (He is now deemed to be among the other Ascended Masters, communicating with the spirit name Lanello.) The mantle of serving as a messenger for the Ascended Masters fell upon her, and today somewhere between 75,000 and 150,000 followers around the world believe she is the absolute authority on all spiritual matters. (Her church, incidentally, is said to have assets in the neighborhood of $50 million.)

The gospel, as preached by the Ascended Masters and dictated through the medium Elizabeth to her *chelas* (disciples), is a mixture of Christian terminology and Eastern/mystical concepts. Each person is believed to be on a spiritual pilgrimage (through a myriad of reincarnations) from his lower self to his higher self. Prophet ignores the warning of 1 John 2:22 that the spirit of antichrist denies Jesus is *the* Christ. She contends that the historical Jesus was a mere human who became *a* Christ. Thus, he is not God who is "able to save to the uttermost" (Heb. 7:25), but merely an example of how we, too, can ascend spiritually by acknowledging our inner Christ-presence.

Chelas are assisted in their pilgrimage by a variety of occult/mystical practices. Foremost among these is the use of "decrees," the mantra-like chanting of incantations. A favorite is "I am that I am," an affirmation of self-deity that ensures ascension. Devotees also seek to cleanse their *karma* by being surrounded by the "Violet Flame," a sacred fire said to be made available by the spiritual merit of St. Germain. As a substitute for the blood of Christ, it provides a source of salvation from any negative influences. In addition to the Violet Flame, Prophet teaches her followers how to enlist the aid of the seven archangels of God in their personal lives. The spiritual smorgasbord in Prophet's theology also includes *chakra* purification, reflexology, healing, fasting, diet, auras, and cosmic astrology.

The cult is currently headquartered at the Royal Teton Ranch in Montana, where large conferences attract more followers each year. Currently, members outnumber the population of Gardiner, a nearby town. At one point a local newspaper discovered and printed a "hit list" that included the names of almost 200 people against which the cult members pray daily, calling for the will of God to cleanse all opposition. Prophet's followers have reportedly built underground shelters, stocked with food for protection from an impending nuclear holocaust. Though she denies it, Prophet has been accused of storing large quantites of unauthorized arms.

As a point of interest, I have received letters of support and appreciation from followers and officials of the *Church Universal and Triumphant*. This correspondence has been in regard to my books on the occult and the immoral aspects of rock music. In fact, these books have been promoted and sold at the public appearance of Mrs. Prophet. In light of the presumption that the Ascended Masters might well be masquerading familiar spirits and that Prophet's messages from them are demonic utterances, how could these same powers then promote the cause of one who represents orthodox, historic Christian theology?

The answer may be that Prophet and her followers are sincere in their religious devotion. In spite of their violation of scriptural commands against attempted communication with the dead (necromancy—Deut. 18:11), they genuinely believe they are defenders of moral purity and opponents of witchcraft. Prophet and her followers should be approached

CHURCH UNIVERSAL AND TRIUMPHANT

with loving concern that they may discover a personal faith in Jesus *the* Christ, who is above all principalities and powers, including the Ascended Masters (Eph. 1:20, 22).

Founder: Mark L. Prophet (1918-1973); Elizabeth Clare Prophet, current leader.

Text: "I am that I am" (Exod. 3:14). In Scripture, this statement affirms the eternal, omnipotent, omniscient nature of God. I AM cults say this phrase can be spoken to testify of the God-presence in each person. Elizabeth Clare Prophet has also written *The Lost Years of Jesus,* in which she supposedly reveals Jesus' experiences in the Orient as a young student of Eastern philosophy before returning to Palestine to complete his mission on earth. She followed this book with *The Lost Teachings of Jesus.*

Symbols: Cross with dove emerging from center of the quadrants; flame representing the sacred fire; chart of "divine self" illustrating man's transition from lower self; pictures of miscellaneous Ascended Masters.

Appeal: Those interested in spiritualism and Eastern religions find a Christian frame of reference for pursuing these beliefs in a syncretistic manner. Some are attracted by the awe of receiving directly from Prophet's lips supernatural messages of departed spiritual masters.

Purpose: Stated—"To publish the teachings of the Ascended Masters and to shed light on the lost and distorted teachings of Christ." Inherent— From a biblical perspective, devotees become entwined in a web of occult practices and psychic experiences that portend a grave risk of spiritual bondage.

Errors: The biblical injunction against necromancy and consultation with familiar spirits (Ascended Masters) is ignored (Deut. 18:9-14). In this context (Lev. 19:31), Elizabeth Clare Prophet fulfills the Bible's description of a witchcraft medium. In Church Universal theology, Christ is not God in flesh worthy of worship (Phil. 2:9-10) but rather "the mediator between God and man, the Christ-self, or the Christ-consciousness." Man's need is not forgiveness by God's grace but rather a purging of his karma to ascend spiritually in future reincarnations, or to join the other Ascended Masters directly.

Background Sources: Church Universal and Triumphant literature and miscellaneous mailings. Among these are *Pearls of Wisdom* (weekly organ), "The Teachings on the Path of Enlightenment," "Only Love," "Sing a New Song," *Climb the Highest Mountain, The Coming Revolution,* Winter 1981; Walter Martin, *The New Cults* (Santa Ana, Calif.: Vision House, 1980), 203-236.

Address/Location: Division of Summit University Press, Box A, Livingston, MT 59047-1390, Royal Teton Ranch, Box A, Corwin Springs, MT 59021.

See also Ascended Masters.

TERRY
COLE-WHITTAKER

"To turn your life around requires that you live a new life in Christ. He overcame the world . . . so can you, now."

"Salvation must be an act of saving yourself from something. If you need to be saved, you must be in danger. The truth is, no one is in danger. You have never broken the laws of God. You are pure and innocent."

To an evangelical observer, the above quotes are obviously contradictory. To followers of Cole-Whittaker, they are truths of the "New Christianity." Cole-Whittaker, a Doris Day look-alike, was momentarily a rising star of the religious electronic media. Her weekly half-hour television program beamed the message of her prosperity gospel to more than a million viewers in major markets.

In the spring of 1985, Cole-Whittaker bade her followers farewell and called it quits. Some said she was burned out. Others thought her mounting debts (estimated at $400,000 to $700,000) had become unmanageable. "I no longer want to be a religious leader. I want to be myself."

Cole-Whittaker, once a third runner-up in the Mrs. America contest, searched through various contemporary human potential cults. She finally ended her quest with enrollment in Ernest Holmes's School of Ministry, a Religious Science sect. Cole-Whittaker's California-style enthusiasm for the good life caught on in the San Diego-area La Jolla Church of Religious Science. Rapid growth led her to form her own group, the Science of Mind Church International.

With a combination of pop psychology, New Age concepts, and beliefs borrowed from est and the occult, Cole-Whittaker declared, "God

185

doesn't forgive; you've never been judged except by your own thoughts."

Among the various disciplines she recommended are the following: *A Course in Miracles,* the occult volume dictated by automatic handwriting; group rebirthing, a breathing technique based upon yogic principles; body massage; nutrition; and affirmations. Among the latter are declarations to "visit only beautiful places . . . to wear only those clothes which are appropriate to upward mobility . . . to associate with those who are prosperous and happy."

The followers of Cole-Whittaker did not visit refugee camps or establish street people shelters. On the contrary, Cole-Whittaker considered poverty the result of irresponsibility. She exhorted those in her church to attend "Dressing to Win" seminars so they could shed the old image of failure for the new personae of "divine wealth."

Such hedonistic and yuppie-appealing pronouncements attracted the Mercedes-Benz crowd. "Our ministry isn't into sin, guilt, disease, pain, or hunger," Cole-Whittaker was fond of saying. What about the appeal of Jesus to deny one's self and take up the cross (Luke 9:23)? Cole-Whittaker declared, "God denies nothing in the world for you."

Cole-Whittaker mastered the lingo of evangelicalism, further confusing her disciples. She spoke of her "prayer ministry," "love offerings," and went so far as to say, "Through the Holy Spirit I was saved." Her ministry tabloid, deceptively entitled *The Good News,* borrowed the trappings of more conventional media ministries.

Cassettes and books expounded her doctrines, along with special videocassette training programs in "Mastery of Living" and "Mastery of Faith." Those who digested the material eventually learned what she called "the principles," an eclectic cafeteria of New Age doctrines teaching that the major religions of the world are "woven together with the thread of light linking the ONE-beyond ISM."

With her chauffeured Cadillac and $180,000-a-year salary, Cole-Whittaker plugged into the good life. Her young and well-to-do parishioners didn't seem to mind, convinced that she really loved them and that they were "walking on the earth as sons of God," exactly as she said. Critics argued she told people what they wanted to hear about themselves. She readily admitted the accusation was true. "I tell people they're wonderful. It's true!" she affirmed.

"I'm an explorer. I'm a metaphysical, evangelical, Pentecostal space cadet," Cole-Whittaker proclaimed. Her audience responded with whoops and hollers, apparently never stopping to ask themselves how someone who failed four marriages could hope to understand transcendent love and guide them out of their own insecurities. On the other hand, her ever-absent injunctions against any divine moral code allowed people to live as they wished, as long as they chose "to look and feel beautiful." Cole-Whittaker affluently affirmed, "The more I prosper, the more others prosper."

After her empire crumbled in the early 1980s, Cole-Whittaker resigned from apparent exhaustion and fatigue. She resurfaced in 1986 as a revitalized New Age advocate with her book, *The Inner Path from Where You Are to Where You Want to Be*. In it, she declared, "God is That Which Includes All Beings. God is All of it and the Everything, and God cannot be apart from it any of it any way." Her new interests are more esoteric: exploring goddess and Mother Earth energies, guided meditations, and channeling higher "knowingness," as pursuits of her Adventures in enlightenment foundation.

Founder: Terry Cole-Whittaker, a divorcée whose great-grandmother, the family matriarch, was married six times and was also an adherent of Religious Science. Cole-Whittaker was trained in the teachings of *A Course in Miracles* as well as the beliefs of Ernest Holmes, who founded the Institute of Religious Science in 1927.

Text: *Prosperity, Your Divine Right,* a gospel of success combining motivational psychology and selfish affirmations such as "It is right for me to prosper."

Symbol: A stylized fountain representing the flow of prosperity from the source of God. The fountain has seven points representing the perfection and completeness of God.

Appeal: Cole-Whittaker attracted three basic classes of people: (1) participants in various New Age and human potential disciplines looking for the latest in-thing to affirm their narcissistic motivations; (2) marginally churched people who wanted an ecclesiastical atmosphere with congregational services, but avoided any theological demands pertaining to guilt and sin; and (3) insecure and introverted individuals for whom Cole-Whittaker provided an alter ego, exuding the self-confidence and charisma they felt incapable of attaining.

Purpose: Conventional religion has failed because of its emphasis upon sacrifice and guilt. Cole-Whittaker taught that no one bears blame for personal misconduct and even suggested that mass murderer Richard Speck was sinless when he murdered eight student nurses because his victims "created" their own fate. She declared her purpose was to "bring you into oneness with God where you can have the direct experience of being limitless."

Errors: Cole-Whittaker borrowed from Christian Science to suggest that everything negative is an illusion, and each human is a "thought in the mind of God." Whereas Jesus told the rich young ruler to sell all that he had and give it to the poor (Matt. 19:21), Cole-Whittaker's best-selling book is entitled *How to Have More in a Have-Not World.* Though she spoke of the Holy Spirit in a personal sense, a closer examination of her theology reveals the term was used more for purposes of conventional religious rhetoric than in reference to any specific divine personage. Terry Cole-Whittaker's Jesus was a gnostic whose references to heaven and hell were merely figurative. Though Titus 2:1 warns us to "speak the things which become sound doctrine," Cole-Whittaker contradictorily declared that traditional dogma should be avoided. "Resist the temptation to buy into those beliefs," she said. She also denied a personal devil by teaching "there is no opposite to God."

Background Sources: Terry Cole-Whittaker, *Prosperity, Your Divine Right,* Terry Cole-Whittaker Ministries, n.d.; Terry Cole-Whittaker, "Prosperity, Your Divine Right," cassette distributed by her organization, 1984; miscellaneous copies of *The Good News,* tabloid distributed by Terry Cole-Whittaker Ministries; *People,* 26 November 1984, 99-106; "A Self-Styled Evangelist Stretches God's Truth," *Christianity Today,* 21 September 1984, 73-75; Paul Zuromski, ed., *The New Age Catalogue: Access to Information and Sources* (New York: Doubleday, Island, 1988), 44; various Terry Cole-Whittaker Ministries publications and fundraising letters.

A COURSE
IN
MIRACLES

For seven years the Voice spoke to Helen Schucman. Claiming to be Jesus, the Voice began, "This is a course in miracles. It is a required course. Only the time you take it is voluntary."

A psychologist at Columbia University, Schucman, when first confronted by the Voice, transcribed its messages by automatic handwriting. She said the process made her uncomfortable. Dr. William Thetford, Schucman's close friend and professor of medical psychology at Columbia University's College of Physicians and Surgeons, typed the manuscript for *A Course in Miracles* from Schucman's notes. The Voice dictated the 622-page text first, then the 478-page *Workbook for Students*, and finally the 88-page *Manual for Teachers*.

Schucman, who was a religious skeptic, took notes almost daily from the Voice. It claimed that guilt is resolved by forgiving others, not through seeking forgiveness from a personal God. The essence of the Course is epitomized in this summation: "Nothing real can be threatened, nothing unreal exists."

In 1976, the Course was published by Robert and Judy Skutch of the Foundation for Inner Peace, which also offers pamphlets, audio and video cassettes, and other books. The 1,200 pages of the three-volume set of books used in *A Course in Miracles* denigrates most Christian orthodoxy. Nevertheless, more than 150,000 sets have been sold without benefit of advertising.

The *Manual for Teachers,* channeled through Schucman during five months in 1972, states, "Christ takes many forms with different names." It also claims man needs no help to enter heaven, since he's already there. Stripping Jesus of divinity exemplifies the Course's unconventional philosophy. Conversely, one of its stated aims is to emphasize "the importance of Jesus as our gentle teacher."

A Course in Miracles claims forgiveness is a "happy fiction," that it's unnecessary to forgive anything God has created. While denigrating God's forgiveness and criticizing Christianity for overemphasis on suffering, sacrifice, and sacrament, the Course proposes that peace becomes attainable only when humans forgive each other. Such borderline blasphemy constitutes a theme throughout the many pages of *A Course of Miracles.*

Founder: Helen Schucman, as channel of the Voice.

Text: *A Course in Miracles,* textbooks Volumes 1 and 2, plus *Manual for Teachers,* Volume 3.

Symbol: Stylized star with beams between the points on a slotted background circle, the word *forgiveness* curved over the top of the circle.

Appeal: Those who wish to affirm a reverence for Jesus are led to believe Christ has actually spoken through the Course. Without abiding by any ecclesiastical structure, adherents can claim to be in direct contact with the truth of Jesus.

Purpose: *A Course in Miracles* seeks to create peace and harmony through self-forgiveness and to correct what the Course views as the errors of Christianity. Removal of all personal guilt is the ultimate aim achieved by the act of forgiving others.

Errors: Salvation is available through self-help methods taught in the Course, not by God's mercy as stated in Ephesians 1:7. Man is already in heaven and needs to exert no special effort to attain what is already his. The Course claims Jesus spoke through a channeler (Schucman) to deliver the messages that contradict basic tenets of Christianity and necessitate the biblically forbidden practice of trance-possession mediumship.

Background Sources: *New Realities,* July-August 1984; Foundation for Inner Peace, *A Course in Miracles* (Farmingdale, N.Y.: Coleman Graphics, 1975).

Address/Location: Foundation for *A Course in Miracles*, RD 2, Box 71, Roscoe, NY 12776.

CROWLEYISM

His mother proclaimed him the Beast, 666, from the Book of Revelation, chapter 13. As a child he gleefully identified with the wicked, horned creature rising from the depths of the sea, blaspheming God. As an adult, he became the most infamous black magician and Satanist of all time. Though he's been dead for four decades, Aleister Crowley, whose motto was "Do what you will," still inspires followers with his philosophies on Satanism.

Jimmy Page, once lead guitarist for rock group Led Zeppelin, reportedly revered Crowley and purchased his Scottish Boleskine House. Page professes to hear chains dragging and feet stepping on the stairs of the home. Heavy metal king Ozzy Osbourne wrote a song of veneration to the occultist called, "Mr. Crowley." Daryl Hall of the pop duo Hall and Oates also admired Crowley at one time, and Crowley's photograph was included on the Beatles' *Sgt. Pepper* album.

Aleister Crowley's life was consumed by the occult. Born in England in 1875, Crowley rebelled against his strict, fundamentalist Christian upbringing. In the 1920s and 1930s, Crowley accomplished with Satanism in England what Anton LaVey did for worship of the Devil in America in the 1960s. Crowley's reputation as a bisexual with voracious sexual proclivities earned him a sinister worldwide reputation as "the wickedest man in the world."

As a young man of 28, Aleister Crowley visited Cairo, Egypt. There a spirit appeared to him, which he referred to as his holy guardian angel—Aiwass (also spelled Aiwaz). The entity commanded Crowley to record a message for all mankind. Aiwass hailed himself as a representative of a Great White Brotherhood, ascended spiritual entities who ruled the earth. Aiwass informed Crowley a new eon would center on occultism and last 2,000 years. Its philosophy would be summed up in the simple dictum, "Do what thou wilt shall be the whole of the law."

Crowley's philosophy was set forth in a volume called *The Book of the Law.* It taught that history could be divided into two eras: the eon of Isis, the domination of matriarchy in Egyptian mythology; and the eon of Osiris, the period of Judaism, Buddhism, Islam, and Christianity, when man dominated. In 1904, however, humanity supposedly entered the eon of Horus, the Egyptian child-god. During this time, the true self of man would predominate. There would be no allegiance to external authorities, priests, or gods.

Crowley built on the concept of man's true will dominating his actions and issued a creed declaring, "Lust. Enjoy all the things of sense. Fear not that any god shall deny thee for this." Aleister Crowley believed sex had magical properties and practiced homosexuality, bisexuality, and child molestation. Borrowing from the Hindu idea of tantric yoga, he taught that sexual union reached its highest realm when the mind, the breath, and the semen were held still.

Aleister Crowley founded the Britain magical association known as A∴A∴—Argenteum Astrum, the Silver Star. The organization constituted the Inner Order of the Great White Brotherhood. The Outer Order was the Golden Dawn. For a time, Crowley coexisted with converts at the Abbey of Thelema (meaning "will") in Italy. Satanism was practiced, and sacrifices were offered to the Devil by the devotees of Thelema. When the Italian government discovered evidence of black rituals and suspected infant sacrifices taking place at the abbey, Crowley was expelled from Italy. During the outbreak of World War I, Crowley shifted his activities to America.

An intellectual exponent of Satanism, Crowley wrote several books, including *Confessions,* as well as his major work on the occult, *Magick in Theory and Practice.* His pornographic novel *White Stains* was published in 1898. An equally illicit book was Crowley's *Snow Drops from a Curate's Garden.* Crowley frequently propositioned prostitutes as partners to practice his black magic. Eventually he acquired the name Baphomet, a Luciferian designation.

Aleister Crowley believed his mission in life was to destroy Christianity and build the magical religion of Thelema in its place. He failed to achieve that goal. Crowley became a heroin addict, and his son mysteriously died during a private ritual that only the two attended. Afterward, Crowley became a babbling, incoherent idiot. A black mass was performed at his funeral. Despite such an ignominious end, thousands in England and America today still follow his teachings of ignoring the conscience and adhering to one's will.

The Order of Thelema was founded as a Crowleyism study group. It rejects attempts by various branches of the Ordo Templi Orientis (O.T.O.), which claims direct lineage dating to Aleister Crowley, to establish their authority by reference to a line of succession from Crowley. The Order believes Aleister Crowley can reach them by psychic means. Such groups are profoundly devil-inspired and without conscience. No true Christian would follow Aleister Crowley's philosophy that uninhibited lust and total licentiousness lead to spiritual truth.

Founder: Aleister Crowley (1875-1947), poet, novelist, and writer of books on magic and esoteric occultism.

Symbol: A∴A∴

Text: Books of Aleister Crowley, including *Confessions, Magick in Theory and Practice, White Stains, Snow Drops from a Curate's Garden.*

Appeal: Crowley's philosophy encourages uninhibited moral abandon without a god to judge one's actions. Intelligent students of the occult who seek an evil rationale for total lustful indulgence discover justification in Crowley's teachings that one can conjure evil entities, devoid of accountability to an avenging God.

Purpose: Since most Satanists are denigrated by mainstream society as evil magicians, Aleister Crowley's ideas facilitate acceptance of demonic supernaturalism through intellectual justification. Though most Crowleyites do not participate in torture, murder, child molestation, or criminal acts, those who adopt Crowley's motto have an excuse for private deviancy and overt support of Satanism.

Errors: 1 Timothy 4:1 declares in *The Living Bible,* "The Holy Spirit tells us clearly that in the last times some in the church will turn away from Christ and become eager followers of teachers with devil-inspired ideas. These teachers will tell lies with straight faces and do it so often that their consciences won't even bother them." As Paul warned Timothy, Crowley rejected his family's stern Plymouth Brethren Christian doctrine upbringing. Likewise, most of his followers preach that Christian doctrine infringes upon their moral license. Crowleyism allows retributive actions and fulfillment of unrestrained lust.

Background Sources: *Passport Magazine,* March 1988, 4; Richard Cavendish, ed., *Man, Myth, & Magic: The Illustrated Encyclopedia of Mythology, Religion, and the Unknown* (Freeport, N.Y.: Marshall Cavendish, 1983); *The Book of the Law* (Kings Beach, Calif.: Thelema Publications, n.d.).

Address/Location: Thelema Publications, P. O. Box 1393, Kings Beach, CA 95719.

See also Black Magic.

DA FREE JOHN

What kind of God would sit by the bedside of a sick person and mockingly tease him about his illness? Or accept a $250,000 gift from a disciple and then forbid him to live in the spiritual resort purchased with the money? Hindus have a term to describe such contradictory conduct on behalf of a god-man: *lilas,* the humorous, irrational disregard of convention.

Franklin Jones (his real name) is not exactly modest about his person and purpose. He claims to be nothing less than an incarnation of God, a guru to be worshiped. "Surrender to me all your seeking, the very sense of your separate self, all thoughts, all desires, every circumstance, even your body." Those who do are promised "freedom" and the joy of constant laughter. All this supposedly comes from being in the presence of one (Da) who is "perfect love," a siddha guru "descended directly from God." In "The Great Confession," followers of Da Free John recite, "Da is the living truth. Da is the way of salvation. . . . I surrender body and mind and all self-attention to Da, the living God."

Jones started out life rather normally as a college student at Columbia and Stanford. He experimented with LSD and studied at a Lutheran seminary. In the late sixties he made several pilgrimages to India, where the Hindu Swami Muktananda influenced him so strongly that he experienced visions of the teacher. He also saw apparitions of the Virgin Mary, whom he considered to be Mother Shakti, the Hindu goddess. By 1970 he felt he had attained enlightenment and hence formed the Dawn

Horse Fellowship, later called the Free Primitive Church of Divine Communion. Other organizational entities under his leadership include the Free Community Order and the Laughing Man Institute. In 1983 the sect, currently known as the Johannine Daist Communion, purchased Naitaumba, one of the Fiji Islands in the South Pacific. On this tiny, isolated island Da's devotees built a retreat center called The Hermitage, where the guru has surrounded himself with certain followers. Others, if they are considered worthy, can come for short-term meditation retreats. Former top-ranking members have alleged that many in the guru's inner circle are using tithes and donations from rich benefactors to live in sensual luxury on Naitaumba and at another center in Hawaii. But devoted followers vigorously defend their leader.

Da's claim of divinity isn't unique in today's marketplace of mystical gurus and cult leaders. But he is the only American-born domestic product available. Thus, when he claims to fulfill the traditions of Moses, Krishna, Jesus, and Buddha, he does so as one who (according to him) only assumed the identity of Franklin Jones to provide a lesson for his disciples. The late Zen authority and Eastern religious gadfly, author Alan Watts, studied Da on videotape. Watts wept and declared, "It looks like we have an *avatar* here. I've been waiting for such a one all my life."

The teachings of Da Free John are dispensed by videotape, film, cassettes, pamphlets, and his four published works: *The Knee of Listening, The Method of the Siddhas, Garbage and the Goddess,* and *No Remedy.* His doctrine is simple: Objective truth and reality do not exist. Life is an unexplainable mystery. One's only choice is to be subjectively absorbed by the impersonal Divine. This is done by sacrificing ego and consciousness and abiding in the presence of a guru. All negative *karma* will thus be dissolved spontaneously. To embark on such a journey and join one of Da's communities, the seeker has to hold down a steady job (and tithe 10 percent to Da's work), adapt to a lactovegetarian diet, confine sex to marriage, and contemplate Free John's teachings every day. These doctrines include the Seven Stages of Life, through which the guru attempts to describe man's current state and the potential toward which he is evolving. Significantly, Da Free John has acknowledged that in addition to himself, several of his disciples have achieved the Seventh Stage. The sect sees this as an indicator that all human beings, not just a few, can attain enlightenment.

Following Bubba (as he was formerly known) is not just a matter of intellectual acknowledgement. His avataristic claims are substantiated by what seem to be amazing supernatural phenomena. Disciples are privileged to see him heal and perform miracles. They credit him with causing violent thunderstorms and creating coronas around the sun. Some students claim to have experienced dynamic *kundalini* phenomena such as *kriyas* (automatic purifying movements), *mudras* (spontaneous yogic postures), visions, revelations, and states of indescribable bliss *(samadhi).* The close comparison of such experiences with similar occurrences in demonism and classical spiritualism should not comfort followers of Da Free John.

Founder: Da Free John, formerly Bubba Free John, born Franklin Jones on November 3, 1939. He changed his name to Da Free John in 1979.

Text: Hindu scriptures; also, Da Free John's *Enlightenment of the Whole Body.*

Symbols: None known.

Appeal: Da's claim to be an *atman,* a self-realized soul and avatar, is stamped "made in America." His pompous claims of enlightenment are rare for a Westerner and thus intriguing to students of Eastern mysticism. Some followers are drawn by hearing stories about his disciples experiencing a spontaneous kind of hilarity in his presence. Others are attracted by tales of devotees receiving powerful psychic experiences by the mere touch of his hand.

Purpose: By abandonment of independent thought and moral judgment, the disciple becomes absorbed by his guru (Da) and thus merges his consciousness with God (since the guru *is* God). "You do not even know what a single thing is. Then rest—abide in that ignorance," Da teaches. Presuming to know and think and be is the cause of all unhappiness. Seeking for solutions to problems is pointless. All dilemmas can be solved by one's abiding in a relationship to a God-realized guru.

Errors: Second Thessalonians 2 describes the nature of the Antichrist, which is to exalt himself above God to the point of actually claiming to be God. Da Free John certainly possesses the same motivating spirit of self-deification. He makes of himself the supreme source of truth and spiritual knowledge and claims equality with Christ as an incarnation of God.

Background Sources: Franklin Jones, *The Knee of Listening* (Los Angeles: Dawn Horse, 1972); Bubba Free John, *No Remedy* (Lower Lake, Calif.: Dawn Horse, 1976); *East West Journal,* May 1976, 60, 67; Ibid, July 1976, 20-25; "Da Free John Charged with 'Sexual Servitude,' " *The Cult Observer,* June 1985, 1-10; Don Lattin, "Free John's Island Paradise: Devotees Build Tropical Home for Their Guru's 'Spiritual Work,' " *San Francisco Examiner,* 14 April 1985, A22-23; "Da Free John Followed Muktananda, Scientology," *The Cult Observer,* June 1985, 10; David C. Lane, "The Paradox of Da Free John," in *Understanding Cults and Spiritual Movements,* vol. 1, no. 2, 50-55.

Address/Location: The Dawn Horse Press, P. O. Box 3680, Clearlake Highlands, CA 95422. The Johannine Daist Communion maintains centers in the Fiji Islands, Hawaii, and Marin County, California.

DIVINE LIGHT
MISSION

(Guru Maharaj Ji)

"God has retired and now resides in comfortable affluence amid the placid splendor of a Malibu, California, mansion." That might well be the epitaph on the tombstone of Divine Light Mission. In the early seventies, Guru Maharaj Ji commanded one of the largest and fastest-growing followings of all imported cult leaders.

At one time he confidently declared, "The key to the whole life, the key to the existence of this entire universe rests in the hands of Guru Maharaj Ji." Then it all fell apart. Reorganizational efforts failed to salvage the momentum of the days when he was worshiped as one "greater than God, because he showed men to God." But don't count him out yet. A hard core of an estimated several hundred to several thousand disciples still believes he is *the* incarnation of God, the Perfect Master for our age.

Guru Maharaj Ji owes the founding of Divine Light Mission (DLM) to his wealthy, revered father, Brahman Samaj Shri Hans Ji Maharaj, who headed the Prem Nagar *Ashram*. Shri Hans was considered to be a *Satguru* (Perfect Master) by many of his countrymen. When Maharaj Ji was born December 10, 1957, in Hardwar, India, no one paid much attention. The family already had three older sons, and one of them was presumed to be next in line as Satguru. But Maharaj Ji was remarkably precocious. By age two he was meditating and giving *satsang* ("holy discourses").

When Maharaj Ji was eight years old, his father died. The boy addressed the grieving devotees by declaring, "Why are you weeping?

200

Haven't you learned the lesson that your Master taught you? The Perfect Master never dies. Maharaj Ji is here amongst you now." As his father's disciples bowed at Maharaj Ji's feet, his mother, Rajeshwari Devi (usually known as Mata Ji), confirmed the passing of the spiritual mantle to him. He was invested with the crown of Krishna, and 13 days later, while praying to his father's cremated ashes, an inner voice spoke. The message was simple: Guru Maharaj Ji was destined to become the savior of humanity.

On November 8, 1970, Maharaj Ji led an entourage of thousands of followers through the streets of Delhi. Arriving at the India Gate, he declared, "I will establish peace in this world." Strange words, indeed, for a ninth-grade dropout from a Catholic mission school. But several million Indian disciples believed his claim, though only a handful of *premies* (devotees — literally "lovers") greeted his arrival in the West as he touched down at Los Angeles International Airport in 1971. Yet, there was something fascinating about this pudgy teenager whose tastes ran from Baskin-Robbins to horror movies.

The turning point came the following year in Montrose, Colorado. Two thousand converts were solicited from an audience of 5,000, and suddenly Maharaj Ji was on his way. By the time another year rolled around there were 480 DLM centers and 35,000 members in the United States. The organization opened up a variety of businesses and communes along with a record company, a film production house, and a printing establishment. Then came "Millennium 1973," an extravaganza held in the Houston Astrodome.

I witnessed the events of that festival that was supposed to draw a potential attendance of 144,000. Though only approximately 20,000 showed up, the worship accorded to Maharaj Ji testified to his uncanny power. Dopers-turned-devotees, fornicators-turned-celibates, hippies, and straights all united in their shouting praise: "Bholie Shri Satguru Dev Maharaj Ki Jai," a Hindi "hip, hip, hooray" to the Lord of the Universe. To my amazement, the entire audience of thousands prostrated themselves before Maharaj Ji's throne, which was elevated nearly 40 feet above the Astroturf.

Controversy soon followed glory. A reporter who threw a cream pie in Maharaj Ji's face was mercilessly beaten by the guru's disciples. Maharaj Ji was accused by Indian customs officials of trying to smuggle $80,000 worth of jewels into his native land. The Astrodome gathering rang up huge debts, and questions were raised about the guru's true age and materialistic preoccupations. Still, dedicated followers declared they would die or kill for the corpulent kid whom Rennie Davis, the ex-leftist radical, called "the power of creation itself."

The biggest upheaval occurred in 1974 when he married a former United Airlines stewardess who was eight years his senior. He pronounced her the incarnation of the ten-armed, tiger-riding goddess Durga. When the new bride refused her mother-in-law access to their $554,000 Malibu estate, that was the last straw. Mother Mata Ji denounced her son as a drinking, dancing, nightclub-haunting meat-eater. She changed the name of the U.S. organization to the Spiritual Life Society and installed Maharaj Ji's eldest brother Shri Satyapal Ji (Bal Bhagwan Ji) as the new Perfect Master. Even the birth of two grandchildren (Premlata and Hans Pal Singh) didn't mollify her anger. However, Maharaj Ji was unperturbed, wondering aloud how anyone could claim to tell God he was no longer qualified to hold office.

For a while things picked up. Income averaged over $400,000 a month, mostly due to a mandatory tithe. Maharaj Ji's passion for automobiles extended to a Jensen, Mercedes-Benz, Maserati, Lotus, and a mobile van. The *Divine Times,* a slick, four-color publication, reported on the guru's activities to communities in 66 countries. He continued holding large festivals and *lilas* (god-games where audiences of disciples were doused with water and red paint from huge pressurized nozzles). But as Goomerajee (as he is affectionately known by close associates) grew more obese, his following conversely diminished.

Plans for his divine city were shelved. Almost 100 DLM-owned vehicles were sold. All but one of 34 food cooperatives were shut down. The staff of 250 at the Denver international headquarters was reduced to a mere 40. Maharaj Ji's scores of hand-picked evangelists, called *mahatmas,* were reduced to 20 and renamed "initiators." Income plunged to less than $100,000 per month. Estimates of followers worldwide remained slightly above a million, but in the U.S. that total went from a heyday high of 50,000 to about 10,000. Some critics suggested the figure might be closer to 3,000. Worst of all, his former head, Bob Meshler, left the DLM amid a series of accusations.

But before any final obituaries on Guru Maharaj Ji are pronounced, it would be wise to ponder the teachings and practices that precipitated his sudden rise to power. In the seeds of his fame may be the genesis of other cult leaders having an Eastern inclination. Understanding what the DLM taught and represented may give a clue forewarning society of other personality cult figures.

Followers of Maharaj Ji are encouraged to live by his Five Commandments: (1) Do not put off until tomorrow what you can do today; (2) Constantly meditate and remember the Holy Name; (3) Leave no room for doubt in your mind; (4) Never delay attending *satsang* (one of Maharaj Ji's discourses of rambling stories and illustrations); (5) Always have faith in God (which is translated as complete devotion to Maharaj Ji).

The theology of DLM may be summed up by understanding its view of God, guru, mind, and Knowledge. God is a form of energy, a cosmic vibration. As such, "the Word" extends itself to everything, making even man's soul part of God. I once heard Guru Maharaj Ji exclaim in a speech that he did not desire a relationship with God. To do so would imply that deity is separate from man, undercutting the doctrine of oneness that is central to Hinduism. Hence DLM has as its ultimate goal the merging of man's soul with the Infinite Absolute—the soul's energy being reabsorbed into the universal energy of God.

Guru Maharaj Ji's variant of Hinduism emphasizes the *Siddha Yoga* school of thought. In this tradition, God-realization can only be accomplished with the aid of a guru who leads one forward on the path of enlightenment. All the better if this guru is a Perfect Master greater than God himself. The Perfect Master is sinless, since his subjective consciousness is the only standard by which he is judged (God is inside him). No external principles of absolute values guide him because he responds spontaneously to his own divinity. This living Master deserves and has the right to demand total submission from his followers. In Maharaj Ji's case, such subservience is reinforced by his ubiquitous visage, adorning every trinket and magazine produced by DLM.

But there is an impediment to following the Perfect Master on the path toward knowledge of God—the mind. Guru Maharaj Ji insists that the rationalistic West has given too much prominence to reasoning faculties. The mind, in his estimation, is delusive, unreliable, and imperfect. It is the spirit that contains the capacity for love and peace. Therefore the Knowledge of God is unattainable by objective information. It can only be received by experience. Maharaj Ji describes the mind as a snake to be killed so the direct revelation of divine Knowledge can be transmitted. "Give it [your mind] to me," he implores. "I am ready to receive it. Because your mind troubles you, give it to me."

The devotee who surrenders his mental capacities is ready to receive the guru's Knowledge. It is this experience that transforms the lives of his disciples and makes them into robots to do his bidding. When pressed to explain this phenomenon, *premies* give glowing testimonials of its benefits but never divulge its process. Only diligent research has uncovered the fourfold procedure that consists of a blinding light (seeing with the so-called third eye), hearing celestial music (supposedly referred to in Rev. 22), tasting a sweet substance called nectar (which presumably has curative powers), and sensing a primordial vibration (representing the internalized Word of God).

A devotee is considered ready to receive Knowledge once his unfettered submission to Maharaj Ji has been proven. This may be evidenced by signing away one's possessions to DLM or listening to extended hours of *satsang*. At the appointed time, the candidate enters a darkened room. He may sit there, draped in a sheet, for several hours. All the while, a *mahatma* lectures him on the importance of the knowledge he is about to receive.

Finally the initiator places his thumb and middle finger on the devotee's temples and presses inward with the index finger at a spot near the center of the forehead (claimed to be the location of the spiritual "third eye," the pineal gland). The optic nerve is pinched, and a neurological light results from pressure upon the retina. *Premies* learn how to duplicate this experience at will by merely closing their eyelids and letting their eyeballs roll back in their sockets.

Divine music is heard with the "third ear." The *mahatma* places his fingers in the initiate's ears long enough for the recipient to be conscious of the sounds of his own internal organs and systems. One *premie* described the sound as "loud rock and roll," while another insisted she was hearing the same vibrations she experienced in her mother's womb.

Tasting divine nectar isn't easy. The substance is said to be a fluid flowing from the brain, the very elixir that sustained Christ 40 days in the wilderness. With the devotee's mouth open, the *mahatma* places his fingers in the *premie's* throat and forces his tongue backward until it rests against the uvula. The resulting mucus of postnasal drip is interpreted as being "sweeter than honey."

Finally, John 1:14 is quoted to justify the theory that God's Word is in man's flesh. The candidate is told that a repetitive pattern of rhythmic breathing actually constitutes a mantra. In reality, this experience of the "primordial vibration of the divine word" is a hyperventilative technique that leaves the *premie* in an altered state of consciousness much like a drug-induced high. This concluding experience conveys a sense of omnipotence producing a feeling of oneness with the universe. Followers of the Guru refer to this ultimate high as being "blissed out."

The dynamics of the four states of Guru Maharaj Ji's Knowledge can be explained on a naturalistic basis. After the *mahatma* has predefined each experience, the candidate can easily be manipulated by autosuggestive hypnosis. At each stage, he is prone to interpret the phenomenon according to the expectations his spiritual leader has previously explained. Undoubtedly the passively receptive state of the willing devotee also allows demonic forces to enhance the dimensions of each aspect of the guru's ritual of receiving Knowledge.

Now that the image of the organization has been revamped, the Perfect Master transmits knowledge in more subtle ways. In 1984 Guru Maharaj Ji retired in Malibu and Miami with his wife and their four children. He made amends with his mother and maintains, "Now I am my own headquarters." Although Guru Maharaj Ji no longer leads an official group of followers, critics estimate that more than a million people worldwide continue to exalt him. Devotees have ceased the Indian custom of *darshan,* literally kissing Maharaj Ji's feet, but they continue to walk in his footsteps.

Founder: Balyogeshwar Param Hans Satgurudev Shri Sant Ji Maharaj (Guru Maharaj Ji), born December 10, 1957, Hardwar, India.

Text: Hindu scriptures.

Symbol: Pictures of Maharaj Ji seated on a throne wearing the Crown of Krishna.

Appeal: During the early seventies, the rebellion of youth against established institutions made them susceptible to a strong disciplinary structure. The age of Maharaj Ji was an ironic contrast appealing to their loss of adult authority. Today's disciples tend to be older and better educated, responding to the DLM's current goals of peace through meditation and selfless service.

Purpose: The only pathway to God is by submission to an *avatar,* a fully God-realized guru. This Perfect Master helps one to remove the resistance of the logical mind that is the only block between man and his divine inner soul. Maharaj Ji's Knowledge is equated with the Holy Spirit, an experience that conveys a heightened sense of well-being and union with the Infinite.

Errors: All the requirements of the DLM are based on pleasing God by the works of submission and service, a contradiction of Ephesians

2:8-9. Since the experience of Knowledge communicates a euphoric feeling, it is wrongly assumed to substantiate the teachings of Maharaj Ji. Proverbs 1:7 states that true knowledge is "the fear of the Lord," not a hypnotic series of psycho-neurological manipulations. Clearly, according to 1 John 2:18-23, Maharaj Ji fulfills the role of an antichrist as prophesied in Matthew 24.

Background Sources: *Who Is Guru Maharaj Ji?* (New York: Bantam, 1978); various issues of DLM publication *Divine Times*; miscellaneous DLM pamphlets and materials published for release to the press; Bob Larson, *The Guru* (Denver: Bob Larson Ministries, 1974); Kenneth Boa, *Cults, World Religions and You* (Wheaton, Ill.: Victor, 1980); *Empire Magazine,* 28 April 1974, 52-61; *The Denver Post,* 2 April 1976; Ibid., 13 August 1976; Ibid., 18 February 1977, 3BB; Ibid., 15 December 1978, 3BB; *Time,* 28 April 1975, 75; Ibid., 13 March 1978, 39; *People,* 15 March 1984, 170.

Address/Location: No current information officially available.

ECKANKAR

Of all the new religions to enter the spiritual marketplace in this century, few are more confusing than ECKANKAR. The individual who picks up one of their promotional pamphlets in the local grocery store may be intrigued by this so-called "ancient science of soul-travel." Followers of ECKANKAR are often intelligent, well-meaning people who constitute an estimated membership of 50,000. (ECKANKAR's leaders claim 3 million followers worldwide.)

Paul Twitchell, a journalist and frequent dabbler in occult and mystical practices (including having served as a staff member in the Church of Scientology), formed the first public ECKANKAR group in 1965. His theology, a restatement of Hinduistic precepts, teaches that ECKANKAR ("co-worker with God") came into being as a result of his contact with two ECK masters, Sudar Singh in India and Rebazar Tarzs in the Himalayas. No documented proof has been presented that Twitchell ever visited either place or that either man actually existed. The terminology of ECKANKAR is said to come from the Amdo dialect of the Tibetan language. Twitchell offered no explanation for claiming such expansive knowledge regarding this tongue, which is unverified by linguists. (One cult expert claims that ECKANKAR is a semantic perversion of "Ek Onkar," the name of the supreme deity in *Shabda Yoga*.)

Sudar Singh and Rebazar Tarzs designated Paul Twitchell to be the 971st Living ECK Master, a *mahanta* (living manifestation of God). Twitchell said such a person is "above the laws of man . . . omnipotent and omniscient." The ECK Master's purpose in life is to lead the souls of men to "that realm of spirit which is known as the Kingdom of Heaven where God (known as SUGMAD) dwells." Life flows from SUGMAD in the form of a cosmic sound and light current called ECK. (ECK is also often used as an abbreviation for ECKANKAR.) Twitchell taught a variety of occult exercises by which the ECK student could tune into this ethereal sound of God. Foremost among these phenomena is an out-of-body experience Twitchell originally called "bilocation" and later changed to "soul-travel," which he declared is "the secret path to God." (Occultists generally refer to this phenomenon as "astral projection.") Twitchell claimed that Jesus, Buddha, and Paul indulged in the practice of soul travel.

The *Shariyat-Ki-Sugmad* are sacred ECKANKAR scriptures, which Twitchell declared to be located in a monastery in the Tibetan mountains. *Anami Lok* is the name given to the true heaven where SUGMAD dwells. *Atma Sarup* is the soul body, which travels astrally from the *Nuri Sarup,* the physical ("light") body. Such language (along with hundreds of other ECKANKAR-invented words) would be of little interest to the average person were it not for Twitchell's contention that by soul-travel one can achieve "omniscience . . . through the release of the soul from the bondage of flesh." In fact, ECKANKAR claims to provide a "key to heaven." Even the inventions of Alexander Graham Bell and the Wright brothers are said to be the results of astral journeys they made to a great museum in the capital of the spirit world, *Sahasra-dal-Kanwal.*

The outward image of ECKANKAR is friendly and tolerant. An advertisement circulated in major newspapers stated that ECKANKAR "does not condemn any person or teaching. If a person is involved in any world religion, he is encouraged to stay there." However, other statements found in ECKANKAR literature do not necessarily support this declaration. Also according to this literature, ECKANKAR is not a cult since it promotes individuality and does not sponsor communal living.

In his book, *ECKANKAR—The Key to Secret Worlds,* Twitchell described God as being "unconcerned about any living thing in this universe. He is detached and unconcerned about man." Christ taught that love is the greatest commandment, but Twitchell asserted that Rebazar Tarzs has instructed man to "love only those whom you must!" *Kal* (an ECK word denoting the devil) is identified in Twitchell's theology as the Father of the Christian faith, and Jesus is "a son of Kal, King of the lower worlds." The inclusive, conciliatory language used in ECKANKAR ads is contrasted by its published claims to be "the path of Total Awareness," "the everlasting gospel," and the one true source of religions, "the most ancient religious philosophy known to man." In Twitchell's booklet, "ECK and Music," he stated, "The ECK, therefore, is the Way. . . . Without this heavenly music, or the WORD, no one can reach God again." Other religions may not be openly condemned, but the teachings of ECKANKAR certainly relegate them to an inferior position.

To replace the Christian doctrines of sin and redemption, Twitchell proposed a Hinduistic concept of *karma* and reincarnation. Those who wish to avoid the countless cycles of rebirth must learn to ascend through a series of eleven astral planes by OBE's (out-of-body experiences). Success on this journey depends on the guidance of a Living ECK Master, who is assisted by other spirit guides. This Master will facilitate astral travel by helping the student discard the karmic debt he has accumulated in past lives.

The ECK Master is no mere way-shower. He is believed to be God-in-the-flesh, an incarnation of SUGMAD. The Master teaches the student that by sensory deprivation, altered states of consciousness, mantra-chanting, trancing, and contact with spirit guides he can advance to higher planes of enlightenment. Twitchell claimed to have witnessed frequent appearances of entities who asserted they were "translated" (ECKANKAR for *dead)* Masters. Students are encouraged to think upon the current living Master until he, too, manifests himself to them as a glowing light-entity.

On September 17, 1971, in a hotel room in Cincinnati, Ohio, Paul Twitchell suddenly died of a heart attack. Living ECK Master number 972 was Sri (an honorific Hindi title) Darwin Gross. Gross claimed to be God's guru for our age, "the most splendid specimen of manhood, the noblest of the noble," "the most gifted spiritual leader alive today," and "a healer who has rescued many from physical ills and mental anguish." As the Divine One, he received Twitchell's Rod of Power, an event said to have taken place in the spirit world since Twitchell died too suddenly for an orderly transfer of leadership. Gross continued "the longest unbroken line of spiritual teachers on this planet."

The teachings of ECKANKAR according to Gross continue Twitchell's tradition. Of love he says, "Many are teaching the masses to love everyone, to love their neighbors, and that's fine, if it's with a detached love. You have to be very careful who you give love to." Morality is described as "an individual thing established by our own inner authority." He supports abortion by declaring that the soul does not enter the body until "after the child has been brought into the outer world, and sometimes later than that." According to Gross, animals have a soul and their own heaven; Christianity adopted the idea of the Virgin Birth from Hinduism; and the current spiritual awakening is "not due to evangelists like Billy Graham. It is due to ECK Masters."

In 1971, Harold Klemp assumed the position of 973rd Living ECK Master. (Darwin Gross continued as a *mahanta;* previously these titles had referred to one person only.) Sri Harold Klemp tells of traveling in his "soul body" to the planet Venus to visit the Moksha Temple of Golden Wisdom.

Evangelical Christians are troubled by the spiritistic overtones of ECK-ANKAR. Others are skeptical about its deified, authoritarian leadership. In "ECK and Music," Twitchell addressed such apprehensions by saying, "If the individual is under the Living ECK Master, then he has no worry, for the Master is taking care of him." ("I am with you always," Twitchell's Master Rebazar Tarzs once told him, an adaptation of Christ's promise in Matthew 28:20.) If ECK advocates believe that Twitchell's Master appeared to him, the stage has been set for Master number 971 (Twitchell) to appear to his followers. A masquerading familiar spirit could easily assume the role of Twitchell (necromancy) to guide students of ECK onward to SUGMAD.

Founder: John Paul Twitchell, born sometime between 1908 and 1912 in Paducah, Kentucky. (Twitchell's biography claims a birthdate of 1922.)

Symbols: A funnel-shaped series of ascending ovals representing the eleven astral planes or "God Worlds of ECK"; a series of five stick-shaped human figures ascending horizontally (the fifth figure encircled), representing spiritual progress on the path of ECKANKAR.

Appeal: ECKANKAR offers dramatic psychic, out-of-the-body experiences and purports to give the student direct access to departed Spiritual Masters, who appear as light-being entities. These astral projection abilities supposedly offer the opportunity to predict one's future, acquire healing, and eventually obtain omniscience. One practitioner claimed he would leave his body while driving to work so he could check traffic flows and avoid any bottled-up intersections that might be ahead.

Purpose: "Soul travel is the means we use as the vehicle of return to our true home." The stated purpose in ECK literature is to preserve the individual through all eternity. Once the techniques of soul travel have been mastered, seekers can travel in different realms, eventually reaching a level of awareness that makes "them co-workers with God."

Errors: Every cardinal Christian doctrine is denied, including original sin, intercessory prayer (called "an occult form of black magic"), the virgin birth, Christ as Creator and sole incarnation of the Father, and the absolute goodness of God (Satan, Kal, is a partial manifestation of God's character). Participants of astral travel may make themselves vulnerable to demon possession.

Background Sources: Paul Twitchell, *ECKANKAR: The Key to Secret Worlds* (New Hope, Minn.: Illuminated Way, 1969), 42; Paul Twitchell, *ECKANKAR: Ancient Science of Soul Travel* (pamphlet); Paul Twitchell, *ECK and Music* (pamphlet) 1971; *Spiritual Counterfeits Journal,* September 1979, vol. 3, no. 1; "Open Letter to All Christians," advertisement placed in various newspapers and paid for by ECKANKAR; Sri Darwin Gross, *Your Right to Know* (Menlo Park, Calif.: Illuminated Way, 1979); "Mutation in Eckankar," *Forward* (Christian Research Institute), vol. 5, no. 1, 1982, 13; Carey Quan Gelernter, "Soul Travelers: Teachings 6 Million Years Old," *The Seattle Times,* 27 January 1983, E2; "ECKANKAR: A Universal Path" (brochure), February 1983, n.p.

Address/Location: Box 3100, Menlo Park, CA 94024; 750 Hawthorne N.E., South Salem, OR.

ESALEN
INSTITUTE

Every summer at least 1,500 people pass through the gates of Esalen Institute to wander through its groves and give vent to whatever suppressed feelings haunt their psyches. Founded in 1962 by Michael Murphy and Richard Price, Esalen Institute is one of the granddaddies of the so-called human potential movement. At its isolated location on Big Sur coastal shores some of the early experiments with encounter groups and sensitivity training first surfaced.

Though Esalen's goals purport to emphasize psychological self-help, the religious overtones are apparent to students of mystical thought. Murphy founded Esalen (its name comes from the local Indian tribe) after studying at an *ashram* in India. His stated goal was to evoke Eastern-style spirituality by allowing participants to vent their true emotions in "the here and now . . . not to adjust, but to transcend." In the process, those who attend Esalen sessions may find themselves seated, facing a naked stranger, and sensuously stroking his or her body. This practice, known as "bodywork," is designed to stimulate self-awareness in attendees, who are also encouraged to pretend they are animals in distress or to simulate the sounds of lovemaking. Sometimes those who attend Esalen sessions are made to stare at white squares until they see visions. Guided imagery and visualization exercises, gestalt therapy, and sensory awakening are a few of the seminars offered. The hot baths, which initiated members may attend in the nude, are considered a rite of passage into a new life. (These are not so popular now, in the age of AIDS.)

A former president of the American Psychological Association has been quoted as saying that Esalen is potentially "the most important educational institute in the world."

In 1983 the Esalen Institute sponsored a Soviet-American satellite link-up with cooperation from the Soviet government and Academy of Sciences. In an attempt to develop relationships that will survive stressful political times, like-minded people in both countries shared — and still do — their common interests in meeting human needs through the development of paranormal perception, stress management, and healing.

Esalen celebrated its twenty-fifth anniversary in 1987. In a special catalog, several innovative thinkers who in some way shaped its major principles were named, among them Aldous Huxley, Alan Watts, Arnold Toynbee, Fritz Perls, B. F. Skinner, and Episcopal Bishop James Pike. While not all of these people agreed, the catalog stated, their "complementary perspective . . . inform Esalen's thinking and purposes today . . . and push us toward further discoveries."

Background Sources: Connie Zweig, "Esalen's Soviet-American Exchange Program," *New Realities,* n.d., 6; David Landau, "Citizen Diplomacy," *New Age Journal,* January 1984, 35-38; *The Esalen Catalog — 25th Anniversary: The Early Years* (Big Sur, Calif.: Esalen Institute, 1987); George Leonard, "First Visit to Esalen: February 1965," 6-9; Richard Leviton, "Job's Body," *East West,* January 1988, 61; John Garabedian and Orde Coombs, *Eastern Religions in the Electric Age* (New York: Workman, 1969).

See also Human Potential Movement.

E S T

"Obviously, the truth is what's so. Not so obviously, it's also so what."
If that sounds like a conundrum, don't be fooled by the apparently harmless confusion of the statement. Behind these words of Werner Erhard
lies a system of religious philosophy rooted in Mind Dynamics, yoga,
Silva Mind Control, gestalt psychology, Dale Carnegie, Subud, and most
importantly, Zen Buddhism and Scientology. Those who indulge in
Erhard's est training are told they are "perfect . . . gods who have created
their own world." This teaching led Erhard to conclude, "How do I know
I'm not the reincarnation of Jesus Christ?"

Born Jack Rosenberg in 1935, Erhard left a wife and four kids in his
early twenties. While traveling on a plane, he met a woman named Ellen
who would become his second wife. (Ellen filed for divorce in 1984, citing Erhard's persistent adultery as the grounds.) He happened to be reading an article entitled "The Men Who Made the New Germany." His long
enchantment with the German nihilistic philosopher Nietzsche (who believed in a super-race, the foundation of Hitler's political approach) compelled Erhard to choose a new identity with a German name. Werner
came from Werner Heisenberg (not Werner von Braun, as est literature
claims) and Erhard from Ludwig Erhard.

In the company of friend Bill Thaw, he explored an interest in a succession of Eastern religions and mind-science cults. Finally (according
to Thaw), Erhard read a book entitled *est: The Steersman Handbook.*

214

The author, L. Clark Stevens, used the abbreviation *est* to denote "electronic social transformation." Erhard borrowed the term and redubbed it Erhard Seminars Training—est (always lower case) for short. While driving his wife's Mustang one day, he experienced a Damascus-road-type enlightenment. Erhard says he "got it," and est became the vehicle for propagating "it."

In the Zen Buddhist tradition of subjective, relative, intuitive enlightenment, no one in est (including Erhard) really knows what "it" is. But the goal of getting "it" is to conclude that there is nothing to get. In est, there is no objective reality, only experience. Being is said to be more important than doing. Logical thinking is forbidden, and terminology is twisted. "Wrong is actually a version of right. If you're always wrong, you're right," est declares. Singer-composer John Denver, an est advocate, extols Erhard's view of life in his song "Looking for Space." ("If there's an answer, it's just that it's just that way.") "Seek and ye shall find," Jesus said. In contrast, Erhard declares, "What isn't, isn't. You can't put it together . . . what you have to do is experience it being together."

Such doublespeak and intellectual dishonesty has been more than a clever way to dispose of the definitions used in normal language. It has also been an elaborate fund-raising vehicle ($16 million per year) and a public extension of Erhard's ego-oriented goal to remake the world. It was all begun when interested parties plunked down $250 to join 249 other people for two weekends of group-therapy encounter sessions, totaling 60 hours. Inductees were initially greeted with smiles and hugs. But all that changed quickly once the hotel room doors were closed to begin the first 15- to 18-hour period. Pen, paper, watches, tape recorders, and cigarettes had to be left outside. Participants needed to be certain they had not eaten or drunk too much before entering, since they were only allowed one bathroom break from start till finish (unless they had a doctor's signed statement indicating physical necessity). Later, numerous trips to the restroom were permitted.

An est seminar was a calculated process of breaking down the inductee's personality and then rebuilding it by harassment and intimidation. A trainer began immediately to abuse the audience verbally with repeated obscenities. All ego defenses were ridiculed by means of demeaning epithets hurled at anyone who resisted the tactics of the trainer. Eyewitnesses reported that scores of people urinated, defecated, convulsed, sobbed, screamed, and vomited (in specially provided silver-colored est bags). The only relief came in the form of "meditation practices" (to acquire an altered state of consciousness) and exercises of lying on the floor to "find one's space." The latter practice had its relaxing effect quickly ended by the trainer, who proceeded to create feelings of fear and danger, causing some to respond hysterically.

After three days of such psycho-manipulative and hemorrhoid-causing activity, participants were expected to "get it" on the fourth day. What they got was not an improved self-image but a totally transformed perception of reality consistent with a Buddhist/occult view of the universe. "You are part of every atom in the world, and every atom is part of you," estians were encouraged to affirm. This all-is-one, merging-of-consciousness doctrine of Eastern thought is what led most est graduates to reject all other belief systems. After all, to know est is to know *you* are God.

The elementary student of psychology can easily recognize est's potential for creating psychosis. By the confrontational stripping away of coping mechanisms, some emotionally unstable individuals can be left in a dangerous, vulnerable condition. Even more serious to consider is the possibility that evil powers may take advantage of such a psychologically defenseless state to precipitate a demonic invasion. At the very least, the destruction of one's concept of self-worth may result in the violent release of suppressed traumas. Without an understanding of God's love, healing, and forgiveness to fill this void, the est participant can only deal with such feeling by retreating from reality and adopting a mystical view of life as an illusion.

In est, Christ's commands to "love your enemies" (Luke 10:27) are replaced with a self-centered approach to life. Since there is no God but one's own ego, moral conduct is judged according to self-serving satisfaction. The cult est doesn't tell you what not to do. It is understood that those who experience their "space" are practicing perfection, no matter what their moral beliefs may be. What an estian graduate decides is good for himself is good. With no gods to worship, some est graduates adulate Erhard to a point of near perfection. His word is *the* word. What they do with guilt is another matter. No reinterpretation of reality can completely assuage one's conscience. That takes much more than four days locked in a hotel room, for it requires the shed blood of Jesus Christ (Heb. 9:22).

By 1985 Erhard had shelved est in favor of his new baby, The Forum. (See this book's separate section on The Forum.) According to *Newsweek,* "Est was about 'getting it together,'" The Forum is about 'making it happen.' " An outgrowth of some of Erhard's satellite TV broadcasts, The Forum foregoes the abusive language of the intense est sessions and emphasizes "dialogue" between leader and participants. The Forum seminars, stretched over two weekends and one evening, involve dialogue on virtually any subject. While the appeal of Forum seminars is to upwardly mobile yuppies (or those who would like to be), the latent mysticism of est still permeates the seminars. Forum spokesmen say that the key element in the seminars is "being," which, they claim, is critical to motivating oneself and one's employees. No one gives a clear definition of what "being" is, and one spokesman happily admits that it is unexplainable, even though "being" is the "magic" of Forum.

This combination of business drive with vague mysticism is not unusual in cults today. Neither is the insistence of Erhard—and dozens of other propagators of cults—that one's logical capacities must be laid aside. In our age, when rock videos set the standard for people's logical thinking abilities, no wonder cults that teach "trust your feelings, not your mind" are popular. We must remember as Christians that, though logic has limits, we are called as children of God to love God with our minds.

Founder: Jack Rosenberg, born September 5, 1935, in Philadelphia. Renamed Werner Erhard. The cult was officially launched in 1971. In 1985 Erhard announced the burial of est and the birth of The Forum.

Text: "What is, is."–Werner Erhard

Symbol: None.

Appeal: Those with a poor self-image learn to assert themselves by ignoring reality. For some it is another "trip" to experience along with involvement in other consciousness-raising groups. People whose lives are meaningless or who have experienced rejection and depression may view est as a quick, cheap form of psychotherapy. The appeal of The Forum is to those who are—or would like to be—upwardly mobile. Like other cults, The Forum appeals to those who seek a vague and undemanding spirituality that combines with their own materialistic interests.

Purpose: Compels people to get "it," though no one, including Erhard, can define what "it" is. The est manual reads: "The purpose of est training is to transform your ability to experience living so that the situations you have been trying to change . . . just clear up in the process of life itself." Life is not to be understood (understanding is irrelevant), but rather experienced.

Errors: Love, concern, compassion, sorrow, and other Christian and human values are considered illusions. For example, the Hunger Project started by est proposes to eliminate world famine by 1997. This laudable goal is not to be achieved by feeding the hungry, but by simply declaring that "the end of hunger is an idea whose time has come." Man is his own god, the center of the universe. Sin does not exist, and all personal conduct is justified by one's own perfection. As in Zen, reality is a matter of perception, not objectivity.

Background Sources: *Newsweek*, 28 August 1978, 50; Ibid., 9 May 1977, 95; Ibid., 15 June 1981, 18-21; *Time*, 7 June 1976, 53; *Circus*, February 1976, 45; *Spiritual Counterfeits Project Newsletter*, March 1976, vol. 2, no. 3; Walter Martin, *The New Cults* (Santa Ana, Calif.: Vision House, 1980), 105-141; "The Fuhrer over est," *New Times*, 36-52 (issue date unknown); *Eternity*, March 1986, 55; *Newsweek*, 1 April 1985, 15.

Address/Location: With a shift of emphasis on The Forum, est centers are no longer operational.

See also The Forum.

THE
FARM

Some folks in the surrounding area view this rural Tennessee commune with alarm. Others begrudgingly bestow kudos for its self-sufficiency and apparent industriousness. Few really understand the historical facts concerning The Farm, or comprehend the teachings and practices of its leader, Stephen Gaskin. Once supporting up to 1,500 members, The Farm includes a school, health clinic, recording studio, and computerized typesetting facilities for a publishing company. The Farm proudly promotes its New York Bronx voluntary ambulance crew and also its relief organization, PLENTY, which dispatches certain of their members to provide aid for Third World countries. But Gaskin and his followers are far from being the respectable band of former hippies they have portrayed in order to earn tax-exempt monasterial status.

In the psychedelic sixties, Stephen Gaskin was an assistant to S. I. Hayakawa at San Francisco State College. He dropped out to drop acid and eventually became a local *guru* celebrity. Gaskin held Monday night counterculture rap sessions, attended by as many as 2,000 supporters. He expounded at length upon revelations from his drug experiences, which were enhanced through his studies in a variety of occult and Eastern practices. In the fall of 1971 he headed a ragtag caravan of 60 school buses carrying his 250 flower children. After meandering across the United States, they settled 15,000 miles later on roughly 1,700 acres of farmland near Summertown, 65 miles south of Nashville. Once, The Farm was recognized as one of the few American communities to have achieved long-term success. In the mid-1980s, however, The Farm was decollectivized. Each member is now self-supporting, although they still help each other and contribute part of their earnings to the land payments. In the early days, commune members lived a carefree life in squalid conditions and frolicked in the effects of peyote, psilocybin, mushrooms, and marijuana (all of which Gaskin proclaimed to be sacraments). The Farm was eventually raided by police, and, in spite of legal appeals all the way to the Supreme Court, Gaskin and three fellow members each spent a year in prison. Group marriages with full sexual privileges were tried (with Gaskin once again leading the way), but also proved somewhat unsuccessful. Now, nuclear families are the rule, though members are, as in the past, complete vegetarians who wear no leather (this would harm animals) and also do not eat dairy products. Visitors to The Farm — there are about 10,000 each year — must obey the no hunting, no smoking, no drinking rules in this idyllic spot that is a veritable nature preserve.

Though monogamy reigns and marijuana is no longer a Farm crop (members freely admit many of them still toke up frequently), Gaskin has not abandoned his spiritual mission. Ex-members accuse him of openly declaring to be a messenger from God. Mystical religious experiences are encouraged, along with a mixture of beliefs ranging from *tantra* (ritualistic sex), *karma,* and *mantras,* to *bodhisattvas* (incarnations of God in Buddhism), the latter fitting nicely into Gaskin's claims of spiritual leadership. His writings declare that Jesus and Buddha were each incarnations of God for their age. For this modern era, another *avatar* is required. Sin is a concept that "is no longer necessary," and the crucifixion of Christ "wasn't exactly what he wanted to teach." The Farm may not be another Jonestown, but neither is its blend of Zen and agriculture the benign enigma that some Summertown, Tennessee, residents view it to be.

Background Sources: Marty Meitus, "After The Farm," *Rocky Mountain News,* 3 August 1984, 70; *Newsweek,* 10 August 1981, 14; *San Francisco Chronicle,* 21 September 1981; *SCP Journal,* n.d.; *East-West Journal,* May 1981, 11; Stephen Gaskin, *Hey Beatnik!* (Summertown, Tenn.: The Book Publishing Co., 1974); Stephen Gaskin, *The Caravan* (New York: Random House, 1977).

F I N D H O R N
F O U N D A T I O N

They don't believe in those that replace pulled teeth with coins or that fly through the air like Tinker Bell, but members of the Findhorn Foundation have faith in fairies and elves, devas that inhabit flowers and plants. Findhorn's purpose is to achieve oneness with God in order to contribute to the emerging New Age, which will herald a culture of world peace and renewed humanity.

Founded near Findhorn, Scotland, in 1962, the Foundation gained early notoriety with its successful production of oversized vegetables and the establishment of elaborate gardens near the Arctic Circle, a horticultural triumph. The organization's founders, Dorothy MacLean and Peter and Eileen Caddy, credit this success to their communication with plant spirits. Professing other metaphysical New Age practices, such as trance channeling and the changing of man's consciousness toward the evolution of a new interplanetary world, the Foundation claims to provide its membership with an international spiritual community, where members strive to create a wholeness of all life.

Through communal living, members contend they are part of the "living laboratory" where sacred works and spiritual ideals are tested and reinforced daily. Findhorn work departments and classrooms are structured to provide the basis from which to create peaceful lives and harmonious relationships. Activities for the Foundation's reported 200 members are carried on at several locations in and around the Scottish town of Forres and the Findhorn Village. Programs such as "The Joy of

Sacred Dance," "Psychic-Spiritual Healing," and "Meditation" are offered throughout the year in a variety of languages.

The Scottish-based community currently consists of Cluny Hill College in Forres, Cullerne House Gardens, Newbold House, the Isle of Erraid, and Caravan Park, upon which a "planetary village" has been planned. Although the Findhorn Foundation is a registered tax-exempt, charitable trust, recommended contributions for the weekly programs begin at 100 British pounds.

Although the Foundation claims no formal doctrine or creed, its basic tenets center around New Age concepts of acquiring expanded consciousness, communion with supernatural beings, and enforcing the belief that God is found in every living thing. Unlike Christianity, which focuses upon the redemptive blood of Christ, the Foundation promotes salvation based upon awareness of the God-within-us and cooperation with cosmic powers toward the creation of a new, more harmonious world.

Founders: Peter and Eileen Caddy with Dorothy MacLean in 1962.

Text: *The Findhorn Garden.*

Symbol: None:

Appeal: Those concerned about man's desensitized relationship to his natural environment are drawn toward Findhorn's ecological ethic, which promises interplanetary harmony, renewed humanity, and the creation of a new civilization.

Purpose: Findhorn believes mankind is involved in an evolutionary expansion of consciousness, which will ultimately create changes in world societies and promote a planetary culture infused with spiritual values. Findhorn is a model of that utopian goal.

Errors: Like most New Age cults, Findhorn adopts a pantheistic belief identifying Deity with the elements of nature. Metaphysical concepts of man finding oneness with God through his own actions, and unique rhythms of life are also promoted. By sacralizing the earth, Findhorn worships the creation rather than the Creator, the sin that is illuminated in Romans chapter one.

Background Sources: Findhorn Foundation Guest Programmes, Autumn-Winter 1984-85; *The Findhorn Garden* (New York: Harper & Row, 1975).

Address/Location: Findhorn, Movay IV36 OTZ, Scotland. One Earth Foundation, c/o Sloane & Hinshaw, Inc., 145 East 74th St., Suite 1C, New York, NY 10021.

THE
FORUM

At age 18, he had an experience about which he says, "I lost the kind of consciousness that locates one in a place. I became the universe." This theology would eventually become the basis for two successful motivational organizations after Philadelphia-born Jack Rosenberg changed his name to Werner Erhard. For several years, Erhard sold used cars, correspondence courses, and encyclopedias. He also studied Zen Buddhism and hypnosis and took courses from Scientology and California's Esalen Institute.

Werner Erhard, founder of est (Erhard Seminar Training), formulated The Forum as an offshoot of est to teach people effectiveness in their lives. A series of addresses he broadcast via private satellite to eager est audiences was the basis for The Forum. The organization advocates philosophical phrases like, "The Forum is about living in the question . . . much more powerful than having an answer, which closes possibilities." That premise is no clearer than another Forum dictum that states, "In all performance, 'being' is that one essential ingredient. . . which gives one human being a decisive edge." The impoverished and infirm need not apply since The Forum welcomes only "successful, healthy people" looking for a "decisive edge" in their "ability to achieve."

Unlike Erhard's famous 60-hour est seminars, which involved verbal abuse, the more casual Forum encourages dialogue between leaders and audience. The training is aimed at healthy, happy people, who are already effective in their lives. It also includes a division called Young People's Forum for children between six and twelve. Other divisions are The Breakthrough Foundation, The Hunger Project, The Education Network, The Mastery Foundation (for religious leaders and ministries), The Holiday Project, and the Werner Erhard Foundation.

Creation of The Forum conveniently coincided with a substantial decrease in est enrollments, a drop of 10,000 within a three-year period. Some observers say The Forum is merely a marketing maneuver, designed to revamp est training. Critics of est have brought their complaints to court, which Erhard reportedly shrugs off. An est-sponsored program, the Hunger Project, which aims to end world hunger through heightened consciousness, has been called "nothing but a big, huge bank account." Nevertheless, Erhard claims to have woven his work into the fabric of American culture.

Contemporary businesses are abandoning stress management seminars and assertive training courses in favor of motivational emphases that will inspire employees toward greater productivity and commitment. Consequently, Erhard has targeted successful corporate clientele and other upwardly mobile individuals, charging $595 for two weekends and one evening during which participants will achieve "a breakthrough to a new dimension of possibility." He claims participants will consider the cost "a joke" after completing the course.

Forum philosophy teaches advocates that commitment is vital, regardless of what the commitment is. According to Forum training, "You simply need to know what you want. . . . Whatever you want is fine. . . . Make a goal. . . . It doesn't make any difference." The organization makes no guarantee of success, claiming results of the Forum's specialized training are unpredictable and difficult to define.

The Forum promises clients will experience "being," while simultaneously admitting the concept defies precise definition. "Your participation in The Forum takes you beyond a mere understanding of 'being' . . . and provides you with direct access to the domain of 'being' itself." Forum advocates are advised to forsake logic and reason before tackling the magic business of "being." Excellence, Erhard says, is a matter of being excellent. He also claims creativity stems from being creative. This simplistic methodology recruited almost 7,700 people eager to discover the enigmatic essence of their "being" within a few months of its inception.

The Forum's philosophy links strongly with Eastern mysticism. Erhard once stated that everyone is "part of every atom in the world." Eastern mysticism is also evident in Erhard's idea that, while "being" alive, one disappears as an identity. Erhard himself confessed that est contained strong Zen Buddhism and Scientology influences, and the redesigned Forum is clearly an est offspring. While claiming not to be a cult, religion, or philosophy, one Forum leader stated that the organization is similar to religion, thus creating further ambiguity.

Christians should be wary of self-motivation training like The Forum, a modern masquerade of Eastern thought. Its obscure terms and aims are designed to conceal a satanic hoax, perpetrated by a man whose own biographer calls "a liar, an imposter, and a rogue." Consult the real expert about "being," Jesus Christ. He uses simple language, and his intent is clear: "Heaven can be entered only through the narrow gate! The highway to hell is broad, and its gate is wide enough for all the multitudes who choose its easy way. But the Gateway to Life is small, and the road is narrow, and only a few ever find it" (Matt. 7:13-14, *The Living Bible).*

Founder: Jack Rosenberg (aka Werner Erhard), former used car salesman, born in Philadelphia.

Text: Zen Buddhist concepts.

Symbol: None.

Appeal: The Forum promises corporate clientele it will galvanize employees to greater productivity and creativity. Forum attendees are taught that man is in control of his life and is at the center of his own universe. There are no rules or regulations, only "being." Such a narcissistic emphasis readily appeals to the financially successful and upwardly mobile.

Purpose: To increase man's awareness of his inner self and his omnipotence. The Forum encourages laying aside all conventional religions and social ideas about achieving success. Once The Forum's state of "being" is acquired, all one wishes will somehow materialize.

Errors: Scripture teaches that God, not man, is the center of the universe. Under the guise of self-motivation, The Forum is an apologetic for Eastern mysticism. God's moral laws must be obeyed to gain salvation, but The Forum claims there are no rules or regulations. Since The Forum terminology is semantically ill-defined, the outcome of the training is equally ambiguous.

Background Sources: "Est Training Changed to 'The Forum'," *The Cult Observer,* February/March, 1985, 2; John Bode, "The Forum: Repackaged Est," *The Cult Observer,* April 1986, 3; J. Yutaka Amano, "Bad for Business," *Eternity,* March 1986, 55; Barbara Zigli, "As Est Training Bows Out, Its Leader Founds The Forum," *USA Today,* 12 December 1984, 5D; "Erhard's Forum: EST Meets the 80s," *Newsweek,* 1 April 1985, 15.

Address/Location: Werner Erhard and Associates Centers located in dozens of U.S. cities. Check local listings.

See also est.

FOUNDATION
FAITH OF GOD

(Foundation Faith of the Millennium)

The Ultimate Evil, a book by Maury Terry, connects the infamous Son of Sam murders to Charles Manson and, ultimately, the Process Church. This church is part of a group whose name is difficult to define, and whose evolving doctrines are even harder to pin down. In the beginning (1963) it was known as the Process Church of the Final Judgment (The Process). In 1974, as a result of a break with its founder, Robert DeGrimston, its name was changed to The Foundation Church of the Millennium (with the word *Church* changed to *Faith* in 1977). Its current name is the Foundation Faith of God.

DeGrimston's original group followed his psychic teachings with rapt enthusiasm. But his theology of dualism (supposing the universe is dominated by two opposing spiritual forces, neither being omnipotently supreme) eventually received bad press. Even non-Christians didn't like being stopped on street corners by robed zealots wearing silver crosses entwined with a red serpent. What Processians taught was even more offensive. "Christ said, 'Love your enemies,' " they declared. "Christ's enemy was Satan. Through love, Christ and Satan have destroyed their enmity and come together for the end, Christ to judge, Satan to execute judgment." Therefore, to worship Satan was to worship Christ, and to kill in Satan's name was to kill in Christ's. Growing out of this doctrine was the belief that "process" by spiritual knowledge would allow members of the church to provide moral leadership in a New Age led by a God-sent Messiah. All this would take place after a Bible-like apocalyptic period when Christ and Satan would finally be reconciled. The Processian philosophy of duality appealed to Charles Manson, whom the group influenced heavily. The prosecutor in Manson's trial did not quite call Manson a member of the Process Church, but he pointed out that Manson stopped mentioning the group after two church representatives visited him in jail.

Eventually the black garb, somber theology, and satanic and Nazi symbolism became too hard to accept, even for Processians. DeGrimston was ousted, though he continues to lead smaller groups of leftovers under the original name. The Foundation clothing was changed to blue suits and white shirts, and lately even these have been abandoned. The serpent-cross was replaced by the Star of David with two Fs, one inverted. Occult practices such as tarot cards, psychic healings, and astrology persist, but elements of Judaism, including Sabbath ceremonies, have been added to upgrade the cult's image. The past and its spooky overtones are de-emphasized, though the belief in a soon-to-appear savior still undergirds Foundation philosophy.

Father Lucius (Christopher de Peyer) and Father Malachi (Peter McCormick), leaders at one time, claimed an estimated 500,000 people were affiliated with their efforts, including 20,000 hard-core members. (Such figures are undoubtedly highly inflated.) Foundation advocates certainly seem more palatable since they no longer publicly promote the Christ/Satan reconciliation theory. But they have not abandoned their basic belief in a coming messiah. Bible students are left to wonder whether such a person might well be the Antichrist, the representative of the once-revered serpent that Foundation Faith advocates now seldom discuss.

In 1980 the Foundation Faith of the Millennium, which remained one of the more successful off-shoots of the original Process Church, again changed its name to the Foundation Faith of God. It has a devoted clergy committed to a vow of perpetual celibacy as a testimony to "the existence of the Kingdom." This group claims 20 ordained ministers with a growing number of followers. One new development is the Crusade of Innocence, a ministry offering counsel to families of seriously ill children. The clown ministry is a hallmark of this crusade, entertaining children in hospitals and private homes. The Foundation has established missions throughout the U.S. and appears to be growing through outreach programs and prayer fellowships.

The Foundation Faith appears to be moving toward more orthodox Christian beliefs, including belief in the Trinity, Jesus' deity, salvation from sin, the need to be born again, and the Second Coming of Christ. Christ has a prominent role in the Foundation's teachings, with special emphasis on spiritual healing. However, its most distinctive doctrine maintains that everyone has a personal guardian angel who can be invoked for guidance in daily living. The clergy will conduct "angel listenings" (for a suggested donation of ten dollars), claiming they can actually hear the angel's voice and write down his instruction. Most angelic messages are generalized and concern removal of barriers preventing one's spiritual growth, but additional questions may be asked of these angels for a tax-deductible fee of three dollars per inquiry.

Two other prominent tenets of the Foundation Faith include reincarnation and the importance of controlling one's own life by personal choices.

Founder: Robert DeGrimston, 1963, London, England.

Text: "Love your enemies — including Satan."

Symbols: Formerly, a cross with a snake entwined upon it; today, a Star of David with two opposing (one inverted) Fs. The symbol of the Crusade of Innocence is a Star of David with a lamb in the center.

Appeal: In the early days of the cult, initiates were intrigued by the exotic doctrines that combined elements of Satanism and Christianity. Through the shift toward more orthodox Christian beliefs, it currently appeals more to the general public, especially to families of acutely ill children through Crusade of Innocence.

Purpose: Originally, DeGrimston endeavored to explain how a good God had created the Devil and evil. (Answer — The Devil is not truly evil and, therefore, he will eventually be a cohort of God.) Today, the emphasis is more on understanding the nature of the coming Apocalypse and the role Foundation members will play in the social order that follows.

Errors: Initially the Process Church exalted Satan as Christ's ally. The church philosophy held that Christ and Satan destroyed their enmity to judge and execute punishment on man. Although dissatisfaction with the growing emphasis on Satan worship in the Process Church led to ousting DeGrimston and the formation of the Foundation Faith of the Millennium/God, the church is still far from orthodox. The Foundation Faith of God is rooted in the evil of the Process Church, which could possibly produce more Charles Mansons and Sons of Sam. The original cross with a snake entwined around it has been substituted by a Star of David with two opposing Fs, which look suspiciously like the swastika symbolizing the original Process Church's love of Naziism.

Background Sources: *The Processians* (cult magazine), March 1974; *The Denver Post*, 27 July 1973; Ibid., 31 May 1974, 5HH; J. Gordon Melton, *The Encyclopedia of American Religions*, vol. 2 (Wilmington, N.C.: McGrath, 1978), 229; *Toronto Star*, 24 January 1981, H6; J. Gordon Melton, "Foundation Faith of God," *The Encyclopedia of American Religions*, 2d ed. (Detroit: Gale Research, n.d.), 578; The Foundation Faith of God, *Statement of Belief*, "God and the Sin of Man," "Jesus Christ," "Salvation for Man," "Baptism," "Duties of the Believer," and "Jesus Lives."

Address/Location: Foundation Faith of God, Faith Center, 3055 S. Bronco, Las Vegas, NV 89102. Also, headquarters in New York, Chicago, New Orleans, Toronto, Miami, and Cambridge, MA. (Some of these offices may no longer be open.)

See also Charles Manson Cult.

FOUNDATION

OF HUMAN

UNDERSTANDING

(Roy Masters)

He reportedly once declared, "Every religion in America is a cult. Only the Foundation is the true church." He claims America is a hypnotized country and that "preachers use the Bible as a fixation point of hypnosis." He considers himself a Christian mystic who can lead each person to perfection. Roy Masters established the Foundation of Human Understanding in 1961. Headquartered in Los Angeles, he offers his self-help brand of religion to 3 million people who listen to his national radio show, "How Your Mind Can Keep You Well."

He optimistically proclaims, "All of us have a natural inclination toward right action," yet Masters believes nuclear Armageddon will occur in the future. He considers himself a survivalist and has been accused of owning a small cache of arms. In 1982, Masters established a 378-acre ranch-retreat near Grants Pass, Oregon, and invited like-minded radio listeners to join him. More than 2,000 disciples packed up their belongings and moved to be near Masters, his wife, and five children. Masters holds seminars and weekend retreats at his ranch and is in the process of establishing Evelyn Street School, a Foundation of Human Understanding institute for kindergarten through twelfth-graders, in Grants Pass. In 1989 I debated Masters on a program of my nationally syndicated broadcast "TALK-BACK," at which time he claimed to have 150,000 people on his mailing list.

The British son of a Jewish diamond cutter, Roy Masters was born Reuben Obermeister in London, England. Fascinated with hypnotism as

232

an adolescent, Obermeister traveled at age 18 to South Africa and apprenticed as a diamond cutter. In 1949, at age 21, he journeyed to America to lecture on diamonds. Obermeister legally changed his name to Roy Masters in 1954, but never became an American citizen.

Propelled by the popularity of the Bridey Murphy hypnosis case (in which an American woman appeared to reveal, under hypnosis, details of a previous life), Masters became a professional hypnotist and founded the Institute for Hypnosis. He claims he can save people by teaching them self-sufficiency meditative hypnosis. In the early 1960s, the American Medical Association incriminated Masters for practicing medicine without a license.

Masters claims over 100,000 people have participated in his Foundation of Human Understanding meditation classes. According to Masters, America's problems stem from the deceptive works of preachers, educators, psychologists, and sociologists. He encourages followers to empty their minds and allow their spirits to guide them to understanding. Masters scorns most men as "wimps" and condemns liberalism and intellectuals. Masters also maintains rock 'n' roll is "written by Satan" and declares education brainwashes youth. He publishes *The Iconoclast* magazine in protest of society.

In Foundation of Human Understanding training, Masters employs meditation exercises based on yoga, hypnotism, and Eastern concepts to help devotees obtain inner direction. He combines Christian terminology with gnostic beliefs. He claims, "One of the biggest curses in Christendom is the false idea the Jesus is God," yet he quotes Scripture and claims he has been saved by the blood of Christ. He says the Bible was written "by men inspired by mystical experiences." Masters maintains the Bible is merely a collection of words on paper.

In his meditation exercise, taught on three cassettes and in a book for a total cost of $25, Masters melodically encourages subjects to obtain an altered state of consciousness so as to contact God without thinking. He hypnotically tells disciples to discover the good within in order to grow in the grace of God. Masters tells participants, "Do not analyze my words. Listen, but do not think." According to Masters, all that's needed to commune with the inner state of intuitive innocence is to empty the mind. On his record album, *How Your Mind Can Keep You Well*, Masters urges subjects to accept the "guidance of an invisible Divine Will" and to "wait, empty, for a new direction." He sells tapes on subjects like "controlling negative emotions and healing through understanding one's relationship to stress."

233

Masters also conducts exorcism seminars, in which he tells participants in a mesmerizing voice that something inside of them is evil and hateful. Then he waves a wooden cross at them until they break down emotionally. In one exorcism, Masters told a possessed person, "All you have to do is be sorry and you'll be all right." Participants pay $1,200 for week-long seminars or $50 for one-day seminars across the country.

Roy Masters believes he's a sinless, perfected being appointed to save America and the world. He explains, "An intuitive innate knowledge . . . gave me a clear vision to see the world for what it was and it protects me from being caught up in various temptations." He boasts, "I can solve the world's problems in a week if I could get on television." Masters says he wants to be remembered in the same category as Moses, Jesus, the apostles, Buddha, Gandhi, Martin Luther King, and John F. Kennedy. He maintains, "I'm not after political power; I only want to save souls."

Founder: Roy Masters (born Reuben Obermeister), talk show host, author of eleven books.

Texts: *How Your Mind Can Keep You Well* and other books promoting self-sufficiency through hypnosis.

Symbols: None.

Appeal: Masters's meditation philosophy and life-style appeal to emotionally susceptible or victimized people who have lost control of their lives. Foundation of Human Understanding participants venerate Masters as a perfected person who can save them from social disintegration. Masters likens the controversy surrounding his teachings to the persecution suffered by Jesus Christ.

Purpose: Foundation of Human Understanding participants seek to relieve stress and attain a perfected state. Through self-hypnosis, they attempt to obtain the solace of inner direction.

Errors: Man can never attain a state of perfected being. He fell from God and remains a sinner, though he may be saved by grace. Roy Masters preaches a doctrine of sinless perfection and maintains knowledge is the enemy of spiritual understanding. Although he doesn't believe the Bible is the inerrant Word of God and denies the deity of Christ and the Trinity, he uses Christian terminology. Masters contradicts himself when he claims Jesus is not God and then says he's been saved by the blood of Christ. And 1 John 4 clearly states that spiritual authority only comes from one whose doctrine declares Jesus is God in flesh.

All Foundation of Human Understanding teachings revolve around Masters's meditation methods, which encourage emptying the mind and exposing it to demonic invasion. The participant clears his mind through a conditioning process that seeks to improve the meditator but gives no consideration to redeeming grace. This false meditation prevents true spiritual renewal through the power of Christ. Foundation of Human Understanding participants believe they have the capability to perfect themselves. Thus they ignore accountability to God for their sins and deny the salvation of Jesus Christ on the cross.

Background Sources: Walter Martin, *The New Cults* (Santa Ana, Calif.: Vision House Publishers, 1980); Roy Masters, *How Your Mind Can Keep You Well* (Los Angeles, Calif.: Foundation Press, 1971); Paul Taublieb, "Masters' Touch," *US,* 23 April 1984, 36-41; Lauren Kessler, "Roy Masters: I Can Do No Wrong," *Northwest Magazine,* 4 September 1983, 5-10; "TALK-BACK with Bob Larson," 27 July 1989 and 1 August 1989 broadcasts.

Address/Location: Foundation of Human Understanding, 8780 Venice Blvd., Los Angeles, CA 90034.

FREEMASONRY

It has been described as the "biggest, richest, most secret and most power-ful private force in the world." Some Baptist leaders have referred to it as "an ungodly brotherhood of satanic darkness," and the Roman Cath-olic church condemns it as incompatible with Christian beliefs and prac-tices. Freemasonry has been denounced over the ages by the Christian community, which maintains Masonic rituals and tenets conflict with Christian beliefs. Members defend Freemasonry, saying it is a religious organization seeking human betterment and service to God.

Freemasonry is a clandestine fraternal order revived in Britain in 1717. Masons claim their organization's roots can be traced to Old Testament stonecutters who built King Solomon's temple. Hiram Abiff, an apoc-ryphal being believed by Masons to have built Solomon's temple, is a celebrated figure of Freemasonry because of his death-defying refusal to reveal trade secrets to intruders. Inspired by Abiff, Masons met in lodges and guilds until the Middle Ages, when the group disbanded, awaiting its renewal in the eighteenth century. With the decline of the Masons' critical role in building construction, "operative" Freemasonry evolved into an esoteric order of "speculative" Freemasonry.

Condemned for centuries by the Roman Catholic church and banned by Greek and Latin American governments, Masons have often been ac-tive in politics. Members have included George Washington, Benjamin Franklin, Theodore Roosevelt, Harry Truman, Gerald Ford, and Chief

Supreme Court Justices William O. Douglas, Potter Stewart, Hugo Black, and Earl Warren. Early nineteenth-century explorers Albert Pike and Albert Mackey wrote and interpreted Masonic literature and rituals. Pike was an admitted occult Luciferian, espousing his beliefs in such books as *Morals and Dogma*, a text of Freemasonry.

Followers of Freemasonry frequently belong to churches and claim the society's traditions are strongly rooted in religious thought. Most lodges of the organization require only the acknowledgement of a Supreme Being and life after death. Masons diligently deny that Freemasonry is a secret society, but admit it has secrets "just like other organizations." The secrets are Masonic rituals, in which advocates orate lessons about the brotherhood of man and Masonic teachings of good and evil. Masons are also required to utter bloody oaths, which they argue are symbolic.

The Blue Lodge is the basic Masonic organization representing the first three Masonic degrees: Entered Apprentice, Fellowcraft, and Master Mason. The symbol for the Master Mason degree denotes a compass, exemplifying male force, and a square, depicting female force. They are combined with the letter *G*, symbolizing geometry and the Masonic Grand Architect of the Universe (God).

Other Masonic symbols include the apron, which must be worn at all meetings and to one's burial, as well as the star and its five points of fellowship. Master Masons may receive more degrees in either the York Rite or the Scottish Rite Masonry. In addition to the Shriners and high-degree Masons, Freemasonry also includes the Order of the Eastern Star for women, the Order of DeMolay for teenage boys, and the Order of the Rainbow for teenage girls.

Masonic members recite oaths to tear open their left breast or have their bowels taken out and burned to ashes should they reveal Masonic secrets. Mason handbooks threaten members who disclose confidences with curses of throat slashing, tongue removal, and burial at the edge of a lake or pond. Third-degree Masons, called Shriners, utter oaths to be penalized for violating rules by having their eyeballs speared and their feet flayed.

Masons profess to be philanthropic, contribute to various charities, and strive to extend charity to Masonic families. Widows of destitute members of Freemasonry are supported, and nursing homes are provided for some elderly. Freemasonry sponsors 22 Shriner hospitals for crippled children, which include three nationally recognized burn units. Recent reports, however, reveal Shriners give their hospitals less than one-third of the millions they raise each year, spending the remainder on travel, food, and entertainment.

Freemasonry and Christianity are incompatible. The symbolic physical penalties advocated by the Freemasons are violent and murderous. No faithful Christian can keep Freemason oaths, which endorse the death penalty for oneself and require members to persecute traitors to the organization. Oaths also obligate lodge members to protect lodge criminals and keep their secrets.

Most Masons join Freemasonry to be part of what they view as a prestigious, socially influential organization. But their society is based on misrepresentations and false explanations. Masons refer to their 33rd degree Masons as "Worshipful Master" and believe Jesus was only a man and teacher. The Bible clearly states that salvation can be attained only through Jesus, God's beloved Son. The brotherhood Masons advocate is false. The only brotherhood spoken of in the Bible is the one entered into by the blood of Jesus Christ (1 John 1:3).

Founder: According to Masons, their history can be traced to Old Testament stonemasons who built King Solomon's temple. Hiram Abiff, purported builder of Solomon's temple, remains a hero in the eyes of Masons because of his refusal to reveal the secrets of his trade to intruders. After the 1717 British revival of Freemasonry, Albert Pike and Albert Mackey were instrumental in laying down the laws of Masonry. Albert Pike is considered a great Masonic scholar and historian by Masons.

Texts: Albert Pike's *Morals and Dogma*; Albert Mackey's *A Lexicon of Freemasonry, Manual of the Lodge, A Text Book of Masonic Jurisprudence,* and *The Masonic Ritualist.*

Symbols: The compass and square combined with the *G* (gnosis, God-Deity). Other symbols are: the apron, which represents the innocence of a lamb; the beehive, which denotes the fertility of a queen bee; the five points of fellowship, which symbolize a third-degree Mason; the Eastern Star; and the All-seeing eye of Horus.

Appeal: Many people seeking social status join Masonic organizations. The society extends help to charities, leading some to believe it is an altruistic organization. Its many levels of membership and elaborate regalia appeal to those who live otherwise austere lives.

Purpose: Masons pledge to better themselves through fraternal association and serve their God and their community by organized philanthropic activities.

Errors: Masons believe Jesus was nothing more than a man and teacher and require allegiance only to a Supreme Being. Though lodges in the South tend to be more Christianized, as a matter of dogma the Bible is only one of many sacred books, and adherents of all faiths are allowed membership. By placing death curses on themselves and others, Masons violate the laws of Christianity. The teachings of Christ in Matthew chapter 5 clearly forbid the uttering of presumptive oaths that one does not have the power to perform (Matt. 5:33-37).

Background Sources: *The Courier Mail Saturday Magazine*, 22 May 1982, 23; *Beaumont Enterprise*, 31 August 1985, 10A; *The Birmingham News*, 12 August 1984; *The Rocky Mountain News*, 30 June 1986, 27.

Address/Location: Throughout the United States, Canada, and Western Europe.

See also Rosicrucianism.

HIMALAYAN INTERNATIONAL INSTITUTE OF YOGA SCIENCE AND PHILOSOPHY

(Swami Rami)

Biofeedback, the psychophysiological technique of mentally controlling body functions and responses, owes its development to the expertise of Swami Rami. Dr. Green, of the prestigious Topeka, Kansas-based Menninger Foundation, developed the principles of biofeedback by observing Rami, who studied with Gandhi, in meditative trance states. Rami not only exhibited the ability to stop his heartbeat for 17 seconds, but by psychokinesis (the supposed ability to affect physical objects by using mental powers) he was able to move an aluminum knitting needle while seated five feet away from it.

Five thousand students a month flock to his Himalayan International Institute of Yoga Science and Philosophy in Glenview, Illinois. Once there, they learn via *Raja Yoga* to "exhale all problems" and "inhale energy" in order to become "a wave of bliss in the ocean of the universe." Rami, who claims to meditate eight hours a day and sleeps only three hours each night, feels his mission is to combine Indian religious therapeutic techniques. As a monk of the Shankaracharya Order, he spent the early years of his life traveling from monasteries to caves throughout the Indian subcontinent and living with various Sadhus. Rather than just popularizing the traditions in which he was trained, he has sought to establish a clear scientific basis for practicing yoga and meditation. As an Oxford-educated and Americanized guru, his life has been dedicated to "creating a bridge between East and West." In creating this bridge, Swami Rami has learned that many spiritually hungry people enjoy the exotic combination of ancient tradition and contemporary science.

Background Sources: J. Gordon Melton, *The Encyclopedia of American Religions*, vol. 2 (Wilmington, N.C.: McGrath, 1978); *People*, 24 October 1977.

H O L I S M

Laurie Cabot, a professed witch, puts a crystal in her moisturizing cream to improve her skin. Pop singer Tina Turner cuddles a crystal to combat loneliness before entering hotel rooms. Actress Jill Ireland meditated with pieces of quartz after her mastectomy. A holism advocate claims, "Crystals are an access tool to other planes of awareness."

Increasing discontent with traditional American health care encourages patients to adopt holistic healing as an alternative to excessively expensive hospital and doctor fees. Researchers report changing a patient's physical and emotional condition can profoundly transform his self-image and worldview. Consequently, some proponents of holism believe anxiety about chronic, catastrophic diseases can be alleviated by guided meditation. The ultimate intent is to unite body, mind, and spirit in an integrated approach to health.

Holism proponents use crystals to promote health and happiness. Others adopt the theories of ancient Greek philosopher Pythagoras, who urged students to cleanse themselves of fear and danger by daily singing. Advocates claim the appropriate music can cure depression, diagnose mental illness, and reduce the effects of surgery. To substantiate their theory, holistic healing adherents refer to the biblical example where David cured King Saul's despondency by playing his harp.

Holism is based on the idea that consciousness can be altered through meditation, visualization, or occult practices. In addition to crystals and music therapy, methods include metaphysical massage, naturopathy, pyramidology, yoga, iridology, reflexology, meditation, trance channeling, biofeedback, acupuncture, and other exotic techniques.

Iridology claims that the entire body can be treated by observing sympathetic body loci in the eye's iris. Reflexology proposes that all the body's organs have corresponding points in the feet, which, when massaged, can relieve physical ailments. Laughter, courage, and tenacity are touted as prime ingredients to holistic healing, since such emotional factors supposedly control the body's ability to heal.

Holism is multifaceted. Macrobiotics, an Oriental theory that divides all energy into opposites, promotes a whole grain diet, augmented by exercise, meditation, and prayer. Rolfing is designed to straighten the body and make it more supple. Psychics use chromotherapy to view otherwise invisible auras. Herbology proposes that its prescriptions are preferable to drugs for treating illness. Polarity therapy, "acupuncture without needles," claims to balance the body's inner energies through deep massage.

Dr. Whit Reaves, certified acupuncturist in West Los Angeles, ran tests on a group of sprinters and found that inserting acupuncture needles in specific body points enhanced athletic performance. Runners reported feeling more energized and efficient. The 200-year-old practice of homeopathy is based on the idea that "like cures like": A substance in large doses that would produce symptoms in a healthy person will, in small amounts, effect a cure.

All such holistic theories hinge upon the idea that man is capable of curing his own diseases. Puncturing the body with silver needles, attaching electrodes to muscles, redistributing energy by laying on of hands, and the myriad other holistic healing practices avoid the primary issue of the sinful origin of many diseases.

Founder: Ancient folk medicine and superstition.

Texts: Various New Age books on self-healing.

Symbol: A circle representing the wholeness of man's consciousness and the link of his body to the cosmos.

Appeal: The failure of conventional allopathic therapy causes some to turn to holistic approaches. Many such therapies are nutritionally sound and are partially beneficial, which is interpreted as an endorsement for the philosophy behind the cure.

Purpose: Traditional medical techniques are viewed as too expensive and intervention-oriented. Holistic therapies purport to be cheaper and more effective because they are based on a preventive approach. The ultimate intent is to restore the body to harmony with universal cosmological laws of health and well-being.

Errors: A severely ill person may circumvent treatment critical to recovery. Through psychosomatic effects, a sense of immediate relief may be experienced, but the real cause of internal organic dysfunction may go unnoticed. Holism purports to treat soul and spirit, as well as the body, without defining those terms in a Christian context. Thus, those who seek such cures are usually introduced to various kinds of mystical concepts and literature. They often adopt a metaphysical world view consistent with Hinduism or Buddhism.

Background Sources: Carolyn Reuben, "It's a Whole New Game with Acupuncture," *East West,* July 1986, 51; Carolyn Reuben, "Homeopathy for Relief," *East West,* July 1986, 52; Stephen Sutphen, "Increasing Crystal Power," *Masters of Life,* January 1987, 14; Pamela Bloom, "Soul Music," *New Age Journal,* March/April 1987, 58.

Address/Location: Traditionally an Oriental concept, rooted in the medical practices of primitive societies using shamanistic approaches to health and healing.

See also New Age Cults.

HOLY ALAMO CHRISTIAN CHURCH, CONSECRATED

(Tony Alamo)

"In a darkened prayer room inside a sprawling mansion atop a remote, guarded ridge in rural Arkansas rests a coffin. Inside the coffin rests the embalmed body of Susan Alamo, patiently awaiting resurrection. The cult leader has been dead more than a year. Encouraged by Susan's husband, Tony, her followers kneel by the coffin in two-hour shifts, 24 hours a day, every day, to pray for Susan's return." So said *People* magazine in a 1983 article about the Alamo cult.

The year was 1970. I stood at the front door of a small frame house just off Sunset Strip in Hollywood. Outside, the sign read *Alamo Christian Foundation.* Inside, a coed crowd mingled in a somewhat disorderly fashion. When I inquired about the nature and purpose of their group, the "elder brother" in charge quickly informed me that I was sent from Satan and ordered me to leave. This small communal flophouse was the inauspicious beginning of an Alamo empire that would eventually stretch from a California ranch to a quiet town in Arkansas.

Tony was born Bernie Lazar Hoffman in 1934 in Missouri. He fancied himself a country gospel star, and eventually changed his name to Tony Alamo. In California he met Susan, who was married to a small-time Los Angeles hood. She was born Edith Opal Horn in Arkansas or Missouri in the 1920s. She and Tony were married once in Tijuana and twice in Las Vegas, to be "triple sure."

Tony and Susan Alamo capitalized upon the early seventies' Jesus Revolution, which they claimed to have initiated. This flamboyant couple with extravagant tastes fashioned an effective organization using Pentecostal-like theology and cult-control techniques. Neither was ordained as a minister. They simply walked up to hippies and drug addicts and asked, "Why are you destroying your mind, your soul, and your body?" They found people who were ready to try religion. The ranks of recruits were filled with disillusioned street kids, who found solace in the regimented life-style of the Alamo ranch complex. These converts seldom questioned their deplorable living conditions, though Tony and Susan lived in secluded splendor. Most Foundation members seldom saw the Alamos except when their Cadillac Fleetwood zoomed by, or when they were bused into Los Angeles to witness a taping of the Alamo TV show.

The Alamos shifted operations to Alma, Arkansas, in the mid-1970s amidst embarrassing press stories, as California agencies began inspecting their organization. Susan's daughter left, charging that the couple was growing rich while taking advantage of their followers. In another ugly scene, a Foundation member severely beat her own mother, aided by Susan's top female lieutenant.

The Foundation quickly settled into its new home. The Alamos owned up to 29 businesses in the small town and soon spread into several other states. This eventually fired up a new controversy: Foundation members were expected to consider themselves "volunteers," running the businesses in return for meager living conditions. The U.S. Department of Labor became interested, and, in a case taken all the way to the U.S. Supreme Court, the Alamos were ordered to pay at least minimum wage to those followers who worked their businesses, from hog farms to hotels.

Even with minimum wage, living conditions were far from pleasant. In California, and then in Arkansas, recruits existed on a diet of harsh sermons and hard labor. Brainwashed into viewing noncult members — including families — as "agents of Satan," they shunned people from their former life and unquestioningly worked long hours. They lived under a siege mentality, and the Alamos occasionally called "alerts," predicting imminent enemy attack. If a member needed anything, from clothes to surgery, the Alamos required a written request, called an "Ask" memo. Members were allowed only books approved by the Alamos. They had no pets, no radios, no vacations, no movies, no newspapers. Single men and women in the foundation were not allowed to speak to each other. Even in marriage privacy was hard to find; Susan decided who would have how many children.

One woman who left the cult stated that when she and her husband were finally allowed a house, it had no phone, and they could not use the kitchen because all cult members were required to eat in the group cafeteria. They could turn the heat on for only ten minutes in the morning and ten minutes in the evening, even on the coldest days of winter.

Alamo theology was bedrock, hell-fire Pentecostalism, though their practice of speaking in tongues appeared to be a hypnotically induced utterance. The Alamos taught that all churches were corrupt, and, in spite of the members having to eat discarded foodstuffs and to labor long hours in order to crucify the flesh, they zealously believed that they were the vanguard of God's spiritual army. The press repeatedly raised charges of sensory deprivation, enslavement, and brainwashing. These allegations only served to reinforce the persecution paranoia that permeated the cult's thinking.

Tony Alamo has spearheaded several campaigns, among them a crusade condemning the Catholic church and calling for the impeachment of then President Ronald Reagan, "one of the pope's little helpers." Another time Tony launched a campaign to recruit unwed mothers to join or give their children to the foundation, which again attracted unwanted attention from the government in the form of social service officials.

Members were instructed to pray diligently for the healing of Susan Alamo, who died of cancer in April 1982. Susan had been the "handmaiden of God" who would miraculously cure herself and then, with Tony, lead a world crusade. Her death shook her followers' faith, and Tony ordered members to pray unceasingly in shifts at her coffin. Tony and his second wife, Elizabeth, whom he married in 1985, now guide what remains of this once prominent (and now declining) seventies youth cult.

Background Sources: Chet Flippo, "Siege of the Alamos," *People,* 13 June 1983, 29-33; "Arkansas Sect Accuses Catholics of Variety of Ills," *Charisma,* August 1984, 98-100; "Wages and Religion," *The Christian Century,* 8 May 1985, 464; G. W. Hunt, "Of Many Things," *America,* 25 May 1985, inside cover; Elizabeth Alamo, *It Was All a Lie!* Testimony published by Holy Alamo Christian Church, P. O. Box 398, Alma, AR 72921, n.d., 1; *People,* 13 June 1983, 29.

HOLY ORDER OF MANS

Publicly distributed literature described the Holy Order of MANS as a "discipleship movement," not a religion. "Seekers" who inquire are told that the Order's purpose is to teach the Universal Law of Creation, revealed by ancient Christian mysteries. A list of Twelve Rules of Living guide the search, including admonitions to tithe ($5 per month for beginners) and render absolute obedience to the Class Master to whom the inquirer is assigned.

Entry into the Order (which is coeducational) starts when the initiate fills out an application form. He must also pledge his willingness to receive the teachings of Master Jesus. This nominal reference to Christ is consistent with the Order's position that Jesus was a great teacher, but only one of several great *avatars*. The Holy Order of MANS purports to have a Christian belief system. There are frequent references encouraging the seeker to maintain "high Christian morals." However, the Order's true mystical nature is revealed by its allusions to concepts such as "Self-Realization," the "Aquarian Age," the "Christ Light Within," the "Esoteric Council," and "Attainment of the Illumination."

The so-called Basic Course takes about two years to complete. Then the entrant (who is now a Lay Brother or Sister) may proceed on to the Advanced Course, or may even pursue the highest level of Discipleship Instructor. From that point onward, each member is expected to exhibit qualities of self-control, charity, and detachment from material and physical desires. Dark-colored clothing with a clerical collar is standard attire, a dress style designed to spiritually distinguish members from "the common folk." Such garb also emphasizes the Catholic-type overtones

248

of the Order. (In fact, the Order has reinstituted many monastic practices of the pre-Vatican II Roman Catholic church. The Order's emphasis on sacraments also reflects a spiritual tie to Catholicism, though some conscientious Catholics would find many of the Order's tactics highly questionable. It is interesting that, after the changes in Catholicism following the Vatican II council, many disgruntled Catholics sought a religion that had the sacramental emphasis of pre-Vatican II Catholicism.)

Rigid moral codes are not assigned. Instead, the Order seems to assume that a subjectively acquired Christ-consciousness will dictate positive conduct. Members are told that they do not need to forsake their existing church or religious faith affiliations because the precepts of the Order are "not doctrines." (For those who make a total commitment to MANS teachings, there are cloister and monastic orders.) By denying that Christ is the only Savior/Creator and relegating him to an infusion of "radiant energy," the Holy Order of MANS places itself in opposition to orthodox biblical belief. The Order also denies the biblical concept of hell, claiming that the only hell we know is of our own making.

More serious spiritual dangers may be encountered by meditation techniques designed to "reach the higher beings and your own inner being." Such a solicitation may result in spiritistic practices, though there is no reason to suggest that any active attempt at spiritualism or necromancy is intended. They do, however, promote involvement in tarot cards, astrology, psychic power, Kabbalah, and parapsychology.

On a more positive level, the Order does operate Raphael House, a San Francisco shelter for the homeless and the abused. Raphael House's inmates can stay until they find work or go on public aid.

The main thrust of the Order is an appeal to achieve a higher consciousness. This exalted state is to be achieved by attaining the same "Christ consciousness" as Jesus, who was merely a God-realized man. Members will then be prepared to enter the New Age of man's spiritual understanding. Their slogan, "And by their work ye shall know them," is paraphrased from Matthew 7:20. The substitution of the word *work* for *fruits* may or may not have been deliberate, but it does reveal the essential difference between the Order and biblical Christianity. The ethical aims of the Order are commendable, but ultimately unattainable. The true Christian is to be known by the Spirit's fruit (Gal. 5:22-23), which comes from the indwelling Person (not consciousness) of Christ. While the Holy Order of MANS is quick to report its acceptance by some Christians, no sensitive Christian can accept the Order's unorthodox theology and its mingling of Christianity with the occult.

Founder: Earl Blighton, an ex-engineer who claims "divine revelation" prompted him to start the Order.

Text: The Bible (preferably the New Testament) with mystical emphasis on the Pauline epistles; seminars and correspondence study.

Symbols: Golden Cross overlaid with a flaming sword. MANS is an acronym denoting *mysterion* (mystery), *agape* (divine love), *nous* (knowledge), and *sophia* (wisdom).

Appeal: Moral asceticism and ethical honesty are strongly emphasized to attract those who have been victimized by society's moral vacuum. The image of the Order is noncontroversial, and so little is known about it that prospective members have no predispositions about its secret teachings.

Purpose: The Holy Order of MANS promises to reveal hidden, ancient Christian mysteries. These "truths" will elevate one's spiritual consciousness and prepare him for the New Age that will soon dawn upon humanity. Members are promised entry into "the Greater Brotherhood," a company of "Christed" individuals who will someday reign with "the Cosmic Christ."

Errors: Christ is not Eternal God but merely a great teacher. God the Father is "the highest initiate among the humanity of the Saturn Period," Jesus is "the highest initiate of the Sun Period," and the Holy Spirit is "the highest initiate of the Moon Period." Mystical wisdom is considered to be a valid source of truth and equal in authority to biblical revelation.

Background Sources: Holy Order of MANS solicitation correspondence; introductory brochure, "Steps Along the Way"; *Spiritual Counterfeits Project Newsletter,* February 1976, vol. 2, no. 2.

Address/Location: Holy Order of MANS, 2101 Seymour Ave., Box 308, Cheyenne, WY 82001 (Discipleship Headquarters). Holy Order of MANS, 20 Steiner St., San Francisco, CA 94117 (International Headquarters).

HUMAN
POTENTIAL
MOVEMENT

Its influence is everywhere—in publications, daily conversations, in business, and on radio and television. As the Human Potential Movement gains momentum, people across the nation are striving to "Master Their Possibilities" and "Be All That They Can Be."

The Human Potential Movement (HPM) claims to provide a quick fix for a society that idolizes human control, comprehension, and expediency. Grounded in humanistic philosophy and psychology, man, not God, occupies the center of the HPM universe. The movement disregards man's sinful nature and considers the universe as self-existing rather than created. Man's emotions and feelings are exalted at the expense of intellect. Jesus, declare HPM humanists, was merely a mortal teacher, who, like Buddha before him, raised his cosmic consciousness to its full potential and became one with the universe. Salvation and divinity are achieved by raising personal consciousness. The most extreme HPM adherents, such as Werner Erhard, founder of est and The Forum, insist man can be his own god.

To attain godship and achieve full human potential, one must regain what has deteriorated through modern scientific thought, specifically, body and soul. Full human potential can be attained only with an elevated consciousness of the God-within-you, a recognition that everything in nature is God and all that exists is one. Through individual conversion to HPM ideals, a new, more harmonious world will evolve.

To achieve this transformation, several means are used. Past life regression therapy frees one from prior traumas and helps attain reunion with

251

the universe. Rebirthing, transpersonal psychotherapy, and a combination of Western self-improvement techniques and Eastern wisdom are also employed.

Conceived in the sensitivity training of the 1940s, HPM concepts of leadership training and group dynamics took on renewed popularity with the self-help movement of the 1960s. As the psychodrama of so-called "self-actualization" evolved, HPM sessions took on a more therapeutic air. By the 1970s, the Human Potential Movement was entrenched nationwide and increasingly emphasized spiritual and transpersonal experiences. Interest in Eastern religions flourished. Psychic phenomena, including the study of man's relationship to the cosmos, took on new meaning and importance.

Today the Human Potential Movement remains the base from which many New Age tenets have emerged. From its roots have sprung such well-known programs, disciplines, and groups as Life Training, est, psychosynthesis, the Esalen Institute, bioenergetics, encounter groups, Gestalt awareness, and Arica training. In all cases, participants are trained to be less analytical and judgmental and to focus on the present.

HPM training programs can be brutal. The practices of marathon sessions, strict discipline, use of buzzwords, verbal abuse, fear, and humiliation to break down an individual's personality have been compared to brainwashing. Negative thinking and past transgressions allegedly cause suffering; therefore, no mention of past failures or sins is allowed. Feelings and emotions are the means by which truth is measured so that one's psychological state becomes an example of pure awareness, once all inhibitions are removed.

The San Francisco Bay area has emerged as the movement's center. At least 25 HPM growth centers are located within the Golden Gate region. A dozen or more universities and colleges conduct related research, and scores of therapists, teachers, and clergy engage in its activities in and around San Francisco. Wherever they are found, HPM promoters charge from a basic processing fee to hundreds of dollars per session. Large donations are actively sought.

One distressing aspect of the Human Potential Movement is its blatant anti-Christian bias. While claiming to be nonreligious, its syncretic, gnostic, and pantheistic ideologies diametrically oppose Christian doctrine.

Founder: Founded partially upon tenets brought forth in the 1933 Humanist Manifesto, restated 40 years later in Human Manifesto II. Beginnings can be traced to sensitivity, leadership, and group training of the 1940s.

Texts: Writings of late psychologist Abraham Maslow and self-improvement teachers, such as Napoleon Hill. The literature of est, The Forum, the Esalen Institutue, and other Human Potential Movement centers is revered.

Symbols: Too diverse for a single representation.

Appeal: Individuals seeking warmth and security in a confusing world turn to motivational therapies to rise above the masses. Promises of control over one's life and destiny draw those who feel powerless in a bureaucratic society. The belief that man can have anything he desires appeals to self-indulgent materialists.

Purpose: HPM seminars promise to eradicate the errors of one's past and create a future of unlimited possibilities. All restraints pertaining to one's religious or social position will be ignored in favor of unlocking boundless powers dormant in each individual.

Errors: The error of Eden was the serpent's lie that man's understanding would allow him to be a god. HPM courses resurrect this falsehood with supposedly pure motives of enhancing self-esteem and improving business environments. In the process, God's sovereign will is ignored, and Christ's call to self-denial refused. A theocentric worldview is exchanged for a man-centered approach to problem solving and personal advancement.

Background Sources: William E. Biewett, Duane C. Beauchamp, Carolyn C. Fouse, and Kathryn K. Kremer, "The Human Potential Movement, est and The Life Training: A Background Paper," 14 September 1984; Ted Peters, "Discerning the Spirits of the New Age," *The Christian Century,* 31 August-7 September 1988, 763; A. J. S. Rayl, "Magical Mystery Tour," *Harper's Bazaar,* April 1988, 158; Donald Stone, "The Human Potential Movement," *The New Religious Consciousness,* 1976, 93-115.

Address/Location: North America and Western Europe.

See also Arica, Esalen, New Age Cults.

I AM

INSTITUTE

OF APPLIED

METAPHYSICS

"Take your metaphysics seriously, but take yourselves lightly." So advises Winfred Grace Barton, who in 1963 founded the I Am Institute of Applied Metaphysics. Her first book, *The Inner Power,* was published in that year. That was followed by ten additional books, including her masterwork, *I Am—The Book of Life.* From her basement classroom in Ottawa, Canada, this occult organization has grown to include campuses, facilities, and representatives on five continents and in nearly a dozen nations.

Barton says her goal is to provide a methodology for "building heaven on earth for all mankind." Like most New Age metaphysical approaches, Barton believes that an unfolding consciousness is the pathway to spiritual health and personal fulfillment. In that sense, Barton says I Am is a kind of "finishing school" to polish the jewel of life so it may reach ultimate perfection. Study courses carry the seeker of higher consciousness through a series of stages with metaphysical designations. The first is The Realization. It requires 20 hours of study. Next comes The Fulfillment. Barton refers to this as "sabbatical," when students spend a month on one of her campuses. The Fulfillment draws students deep into its teachings, which are designed to free the mind from inhibiting constraints. Next is The Opportunity, at which stage Barton believes students become "full co-creative partners in planetary transformation." During The Opportunity, I AM students are asked to commit five months of their lives, one month on an I Am campus, the next four at home, after which they become licensed affiliates and "profit-sharing participants in the establishment of the New Age."

Barton admonishes students to read her books faithfully as "the Link." Topics in her volumes include human auras, psychic phenomena, meditation, astral projection, and dream power. The cost for a single course? Around $250, including textbooks—expensive for some, but for others a small price to acquire "the super magic vibrance that fills the air."

Founder: Winfred Grace Barton, 1963, Ottawa, Canada.

Text: Promotional material from the I AM Institute of Applied Metaphysics.

Symbols: A pair of wings with an encircled human figure, arms raised in the center with the motto "I Am All in All."

Appeal: New Age seekers of wisdom who have dabbled in metaphysics are attracted by Barton's intellectual approach to the paranormal and the academic presentation of the courses.

Purpose: The I AM Institute seeks to develop a methodology by which dedicated people can change the world by changing themselves. This transformation occurs by an altered perception of reality, consistent with metaphysical explanations of being.

Errors: The I Am motto, "I Am All in All," suggests in a humanistic way that man is the center of the universe and self-sufficient. In contrast, Christianity teaches our universe is sustained by God's power alone. Man is incapable of overcoming his moral insufficiencies because of original sin. Instead of being "All in All," mankind is under the curse of Eden's sin.

Background Sources: I AM Institute of Applied Metaphysics promotional material.

Address/Location: I AM Institute of Applied Metaphysics, 3940 Hancock Street, Suite 205, San Diego, CA 92110.

See also Human Potential Movement, New Age Cults.

INTERNATIONAL COMMUNITY OF CHRIST / THE JAMILIANS

Would you be willing to believe that Christ has come again in the form of Jamil Sean Savoy, the child of Eugene Douglas Savoy, born in the United States (1959) and passed away in the Peruvian Andes in 1962? And would you also be willing to accept the fact that the miracles of Christ were performed by solar energy? If not, then this "secret community" based on "the System" as revealed by Gene Savoy is not for you. If these beliefs do seem plausible, you are welcome to enroll in The Academy and Sacred College (with a minimum pledge of $734.40 annually) to discover the esoteric, true teachings of Jesus as revealed in *The Decoded New Testament*. To begin, just fill out the "Spiritual Awareness Aptitude Test" advertised in major occult journals.

Savoy, a writer and explorer of some renown, was the grandson of a Baptist minister. At the age of six he witnessed the first of several visions and psychic experiences that led him into a study of world religions. At age 28 he came upon the teachings of the Essenes and other Middle-Eastern mystic orders. Savoy became convinced that Jesus was a mere "inspired man of God" whose most important teachings were not included in the New Testament. He concluded that Christ orally communicated a secret closed system to his followers that is only cryptically revealed in the Gospels. The time has now come to restore to the church this message that has been lost for centuries.

As a result of explorations in the Peruvian mountains, Savoy became convinced that ancient sun worship was based on the premise that all humans are actually "light-beings." By a technique of gazing at the sun, initiates of the cult are taught to absorb solar energy so they can experience a "new birth" and increase their life span by "15 to 20 percent." By "feeding upon the invisible light that is being shed through the sun," each person can become more aware of his "true nature" as a "light body." Savoy contends that "the creative energy of the universe begins in the sun." His ultimate goal is "intercommunication with some greater intelligence via the sun."

The rationale for his "co-solary" teachings lie in the assertion that his only child, Jamil, was actually a divine being who came to earth as Christ. Taking his cue from Christ's references to receiving the kingdom of God as a child (Matt. 18:3) and Isaiah's prophecy that "a little child shall lead them" (Isa. 11:6), Savoy claims Jamil is the fulfillment of these Scriptures. Jamil's purpose was to amend Christianity through his prophecies and restore its original form. Though any adept student of occult and Eastern philosophy will find nothing new in Jamil's discourses, Savoy is convinced that the child's words were divinely inspired. When Jamil died in 1962 ("returned to the World of Light," is Savoy's way of putting it), Savoy came back to the United States. In 1972 he established the Community near Reno, Nevada. The ministry went public in 1975. There are presently about 500 members worldwide.

In Savoy's scheme of theology, "Christ is a universal force to be experienced [instead of worshiped as a deity]" and "man, too, is a son of God." His writings denigrate the blood atonement and promise to "open the Book of Life." When Christ returns, he will not be a "man-savior . . . to redeem mankind, but a new spiritual Sun, unlike any sun that ever shone." Among the practices used to develop Savoy's concept of solar energy are pyramidology, dream analysis, altered states of consciousness, vision analysis, biorhythms, auras, the study of light and color bodies, and other indulgences from the world of spiritualism. The promotion of occult phenomena, along with persistent references to "light-beings," are uncomfortable reminders of the Apostle Paul's warning of 2 Corinthians 11:14 — "For Satan himself is transformed into an angel of light."

Though Savoy's religion is a false one, civic officials are not so sure it's a religion at all. In 1986, county officials revoked the tax-exempt status of the group's large land holdings outside Reno. The county apparently did not feel that the group's sun-gazing ritual or the 30 crosses scattered around the property qualified the group as a church.

Founder: Eugene Douglas Savoy, born May 11, 1927, in Bellingham, Washington.

Texts: *The Essae Document, The Decoded New Testament, The Lost Gospel of Jesus, The Jamilians* and *Jamil, the Child Christ.*

Symbol: A four-pointed cross with radiants of equal length.

Appeal: Those with a nominal Christian background and metaphysical inclinations may be fascinated by the idea that Savoy has discovered the true, hidden teachings of Jesus.

Purpose: The Community reveals the secret teachings of Christ orally communicated to his disciples and now interpreted through the writings of Savoy. These doctrines are substantiated by the "prophecies" of Savoy's late three-year-old child, Jamil.

Errors: Savoy refuses to accept the Bible as inerrant and assumes that the supernatural power of Jesus was from solar energy. Christ is a mere prophet of no greater significance than others. Jesus was a messenger, not the Redeemer.

Background Sources: Miscellaneous Community documents, advertisements, and published texts by Gene Savoy: *The Emerging New Christianity, A Confidential Prospectus,* 1975; *The Child Christ,* 1973 (all Reno, Nev.: International Community of Christ); "Dawning of a New Creation," *East/West Journal,* December 1976, 19-21; Ibid., April 1981, 7; membership solicitation letter, 19 May 1976 (signed by Gene Savoy); *East-West Journal,* March 1980, 40-49; *Project X: The Search for the Secrets of Immortality,* 1977, Gene Savoy.

Address/Location: International Community of Christ, Chancellory Building, 643 Ralston, Reno, NV 89503.

INTERNATIONAL SOCIETY OF KRISHNA CONSCIOUSNESS

(Hare Krishna)

"Get out of here! You're a demon—a fornicating meat-eater." That kind of rebuke would be harsh anywhere, let alone in a crowded airport concourse. The epithet was directed toward me for butting in on what, to that point, had been a successful attempt to con an unsuspecting tourist out of his money. He was an Israeli citizen visiting America. If I hadn't stepped in, he might never have known he was the victim of what Hare Krishna devotees call "transcendental trickery." The victim had been told he was giving his $100 traveler's check "donation" in exchange for a book about the Jewish religion.

Of all the imported cults to land on American shores in recent times, none is more ubiquitous and scorned than Hare Krishna. (The official organizational name is the International Society of Krishna Consciousness. For the sake of brevity, the rest of this analysis will use the acronym ISKCON.) Even though the saffron robes and shaven heads publicly have given way to wigs and conventional clothing, the public image of ISKCON remains negative. Members are seen as deceptive, pushy beggars who frequent public places to prey on the naive. But beneath the *dhotis* and *saris* they wear is more than a collection of societal dropouts with brainwashed minds.

Thirty percent of the devotees have spent a least a year in college, and 70 percent formerly attended church with regularity. What they found in Hare Krishna is not just an exotic system of authoritarian asceticism. The 50 percent who remain permanently with the cult claim a deeply personal relationship to their Lord similar to the devotion expressed by

259

evangelical Christians to Christ. ISKCON members are dedicated to a set of sacred scriptures and seek to surrender their lives to a supreme power. They acknowledge man's inherent desire to worship a deity beyond himself and have plunged into their belief system with total commitment. This is not to suggest that Christianity and Krishna Consciousness are in any way compatible. Far from it. An exploration of the history and nature of ISKCON readily establishes the pagan and mythological roots of this fervent faith. The worship of Lord Krishna began in the sixteenth century in Bengal, India. It was then and there that Caitanya Mahaprabu, inspired by the *Bhagavad-Gita* (one of Hinduism's sacred books), sought to revitalize a religion that had become heavy on philosophy and weak on participative devotion. Hinduism had split into two schools: those who worshiped Shiva as the greatest of the godhead (Brahma, Vishnu, Shiva), and those who considered Vishnu to be supreme. Caitanya insisted that Vishnu was actually an incarnation of Krishna (chief character of the *Gita*) and that Lord Krishna was the ultimate god. Even more revolutionary was his idea that Krishna would intimately commune with his devotees on a personal level, a foreign concept to the traditional Hindu perception of God's impersonality. This communion could be possible by the practice of exuberant chanting and dancing, known as *sankirtana*.

This concept of worshiping Krishna was revived in the early 1900s by the Indian sages Bhaktivinode Thakur and Sri Srimad Bhaktisiddhanta Saroswati Gosvami Maharaj. One of the latter's disciples was a University of Calcutta philosophy and economics major named Abhay Charan De. In 1922 Gosvami initiated Charan De into the discipline of *Bhakti Yoga* and instructed him to take the message of Krishna Consciousness to the Western world. Abhay Charan De became known as Bhaktivedanta Prabhupada ("at whose feet masters sit"). At age 58 he left his wife and five children and a prospering pharmaceutical business to pursue the life of a *swami*. In 1965 he boarded a steamer for the United States and on September 18 sailed past the Statue of Liberty with eight dollars in his pocket. At the time of his death, His Divine Grace A. C. Bhaktivedanta Swami Prabhupada was chauffeured in black limousines and could claim to his credit 40 Krishna temples and an estimated 5,000 to 10,000 followers in the United States alone.

At any other time, this 70-year-old man sitting in a Greenwich Village park and chanting strange words would have been an oddity. In the burgeoning counterculture milieu of the sixties, he was considered hip. Beat poet Allen Ginsberg, along with an array of hippie-types, gravitated to Prabhupada's message. Ex-Beatle George Harrison wrote a song extolling Krishna's virtues ("My Sweet Lord") and dedicated an entire album (*Living in the Material World*) to ISKCON belief. With the proceeds from these and other activities, Harrison bankrolled Prabhupada's efforts to evangelize. In those days Bhaktivedanta had confidently declared, "This is a prediction that in all the villages and towns of the entire world, the Krsna [his preferred spelling] Consciousness movement will be known." For a while, it looked like he might be right.

What was the message he brought? Many people have heard of the repetitive Hare Krishna chant and have witnessed devotees ecstatically dancing on urban street corners. But few understand the aim of such activity, and even fewer have any knowledge about their object of devotion, Lord Krishna. Dismissing ISKCON antics as weird and offensive is an understandable response of Westerners. What may not be apparent to the occidental mind is the complicated system of religious philosophy behind the conduct of Krishna devotees.

The religious philosophy of ISKCON is found in the *Bhagavad-Gita*, a long Hindu poem written (according to most credible scholars) sometime in the first century A.D. (not 5,000 years ago as Krishna devotees claim). The *Gita* is a virtual bible to devotees, so long as it is consulted in the form of Prabhupada's commentary, *Bhagavad-Gita as It Is*. The *Gita* is an allegorical story of a certain war. The dialogue between Krishna and the warrior Arjuna is purported to represent a conversation between deity and humanity. This exchange is said to embody the ultimate wisdom of the ages.

Arjuna bravely enters the battle until he learns that his relatives are among the opposing forces. He hesitates to fight and is understandably overwhelmed with concern for the coming death of his kinsmen. Krishna spurs him on, advising him to avoid feelings of attachment to his loved ones. This approach of detachment from earthly desires and emotions is central to Krishna's message and ISKCON's theology. *Gita As It Is* contains a picture of devotees calmly walking past the poor and suffering. The caption explains such indifference by quoting Krishna's command, "Those who are wise lament neither for the living nor the dead." Prabhupada agreed. He wrote, "Philanthropists who build hospitals and churches are wasting their time."

Such a callous rationale is nothing compared with the twist in logic necessary to justify Krishna's character. Hindu legends portray ISKCON's deity as a blue-skinned (blue symbolizes divinity in Hinduism), flute-playing prankster. He hides the clothes of girls bathing in a river and entices the wives of other men to frolic with him in the moonlight. They become so overwhelmed by his romancing that each feels as if she is the only one having intercourse with him. Though Krishna does have a favorite mistress named Radha, he also consorted with 16,108 *gopis* (women cowherds). Over a period of 125 years he fathers ten children with each of them.

Such orgiastic abandon is a far cry from the behavior demanded of present-day Krishna devotees. Their lives are carefully regimented in a fashion that eradicates the need for personal choices or decisions. Everyone rises at 3:00 A.M. for a cold shower before "awakening" the temple idols. These "deities" are then dressed and "fed." Devotees chant, count their japa beads, and head for the street to solicit funds and fill the surrounding landscape with Krishna's praises. Evenings are spent with more chanting and idol worship before an early retirement. Six hours of sleep on a hard floor is all that is between most of Krishna's disciples and another day.

Life is austere in many other ways. No alcohol, drugs, coffee, meat, fish, gambling, or conversation unrelated to Krishna devotion is allowed. Reading of magazines or newspapers is strongly discouraged. Contact with the outside world, including family and friends, is infrequent and sometimes nonexistent. Personal possessions are disposed of, leaving the devotee solely dependent on the temple for food and shelter. Children born of temple-sanctioned unions are taken from the parents to be placed in special ISKCON schools.

In fact, the marriage relationship is viewed as an inferior state for those unable to answer the higher calling to celibacy. Couples live in separate quarters, and sexual intercourse is allowable only by permission of the temple priest. At the most, conjugal relationships are restricted to one visit per month at the wife's optimum time of fertility, preferably at the time of a full moon, and only then for the purposes of childbearing, not pleasure. In addition, consummation is possible only after each partner has completed chanting 50 rounds of the Krishna mantra, a feat requiring about five hours. Finally, avoiding hand-holding and kissing, the act is performed to the accompaniment of a cassette recording of Prabhupada's voice. It should come as no surprise that one former member claims 90 percent of ISKCON marriages fail.

Obviously, the mind and body of a Krishna devotee is not his own. To signify this fact, every day each member places 13 clay markings (*tilaka*) on his body. The clay is flown in all the way from India, and these marks signify one's total servitude to Krishna. Those who stay in the cult more than six months are given a new Sanskrit name and a secret mantra. Men must shave their heads, leaving only a handful of hair (a *sikha*) by which Krishna can pull them up to heaven if he so desires. The shaved heads also remove what Prabhupada declared is the symbol of man's vanity. Bald pates are to be indicative of denying any means of sexual attraction. Women, who are said to have inferior brains and be worthy only of serving men, must adorn themselves in plain Indian *saris*. This long, loose-fitting garment is prescribed as a deterrent to arousing male passion. Such practices are central to the Krishna doctrine that all desire must be suppressed. The body is the enemy of the spirit, and only by denying it comfort and attention can one reach the high goal of intimacy with Krishna.

Prabhupada expounded a strict, fundamentalist form of Hindu philosophy. In essence his main goal was to help disciples liberate their pure souls from the spiritually inferior nature of their bodies. "I am not this body," devotees are fond of saying. What they mean is that all matter is *maya* (illusory and transient), and only the spirit is worthy of eternal attention. Man's primary dilemma in life is his ignorance of the Krishna god-nature of his spirit. This unfortunate state has been caused by the bondage resulting from the spirit's encasement in flesh. The only merit of having a human body at all is the alternative of having been incarnated in a lower animal form. At least having a human body means one's previous incarnation must have exuded good karma.

How does one escape the confines of the sensory temptations of flesh and blood? ISKCON teaches that the way of salvation can be shown only by a guru whose spiritual succession is legitimate. Prabhupada lays claim to such a lineage, insisting he is the spiritual heir of Caitanya (mentioned earlier) who was Krishna's incarnation for this present age. (Some devotees believe that Prabhupada was himself an incarnation of Krishna and thus greater than Christ.) Prabhupada taught that liberation of the soul in this age, called *kali-yuga* ("the dark age"), is possible only by *kirtana:* reciting the Hare Krishna chant. The devotee who does this is freed from *samsara* (endless cycles of reincarnation) and begins his pilgrimage "back to the Godhead."

One must admire the zealous success of Krishna devotees. Their relatively few numbers have managed to familiarize the public consciousness with their 16-word chant: "Hare Krishna, Hare Krishna / Krishna, Krishna, Hare, Hare / Hare Rama, Hare Rama / Rama, Rama, Hare, Hare." Even though it is brief, amazing powers are claimed for the mere utterances of this *maha* ("great") mantra. Accompanied by the "transcendental sound vibrations" of drums and finger cymbals, these words are said to embody Krishna himself. (*Rama* is an alternate name for Krishna and *Hare* expresses his creative energy.)

Devotees often do the chant in correspondence with each of the 108 japa beads on the "rosary" kept in a bag hanging around their necks. They may repeat the entire cycle as many as 16 times a day. It is of no concern to the chanters that the curious observers who watch them during public displays may mock or listen with disinterest. Prabhupada told them that "there is no need to understand the language of the mantra." Anyone who hears it will be automatically affected by Krishna's name. For a similar reason, ISKCON's own "spiritual sky" incense is often burned during chanting to provide an aroma in which Krishna may dwell. Devotees believe that those who smell it will literally inhale Krishna. And there's more to chanting than that silly, blissful smile on the face of devotees. They are promised by His Divine Grace that eventually they may experience hair standing up on their bodies, dislocation of the voice, crying in ecstasy, and going into trance states.

The result of this form of suggestive hypnotism is that the participant may enter a condition that would facilitate control by demonic possession. At the very least, such an enforced method of divorcing the mind from reality can turn devotees into robots who will act blindly in response to whatever they perceive to be Krishna's will. The potential misuse of such exaggerated devotion should cause alarm to those initiates who are just beginning the pathway of temple service.

The Hare Krishna chant is essentially an invocation to the pantheon of Hindu deities. Such paganism is also evident in a variety of temple duties and rites. Krishna is believed to be resident in the metal and wood idols maintained in ISKCON facilities. These statues are offered food six times a day, which is later eaten by devotees (an act called *prasada*) as a way of actually ingesting Krishna. (This ritual is a kind of Hare Krishna eucharist.) When water is used to bathe the deities, it is collected for the disciples to drink. A sample of the Indian *Tulasi Devi* plant is kept in each temple as an object of worship to eradicate sin and disease.

In spite of all this, Prabhupada declared his religious system is not idolatrous. To him, idolatry was the "worship of a material *form* of God." He insisted that in Hare Krishna the devotee is not worshiping a *form* of God. "The form *is* God," Prabhupada declared. In Krishna's case, "There is no difference between the form of the Lord and the Lord himself." Whatever the excuse, such practices are inconsistent with Exodus 20:4-5.

But accusations of idolatry are mild aberrations to defend compared with more recent charges leveled at ISKCON. Since the passing of Prabhupada, the organization has faced accusations of drug-smuggling, firearms-hoarding, suicides, murder, and outright thievery. The solicitation methods directed toward nonbelievers (*karmi*) have fostered court investigation of tactics including shortchanging donors, participating in false pretense, and even using experienced thieves to train devotees on how to lift wallets. Critics suggest that such sources of income enabled the cult to erect its elaborate onyx, teakwood, ebony, marble, and gold-adorned temple at its center in the West Virginia hills. This center, called New Vrindaban, is the largest of about 300 centers worldwide.

Prabhupada died of heart failure in 1977, leaving few instructions on who should lead ISKCON or just how it should be run. Consequently, leadership passed on to eleven gurus, each with his own geographical jurisdiction. These gurus divided up the world, competing for members and money. Disillusioned devotees began to leave. Today ISKCON claims a membership of 3 million, 1 million of whom are in the United States. Only about 10,000 hardcore members remain. A governing body was established, which excommunicated six of the eleven gurus between 1982 and 1987 for reasons such as seduction, violent behavior, homosexuality, and drug abuse.

Other troubles have plagued ISKCON. In 1983 a California jury leveled a $32 million judgment against the organization for kidnapping and brainwashing a 15-year-old girl and actions that led to the death by heart failure of her father. Though the judge reduced the actual payment to $9.7 million, it was at the time the largest award against a cult. Critics charged that the Krishnas set up large companies to launder illegal money. It was discovered that New Vrindaban disciples were stockpiling weapons. A New Vrindaban devotee was convicted of murdering a fellow Krishnaite, whom he shot, stabbed, and bludgeoned to death in 1983. Other Krishna followers have mysteriously disappeared.

ISKCON still defends its fund-raising policies by insisting that even deceptive tactics serve a useful purpose. The *karmi* who is unwittingly separated from his money partakes in his own salvation by giving to Krishna. Thus, the solicitor has actually favored the donor by enticing him to give back to Krishna what really belonged to him in the first place.

Some of the practices offensive to non-Krishnaites are being modified. In the future, members will not necessarily need to forsake everything and move into the temple, so long as they maintain a vegetarian diet and construct an altar in their home. Health food stores and society-owned farms will channel energies that may result in less public chanting exercises. And other religious viewpoints may be viewed a little more tolerably. Krishna is reported to have said, "There is no truth superior to me." What he will think of such liberalization is anyone's guess. What is certain is that after 100 million books distributed (plus 500,000 copies per month of the periodical *Back to the Godhead*), the innocence of those flower-power days is gone. Hare Krishna faces a more skeptical world where promises of ecstasy by chanting will no longer keep either the coffers or membership rolls filled.

Founder: His Divine Grace, A. C. Bhaktivedanta Swami Prabhupada, born Calcutta, India, September 1, 1896, as Abhay Char De. Died of heart failure November 14, 1977.

Text: The Hindu sacred texts, especially *The Bhagavad-Gita* according to Prabhupada's interpretation.

Symbols: Traditional Indian-style devotional paintings of gods and demigods, especially Lord Krishna as the Supreme Personality of the Godhead driving the chariot of Arjuna.

Appeal: Youth in the sixties were ripe for exotic, simplistic answers to questions unfulfilled by technological advances. Even today, those frustrated by the vanity of materialism may resort to a system that totally rejects all pleasure from sensory gratification. The authoritarian structure of temple life may fill a need for the disciplinary life-style being sought by some victims of this permissive age.

Purpose: ISKCON offers a highly religious life with dedication and the fellowship of like-minded adherents. All rituals and devotions are designed to free man from the ignorance of having forgotten his true personal relationship with Lord Krishna. This can be accomplished only by freeing the spiritual body from the physical body. Chanting Hare Krishna bypasses the intellect to cleanse the mind and heart of their false concept of concern for the material world.

Errors: The entire religious system of ISKCON is built upon mythological scriptures of legendary events and people (including Krishna). There is no sin to be saved from, there is only the illusion of evil to be eradicated. Jesus warned in Matthew 6:7 that "vain repetition" was a fruitless form of prayer. According to 1 Corinthians 8:6, there is but one Lord, Christ, and not Krishna. Jesus died of his own choice and rose from the dead. Krishna expired from an arrow in his foot and failed to conquer death.

Background Sources: Bhaktivedanta Prabhupada, *The Nectar of Devotion* (Los Angeles: Bhaktivedanta Book Trust, 1970); Bhaktivedanta Prabhupada, *The King of Knowledge* (Los Angeles: Bhaktivedanta Book Trust, 1973); Bhaktivedanta Prabhupada, *Bhagavad-Gita As It Is* (Los Angeles: Bhaktivedanta Book Trust, 1975); ISKCON Pamphlet, "On Chanting Hare Krishna"; various issues of ISKCON periodical *Back to the Godhead,* especially vol. 10, no. 7; *The Denver Post,* 11 July 1975, 3BB; Ibid., 15 April 1977, 4BB; Ibid., 26 August 1977, 2BB; Ibid., 17 March 1978, 1BB; Ibid., 6 March 1981, 5BB; Ibid., 29 May 1981, 1BB; *Newsweek,* 27 December 1976, 26; Ibid., 30 January 1978, 57; Ibid., 29 September 1980, 83; *Circus,* 28 February 1977, 48; *Life,* April 1980, 44-51; *Time,* 15 September 1980, 71; Pat Means, *The Mystical Maze* (San Bernardino, Calif.: Campus Crusade for Christ, 1976); Jack Sparks, *The Mind Benders* (Nashville: Thomas Nelson, 1977); Kenneth Boa, *Cults, World Religions and You* (Wheaton, Ill.: Victor, 1980); J. Isamu Yamamoto, *Hare Krishna, Hare Krishna* (Downers Grove, Ill.: Inter-Varsity, 1978); *Forward,* vol. 4, no. 1; R. E. Schecter, "$32 Million Judgment Against Krishna," *The Advisor,* August-September 1983; "One Generation of Hare Krishna," *SDP,* 22 March 1987, 10A; John Hubner and Lindsay Gruson, "Dial Om for Murder," *Rolling Stone,* 9 April 1987, 53; Sue Lindsay, "Krishna Devotee Linked to Crimes," *The Rocky Mountain News,* 5 February 1989, 8.

Address/Location: International Society for Krishna Consciousness, 3764 Watseka Avenue, Los Angeles, CA 90034.

JEHOVAH'S
WITNESSES

She died on her sixth birthday. She could have lived. A blood transfusion would have saved the life of Ricarda Bradford, who was critically injured in a car accident. But her father, a chiropractor and devout Jehovah's Witness, refused the life-giving procedure. He quoted Genesis 9:3-4 and Leviticus 17:10-15, explaining that Witnesses consider taking blood in the veins to be the same as eating it.

Refusing to accept blood transfusions is just one of several distinctive beliefs associated with Jehovah's Witnesses. They do not donate vital organs or receive transplants. Until 1952, they refused smallpox vaccinations. They also refuse to vote, salute the flag, sing "The Star Spangled Banner" (or any nationalistic anthem), and will not serve in the armed forces.

In 1879 a Bible study leader named Charles Taze Russell was looking for a way to expound his somewhat peculiar teachings. He had departed from orthodoxy by denying the existence of hell, the Trinity, and the deity of Christ, and felt compelled to reach a larger audience. He copublished *The Herald of the Morning* magazine with its founder, N. H. Barbour, and it is here that we find the first records of Russell's movement. By 1884 Russell controlled the publication, renamed it *The Watch Tower Announcing Jehovah's Kingdom,* and founded Zion's Watch Tower Tract Society (now known as the Watch Tower Bible and Tract Society). The first edition of *The Watch Tower* magazine was only 6,000 copies each month. Today the Witnesses' publishing complex in Brooklyn, New York, churns out 100,000 books and 800,000 copies of its two magazines – daily! Russell's theology established the foundation for the Witnesses' militant opposition to all other church organizations. Until his death in 1916 aboard a train in Texas, Russell insisted that the Bible could be understood only according to his interpretation. At the heart of his system was a prophetical chronology that predicted the Gentile era would end in 1914. (Russell had already concluded that Christ had returned in 1874, but as a "presence in the upper air," not a visible manifestation.) The end of the sealing of the 144,000 saints who would be "kings and priests in heaven" was also designated to occur in 1914. Those saved after that would belong to a servant class, "the great company," who would rule on earth under the tutelage of the 144,000. In these early days, abstention and strict doctrinal discipline were not mandated.

After the death of Russell, a Missouri lawyer named Joseph Franklin Rutherford took over the presidency of the Watch Tower Society. At a Columbus, Ohio, convention in 1931, he cited Isaiah 43:10 as the pretext for changing the name of the organization to "Jehovah's Witnesses." Thus, the stigma of Russell's questionable scholarship (he had only a seventh-grade education) and morals was resolved. Rutherford assumed total charge of the organization, and from then on his prolific writings were the source of divine mandate. This consolidation of power enabled him to discard some of Russell's less desirable teachings about the gathering of the Jews and the great pyramid theory.

After Rutherford's death, Nathan Knorr took over. In the same way that Rutherford had sought to supplant Russell's influence, Knorr ignored the works of Rutherford. Today, the Society is led by Frederick William Franz, now in his eighties, who wields papal power over the lives of Witnesses all over the world. The Society has evolved into a two-class system where governors maintain strict control over believers' lives and thoughts.

The pronouncements that issue forth from the Brooklyn headquarters (known to members as Bethel) are binding, and no deviation is tolerated. Witnesses who depart from such injunctions are "disfellowshiped" (their term for excommunication). From then on, Kingdom Hall worshipers (even family members) consider them as dead and are forbidden to speak with them. The excommunicated "apostate" is told he will not rise from the grave on Judgment Day. Many former Witnesses have revealed that in the early 1980s grounds for this shunning increased to include reading books written by ex-members, eating with suspected dissenters, and even, for some women, wearing pantsuits.

Strict theological control insures a consistency of doctrine. Witnesses avoid contact with outsiders, and the rare chance to meet one usually occurs when they knock on the door. Society statistics indicate that 740 house calls are required to recruit *each* of the nearly 200,000 new members who join every year. During the 1970s the Society grew 45 percent worldwide; in 1985 alone members spent 590,540,205 hours in missionary outreach worldwide.

Never identifying themselves, these friendly but persistent zealots deserve high marks for perseverance. The first thing to notice once they're inside the front door is that they do bring a Bible, *The New World Translation*—their especially prepared version. Its translators are anonymous, so neither credentials nor their manuscript sources can be checked. But astute students of the Word will readily notice that the Society's theological stance is enhanced by significant changes from the Authorized Version.

Debating a Witness requires skill and a thorough knowledge of Bible doctrines. They have been taught that all other beliefs are satanic and have been programmed with stock answers for questions that are often raised. Even if they don't know an answer, they're confident that their leaders back at the Kingdom Hall will provide the correct response. Evangelical Christians need to be aware of Witness beliefs so that a clever choice of words doesn't disguise their extremely unorthodox doctrine. The following paragraph points out some of their more controversial views.

To begin with, the Trinity is seen as a demonic doctrine. The Holy Spirit is robbed of his personality, and Jesus is stripped of his deity. Their *Translation* renders John 1:1 "the Word was *a* god," introducing the Witness belief that Christ, the Archangel Michael, was created by Jehovah. The appearance of Jesus on earth was not an incarnation but an example of human perfection in response to Jehovah's moral law. Witnesses do not consider Christ to be Eternal God, the Creator of the universe, and our Great High Priest as declared in Hebrews 4:15 and Colossians 2:9-10. Each year around March, Jehovah's Witnesses hold a "Memorial" service, which all members and potential members are expected to attend. This occasion commemorates Jesus' sacrifice, which began the covenant between the 144,000 and Jehovah. While it is similar to the biblical ordinance of Communion, only a few Witnesses partake of the meal. The Memorial is considered merely symbolic. No spiritual significance is attached to the event. Even October 2, their estimated date of Christ's birth, is largely ignored. (The only birthday the Witnesses acknowledge is that of the Watch Tower Bible and Tract Society, which celebrated its hundredth anniversary in 1984.)

Other Jehovah's Witness doctrines that may be encountered are soul-sleep and the annihilation of the wicked (along with Satan and his demons). They deny the existence of a soul that can exist apart from the body. To Witnesses, the soul is just the life-animating force that gives life to a material body. When a human being dies, his soul ceases to exist and his body ultimately deteriorates. There is no hell since there is no conscious existence after death. Hell, for the Watch Tower, is the grave. Faithful Witnesses hope one day to be recreated (resurrected) from Jehovah's memory. Those destined for resurrection will inhabit either paradise, earth (the large earthly class), or heaven (the elite spiritual class, the 144,000 of Revelation 7 and 14). The earthly class will live as they have here with a body and life-animating force (soul). The heavenly class will "give up" any right to a resurrected body and will live as spirits, as they believe Jesus did after his "recreation" or spirit resurrection.

Witnesses make much of their devotion to Jehovah and eschew any reference to God by another name. Ironically, respected Greek and Hebrew scholars tell us that the word *Jehovah* is nonexistent in the original Scriptures, no matter how many times it appears in *The New World Translation*. (No one is exactly sure how the Hebrew consonants referring to God—*YHWH*—were pronounced. Probably it was "Yahweh." The word *Jehovah* did not appear until William Tyndale's English translation of the Bible in the 1500s.) There is no sufficient proof that any designation other than Jehovah is a deliberate distortion of God's name. The greatest challenge to Watch Tower Society doctrine is the fact that the Bible presents Jesus as God incarnate, a fatal blow to their entire belief system.

But one need not be a Hebrew scholar to be aware of the most glaring inconsistency in the teachings of Jehovah's Witnesses. A brief study of the Society's history shows a confused view of the end times as indicated by their record of erroneous dates for Christ's return. The world's end has been prophesied for 1914, 1918, 1920, 1925, 1941, and 1975. Since Adam's creation was presumed to occur in 4026 B.C., Witnesses taught that 6,000 years of human history would end in A.D. 1975. When the date passed, thousands of disillusioned members left the sect. But President Franz had an explanation ready. The 6,000-year chronology was set forward to begin with Eve's creation, and how long that occurred after Adam's advent is an interval not yet revealed by Witness leaders.

Still, members believe the end can't be far off, and in fact the society has mathematical reasons to delay Armageddon only until the early

2000s. They have been told that the war of Armageddon will be waged, and the Millennium must dawn before all of the 144,000 "anointed class" from 1914 have died. Less than 10,000 of the "anointed" are left, and some younger Witness members, anxious for the start of the Millennium, believe that Michael Jackson, the society's most well-known former member, is actually the Archangel Michael.

Founder: Charles Taze Russell, born 1852 in Pittsburgh, Pennsylvania. Died 1916.

Text: Isaiah 43:10 — "Ye are my witnesses. . . ."

Symbol: The ubiquitous castle-shaped watch tower that appears on almost all their literature.

Appeal: Those with an apocalyptic mentality may be enticed by the zealous desire of Witnesses who want to evangelize all the world before the end. Some not well-versed in Scripture may be attracted by what seem to be logical and reasonable explanations for hard-to-explain doctrines, such as the Trinity and the eternal punishment of the wicked.

Purposes: To usher in the Kingdom Age of the Millennium and join Jehovah's forces, who will triumph at Armageddon. Only faithful Witnesses will survive the battle. Since the 144,000 already sealed will remain in heaven with Christ, most current-day Witnesses look forward to living eternally on a perfected earth.

Errors: Faulty biblical scholarship and out-of-context interpretations allow Witnesses to discard most orthodox doctrines. The 144,000 cited in John's Revelation obviously refer to 12,000 Jews out of each tribe of Israel, not a sealed company of heavenly "spirit brothers," as Witnesses contend. The death of Christ is not seen as a ransom for sin but rather as the procurement of a second chance to be offered in the Millennium.

Background Sources: Kenneth Boa, *Cults, World Religions, and You* (Wheaton, Ill.: Victor, 1977); Walter Martin, *The Kingdom of the Cults* (Minneapolis: Bethany, 1977); Watch Tower Society, *The Truth That Leads to Eternal Life; The Denver Post,* 10 June 1977; *Time,* 11 July 1977, 64-65; *Christianity Today,* 12 December 1980, 60-71; Kenneth Woodard, "Witness for the Millennium," *Newsweek,* 15 October 1984; "Watch

Tower World View," *Christianity Today,* 22 November 1985, 43; Walter Martin, "Jehovah's Witnesses," *The Insider,* March 1986; Ruth Tucker, "Nonorthodox Sects Report," *Christianity Today,* 13 June 1986, 48.

Address/Location: Watch Tower Society, 117 Adams Street, Brooklyn, NY 11201.

K I R P A L   L I G H T   S A T S A N G ,   I N C .

The organization is noted for its belief that one spiritual master (*avatar*) exists in the world at all times and that, by following him, devotees can burn away past karma. Its advocates are vegetarians who meditate three hours daily and regularly practice introspection. Kirpal Light Satsang members are forbidden to participate in political campaigns and must pledge total obedience to their master.

Literature of Kirpal Light Satsang describes its organization as primarily service-oriented. According to the organization's founder, Sant Thakar Singh, the cult services the self/soul as well as the body/vehicle. Singh stresses, "Any service to the body which is not accompanied by service to the soul is of no use."

Initiation into the group is free, and the organization professes to be funded by private donations from members only. Thakar Singh tells his followers they must not believe in him until they verify the truth of what he says. He insists, "If you follow blindly, there is a 99 percent chance you may be led astray because you have only blind faith, which leads to blindness."

But Singh followers are blind if they believe his claim that he needs no money and lives off his own retirement pension. He and his organization plan to build a $1 million school in Oregon. In contrast, Thakar Singh says his wealth will accumulate in his spiritual believers when he dies, not in material things.

Sant Thakar Singh travels around the world each year claiming he has no followers, only cherished brothers and sisters. He says he serves people and lives with them in harmony and in faith of God. To Thakar Singh, success is achieved through the amount of service and love he teaches his cult members to give to each other. He believes this is a basic necessity and the "greatest service we can do for humanity."

Kirpal Light Satsang was founded by Sant Thakar Singh in 1976. The organization sells itself as a spiritual and social group dedicated to helping others. The organization's headquarters is in Kinderhook, New York. Satsangs, or spiritual centers, are located throughout the country.

There are approximately 2,000 active Kirpal Light Satsang members in the United States. The national organization is operated by a board of directors and chaired by the U.S. national representative. The organization claims 130,000 members worldwide, with branches in 16 countries.

Sant Thakar Singh was born in 1929, the only child of a devoutly religious Sikh family. His father, a rural blacksmith and carpenter, died when Thakar was eleven years old. Thakar worked to support his family and finish his education. He gained admittance to an engineering school and worked as an engineer with the Irrigation Department of the Punjabi government.

Thakar Singh searched for truth and the perfect religion throughout his youth. His life was changed by Sant Kirpal Singh, a reputed Indian guru, whom he met in 1965. Born in India in 1894, Sant Kirpal Singh was considered a leading spiritual figure of India during his lifetime. He was an avid religious scholar and wrote numerous books on spirituality. Sant Kirpal's master, Baba Sawan Singh, died in 1948, at which point Sant Kirpal became successor to a long line of spiritual masters. Sant Thakar Singh eventually followed in his footsteps.

In the 27 years that followed Baba Sawan Singh's death, Sant Kirpal Singh organized and presided over the World Fellowship of Religions and sponsored the first World Conference on the Unity of Man. Sant Kirpal has traveled to more than 50 countries, talked with Pope Paul VI, met with royalty, diplomats, and high government officials.

After days of questioning Sant Kirpal Singh about truth and religion, Thakar was initiated into Surate Shabd Yoga (the meditation of the Inner Light and South Current, which the group considers the Word of the Bible). Before he was initiated, Sant Thakar struggled spiritually because his Sikh religion taught that Guru Gobind Singh was the last master and there could be no other living master on earth. But once he accepted Sant Kirpal Singh's beliefs, Sant Thakar quickly advanced as a student of Surat Shabd Yoga. He practiced spiritual meditation six hours daily.

In 1974 he retired from the government of India to devote himself to the task assigned by his master, Sant Kirpal Singh. Sant Thakar Singh explains, "I was given this Mission by him: to carry on and share this help with other needy souls. It is by his orders and by the Will of God I am going on. These are his powers working. I am only being used as an instrument."

Sant Thakar Singh believes he accepted the "mission" from Sant Kirpal Singh because he had yearned to find God in previous lives. By establishing a cult based on the teachings of Sant Kirpal Singh, Sant Thakar Singh feels he found God. He teaches from the Bible in Western countries. When in the East, he teaches from the Hindu scriptures, such as the *Vedas* and *Adi Granth,* the *Mahabharata* (which includes the well-known *Bhagavad-Gita*) and the *Ramayana.*

Sant Thakar Singh acquired from Sant Kirpal Singh the concept of the Manav Kendra of Man-Center. For Kirpal Light Satsang members, Manav Kendra services humanity. These man-centers offer free food, retirement homes, and free spiritual schools for orphaned children or those with poor parents. Handicapped people are also helped, and medical assistance is available through the man-centers. They also serve as an altruistic trap for spiritually searching individuals.

Kirpal Light Satsang claims to be a worldwide spiritual and social service organization expanding to Western countries. Members come from all walks of life, but must possess idolatrous devotion to their master and tolerance for his frequent and harsh discipline. Advocates are not asked to abandon their religions, but must practice daily the ideals expressed in the scriptures of all the world's religions. Meditation, vegetarianism, and introspection are basic tenets of the cult.

Spiritual risk permeates Kirpal Light Satsang practices. Initiation, or the reconnection of the soul to its God-Source, is taught through Surate Shabd Yoga (literally, the practice of light and sound), the meditation practice of the organization. Kirpal Light Satsang enthusiasts believe light and sound can be awakened within every human being through initiation. Meditation is single-minded attention on that highest entity—God—which is to be seen, heard, and enjoyed. Meditators are supposed to feel the blissful and peaceful "inner music of God." Initiation usually takes about two hours at the aspirant's home or at the Satsang Center. During initiation, the master "burns away" the seeker's past karma, which has "accumulated for ages," so the soul can be as new. Through daily practice of introspection, the student can realize and see for himself that God resides in his own soul.

For some, Kirpal Light Satsang meditation is not peaceful. Six former female disciples of Thakar Singh have publicly accused the guru of physical and sexual abuse. One woman described a 45-minute session of beatings, including karate chops to her head, as an exercise the guru inflicted to free her of negative emotions. Other women have complained of sexual assault committed under the semblance of meditation massages.

Initiates into Kirpal Light Satsang are staunchly disciplined. Members must become vegetarians, since meat, fish, fowl, and eggs are considered bad for the body and the soul. Kirpal Light Satsang seekers are also expected to be ethical and honest, with an unwavering devotion to their master. They must meditate at least three hours daily and abstain from intoxicating drugs. Receiving the holy initiation does not signify joining any group or membership.

The charter of Kirpal Light Satsang, Inc., also forbids its members to participate in or interfere with political campaigns or legislature. Members may not own any kind of business in the name of the organization, which stresses that it is not a political or money-making group. Its sole function is to encourage people to attain God-realization.

The organization has a monthly magazine called *SAT,* which means truth, obtained by writing to the national headquarters address. Sant Thakar Singh calls Kirpal Light Satsang a universal religion of love and service and wants to build a school in Oregon to have his concept carried on by younger generations.

The Lighthouse School has been the center of much controversy. The $1 million boarding school is to be constructed near Umpqua, Oregon, but issues of fire danger, water quality, and traffic control have been raised by critics. Oregon citizens remember Guru Bhagwan Shree Rajneesh and his immigration fraud, attempted murder, and wiretapping. Thakar Sing is also a God-realized guru, causing fear about any unknown agenda the group might have.

The Lighthouse School would be owned and operated by Kirpal Light Satsang, Inc., as a moral education school. It would teach that "all mankind is one" and stress full development of body and mind. The school would accommodate parents who want children otherwise exposed to violence, drugs, and other immoral behavior to learn occupational skills and standard academics in a harmonious setting.

The initial expected enrollment of the Lighthouse School is 32 students, increasing to 80 over five to six years. The children would be from ages four to twelve. Meditation and Bible study would be taught to "those who want it." Impressionable children would be taught the ways of the cult at a very young age. The school would be funded through donations by members and nonmembers, as well as by a sliding scale tuition.

Founder: Sant Thakar Singh, born in 1929 in India of a pious Sikh family and educated as an engineer. He was inspired by his guru, Sant Kirpal Sing (1894-1974).

Text: Monthly magazine *SAT,* which means "truth." The magazine may be obtained by writing to the national headquarters address.

Symbols: Lighthouse on Kirpal Light Satsang stationery. Slogan—"The masters come to fulfill existing religions, not create new ones." Also, "All mankind is one."

Appeal: Kirpal Light Satsang appeals to the altruistic, as well as to parents who feel society destroys the values they try to instill in their children. The emphasis on service to others contrasts with the obvious self-centeredness of most Hindu cults.

Purpose: The purpose of Kirpal Light Satsang is to help others and to attain God-realization within oneself. The organization teaches its followers not to surrender personal religions but to connect with all humanity through universal love and brotherhood.

Errors: Kirpal Light Satsang conflicts with Christianity and the Bible. Christians believe Jesus Christ was God's only begotten Son, that he was the world's only Savior. In contrast, Sant Thakar Singh (founder of Kirpal Light Satsang) says, "I think the Christians have not read all the other Scriptures. They are not wrong in saying Christ was the only begotten Son of Lord God, but as he himself said, 'As long as I am in the world, I am the Light of the world.' He was the Light of Life as long as he was in the world." Sant Thakar Singh claims that since Jesus is no longer in the world, someone else (himself) must be the new master and the present light. The cult exalts itself and its leader, not Christ or God. Kirpal Light Satsang is a dangerous cult that misinterprets the Bible and throws in Eastern philosophies and beliefs. Sant Thakar Singh manipulates his disciples spiritually and stands accused of assaulting some of them physically and sexually.

Background Sources: Kirpal Light Satsang, Inc. and the Lighthouse School brochure, 1 March 1988; publicity cover letter by Michael Robinson, 1 March 1988; biographical history cover letter with material, 1 March 1988; excerpts from interviews with Sant Thakar Singh; cover letter with material, 1 March 1988; *The Register-Guard*, 31 July 1988; Ibid., 2 August 1988, 1B.

Address/Location: Kirpal Light Satsang, Inc. National Headquarters, Merwin Lake Road, Kinderhook, NY 12106, (518) 758-1906; (Contact Mrs. Joanie Soloman, U.S. National Representative); Kirpal Light Satsang, Inc., Lighthouse School, 7637 Tyee Road Umpqua, OR 97486, (503) 459-1181.

KRISHNAMURTI
FOUNDATION
OF AMERICA

Annie Besant, a guiding force behind the Theosophical Society, believed him to be an incarnation of God, the divine spirit in human form. A periodical, *Herald of the Star*, was printed and an organization was formed — Order of the Star of the East — to announce his appearance to the world. Unfortunately for Annie and more than 100,000 members of the Order, Jiddu Krishnamurti wasn't interested in being worshiped. He repudiated the ideas of his followers and commenced to travel the world, proclaiming his philosophy that mankind's crises are psychological in nature. Though he was born the son of a devout Brahman, Krishnamurti declared, "Discard all theologies and all beliefs." Krishnamurti believed that all problems could be solved when human beings achieved a "right relationship with each other."

The Krishnamurti Foundation was not started by Jiddu Krishnamurti himself. Annie Besant, then president of the Theosophical Society, spotted the young teenager playing on a beach in southern India. Attracted by his "aura," she adopted Jiddu and raised him in Europe, all the while grooming him for the role she had in mind. Besant, with other Theosophists, believed in a high entity called Lord Maitreya. She believed Maitreya had come to earth as Buddha and as Christ and would now manifest in Krishnamurti. In 1911 she founded The Order of the Star, with Jiddu as World Teacher.

At first he accepted the situation, but in 1929 he dissolved the order, declaring that he was not the Messiah, was not divine, was not even a spiritual leader. Eventually he reconciled with Besant and the Theosophical Society. He spent the rest of his life traveling between England, India, and California. California was the site of his meditation and retreat center in Ojai.

Krishnamurti's most consistent teaching was that there is no path to truth. Man cannot reach it through creeds, doctrines, organizations, or knowledge. He stated over and over again that he believed in nothing. He encouraged those who looked to him for spiritual wisdom to "look within for the incorruptibility of self."

Even as an aged "non-guru" who disdained devotees, he continued to draw large audiences in the seventies composed mostly of young people anxious to observe a mystic of "elevated consciousness." Until his death in 1986 at age 90 he traveled less frequently than when he was younger but still conducted several world tours each year. His trips to the United States were often sponsored by New Age consciousness groups.

Theosophists have not rejected him entirely; they carry his writings in their bookstores. In *The New Religions,* Jacob Needleman observed, "Many people still think of him as the World Teacher, even when he tells them to their faces that there is no such thing as spiritual authority and that he is not anyone's teacher. American students, who do not know his background and reputation, often hear his talks mainly as a profound expression of their own disgust with society, its hypocrisy, its ideas of national honor, duty, race and class, its bourgeois ideals and morality."

Background Sources: Karin Stephan, "The Man Who Would Not Play God—The Life of Jiddu Krishnamurti," *East West Journal,* July 1983, 36-39; Catherine Ingram and Leonard Jacobs, "I Don't Believe in Anything," *East West Journal,* July 1983, 34-40; Harriet Shapiro, "Picks and Pans," *People,* December 1985; Gretchen Passantino, ed., "Jiddu Krishnamurti Dies at 90," *CRI,* 1986; "Milestones," *Time,* 3 March 1986, 79; *Time,* 7 June 1971, 4; *The Denver Post,* 1BB, 23 July 1976; Jacob Needleman, *The New Religions,* (New York: Dutton, 1970), 154.

See also Theosophy.

KU KLUX KLAN

It was no ordinary picnic. White-robed figures mingled in the Alabama countryside with mothers and children, teenagers, and college students. People clustered around a hot dog stand. A man in a booth sold bumper stickers, belts, wallets, knives—all marked KKK. Later, hooded Ku Klux Klansmen solemnly lit torches. At their leader's command, the disguised men tossed their blazing torches at the foot of a large wooden cross. Flames shot upward and to each side of the cross. A man nearby exclaimed proudly to his small daughter, "That's white power!" An attending Klansman attested, "We don't burn crosses, we light them!"

The KKK insists it is a Christian organization and that torching a cross is a "religious celebration and ceremony . . . [not] an act of desecration." Many members use the Klan as a church substitute, citing the fellowship and support as reasons for joining. Its elitist tenets demand that prospective members be white, non-Jewish American citizens, who favor a white government and racial separation. The Klan also targets homosexuals for harassment and physical violence, but it has changed its attitude toward Catholics and now accepts them as members.

The Ku Klux Klan (from the Greek *kuklos,* meaning circle or wheel) grew out of the Civil War. Alarmed at the changing social scene in the South—blacks were no longer slaves, and the unscrupulous Northerners known as carpetbaggers moved into the South, taking advantage of the defeated Confederates—many ex-Confederate soldiers and sympathizers formed the KKK out of desperation. It was natural that in the changed South, with former slaves and sneering Northerners wielding political and social muscle, white Southerners would react in some way. But the Klan didn't become a serious social force until the movie *Birth of a Nation* was released in 1915. The film so romanticized the KKK and encouraged racial prejudice that, by the 1920s, the Klan counted nearly 5 million members. For the next half century, it enjoyed a heyday that included substantial political influence, listing several senators and governors among its members. Throughout much of this century the Klan was a respectable—albeit secret—fraternal organization in many areas, and hooded Klansmen often marched en masse in civic parades, reminding both white and non-white onlookers that white supremacy was still a cherished concept.

The KKK states its primary goal is to protect and preserve the white race and ensure voluntary separation of the races. Its violent history has included lynchings, murders, and bombings. In the late 1970s, 125 Klansmen wielding ax handles and guns clashed with a hundred black protesters in Decatur, Alabama. After the brutal brawl ended, the state prosecuted only one participant on a felony conviction: a black man who shot a robed Ku Klux Klansman. During the sixties and seventies, many Klansmen went underground or quit the KKK because of internal splits and rivalry.

A young minister who recently refused to allow Klan recruitment in his Cambridge, Massachusetts, church was warned that he had only two weeks to live and would be shot in the pulpit. A large butcher knife was plunged into the upholstered backrest of his desk chair with a note that read, "You will be dead." Lydia Jackson, president of Harvard University's Black Students Association, was threatened by the KKK with rape if she didn't "stop creating trouble and making noise on campus."

According to *Klanwatch*, a publication that monitors KKK activities, combined national membership of 25 public Klan groups in 1984 numbered fewer than 10,000. *Klanwatch* stated that virtually all the groups claim their "Christian calling" is to separate or eradicate all minority races. A former Grand Wizard of the White Knights of America Klan said, that 'minorities were placed here by Satan to overthrow."

KKK leaders arbitrarily interpret various biblical passages to support their prejudices and to Christianize their viewpoints. One prevalent view is that Eve had sexual intercourse with Satan and bore Cain, from whom the Jewish race descended. The Klan teaches that the Jews then fled to the forest where they had sex with animals, thereby creating all other minority groups. Only the chosen people—the white race—descended from Adam. Klan doctrine evades the issue of Jesus being a Jew by claiming he descended from Adam and is, therefore, part of the Aryan race.

The KKK embraces neo-Nazism while claiming its solutions are more moderate than its swastika-emblazoned brother groups. During the 1970s, a Klan revival was fueled by economic troubles, social changes, and a white backlash. But its agenda of hate and elitism met with unprecedented opposition. Many states enacted laws dealing with racial and religious terrorism, cracking down also on paramilitary camps, where the KKK, the neo-Nazi National Socialist Party of America, and the National States Rights Party practice guerrilla warfare. One such camp in Alabama, named My Lai, trained 30 boys and girls with M-16 rifles in the summer of 1979. No greater travesty exists than when men play God and decide who is worthy of human dignity. The Ku Klux Klan abuses Christian charity by claiming godly direction in its diabolical schemes to eradicate minority groups. Terrorism and murder are examples of satanic activity, devoid of the tolerance and love Christians should extend to others, regardless of race, color, or creed. Carefully crafted rhetoric cannot alter the fact that a burning cross symbolizes hatred and profound prejudice against God's handiwork.

Founders: Small group of ex-Confederate soldiers in Tennessee after the Civil War.

Text: Bible passages quoted out of context and misused to justify racial intolerance.

Symbols: White hoods and robes, burning crosses.

Appeal: The economically disadvantaged have historically been exploited by scapegoating explanations. In this instance, America's problems of unemployment, crime, and civil strife are blamed on racial minorities. Such simple answers are attractive to the uneducated, who cannot comprehend the complex causes of social unrest.

Purpose: The KKK proposes total separation of the races and the eradication of minorities. Some favor a back-to-Africa solution, while other racial separatists advocate partitioning the United States into segregated sections. KKK followers believe they are elevating white ethnic pride.

Errors: The New Testament teaches that all born-again believers are one family in Christ. To the Apostle Paul, there was no Jew or Greek, male or female, but all disciples of Christ were of one body (Gal. 3:27-28). Ironically, the theory of Eve's sexual seduction by the serpent was borrowed from occult Jewish rabbis.

Background Sources: *Christianity Today,* 20 April 1984; *Denver Magazine,* 1978; *Cornerstone,* 1981.

Address/Location: Originally, the rural South. Today, also found in urban areas of the U.S., mainly in the Midwest.

LIFE TRAINING

Headlines read: "NOW you can live your life powerfully and meaning-fully. THE LIFE TRAINING: An intensive educational experience." Brochures proclaim, "You can ease the effects of . . . disorders in your life and begin to live . . . the vision you have always had!" Advertisements promise, "You become free to contribute what you are to the benefit of all." This and more can be yours if you raise your consciousness and awaken your self, your heart, and your soul through the miracle of Life Training.

In the late 1970s, two California est-trained Episcopalian priests, W. Roy Whitten and K. Bradford Brown, founded Life Training. Rooted in the New Age and Human Potential Movement, Life Training tells students they "can be free from fears, decisions, judgments, expectations, and beliefs" if they learn to change their basic reactions to life's problems. Since 1979, over 5,000 students have sought to discover the truths of Life Training through reawakening or conscious awareness. Life Training is offered at several sites throughout the United States and England.

At the heart of Life Training is the humanist philosophy of noted psychologist Albert Ellis. According to Ellis, all suffering is created by illogical thinking. By his definition, man, not God, is the center of the universe, and all religious thought is irrational.

In spite of Life Training's founders' claims that it is "proto-evangelism," there is more similarity to New Age programs such as est than to Christianity. Specific examples include the two-weekend format, group size, the use of neutral hotel facilities, creation of a controlled environment, intimidation, transformational New Age buzzwords, group manipulation, a mystical worldview, public exposure of painful past experiences, and catchphrases such as "Transformation begins with Life Training." Founder Whitten admits he believes that a nonreligious approach reaches more people than a religious one. As a result, man's sinful nature and the fallen state of the world are ignored. Though not directly stated, using this technique eliminates the need for a Savior.

A slick manipulator of crowds, Whitten uses physical touch, eye contact, humor, and affirming applause to disarm people. He quotes the Scriptures but carefully avoids revealing his opinion of who Jesus is. He categorizes as holy books the Hindu *Upanishads* and the *Bhagavad-Gita* and the Muslim Koran, as well as the Bible. He states his training would benefit members of all religions. Life Training brochures declare the group's diversity, claiming that "approximately one-third of the participants are involved in a church, synagogue, or temple, another third consider themselves 'spiritual' but unaffiliated with a religious group, and the other third are burned out on the subject of religion or simply not interested."

Typical sessions consist of two weekends, 17 hours per day, and conflict with traditional Sunday worship. Instruction is intensive, running from 9:00 A.M. to 2:00 A.M. An average of 150-200 students are accepted per training session. Detailed directions offer suggestions on seating, when and how to talk, and what to do in case of drowsiness. Chewing gum, watches, and outside reading material are forbidden, as are the names of Jesus, God, Christ, and Buddha. Members of the audience are encouraged to share painful personal moments. For additional instruction, "mastery training" is available. Once certified by Brown or Whitten, graduates assist in staffing weekend seminars.

Special programs, such as Lifework, provide routine follow-up lectures, workshops, and seminars to prevent graduates from slipping back into old habits. Life Training supporters claim this reinforcement gives followers the means to attain a higher mastery of self and service. Upon achieving higher consciousness, graduates are encouraged to bring guests to Lifetalks and are used as ringers in the crowd to evangelize and evoke appropriate cues and responses.

Life Training is operated by the Kairos Foundation, a nonprofit educational organization created in 1983 by Whitten and Brown. Potential participants are told the programs are free, a gift paid for by contributions of satisfied customers. Although suggested donations can range between

$350-$1,000, Life Training says its $20 nonrefundable processing fee is the only levied charge. That may be a small monetary investment, but the spiritual cost may be one's soul.

Founders: W. Roy Whitten (M.Div.) and K. Bradford Brown (Ph.D.). Founded in San Jose, California.

Text: Nothing specific. The Bible is quoted to those who want to hear it. During the training, certain exercises or disciplines are handed out in printed form.

Symbol: A squiggly line that represents the ups and downs of life.

Appeal: Life Training offers empowerment to transform oneself and the world through a simple set of psychological techniques similar to the rational-emotive therapy of Albert Ellis. Founders claim that "telling yourself the truth" can cure pain and suffering. Troubled persons with low self-image and feelings of powerlessness and hopelessness see Life Training as a solution to their maladies.

Purpose: Life Training literature states its purpose is "to awaken you with an experience of life, which will radically enhance your ability to handle everything else in life."

Errors: According to Life Training, life's pain and suffering is the result of "mindtalk," which is counterproductive and untrustworthy. A psychological technique called process supposedly will solve all problems. Self-awakening is said to be a God-realization experience. In keeping with the Human Potential mind-set, Life Training contends that man creates his own universe. The Training reveals a strong obsession with self and falsely claims human experiences and emotions can measure truth. Sin is ignored, and salvation is offered without Jesus Christ.

Background Sources: William E. Biewett, Duane C. Beauchamp, Carolyn C. Fouse, and Kathryn K. Kremer, "The Human Potential Movement, est, and The Life Training," 14 September 1984.

Address/Location: 15810 Los Gatos Boulevard, Los Gatos, CA 95030; 634 W. Peachtree N.W., Atlanta, GA 30308; 3013 Fountain View, Suite

50, Houston, TX 77057; 203 Lake Ridge Village, Suite 211, Dallas, TX 75238.

See also Human Potential Movement, New Age Cults.

LIFESPRING

Cult researchers familiar with est (discussed earlier in the book) are aware that some of its concepts are rooted in Mind Dynamics, a San Francisco organization that taught mind power techniques until its demise in 1975. Werner Erhard (founder of est and The Forum) was a Mind Dynamics employee, as were John Hanley and Randy Revell, originators of Lifespring. Hanley, who looks like the quintessential California golden boy, states his movement is influenced by the such thinkers as Søren Kierkegaard, Martin Heidegger, and Abraham Maslow. Following these thinkers' lead, Hanley has chosen to be deliberately anti-intellectual and nonlogical. Approximately 150,000 people have been trained (each at a cost of $350-$750) by this "personal growth" movement that freely admits its similarities to est. (One difference is that Lifespring concentrates more on personal relationships than est did.) In the course, "lecturettes" suggest principles against which participants can test their beliefs and habits, though the "lecturettes" do not present a particular doctrine that should be believed. Lifespring concepts reflect a mystical perception of reality. Even though no specific theological precepts are promoted, trainees are encouraged to indulge in parapsychology, meditation, and "guided fantasies." Self-love is promoted as being "the greatest love" one can experience. In fact, Hanley states that the first goal in the course is to get people to realize "they're enough." Such practices and teachings inherently condition the trainee to view life in a non-Christian mode. Exposés in the media and lawsuits by former participants have marred the image of Lifespring and raised serious questions about its techniques. Critics wonder if it really can aid individuals in discovering their "core . . . a perfect, loving, and caring being." But the movement still has training centers in 13 major cities, an expense budget of over $10 million, and a full-time staff of over 100.

Background Sources: Elliot Miller, *Lifespring* (San Juan Capistrano, Calif.: Christian Research Institute, 1979); "Lifespring—New-Age Danger," *Forward,* vol. 4, no. 1 (San Juan Capistrano, Calif.: Christian Research Institute).

MACUMBA

Black roosters with their throats slit, lighted candles tied with brightly colored ribbons, and bottles of sugarcane whiskey placed at special cross-roads in Brazil are commonplace signs of Macumba. In a nation where hunger is epidemic, no one touches offerings of cooked chickens left at such road junctions, for fear of angering the gods of Macumba.

On New Year's Eve, Rio de Janeiro's world-famous Copacabana Beach glitters with lighted candles placed in holes scooped out in the sand in ritual homage to Iemanjá, goddess of the sea. White-robed, cigar-smoking *macumbeiros* (priests of Macumba) hold court in front of flower-strewn altars made of sand. At midnight thousands of devotees wade into the water, carrying fresh flowers and other ritual offerings, which are floated away on toy boats to the goddess. Once the sea claims its gifts, those placating the gods believe their wishes are granted for the year ahead. On a recent Macumba holiday, about 2 million people gathered on Brazil's Atlantic beaches to honor Iemanjá. They offered money, jewels, and champagne by tossing them into the ocean.

Although Brazil is the world's largest Roman Catholic country, its more widely practiced, unofficial religion is Macumba. An Afro-Brazilian cult that blends spiritualism, Catholicism, and voodoo, Macumba was imported by sixteenth-century African slaves who worked on sugar plantations. While most of the nation's cults tend to be regional, Macumba and the related cults of Umbanda and Condomble have adherents in most parts of Brazil. An estimated 25 percent of Rio de Janeiro's 8 million people believe in Iemanjá, and about 40 million Brazilians combine

Christian beliefs with spirit worship. Macumba stores are found on nearly every street throughout Brazil's major cities. The faithful choose their gods from a pantheon of Christian/African deities and make offerings to win their favor. During Macumba rituals, gods speak through mediums in trance to offer help and advice. The Mother of the Gods, the ceremonial leader, is forbidden to enter into trances and oversees the rituals while making her own special contact with Macumba deities. Candomble, like Macumba, blends African spiritism and Portuguese Catholicism. On any Catholic saint's day, Candomble practitioners pray and sing to the *orixa,* an African deity affiliated with the saint. But Candomble, unlike most cults, is monotheistic and claims the supreme being, Olorun, Lord of the Sky, created heaven and earth.

Macumba gods are supplicated by illiterate, middle, and upper-class advocates. The cult is embraced throughout Brazil, and an estimated 62,500 temples exist in the state of Rio de Janeiro alone. A Brazilian state assemblyman won an election by promising state support of Macumba, and popular athletes and singers openly profess their adherence to the cult. One upper-class Macumba practitioner said, "It's OK to come out of the closet now."

To demonstrate his faith in a dead Catholic priest, canonized after allegedly turning the host into blood, a young Brazilian walked on ground glass and hot coals, swallowed razors, nails, and screws, ate light bulbs, and jabbed nails through his cheeks. He emerged unscathed from the Macumban practices, claiming he could do such things without feeling pain because of his faith in the dead Catholic priest.

When Portugal ruled Brazil, the Roman Catholic Inquisition tried to destroy heretical cultists, and failed. In the late 1800s, a troublesome mystic, Antonio Conselheiro, persuaded thousands of followers to ignore the Catholic church and to deny the authority of the state. It took four military campaigns to obliterate the sect's stronghold by killing the mystic. Subsequent Brazilian regimes decided it was simpler and more prudent to tolerate the Macumban cultists.

Founders: West African slaves transported to Brazil.

Text: Oral traditions.

Symbols: Many, including drawings in dirt, charms, signs, primitive idols representing the gods, offerings of money, liquor, cigars, flowers.

Appeal: The promises of wealth, health, and revenge appeal to an illiterate majority. More educated devotees are fascinated by Macumba's promise of instant gratification and its immediate response to petitions. The popularity of spiritistic cults in Brazil can be traced to a hunger for transcendence many churches fail to satisfy.

Purpose: Adherents seek favor with the gods or desire revenge upon an enemy through intercession by the gods. Material gains and social successes lure those who have no other way to acquire economic wealth in Brazil's fragile economy. Many educated people embrace Macumba because it makes few ethical or moral demands, and, they claim, such faith is a logical completion of Judaism, Christianity, and Islam.

Errors: Macumba supports a pagan polytheistic belief system that refutes the Christian concept of one God. Pagan deities are identified with Christian saints, compounded by the weakness of the Roman Catholic church in permitting such syncretism. Evil spirits, fetishes, charms, symbols, and signs are tools of Satan, as are all manifestations of witchcraft and black magic. Macumba spiritually oppresses a people already steeped in superstition and illiteracy and distorts Christian missionary work in Brazil.

Background Sources: "Brazil, Paying Homage to Goddess of the Sea," *To the Point International,* 26 December 1977, 12; "Brazil's Bizarre Cults," *Newsweek,* 27 February 1978, 39; David R. Phillips, "Brazil: The Spiritual Climate," *Christianity Today,* 4 April 1980, 32; Richard N. Ostling, *Time,* 21 July 1980, 43.

Address/Location: Brazil, South America.

See also Black Magic, Macumba, Voodoo/Santeria.

CHARLES MANSON CULT

He envisioned a racial holocaust and an elite "family" emerging victorious. Charles Milton Manson masterminded a plan to launch a bloody war between whites and blacks and convinced his slavishly faithful disciples to do the dirty deeds. On August 9 and 10, 1969, Manson mandated the murder of several prominent Caucasians, heinous crimes he hoped would be blamed on the black community and ignite a racial battle. In all, seven people were slain, including actress Sharon Tate, coffee heiress Abigail Folger, and wealthy supermarket president Leno LaBianca. The Tate-LaBianca murders exposed the Charles Manson cult.

The philosophy Manson preached is based in the Process Church, also known as the Foundation Faith of God. In late 1967 Robert DeGrimston published *As It Is,* which spelled out the Process philosophy that Christ and Satan destroyed their enmity and came together for the End. Christ is considered the judge and Satan the executor of the judgments made by Jesus. Therefore, to love the Devil and kill for him is a divine mission of love for Christ. This duality of Christ and Satan greatly appealed to Charles Manson, who became known as the Christ/devil to his advocates.

Charles Manson and the "brothers and sisters" of his familial cult were also heavily influenced by Adolf Hitler. Vincent Bugliosi, prosecutor in the Charles Manson murder trials and author of *Helter Skelter,* wrote, "Manson looked up to Hitler and spoke of him often. He told his followers that 'Hitler had the best answer to everything' and that he was 'a tuned-in guy who leveled the karma of the Jews.' " The swastika Manson carved on his forehead testifies to his admiration of Hitler. Manson, like Hitler, is viewed by his devotees as a leader who strived to save the Aryan race, his all-white family.

The Process philosophy gained further popularity with the publication of *The Process,* a magazine devoted to the cult. In one issue, a band of marching Nazis spewed from the mouth of a fiery pink skull, trampling people perishing in a fire. In the same issue, Hitler's face appeared on a funhouse mirror, and a human being was shown burning to death. Fear was portrayed as power.

Vincent Bugliosi picked up on Manson's use of fear. Bugliosi said, "Manson's attitude toward fear was so curious I felt it to be almost unique . . . until reading a special issue of *The Process* magazine devoted to fear." Bugliosi said Manson preached about fear as an energizer and weapon, enabling a person to reach new heights and leave bitter failures behind, just as the magazine sermonized. Manson still favors fear and has been cited for behavioral problems in prison.

Incarcerated for masterminding the Tate-LaBianca murders, Manson continues warring with society. He was recently denied freedom for the seventh time. Albert Leddy, chairman of the State Board of Prison Terms, declares Manson is "definitely a danger." But Manson's family awaits his return. Still revered as the Christ/devil by disciples, Charles Manson serves as an inspiration for those who bastardize the Bible and attempt to justify murder, butchery, and such crimes as child pornography and sadomasochism. Racial Armageddon remains a vision for cult members.

The cult of Charles Manson has persisted over the years. Glorified by heavy metal masters like Ozzy Osbourne in such songs as "Bloodbath in Paradise," Manson continues to lure fascinated followers. Testifying at his murder trial, Manson taunted, "You say there are just a few? There are many, many more, coming in the same direction. They are running in the streets—and they are coming right at you!"

People are attracted to the Manson cult because of its twisted philosophies of Aryan superiority and the worship of the Devil and Christ as one. The torch that Manson lighted in 1969 continues to blaze and singe the lives of those who revere him as a visionary leader and sanctified savior.

Founder: Charles Manson, inspired by the Process Church and its Christ/devil duality.

Text: Robert DeGrimston's *As It Is,* as well as issues of *The Process,* a magazine published by the Process Church in the 1960s.

Symbols: The official Process symbol is a form of inverted swastika. The Mendez goat of Satan is also used.

Appeal: Charles Manson appeals to the socially maladjusted because of his hatred of society and visions to make things better. His fame as the mastermind behind the Tate-LaBianca murders also makes him a god to some.

Purpose: The purpose of following Charles Manson is to become part of his family. By being on Manson's side, if indeed a racial Armageddon occurs, that person will be saved along with the rest of the elitist family.

Errors: The idea that Christ and the Devil are no longer enemies is erroneous (Rev. 20:2). Manson followers feel that by killing for Satan they're conducting a noble mission for Christ. But Satan ("adversary") is the enemy of God. The two will never be allies, as John's Revelation clearly instructs us.

Background Sources: Maury Terry, *The Ultimate Evil* (New York: Doubleday, 1987), 175, 177, 511-512; Vincent Bugliosi, *Helter Skelter* (New York: Bantam, 1975), 637-638; *The Rocky Mountain News,* 9 February 1989, 33.

Address/Location: Most cult members reside in California.

MARTIAL
ARTS

He stands motionless, draped in his flowing white uniform called a *ghi*. Silence fills the room. With eyes closed in mute contemplation, one thought possesses his mind. Finally, he is ready.

Bowing slightly to his *sensei* (honorable teacher), he steps near the object of his concentration. In the center of the main room of the *dojo* (training center), someone has stacked six one-inch-thick pine boards on top of each other. Each end of the pile rests on two cement blocks that suspend the center of the boards about 12 inches off the floor.

For several moments he glares at the inanimate boards as if attempting to stare down a dangerous opponent intent on his harm. Suddenly, he draws several deep, quick, rhythmic breaths and lunges toward the stack. His arm is raised in the air as though it were a chopping axe, and he lets forth with a piercing yell *(kiyai)*. Almost simultaneously, faster than the eye can follow, his hand strikes the center of the stacked boards with one violent thrust.

Crack! Six one-inch pine boards splinter and fall to the floor, victim to the force of nothing more substantive than human flesh.

An audible sigh of relief is heard from those watching. Some nod in approval while others shake their heads in disbelief. Few, if any, realize that what they have just seen is an ancient spiritual discipline designed to harmonize the body with the energy forces of the universe in order to achieve religious enlightenment.

Tales abound (some spurious, some true), relating the paranormal feats of adept *senseis.* Such claims are astounding. Bullets can be caught between one's teeth. Punches can be pulled (i.e., stopped short of striking the body) and yet their effects can still be felt. Psychokinetic phenomena (the movement of material objects by immaterial "mental" power) may be displayed.

These accomplishments have a name: *noi cun.* The source of power for such feats is said to be *ki* (sometimes written as *ch'i*). *Ki* is widely known in the occult arts as the "life-energy-creative force of the universe." Advanced practitioners of the marital arts credit *ki* with enabling them to knock a man down by barely touching him or by merely pointing a finger at him. Some have cultivated *ki* to such an extent that they can floor a man by their breath or a look from their eyes. One martial arts practitioner I interviewed said his *sensei* could place his knuckles on a man's chest and send a burning electric shock through his body, driving him up against a wall.

Most people are interested in the martial arts for less exotic reasons. Concerned with warding off muggers or attaining physical prowess, they spend evenings at a store-front *dojo* learning kicks and punches. They are more concerned with downing an opponent than with attaining spiritual insight. Some may be seeking an effective means of self-protection that will enhance a macho image to friends and lovers. But the inherent principles of paganism underlying the martial arts promise the novice he may get more than he bargained for.

Interestingly enough, the centuries-old practices of martial arts are relatively new to the Western world. The boom started when returning World War II servicemen brought back such arts from the Pacific. Later, the movie industry churned out films such as *Five Fingers of Death* and *Duel of the Iron Fists.* But it took American actor David Carradine to popularize the arts for the masses. In the 1970s his successful TV series "Kung Fu" helped spin off magazines and T-shirts with an appeal far beyond board-breaking. Martial arts film star Bruce Lee, to whom kung fu was more than a physical practice, explored its spiritual depths until he met an untimely, mysterious death. Carradine told his fans, "When Bruce Lee died, his spirit went into me. I'm possessed."

There are many conflicting historical theories regarding the origin of martial arts. The account stated here is a widely accepted survey that traces the general history of the martial arts and goes back to the dawn of civilization in India. Three millennia ago in China the arts were developed even more extensively. By the establishment of the Feudal States in 770 B.C., kung fu was widely practiced. Only during the Boxer Rebellion of 1900 were the martial arts partially eliminated from the mainland. In 1928 they were renamed War Arts and were accorded national recognition.

Over the centuries various aspects of the arts were modified and eventually evolved into more or less violent types. Northern and Southern schools and hard and soft forms also developed. Kung fu was the original all-inclusive term describing the martial arts. Later, specific names were applied to its variations: karate, tai chi, judo, jujitsu, and aikido. In Korea, the arts were known as Tae Kwon Do, and they were honed into their highest forms of proficiency in Okinawa. Though one often thinks of the arts as "made in Japan," they have many roots and cultural variations.

The original religious philosophy of kung fu dates back as far as 2696 B.C., where it was rooted in the occult forms of divination known as the *I-Ching* and the "Book of Changes." Lao-Tse, the Chinese sage born in 604 B.C., added further embellishments. His teachings were set forth in a 5,280-word manuscript called *Tao Te Ching,* often called simply "the tao," or "the way." He taught that salvation could not be found in prayer but rather by the observance of nature, the natural way. As the trees bend with the wind and the rivers follow the path of least resistance, so must man adapt to the rhythm of coexistence with evil and wrong.

The next development in the history of kung fu took place when a monk named Bodhidharma brought Buddhism to China in the sixth century A.D. When he discovered the monks sleeping during his lectures, he introduced exercises to assist them in meditation. Known as *I-chin Sutura,* his system combined kung fu with the philosophical principles of Zen to develop a highly sophisticated form of weaponless fighting. The monks at his Shaolin Temple became famous for their savage abilities of defense, which they employed whenever they were attacked in the course of pilgrimages. Eventually two schools of martial arts evolved: *Ch'uan Fe* (kung fu) based on the hard (external) school of Buddhism, and other arts founded on the soft (internal) school of Taoism. As martial arts spread beyond the monastery to the fields of war, some of the religious flavor was lost. But the essential belief system behind these disciplines has never been completely abandoned, even today.

After centuries of countless adaptations, the martial arts have evolved into six basic forms by which they are known in the Western world. Other variations exist, but, for the sake of brevity, categorizing these six headings will be sufficient.

KUNG FU

Originally used as a colloquialism referring to any martial art, kung fu is considered to be the mother of all such physical disciplines. The alchemists who developed it were said to be literally "possessed" with kung fu. In *The History and Philosophy of Kung Fu,* Earl C. Mederiros states, "Kung fu represents the development of man as a complete person. It combines the theological with the philosophical and blends these with the physical, thus evolving those attitudes that are in keeping with the natural laws . . . a perfect harmony of the physical and metaphysical."

Kung fu is known best for its "hard" school, which emphasizes kicking, striking, and punching with strength and speed. The power is said to be derived from *ki* and may also be directed toward improvement of one's health as well as for self-defense. But its appeal to the average person lies more in its offensive character, which emphasizes force to break force. It also may include the striking of vital points, delayed action "death touches," and the use of psychic powers.

T'AI CHI CH'UAN

Some historical evidence indicates that this art evolved from the "soft" school of kung fu. It was founded by Chang San-feng who meditated on the occult I-Ching for three weeks while watching a snake and crane fight. Like Lao-Tse, he was interested in the balanced interplay of opposites known as *yin* and *yang.* In T'ai Chi Ch'uan, these negative (*yin*) and positive (*yang*) principles are supposed to reach a harmonious duality when mind, breath, and sexual energy come together. In this state, *ki* will produce quietness and cure impotency and depression.

All this is achieved by practicing "shadow-boxing" while concentrating on the body's psychic center located below the navel. Participants often arise early to practice the fluid, rhythmic motions of T'ai Chi. Some claim it produces natural health (a famous participant was said to have lived for 250 years). One of the West's foremost T'ai Chi teachers, T. T. Liang, states, "The ultimate goal of learning and practicing T'ai Chi is to become an immortal." This is accomplished by placing the body in harmony with the laws of nature. Some proponents claim supernatural strength and warn of its devastating power as a combative form.

KARATE

For Westerners, this is the best known and the most practiced of all the martial arts. Today it is used basically as a form of self-defense and sport-fighting, using bare hands, arms, and wrists. American occupation forces brought karate back from Japan where it had been imported from Okinawa and China. It developed in these countries because the Japanese rulers had forbidden their people the use of weapons. Gichin Funakoshi, who developed it as Shotokan Ryu, emphasized that the student must empty his mind of wickedness in order to react cognitively, and from this philosophy we get the term *karate*, meaning "empty" *(kara)* "hand" *(te)*. In Okinawa, karate became imbedded with Zen philosophy.

The undercurrent of Buddhism found in some martial arts is illustrated by the emphasis on bowing, breathing exercises, seated meditation, intense concentration, and heightened awareness. Reflective thinking is discouraged—another influence of Buddhism. Since karate is a practice of the spirit, its stated purpose is to unite mind, body, and spirit to achieve the unity envisioned by Zen.

The most distinctive practice in karate is called *kata*, a choreographed combination of kicks, punches, and breathing techniques. It is like a graceful, yet powerful dance performed alone because the blows are deadly enough to kill. Fortunately, sport karate does not cultivate the intent of taking another life or painfully disabling an opponent. And most instructors do not pursue the spiritual purpose of cultivating *ki* to achieve union with an internalized god. But it is questionable whether any devotee taught by a traditional sensei may be totally free of the distinctly pagan frame of reference associated with karate.

AIKIDO
This martial art is the most overtly religious. Literally, it means "the road" *(do)* "to a union" *(ai)* with the "universal spirit" *(ki)*. It was founded by Morihei Uyeshiba, who became concerned that he couldn't control his strength without controlling his mind. Ultimately, after entering many temples, he arrived at "enlightenment" and viewed himself, in the Buddhist theological concept, as "at one with the universe." At that moment, he declared, "The fundamental principle of the martial arts is God's love and universal love. The true martial arts," he said, "regulate the *ki* of the universe."

All of the body movements of aikido are said to agree with the universal laws of nature and bring to the follower the power of *ki*, which is inhaled into the lower abdomen and exhaled through the hands. When the innate psychic powers of all men are united with the spirit and body, aikidoists predict the world will be composed of one family.

A tenth-degree black belt aikido instructor from Japan states of his art, "We create a universal harmony that ties together all of the worlds, the phenomenal world we see around us, the world of the kind of spirits we cannot see, and the pure world of energy. This building of harmony and harmonizing the universe with ourselves so we may become one is the essence and ultimate purpose of aikido."

Morihei Uyeshiba (O'senei as he is known by devotees) once described a strange psychic/occult visionary experience of seeing rays come down from the sky. "I felt my body growing larger and filling the entire cosmos. While I was exalted by this vision, I acknowledged suddenly I should not want to win: a martial art should be a form of life."

JUDO AND JUJITSU

Jujitsu is a blending of kung fu and Japanese martial arts. By the twentieth century, it was the Japanese national sport. A basic factor is knowing the vulnerable portions of an antagonist's anatomy and how to attack those areas.

Judo is basically jujitsu minus the killing aspects. It was founded in 1882 by Jogoro Kano, a student of jujitsu. Unlike karate, which may be compared with boxing, the gentler art of judo is similar to wrestling. It employs the use of balance and leverage to throw an enemy. Devotees are warned in some judo manuals that the art should not be learned without the inclusion of meditation exercises. Its founder agrees, calling it a "method of arriving at self-realization."

While it may be true that the various disciplines of martial arts have different forms, they all have similar religious backgrounds and goals. Because of their roots in Taoism and Buddhism, they view the entire universe as an interplay of harmonizing opposites, the *yin* and *yang*. These principles are expressed by the relaxed state of movements. "The way" of Tao is accomplished by yielding and never resisting, and by responding sympathetically to each action of one's opponent. As illustrated in kung fu, each movement is uninterrupted and flowing. The end of one action is the beginning of the next, thus balancing the *yin* and *yang*. When the Zen goal of stilled senses is also achieved, this balanced harmony is supposed to help one merge with the Universal Consciousness.

To the Christian, salvation comes by the finished work of the cross where Christ was sacrificed for man's sin. And it is by his resurrection that man has hope of eternal life. Salvation in Zen is achieved by comprehending the divine essence of man, who is a manifestation of the

Universal Soul. Followers of Zen believe that such enlightenment may be shared by sending forth *ki* to illuminate the spiritual darkness of the world. Whether the form of martial art one practices is based on the doctrine of naturalism found in Taoism or the doctrine of illusion found in Buddhism, the philosophical basis of both explicitly deny the blood atonement of Christ. The Christian practitioner of the martial arts must ask himself whether or not any involvement in such physical disciplines implies an inherent approval of the religious principles behind them. He should also take care to be certain his instructor adequately divorces the mystical aspects of the martial arts from their strictly physical components.

Founder: Most historians credit the Buddhist monk Bodhidharma in the sixth century A.D.

Text: Zen Buddhist doctrines; *Tao Te Ching.*

Symbols: So-called "spiral configuration" from the *I-Ching* representing the belief in reincarnation and cyclical evolution; double fish shown as a curved line in the shape of an *s* bisecting a circle. One side of the *s* is dark and the other is light. This represents the harmonizing opposites of yin and yang.

Appeal: Self-defense as a crime deterrent; physical conditioning; sport; fascination with martial arts movies and TV idols; desire to achieve physical and spiritual composure; as a way of life to arrive at immortality.

Purpose: The intent depends on the form of discipline and the instructor. Traditional Eastern *senseis* will possibly present the arts as a religion with meditation techniques and idolatrous trappings. Western instructors will more likely emphasize the initial sport stages and appeal to a more casual fascination with the arts as a fad.

Errors: The religious and philosophical roots of most martial art forms presuppose a pantheistic perception of the cosmos. Even the cautious student runs the risk of being conditioned by the techniques that pursue a goal of impersonal oneness with the universe. The Taoistic and Buddhist overtones represent more than a historical root. These principles are an integral part of fulfilling the ultimate spiritual aims of most art forms.

Background Sources: Koichi Tohei, *Aikido in Daily Life* (Tokyo: Rikugei, 1966); William Logan and Herman Petras, *Handbook of the Martial Arts and Self Defense* (New York: Funk and Wagnalls, 1975); Earl Mederiros, *The History and Philosophy of Kung Fu* (Rutland, Vt.: Charles E. Tuttle, 1974); "Women Liberating Themselves with Karate," *East West Journal*, September 1976, 14-16; Ibid., November 1978, 72; *Sports Illustrated*, 18 August 1975; *Newsweek*, 2 January 1978, 40.

Address/Location: Martial arts training centers *(dojos)* in most major cities.

MIND

SCIENCES

"If by Christian you mean that we are saved by the blood of Christ on the Cross, then we're not." That explicit admission by a Church of Religious Science minister points out the essential distinction between the mind science cults and historic Christianity. Mind science organizations include some better-known groups discussed elsewhere (Christian Science and Unity School of Christianity), as well as other entities that more specifically base their teachings on the ruminations of Ernest Holmes. They go by such names as Religious Science, Divine Science, and Science of Mind.

Drawing upon the metaphysical heritage of Charles and Myrtle Fillmore, Warren Felt Evans, Mary Baker Eddy, and Phineas Parkhurst Quimby, Holmes founded the Institute of Religious Science in 1927. *Science of Mind,* published by Holmes in 1938, is the textbook of mind science teachings, emphasizing that the law and love of God (the "Thing-in-Itself") are perfect. Applying this theory to living is a nonsupernatural process of "science." Realizing one's inherent self-worth as emanating from a divine spark is the thrust of Holmes's emphasis. "When an individual recognizes his true union with the Infinite, he automatically becomes Christ," he wrote. By using the definitive article "the" when referring to Christ, mind sciences distinguish between Jesus the man and the divine idea of Christ-realization attainable by all men.

Christ's incarnation and divinity are not the only orthodox doctrines denied by mind science cults. In the process of spiritualizing all biblical truth, they also relegate heaven and hell to mental states and suggest that the Resurrection did not produce a bodily risen Lord. While ignoring scriptural doctrine, mind scientists willingly accept a variety of non-Christian philosophies and sacred books, amalgamating these diverse viewpoints into a syncretistic whole. In spite of their special emphasis on the contemporary interest in healing and positive thinking, the basic presuppositions of Mind and Religious Science groups differ little from the Gnostic heretics that the Apostle Paul confronted over 1900 years ago.

Background Sources: J. Gordon Melton, *The Encyclopedia of American Religions,* vol. 2 (Wilmington, N.C.: McGrath, 1978); Todd Ehrenborg, *Religion, Science or Science of the Mind* (San Juan Capistrano, Calif.: Christian Research Institute Inc., 1979).

See also Christian Science, Unity School of Christianity.

MORMONISM

They're easy to spot. First of all, they always come in twos. Then there's that closely cropped hair and regalia of dark suits, white shirts, subdued ties, polished shoes, and plastic name cards with the impressive title "Elder." Their sincerity is beyond question. And they represent the most basic of human values—patriotism, sobriety, familial responsibilities, and hard work.

While they spend two years of their lives propagating the gospel of Mormonism, these young missionaries are subsidized by their parents, friends, and relatives. Each of them must file a weekly report accounting for every hour of the day. Their task isn't easy. Only nine of every thousand doors they knock on is opened to them. But it's worth it. In one and a half centuries, the Church of Jesus Christ of Latter-day Saints has grown from six adherents to nearly 6.5 million members worldwide.

Why such zeal? Founder Joseph Smith declared that he had a vision of God the Father and Jesus Christ. They revealed to him that all churches and creeds were an "abomination" unto the Lord. He, Smith, was to be a prophet proclaiming a "restored" message of the true gospel. Today, 30,000 Mormon missionaries garner 200,000 converts each year, while the church pulls in an estimated $1.3 billion annually. (The wealth of the Mormon empire is conservatively estimated at $8 billion.) Mormon-owned Brigham Young University is the largest private university in the U.S., and the Mormons are the largest religious media operator in the world. The 28-story headquarters in Salt Lake City, Utah, might well bear the inscription "Success" emblazoned from its top.

Mention Moonies or Hare Krishna to the average person and he'll respond with disdain. But the word *Mormon* generally evokes an immediate nod of approval. The morally austere image is no sham. Mormons are known to eschew tobacco, cigarettes, caffeine, and premarital sex while revering family life and free enterprise. They have a low cancer rate and score higher than the general populace when it comes to physical fitness. Who wouldn't admire a religious group that promotes the Boy Scouts and receives "fast offerings" to care for widows as well as the poor and indigent? The suspicious history and strange beliefs of Mormonism are often overlooked on the assumption that sound morals make a good religion. (Apparently the U.S. government is impressed by Mormon integrity. The FBI and CIA recruit heavily among Mormons, and the Reagan Administration employed more Mormons than any previous administration.)

Most people know little of Mormonism's doctrines and beginnings. They may be familiar with the names Joseph Smith or Brigham Young. Ezra Taft Benson and George Romney have been visible Mormons on the political scene. And Mormon Tabernacle Choir concerts have earned the respect of music critics. Only a few have heard about the odd practices of proxy baptisms and celestial marriages. To truly understand Mormonism, one must sift through all the arcane doctrines and public relations ploys of Latter-day Saints and go back to the small town of Palmyra, New York, in the year 1820.

Joseph Smith, Jr., is revered by millions of Mormons as a seer and prophet. The contemporaries who knew him and his parents were less gracious. Neighbors viewed the Smith family as "illiterate, whiskey-drinking, shiftless, and irreligious." Joe (as he was known) was said to be indolent, with a penchant for exaggeration and untruthfulness. His mother, Lucy Mack, practiced magic and had visions. His father, Joe, Sr., was known as a persistent treasure-seeker, always trying to dig up the fabled booty of Captain Kidd. The founder of Mormonism often accompanied his father on these expeditions and was himself fond of the occult, especially divining and fortune-telling by "peep stones."

Then one day in 1820, while praying in the woods, Joseph Smith received his fabled vision of God and Jesus. In 1823 another personage, an angel named Moroni, appeared at his bedside. The visitor claimed to be the son of Mormon, the departed leader of an American race known as Nephites. Moroni told him about a book of golden plates that contained "the fullness of the everlasting Gospel." Four years later, in the hill named Cumorah (near Palmyra, New York), Smith unearthed the plates. Buried with them was a pair of large, supernatural spectacles known as the "Urim and Thummim." They were to be used in translating the hieroglyphics on the plates, a language called "reformed Egyptian." (Archaeologists and Egyptologists deny there is any historical evidence to validate the existence of such a form of communication.)

Joseph immediately began his work of translating the plates. He claimed that later during this time John the Baptist (sent by Peter, James, and John) appeared to him and administered a divine ordination. When the translation work was completed (with the help of Oliver Cowdery, an itinerant schoolteacher, and Emma Hale, his first and only legal wife) he returned the plates to Moroni. The *Book of Mormon* was published in 1830. A subtitle, "Another Testament of Jesus Christ," was recently added to make the *Book of Mormon* appear to be more closely linked with orthodox Christianity. On April 6 of that same year, Cowdery, Smith, and his brothers, Hyrum and Samuel, officially formed the Church of Jesus Christ, now known as the Church of Jesus Christ of Latter-day Saints.

The *Book of Mormon* is the cornerstone of Mormon faith. Along with the other Smith volumes, *Doctrines and Covenants* and *The Pearl of Great Price,* it is considered to be a divine revelation superior to the Bible. In actual practice, whenever the *Book of Mormon* contradicts the Bible, the former is considered to be the final authority. What exactly does the Book of Mormon contain?

It purports to tell the story of two Middle Eastern peoples who migrated to the Americas. The tale unwinds in a series of books written between 600 B.C. to A.D. 400. An ancient civilization called Jaredites came from the Tower of Babel to Central America. A wicked group, they perished as a result of their own immorality. (I have visited a number of ancient Mayan ruins in Central America where Mormon archaeologists search for clues to verify Mormonism's historical claims. At Tikal in Guatemala and Copan in Honduras I have viewed carvings resembling a Star of David, which Mormons say prove their assertions.)

A later group of Jews led by a righteous man named Nephi fled Jerusalem to avoid the Babylonian captivity and ended up in South America. They divided into warring factions, the Nephites and Lamanites. The latter annihilated the Nephites in a fierce struggle near Palmyra, New York in A.D. 428. The victory earned them a curse—dark skins. They continued populating the continent and became the American Indian race. Before his demise, Mormon, the Nephite leader, compiled a record of his civilization and of the appearance Christ is supposed to have made to them after his resurrection. He described how the Lord met them in South America and commissioned them to institute the ordinances of communion, baptism, and the priesthood. The entire account was recorded on the golden plates that Mormon buried and were found by Joseph Smith 1,400 years later.

Before continuing with the historical saga of Smith and his successor (according to the Utah branch), Brigham Young, the *Book of Mormon* deserves some scrutiny, for it claims equality with the Bible. It purports to be the sealed book mentioned in Isaiah 29 and a record of the "other sheep" Jesus spoke of in John 10:16. But its proofs are questionable, and its inconsistencies glaring.

While it aspires to be an additional revelation to the Bible, it contains verbatim references in King James English, though it was supposedly written many centuries before the 1611 Authorized Version. These analogous passages even include some seventeenth-century translators' errors, a strange coincidence for a book supposedly predating the KJV scholars' efforts. In addition, the *Book of Mormon* credits these New World immigrants with metal-producing capabilities, a claim not confirmed by archaeological research. Mormon even described elephants roaming the Western hemisphere, though no skeletons have ever been found.

The Smithsonian Institution flatly denies any correlation between American archeological discoveries and the information contained in the *Book of Mormon*. A Mormon publication, "Joseph Smith's Testimony," concludes its glowing appraisal of the *Book of Mormon* by citing a total of eleven witnesses. What the pamphlet's author failed to note is that three of them, Oliver Cowdery, David Whitmer, and Martin Hanes, were later denounced by Smith. The other eight include five who were related to David Whitmer. Of the final three witnesses, one was Smith's father and the other two his brothers, hardly an objective company of jurists.

Who wrote the *Book of Mormon*? God, Satan, Smith, or another mortal are the only possible sources. Some who doubt its divine inspiration suggest that Smith may have been a fanciful thinker who borrowed King James English and nineteenth-century historical speculation to produce a fictitious novel. Others contend that one of his converts, Sidney Rigdon, stole a manuscript entitled *Manuscript Story* by Solomon Spaulding, a minister-writer who died in 1816. A few insist Smith's writings bear strong similarity to those of the Rev. Ethan Smith who authored *View of the Hebrews*. Most evangelical critics espouse the Spalding-plagiarism explanation, noting that Smith always dictated his writing from behind a curtain.

No matter who really wrote the book, its revelations and its followers caused quite a stir wherever they went. Mormons were a combative lot, challenging all other sects, and flaunting their polygamous ways. (Smith, it was said, had 27 wives, though one authority estimates Smith may have had 60 or more.) Persecution drove them from New York to Ohio and then Missouri, where the governor asked them to leave. Smith's clan ended up in Nauvoo, Illinois, where, with hard work and dedication, they built the largest city in the state. He told his followers that Nauvoo meant "beautiful plantation" in Hebrew, and obtained a charter that made it a city-state with its own military. But Joseph and his brother Hyrum ran afoul of the law and ended up in jail in 1844. An outraged mob beset their Carthage, Illinois, cell and murdered both. This tragic, lawless act of intolerance insured instant martyrdom for Smith.

A split immediately followed the shooting. One group led by his widow felt that the mantle of leadership should fall on Joseph's sons. They left for Independence, Missouri, to settle on the site where the prophet had declared Christ would return. That body, now known as the Reorganized Church of Jesus Christ of Latter Day Saints, parted ways with some major Mormon doctrines. Though they claim a common origin and reverence for the *Book of Mormon,* the Reorganized Church repudiates several vital beliefs of the Utah group—i.e. secret rites, a plurality of gods, and sealed marriages. Above all, they claim to be the only legitimate Latter-day Saint body, saying that Joseph Smith appointed his son to succeed in the church presidency. A recently discovered document in Smith's handwriting, dated January 17, 1844, seems to confirm their contention. (See the entry on the Reorganized Church.)

But such historical verification matters little now. The fact is that after Smith's assassination, Brigham Young persuaded a majority to follow him on the arduous trek to Utah. In July 1847 Young and his band looked on the Salt Lake Valley and declared, "This is the place." Brigham Young encouraged polygamy, took 25 wives, and by the time of his death in 1877 had collected 140,000 followers. He strongly adhered to the little-talked-about Mormon doctrine of blood atonement. Christ's blood, he believed, could not atone for certain sins. Such deeds required a man's own blood. Another could kill him as a righteous act he described as, "loving our neighbor as ourselves . . . if he wants salvation and it is necessary to spill his blood . . . spill it." Modern Mormons have suppressed (but not officially repudiated) the doctrine. But they still have stinging memories of the day their second "prophet" ordered his fellow Mormons to attack and slaughter 120 men, women, and children of the Fancher party, who crossed Mormon land on their way to California.

Brigham Young also espoused two other doctrines that Mormons would like to forget. He taught that Adam was actually God who took on a body and came to Eden (in Missouri) with one of his heavenly wives, Eve. This Adam-God (the Archangel, Michael) begat Jesus by sexually cohabiting with the Virgin Mary in a physical, flesh relationship. "He [Christ] was not begotten by the Holy Ghost," Brigham declared emphatically. It was Young's espousal of polygamy that gained Mormons the most bad publicity. He instructed his followers, "The only men who become gods are those who enter into polygamy."

Even today, Utah is pocketed with an estimated 30,000 fundamentalist Mormons who engage in plural marriages. They are devout in their belief that they will be barred from heaven unless they follow the covenant of polygamy set forth by Joseph Smith in 1843. In the late 1800s, the U.S. Congress became so concerned with the conduct of Mormons that it passed the Edmunds-Tucker Act, threatening to confiscate Mormon property and jail its leaders. The church recanted in 1890, and today most mainline Mormons maintain an image of monogamous bliss.

But polygamy and the Adam-God theory are not the only unorthodox doctrines of Mormonism. They subscribe to the idea of an anthropomorphic God with physical, material dimensions. He is a procreating father (all humans were preexistent spirits he begat) with a divine mother-wife. It is this conviction that undergirds the Mormon emphasis on marriage and parenthood in this life and the next. Some Mormons believe that Jesus was married to both Mary and Martha and that he bore children on earth. Good Mormons enter their secret temples and don white garments to indulge in esoteric, Masonic-like rituals that seal their marriages for eternity.

The most famous of all Mormon aphorisms declares, "As man now is, God once was; as God now is, man may become." God himself was once procreated in another world, and now humans' may aspire to the status of procreator that he has obtained. Adam did right by eating of the forbidden fruit because it made him capable of fathering the human race. In other words, "Adam fell that men might be." The right to godhead is not earned by the grace of Jesus, but by being a good Mormon. Followers of Joseph Smith prove their faithfulness by being baptized and married in the temple, being a member of the priesthood, and tracing genealogies. As potential father and mother gods, Mormons will ultimately have their own planets to populate.

All those born prior to Mormonism's founding in 1830 cannot enter the celestial state without a little help from present-day adherents. The Church has blasted a tunnel out of Utah granite (capable of withstanding a nuclear explosion) to house the ancestral records of devout Mormons. Once departed kin have been identified, posthumous proxy baptisms are performed. Mormons spend $10 million a year to maintain the facilities, but for them it is well worth it. Some go through the three-hour ceremony on behalf of a nonrelative they have never known. Mormons are universalists and believe that everyone will eventually have immortality with only baptized Mormons attaining godhead. (Article of Faith Number Three states, "We believe that through the atonement of Christ all mankind may be saved.")

The priesthood concept, a belief in a restored priesthood of Aaron and Melchizedek, represents one of Mormonism's most distinctive departures from Christian tradition. All Mormon males over 14 years of age are eligible for the Aaronic priesthood. At 20 years of age they may enter the higher office of Melchizedek and be designated an elder. Until 1978, those with black skins were forbidden this status. Mormonism's temples (there are now 40 temples around the world) were off limits to blacks because Joseph Smith taught that they were the descendants of Cain and therefore cursed. The church rejects the doctrine of original sin and believes that sinners are punished on earth for failure in their past spirit lives. Blacks were thus guilty of the preexistent sin of rebelling with Lucifer and barred from the priesthood until Mormonism's leader, First President Spencer Kimball (who died in 1985, succeeded by Ezra Taft Benson), received a "revelation" abrogating this injunction.

Most aspects of church structure are seldom known to outsiders. The First President is considered to be a prophetic successor to Smith and thus is a prophet and revelator who speaks in God's name. From there, authority descends in a nondemocratic fashion to the President's advisors (two other high priests), the 12 apostles, the presiding quorum of 70, and the presiding bishopric. Individual members are organized into *wards* of 500 to 1,000. Wards are consolidated into *stakes*. Space does not permit a detailed discussion of unique Mormon practices. Some of them are as follows: de-emphasis of Easter and the Cross, speaking in tongues and spiritual healing, the ability of individuals to receive private revelations from God, emphasis on Monday as family night, storing of food supplies for times of famine, insistence that the U.S. Constitution is divinely inspired, believing that the state of women is inferior to that of men, opposition to the use of birth control, opposition to interracial marriages, binding temple oaths (breaking them can jeopardize one's hope of eternal life), and belief in the brotherhood of Jesus and Lucifer. Mormons also believe in a three-tiered heaven with separate sections for heathen, non-Mormon Christians, and those with sealed marriages whose earthly matrimonial unions will endure forever.

Some may wonder how such exotic ideas could be compatible with the seeming love and care exhibited by most Mormons. The evangelical Christian questions how such unorthodox theology could produce such pleasant people who knock on doors and warmly present their case. This irony is not so hard to understand when one comprehends why an individual may have joined the Mormon Church. For one thing, the new Mormon finds an instant social community of God-conscious values. The positive emphasis on Christian virtues and the intense involvement on a layman's level cause most new members to simply overlook the blemished history of the LDS's origins. Family pressure prevents many disillusioned Mormons from forsaking the church, particularly if they are second- or third-generation adherents. People today often have a pragmatic approach to religion that tends to see theology as a cumbersome commodity. They want something that *works,* something that will bring them emotional security and shared goals. Mormonism delivers, and for millions that is good enough. While their unorthodoxy—and their success—may alarm us, they should also inspire us to equal or excel them in showing love and concern to searching people.

Founder: Joseph Smith, born in Sharon, Vermont, December 23, 1805. Killed June 27, 1844, Carthage, Illinois. The *Book of Mormon* was published in 1830 and the Church of Jesus Christ of Latter-day Saints was founded April 6, 1830. (It was originally named the "Church of Jesus Christ." The current official name was adopted in 1837.)

Text: John 10:16, "Other sheep I have, which are not of this fold," supposedly refers to a Middle Eastern civilization that migrated to the Americas. Christ preached to them (the Nephites) after his resurrection. The Bible is the Word of God only "as far as it has been translated correctly." A Mormon article of faith states that "we also believe the *Book of Mormon* to be the Word of God."

315

Symbol: The angel Moroni, usually perched atop temple spires, with trumpet in hand.

Appeal: Outside observers who do not scrutinize Mormon doctrine may be attracted by their avoidance of unclean physical habits and the seriousness with which members take their faith. They believe in the continuing function of divine revelation that gives a vitality and authority to their faith.

Purpose: Since Mormonism is the only restored, true church, its concept of salvation must be strictly followed. The highest heaven is open only to faithful Mormons, who will become gods and join in procreative partnership with God who was once as humans are now. Life on earth is a discipline where one develops one's potential to rule a celestial kingdom with a spouse and children. Marriage and large families on earth are encouraged as part of this evolving process toward equality with Christ, who is the Mormon "elder brother." After death, Mormons in the heavenly realms seek to convert non-Mormons who dwell in the lower realm, so these "gentiles" can also accept the revelations of Joseph Smith.

Errors: Mormons find themselves in the conundrum of having to modify or deny some of their more embarrassing past doctrines (e.g., blood atonement, the Adam-God concept, polygamy, anti-Negroid beliefs) while according prophetic status to the men who taught such beliefs (i.e., Joseph Smith, Brigham Young, et al.). The priesthood concept is repudiated by Hebrews 7 and 1 Peter 2:9-10. The Aaronic and Melchizedek orders were consummated in Christ, and now all believers are part of a "royal priesthood." The Mormon Jesus is not eternal God-Jehovah (Elohim), able to "save them to the uttermost" (Heb. 7:25). He is therefore "another Jesus," and Moroni is the false angel of the "accursed" gospel of which Paul speaks in Galatians 1:8-9.

Background Sources: "Joseph Smith's Testimony," *Desert News Press,* LDS publication; *Book of Mormon, Doctrine and Covenants, The Pearl of Great Price,* books by Joseph Smith; *Moody Monthly,* June 1980, 32; *Newsweek,* 21 November 1971, 113-119; Ibid., 1 March 1976, 71; Ibid., 1 September 1980, 68-71; Ibid., 27 April 1981, 87-88; Walter Martin, *The Kingdom of the Cults* (Minneapolis: Bethany Fellowship, 1977); *Time,* 11 July 1977, 69; Ibid., 19 June 1978, 55; Ibid., 7 August 1978, 54-55; Ibid., 4 December 1978, 30; Ibid., 21 October 1977, 38-39; Ibid., 23 May

1980, 42-43; Ibid., 24 April 1981, 42; *The Vancouver Sun,* 19 April 1980, 5B; *The Denver Post,* 1 October 1976, 4BB; Ibid., 1 July 1977, 4BB; *Newsweek,* 25 November 1985, 87; *Christianity Today,* 5 September 1986, 29; *Journal of Discourses* (Salt Lake City: Bookcraft).

Address/Location: The Church of Jesus Christ of Latter-day Saints, 47 East North Temple Street, Salt Lake City, UT 80150.

See also Reorganized Church of Jesus Christ of Latter Day Saints.

M U K T A N A N D A
P A R A M A H A N S A

(Shree Gurudev Siddha Yoga Ashram)

Joe Don Looney was a terror off the field as well as on during his pro football days of the sixties. Now he's a docile, disciplined truck driver. John Denver sang of being "Rocky Mountain High," with literal reflection on the drug-induced altitude in his own life. Now he sings of nothing higher than transcendental bliss. Both Joe and John credit their transformation to the pressure of two fingers placed against their closed eyelids. The fingers belonged to Swami Muktananda Paramahansa.

Baba (father) Muktananda, once surrounded by 2,500 blissed-out showbiz folk who came to do him honor, came a long way from his home in Mangalore, India. At age 15 he left his parents to spend more than 20 years seeking spiritual truth. In 1947 he met Guru Bhagwan Sri Nityananda. Nityananda claimed to be a *siddha* yogi, a person whom Hindus believe is a Perfect Master capable of awakening the latent spiritual power of *Shakti*. (Shakti is the Hindu Supreme Mother goddess lying at the base of the spine.) He told Muktananda that man has forgotten his divine nature and that awakening Shakti brings forth God-realization. Unlike most gurus, who may take years to arouse a student's Shakti power, Nityananda transmitted the experience to Muktananda immediately. He was instantly overwhelmed by rays of light and a hot, burning fever.

This system of enlightenment known as *shaktipat* was passed on to Muktananda. When Nityananda died in 1961, the Shree Gurudev Siddha

Yoga Ashram was founded. Muktananda came to America on his 1970 world tour and was accompanied by Baba Ram Dass. Just before his death in 1982, Muktananda was estimated to have over 300,000 Western followers who experienced *shaktipat* at his hands. Three hundred meditation centers carry on the work in the United States (est founder Werner Erhard sponsored one of his American tours). Followers say they have seen visions, heard ethereal sounds, and even, among women, undergone orgasms. "God is within you," Muktananda declared. "Honor and worship your inner being." The audiences were relatively mature, containing a high proportion of professionals. To Westerners geared to instant-everything, this version of God-realization is particularly appealing.

Founder: Swami Muktananda Paramahansa, born 1980, Mangalore, India. Died 1982.

Text: Hindu scriptures.

Symbols: None.

Appeal: Muktananda was less secretive and not as ostentatious as most Eastern gurus. This made him appear to be more credible. Followers testify of spontaneous, emotionally and physically charged experiences resulting from his initiation ceremonies. They feel this encounter gave meaning to their lives without having to believe or renounce any religious dogmas.

Purpose: With a brush of his peacock feather fan or the thrust of his fingers into a disciple's eyes (an old Hindu ploy of creating neurological pressure on the retina), Muktananda claimed to awaken the elemental energy force of Shakti. Followers were admonished to direct their devotion and meditation toward Muktananda with unconditional zeal. In exchange, they received God-realization.

Errors: The entire system of Siddha Yoga is based on the false premise that a human being can be a channel to God-realization. First Timothy 2:5 states, "There is one God, and one mediator between God and men . . . Christ Jesus." The so-called awakening of the *Kundalini* power of Shakti may be the result of an anticipatory psychological response. This experience may also be induced by demon activity.

Background Sources: *People,* 24 May 1976, 83; *People,* 3 December 1979; *People,* 9 March 1981, 89; *Time,* 26 July 1976, 78-79; "Update," *SCP Newsletter,* October 1982, 6.

Address/Location: In India, Muktananda's Center is known as the Shree Gurudev Siddha Yoga Ashram. U.S. Centers are known as the Siddha Yoga Dham of America, with headquarters in Oakland, CA. His meditation community, formerly in New York's Catskill Mountains, has been moved to a Miami Beach hotel, address not available.

NEO-GNOSTICISM

As the infant church sought to formalize its beliefs into a doctrinal structure, the heresy of Gnosticism prompted Paul to write an epistle to the Colossians. Taking their name from the Greek word for "knowledge" (*gnosis*), the Gnostics taught that Jesus was either a magician, an ascetic, or a sexual deviate who initiated his followers by means of secret ceremonies. The apostle found it necessary to defend the uniqueness of the *person* and redemptive *work* of Christ in the face of suggestions that Jesus was only one of many angelic intermediaries between God and man. He also emphasized that salvation was completed in Christ, countering the legalistic asceticism of Gnosticism (Col. 2:20-30).

A major conflict erupted between the orthodoxy of codified beliefs as expressed in the Bible and mystical philosophical concepts held by those who claimed they were the true followers of Christ's esoteric teaching. Orthodoxy eventually triumphed. Today, however, this early A.D. heresy is alive and well and debated in prestigious seminaries. Neo-Gnosticism forms the theological foundation for many modern cults and has even formalized a belief structure of its own. Though it has no official organizational apparatus, the tenets of Neo-Gnosticism are held by an increasing number of the educated elite.

Gnostic belief, as expressed in the fourth-century Nag Hammadi Codices (and more recently published volumes such as *The Secret Gospel, The Gospel of Thomas,* and *The Forbidden Gospel*), may be summarized as follows: God is actually an abstract figure in an invisible realm. The Judeo-Christian Creator is replaced by another deity named Yaldabaoth. The serpent in Eden heroically revealed to Adam and Eve secret knowledge that Yaldabaoth had hidden from them. The Gnostics guarded this knowledge carefully throughout history. The Flood and the destruction of Sodom and Gomorrah were Yaldabaoth's way of getting revenge upon the Gnostics. However, that divine light of *gnosis* has continued in some enlightened souls even to our present age.

Jesus, according to Gnostic belief, was one of those who possessed a higher consciousness. How he attained this knowledge and what he did with it is a point of conjecture among current Gnostics. Some believe he clandestinely traveled to India to learn the way of the Buddha and the wisdom of the Brahmans. Others suggest that Christ was actually raised by the hermetic Essenes, who schooled him in mysterious rituals. All Gnostics agree that Christ did not die for man's sin, even suggesting that the Savior tricked Simon of Cyrene into enduring the fate intended for him.

Gnosticism finds fertile ground in two camps. The atheist and agnostic find comfort in believing that Christ was a mere man whose charisma was due to hypnotic techniques or sexual baptismal ceremonies. The mystically inclined student of Eastern philosophy discovers a presumed harmony between the Gnostic Jesus and the avataristic concept of spiritual leadership as expressed in Hindu texts. Though Neo-Gnosticism expounds theories too abstract to interest the average person, it does appeal to those whose education has placed them in the upper socio-economic strata. As an elitist cult, Neo-Gnosticism is a serious intellectual challenge to Christianity. Those interested in its teachings will acquire an elaborate rationale for rejecting the deity and sacrificial atonement of Christ.

Founders: First-century heretics or earlier mystical religions.

Texts: Nag Hammadi scriptures; miscellaneous Gnostic manuscripts; modern books with conjectures based on ancient texts; the Bible.

Symbols: None known.

Appeal: Secret knowledge not available to the uninitiated is the main lure of Neo-Gnosticism.

Purpose: Orthodox Christian doctrine is refuted and replaced with an alternate explanation for Creation, the Fall, and Redemption.

Errors: The inspired Scriptures are denied in favor of the "true" teachings of Christ. These esoteric doctrines are available to the adepts of Neo-Gnosticism, who achieve the same level of consciousness as Jesus.

Background Sources: *Time,* 4 June 1973, 73; Ibid., 9 June 1975, 46-47; *Newsweek,* 3 March 1975, 65; *The Denver Post,* 2 December 1977, 6BB; *East West Journal,* January 1978, 76-87.

Address/Location: Primarily Western countries, especially the United States and Europe.

N E W
A G E
C U L T S

She channels information from bodiless beings called Theos and conveys messages from the cosmic creatures to clients for $85 an hour. Sheila Peterson-Lowary has written *The Fifth Dimension: Channels to a New Reality* to chronicle her encounters with Theos. Peterson-Lowary claims a New Age called the Fifth Dimension has ushered out a 26,000-year-old cycle. The Theos she channels from beyond offer customers strategies for entering the new era of enlightenment.

"A strange mix of spirituality and superstition is sweeping the country" — so said *Time* magazine. *Choices and Connections,* a New Age resource journal, declared, "Many of us are still asking what the New Age is. First and foremost, it appears to be an explosion of human curiosity and creativity. It is a time when individuals are passionately seeking to unlock their undiscovered potentials. And while some of this may represent dreams of grandeur, for many it seems to spring from a deep desire to realize the innate goodness that lies within each person." What is it, and who started it? The name *New Age* has been around for decades. Its practices have enchanted mystics for centuries. So, what's new about the current New Age?

The time seems to be right for what New Agers refer to as a "paradigm shift in evolutionary consciousness." Successful businessmen consult astrological charts. Yuppie investment bankers talk about past lives. Ethical stock purchasers question a company's worthiness on the basis of its societal contributions. Books like *Love, Medicine and Miracles* by Bernie Siegel, M.D. and *The Relaxation Response* by Harvard M.D.

Herbert Benson make the best-seller charts. The National Institute of Health earmarks $70 million for research on biofeedback and hypnosis. The New Age is an old adage. Like medieval metaphysicians and ancient Eastern mystics, the cult of the New Age hails man and his paramount powers as the center of the spiritual universe. For centuries, people have endeavored to deify themselves and evoke the mysteries of spirituality. The oracles of Greece, the *Vedas* of the Hindus, and the mysteries of the Pharaohs supposed that a secret of existence lay beneath reality. In secluded woods, musty caverns, and passageways of pyramids, these cryptic truths were sought through ritual and ceremony. Today New Age cults pursue these mysteries of religion more diversely and ingeniously.

Implicit in this quest is the assumption that beyond observable reality there is an even more real hidden universe where unmanifested order is unified into a whole. New Agers believe a "Copernican threshold" must be crossed to uncover the mystery of mankind's relationship to universal spiritual truth. Then, the present confrontational system of differing faiths will be replaced with a worldwide oneness of soul and spirit.

Discovering this spiritual symbiosis is the globalistic goal of all New Age religious pilgrimages. Whereas past religions looked outward to the sun, moon, stars, and cosmic forces, those in the New Age who aspire to know hidden truths journey inward to find collective connection with the One Cause. The term *New Age* represents this consciousness, as well as the astrological prediction of the end-of-the-century arrival of an era called the Aquarian Age.

New Age cultists seek a divine being within themselves and strive to be an integral, conscious element of the universe. God becomes the self, and the self becomes God. Marilyn Ferguson, who sums up her support of the New Age movement in *The Aquarian Conspiracy,* describes the New Age as a time for people to unleash the deity within. Ferguson encourages New Agers to "Go to the depths of the soul . . . for all that God can do is focused there."

New Age advocates insist that ultimate reality can only be experienced when the mind is stilled of daily distractions. Through New Age practices such as mystical meditation, proponents alter mental states and enter into a collective cosmic consciousness. In the process, most New Agers adopt the philosophy of relativism, the idea that the meaning of the moment governs behavior, not predetermined rules. Reality is individualized, created minute by minute. By practicing this theory, New Agers believe they can access enlightening energies and implicit powers to become a co-creator with the Divine.

New Age beliefs saturate every aspect of American society, from business to sports, education to government. Meditative techniques, such as self-hypnosis, guided imagery, yoga, and centering, are used as part of stress management work strategies. The Human Potential Movement rakes in $4 billion annually from American companies that urge or require employees to enroll in motivational training seminars.

Beyond the public arena, the cult of the New Age infiltrates family households with its philosophies of how to achieve self-realization. Housewives hail holistic healing as a new way to tend suffering children. Copulating couples praise pyramid power as a way to channel energy and improve orgasms. Parents and children alike consult astrological charts to foretell their futures.

New Age mind control techniques are employed everywhere. At work and at home, people attempt to achieve self-actualization and manage their lives through visualization. Neurolinguistic trainers observe body language and help clients overcome learning disabilities and insecurities. Creative visualists, frequently found in school systems, use imagery to unleash inner creativity. Teachers encourage ingenuity by asking children to visualize themselves as animals or objects. One teacher instructed students to imagine tiny vultures living inside them that grew if the child was bad or diminished when the child was good.

The New Age philosophy that consciousness can be used to influence the body is apparent in the holistic health movement. Some practitioners recommend rolfing to eliminate ailments by using hands and elbows on connective tissues to achieve bodily "synchronicity." Still others favor reflexology, viewing the sole of the foot as a microcosm of the body, and manipulate key energy points to treat ailments. Polarity therapists teach that sickness results from energy blockages that can be relieved by maneuvering energies around the body. Herbologists use plants to cure minor illnesses.

Most New Age disciples adopt the doctrine that they can cure themselves through positive perception. Some venerate visualization to destroy disease through inner power. Holistic healers advocate therapeutic touching to restore bodily balance and heal the sick. More than 50 nursing schools nationwide teach the therapeutic touch technique. Homeopathy proponents use a theory of like-cures-like and treat the patient with the same substance that sickened him.

Danger exists for New Agers who use consciousness to influence the body. The body may also control the mind to the detriment of the entire person. Dr. Carl Raschke, professor of Religious Studies at the University of Denver, describes the dangers of the Human Potential Movement on a medical and spiritual level. Raschke refers to New Age activity as "the spiritual version of AIDS" because "it destroys the ability of people to cope and function."

The cult of the New Age also encompasses psychic phenomena. A recent poll by the University of Chicago reveals that 67 percent of the public claims psychic experience. Psychics seek inner deification through extrasensory perception and psychokinesis, the exertion of energy on an object, event, or situation. Parapsychologists research mental and physical effects of extrasensory occurrences. Clairvoyants receive information from an object or event. Telepathists transfer thoughts into the mental states of others. Rebirthers relive the first moment of their birth and release the trauma to experience a higher self.

Steven Rogat, who teaches New Age psychic seminars, claims intuitive counseling promotes spiritual and physical fitness. Rogat counsels clients on karmic relationships and predicts their futures through dream therapy, numerological consultations, and tarot card readings. A licensed massage technician, Rogat also says magnetic therapy provides relief from menstrual cramps and other bodily discomfort. He routinely rids clients of what he calls "dis-ease" with New Age techniques.

New Age advocates also employ occult divinatory devices to achieve mortal omnipotence. Many consult the Chinese *I Ching* before making crucial career or personal decisions, or commission tasseographers to read tea leaves and calculate kismets. Still others reach for runes to provide answers to dilemmas. People undergoing dream therapy are told they must acknowledge their dreams and commit to realizing them. New Age devotees celebrate auras, supposed fields of multihued colors surrounding one's body as an emanation of one's higher self. Aura advocates have ambiances analyzed to detect health, emotions, and confidence levels.

Through mass marketing of books, music, and periodicals, New Age philosophies and practices taint every intersection of society. Advocates of New Age consciousness meditate to New Age music to elevate inner excellence. The public is familiar with the works of Shirley MacLaine, New Age cosmic superstar. *Out on a Limb,* published in 1983, relates the beginning of MacLaine's transformation from an agnostic to a believer in the spirit realm. *Dancing in the Light,* her second book, describes the use of crystals and Hindu mantra-chanting for spiritual power. In *Dancing in the Light,* MacLaine relates that her spirit guide revealed the law that "everyone is God. Everyone."

MacLaine's latest book, *Going Within,* promotes yoga and aligning seven spinning wheels of consciousness, called *chakras.* MacLaine, an Academy Award-winning actress, recently released her meditation videotape called *Shirley MacLaine's Inner Workout.* MacLaine maintains exercising the seven batteries of energy permits people to reach ultimate levels of relaxation and higher consciousness.

Some New Agers insist they have encountered their higher selves through a rebirth of their sense of the sacred in near-death experiences. According to a recent Gallup poll, 8 to 9 million Americans have reported mystical encounters while temporarily "dead" or on the verge of death. Dr. Raymond A. Moody, Georgia psychiatrist, says near-death encounters evidence life after life. Moody maintains, "Near-death experiences totally transform those who experience them and demonstrate their reality and power."

The cult of the New Age also advocates past lives therapy to uncover the mystery of previous incarnations. New Agers exercise the strategy to solve current fears and phobias stemming from events in past lives. Dr. Ronald Wong Jue, president of the Association for Transpersonal Psychology, places patients under hypnosis to evaluate past-life memories and dreams. The licensed clinical psychologist believes the material world and the consciousness are interconnected.

Dr. Jue teaches that the past, present, and future can be retrieved by examining linear and mythic time zones of patients. For example, he postulates that someone with a vanity problem may have led a previous Cleopatra-type life. Among Jue's theories is the notion that victims of violent crimes were exploiters in past lives. He attempts to get the client to recognize problems on a mythic level to effect a therapeutic cure.

Still other New Age proponents like the Findhorn Foundation and the Perelandra community communicate with plants, believing them to be inhabited by elemental spirits called *devas.* Plant communicators seek wisdom and guidance from the spirits, whom they believe possess feelings and intelligence. Other New Agers advocate astral projection to reach spiritual purity. They claim the soul, when propelled into the astral realm, is a temporary manifestation of a higher, eternal spirit that identifies with Christ.

Critics say this New Age search is really a very old examination of occultism's principles and practices. Reincarnation, astral travel, shamanism, astrology, goddess worship, visualization, and affirmations of inner deity aren't new modes of spirituality. They are ancient ways of claiming to reveal the link between man and God. In fact, antagonists of the movement say that New Age discoveries aren't really mysteries at all. They are only examples of pagan spiritism rediscovered by those with little sense of religious history and no healthy fear of the unknown.

New Age theoreticians are forcing a revolution in man's relationship to his macrocosm as eventful as the way Copernicus and Einstein altered their worlds. The nature of man's body, mind, and spirit will never be the same. Positive visualization, therapeutic healing, guided meditation, and creative imagery all evoke a single transcendent, unifying force. Instead of Gandhis, Jungs, and Christs to guide the way, there are millions of alternate thinkers, each seeking separation from the past while favoring new explanations of reality. Carl Raschke said it well. He claims the New Age movement is "essentially the marketing end of the political packaging of occultism . . . a breeding ground for a new American form of fascism."

The New Age motivation is no longer to be one's brother's keeper. Number One is who matters. New Agers have their own buzzword for it—*autarchy.* Basically, it posits government by self. Hence, the political agenda of the New Age movement ranges from abortion rights to gay rights, even animal rights. For some, it includes polygamous privileges, prostitution, gambling, and, for the most extreme, drugs. And why not? In the New Age, one's own transformed self automatically seeks moral goodness without interference from external laws.

Simply said, New Age truth is not ultimate but evolving. In fact, any kind of moral absolutism is seen as a dogmatic form of spiritual stagnation. As New Age thinker and writer Marilyn Ferguson puts it, the transformative methods of New Age philosophy "lead to the realization . . . there will be no ultimate answers." If truth is a constantly changing reality perceived momentarily, then rightness and wrongness are up for grabs as each instance presents itself. Consequently, androgyny, sexual ambiguity, is a preferred state, and homosexuals may be the most enlightened among us.

The New Age rage is intended to become a new world order in which all becomes one. Theology, philosophy, economics, and sociology will unite as common sciences to obliterate all national boundaries. A central authority could then achieve a consolidated consensus concerning all issues of importance to government and religion. If that sounds a little demagogic, with the potential for Big Brother abuse, never mind. Remember, all is one, one is God, you are one, and you are . . . that's right, God. And since the God in you makes all the decisions, then whatever you decide is right. And if someone disagrees? There's the rub.

The Christian worldview is quite different. God's "shalt nots" are not an oblivious avoidance of each circumstance's merit, but rather a divine perspective that knows the source of ultimate good. Disobedience to God always brings heartache and dysfunction, not because God has arbitrarily ruled so, but because his character is the stabilizing force of the universe. Thus, divine law is an extension of divine character. The Ten Commandments weren't meant to be the Ten Suggestions. They represent truth that is fundamental to the perpetuity of human good, just as the laws of thermodynamics are crucial to the continuance of the material universe. One must wonder what's next on the New Age agenda. When they have exorcised all moral law from society's cognizance, will they next deny gravity its binding role in the universe?

Founders: Rooted in many sources, some ancient, some modern. Marilyn Ferguson, David Spangler, Michael Harner, Jean Houston, Robert Muller, Shirley MacLaine, and others are major theoreticians.

Texts: Marilyn Ferguson's *The Aquarian Conspiracy,* Fritjof Capra's *The Tao of Physics,* Shirley MacLaine's *Out on a Limb, Dancing in the Light,* and *Going Within,* as well as the writings of José Arguelles, Ram Dass, Barbara Marx Hubbard, and many others.

Symbols: Rainbow, globe, lotus flower, mandala, dove.

Appeal: By practicing the philosophies of the New Age movement, advocates elevate themselves to a deity and deny the Christian concept of original sin. Free from accountability to God, New Agers feel personal power and superiority over others.

Purpose: The purpose of the cult of the New Age is to unleash inner gods and attain mortal omnipotence. Advocates attain self-realization by tapping into their subconscious through New Age techniques. They believe the subconscious will conquer all foes and resist all negativism. They restructure perceptions of the world, leading them to a state of personal happiness and power.

Errors: Most New Agers conclude God erred by forbidding man to eat of Eden's tree, which they say had the puissance to unleash man's dormant powers. Thus, they blaspheme God's wisdom. Man's problem is not blindness to his innate goodness and potential for divine conduct, but his incapacity for humility in the face of God's omnipotence. Christians believe humanity needs a mass transformation of its value systems and methods of achieving global harmony. But the transmutability of social institutions and the recasting of human conduct can only occur as individuals are converted by God's grace. Any solution to the human condition that ignores the heart's depravity and God's transcendent wisdom will not usher in a New Age. It can only perpetrate an old lie. Esoteric half-truths do not lead to God. They are manifestations of the "mystery of iniquity" spoken of in 2 Thessalonians 2:7. The marvelous insights and fascinating knowledge New Agers acquire are the "signs and lying wonders" of Satan and his Antichrist.

Background Sources: Marilyn Ferguson, *The Aquarian Conspiracy* (Los Angeles: J. P. Tarcher, 1980); *Straight Answers on the New Age* (Nashville: Thomas Nelson, 1989), 18, 20, 123; *Christianity Today,* 16 May 1986, 17-18; *The Denver Post,* 23 September 1988, 1F; *New Age Journal,* May-June 1988, 67; International Transpersonal Conference 1988 notes.

Address/Location: Worldwide.

See also Holism, Human Potential Movement, I AM Institute, Spiritualism, Trance Channeling.

N I C H I R E N

S H O S H U /

S O K A   G A K K A I

Most Eastern cults offer psychic experiences, authoritarian father-figures, or ascetic rules that are in contrast to hedonistic Western life-styles. How could anyone be attracted by the thought of chanting strange syllables while kneeling before a black-lacquered box containing a small, sacred scroll? Until a scandal involving charges of misappropriation of funds and sexual misconduct by its leader jolted the Nichiren Shoshu organization, 200,000 Americans and 10 million foreigners were performing this ceremony each day. (There are an estimated 10 million adherents in Japan. Total world membership including all the various subsects may be as high as 30 million.) If that seems hard to believe, then consider the testimonials of practitioners who claim that Nichiren Shoshu has brought them love, health, wealth, and whatever else their hearts desire. Jazz musician Herbie Hancock is only one of many people who claim that Nichiren Shoshu has brought harmony to their lives.

In his search to discover the essence of diverse Buddhist teachings, a thirteenth-century Japanese monk named Nichiren Daishonen claimed to have found the "true Buddhism." It was embodied, he said, in the *Lotus Sutra,* a writing attributed to Buddha but actually written much later. Nichiren wrote scores of books, but the real growth of his teachings awaited the formation of the Soka Gakkai (Value Creation Society) in 1930. (Soka Gakkai is the politically active, evangelistic branch of the organization. It operates a 4.5-million-circulation daily newspaper and has a huge temple near Mount Fuji.)

After World War II, the movement grew rapidly under the leadership of Daisaku Ikeda. He made Soka Gakkai a significant force in Japanese politics by establishing its own political party under the name Komei ("Clean Government") party. In contrast to Christ's teaching that the chief should be servant of all (Matt. 20:27), Ikeda declared, "You have to have power to do anything at all meaningful."

This power originates in a series of pagan rituals and beliefs. Members are acquired by a conversion technique known as *Shakubuka* ("brow-beating"), a controversial kind of forced persuasion that borders on brain-washing. An NSA (Nichiren Shoshu of America) document calls it "a merciful method of introducing True Buddhism to nonbelievers." Once they join, many believers become convinced that NSA holds the keys to world unity and peace. Such laudable goals are to be obtained by chanting *nam-myoho-renge-kyo* ("glory to the lotus sutra of the mystical law") before an altar upon which sits the *butsodon* (a black box) containing the *Gohonzon* (sacred scroll). All the while, the devotee fingers the 108 beads of a rosary.

The goal of such devotion is to merge one's self with the essence of Buddha. (Curiously, Nichiren Shoshu differs from other Buddhist sects in that it elevates Nichiren to a rank higher than the Buddha.) Repeated chanting of the *Diamoku* (worship formula) is said to place one in tune with the rhythm of the universe. As a substitute for psychotherapy, chanting *nam-myoho-renge-kyo* is much easier and cheaper. Perhaps more important, its spiritual goals of working out one's karma take second place to the more immediate purpose of satisfying selfish desires. "Happy individuals can build a happy world" is NSA's creed, a hedonistic motto that is well received in affluent, Western cultures. If he were alive, Buddha, who taught principles of denial and withdrawal from material pursuits, might look askance on such egocentric goals.

While most of NSA's emphasis is on acquiring wealth, power, and personal happiness, the pagan religious overtones cannot be overlooked by evangelical Christians. Chanting to the *Gohonzon* constitutes an idolatrous act, and the belief in its supernatural properties could be a dangerous opening for demonic subjection. The *Gohonzon* takes the place of God, while implying at the same time a pantheistic version of deity. NSA's espousal of karmic philosophy and reincarnation place it yet another step away from biblical Christianity. The Buddhist goal of fusing one's nature with the universe negates any individual accountability for sin or salvation. While certain material benefits may be incurred by NSA's chanting, conformity with God's moral laws and forgiveness of sin are something that meaningless repetition can never achieve.

333

Founders: Nichiren Daishonen (1222-1282); modern founder, Tsunesaburo Makiguchi (1930). The cult's main growth occurred under the leadership of Daisaka Ikeda, who was ousted in 1979 due to charges of sexual misconduct and misappropriation of funds.

Texts: The *Lotus Sutra* (writings erroneously attributed to Buddha) and *Gosho* (collected volumes of Nichiren Daishonen).

Symbols: Prayer beads, *gongyo,* a booklet with the words of the *Lotus Sutra, butsodon,* black box containing the *Gohonzon* (sacred scroll).

Appeal: Some members are attracted by the admirable goals of world peace, nuclear disarmament, and abolition of war. Others join in the pursuit of personal desires without moral regard for Christian beliefs or the wishes of others.

Purpose: New members are proselytized with the eventual goal of world domination through political power.

Errors: Nichiren Shoshu promotes a Christless belief with a Buddhist view of reality, while denying Buddha's basic teachings. Salvation is by enlightenment and the attainment of Buddhahood. Occult and spiritistic practices of idol worship, shrines, talismans, false scriptures, and repetitious chants are included.

Background Sources: *Newsweek,* 5 June 1973, 68; Ibid., 27 August 1973, 60; *Time,* 13 January 1975, 12; Walter Martin, *The New Cults* (Santa Ana, Calif.: Vision House, 1980), 321-350; Pat Means, *The Mystical Maze* (San Bernardino, Calif.: Campus Crusade, 1976), 169-180; *Christianity Today,* 23 January 1981, 57; *Time,* 1 August 1983, 60; *Encyclopedia Britannica* (1986), vol. 8, 681.

Address/Location: Headquarters and main temple in Japan. Cult branches throughout the Western world, especially the United States.

NOSTRADAMUS

He supposedly predicted the coming of two antichrists, who materialized as Napoleon and Hitler. Many believe Nostradamus, sixteenth-
century physician and mystic, made those predictions 400 years ago and
that his prophecy of a third antichrist will also be fulfilled. Believers in
Nostradamus also claim he predicted air travel, air warfare, the space
race, electricity, submarines, and even a future bombing of New York
City. His book of prophecies, *True Centuries,* remains popular today.
The word *century* in the book refers to its hundred quatrains, which were
written in convoluted language to obscure meaning, since Nostradamus
feared prosecution as a magician.

Born in 1503 of Jewish heritage, Nostradamus was influenced by the
Catholic church. Although he attained a doctor's degree and was known
as the "healer of the afflicted ones," he studied the occult, alchemy, and
magic. He also taught astrology. Nostradamus predicted the end of the
world in 3797. For those worried about nuclear war, he wrote: "In the
year 1999 and 7 months, there will come from heaven the great king of
terror, to raise again the great king of the Mongols, before and after Mars
shall reign at will."

Other physicians of his time deemed him unorthodox for using home
remedies. One of the plagues that marked the era killed his wife and children, instigating many years of travel. Nostradamus finally settled in
Salon and published his first almanac, which contained prophecies for
the pending year. The almanac was so successful that he continued to
publish a new one each year thereafter. Nostradamus's fame as a prophet
fired up much controversy. Followers visited him from all parts of France.

Catherine de Medici summoned him to the royal court to plot horoscopes for the king and his children, while detractors claimed he represented the devil.

Hitler became fascinated with Nostradamus after Frau Goebbels, wife of the Nazi propaganda minister, introduced him to the *Centuries* in 1939. During World War II, pamphlets based on a forged Nostradamus prophecy that Germany would win the war were dropped from Nazi aircraft.

Nostradamus said all his visions came from God. He admitted that the Bible condemns his methods, which included employing the occult. *True Centuries* may have been written through necromancy or tarot cards, witchcraft or psychic inspiration. The Bible clearly reveals that such foretelling is forbidden and that Christ did not make specialized prophecies about future Nazi political regimes.

Founder: Michel de Nostredame (Nostradamus).

Text: *True Centuries.*

Symbols: None.

Appeal: Many forms of divination are popular today, and ancient occult wisdom is particularly revered. For them, the idea of forecasting the future holds fascination in an uncertain age. The Third Reich's use of Nostradamus reminded many who had forgotten his obscure quatrains.

Purpose: *True Centuries* supports belief in the supernatural, that man can look into the future and arrange the present to his advantage.

Errors: Nostradamus's prophecies were construed through occult methods; therefore, they are the work of Satan. Only God knows the future (Rev. 1:8). It cannot be divined by man. The Bible forbids forecasting the future through divination of any kind (Deut. 18:22).

Background Sources: *The Prophecies of Nostradamus,* edited by Erika Cheetham (New York: Berkley Books, 1973); *The Complete Prophecies of Nostradamus,* edited by Henry C. Roberts (New York: Crown, 1982); *The Plain Truth,* April 1983, 33-34.

P E N I T E N T E S

High in the remote mountain areas of southern Colorado and northern New Mexico live a people caught in a time warp, playing out centuries-old rituals of penance. Each year at Easter, members of the Brothers of Our Father Jesus – the Penitentes, as they are commonly known – reenact Christ's crucifixion. Their devotion includes painful self-flagellation and stark suffering. According to some witnesses, actual crucifixions take place every year during Holy Week. Spokesmen for the Brothers deny this claim, but several outsiders who have observed the ritual insist that the ceremony concludes with a man being raised on a cross. There are also tales of literal nails being used and of the participants actually dying, though such versions of this religious drama are hard to verify.

The history of Penitentes can be traced to a fifth-century movement within the Roman Catholic church. Spanish followers of the discipline emigrated to the New World and subsequently retreated to the rugged mountain regions of the Southwest where they were cut off from civilization. Two centuries later, public knowledge of their activities began to emerge. Though the Catholic church officially denounced their gory activities, the bizarre and clandestine nature of their devotion continued to attract followers.

Unlike their bloodier, better-known counterparts in Brazil and the Philippines, the American Penitentes rigorously guard their secrecy. Eyewitness accounts of present-day cross-bearing, self-whipping, and other torturous acts of penance are hard to verify. Some who claim contact with this strange sect believe that it is currently experiencing a resurgence of interest from those wishing to join its ranks. It has even been suggested that chapters exist in some urban centers of the West. Whether the present fascination with the darker side of occult practices has contributed to such a revival of these ancient masochistic techniques is open to question.

In an age of apathy and contentment, it is only logical that the sufferings of Jesus would incite fascination in the human spirit. To those who fail to see these agonies as the finished work of atonement, there may still lie the haunting appeal of personally reliving such pain to seek favor with God. Known Penitentes in America are confined to the active involvement of several thousand Hispanics. But the ritual has an uncanny attraction for new, curious members who seek to share the Lord's passion. They remind us that the church may have lost a valuable incentive for spiritual fervor by emphasizing the glory of Christ and forgetting that "learned he obedience by the things which he suffered" (Heb. 5:8).

Founders: Spanish Catholic immigrants, circa 1700.

Text: Bible, folklore.

Symbols: Revered religious statues and icons.

Appeal: Adherents share companionship with Christ's passion.

Purpose: To obtain favor with God by self-inflicted penance.

Errors: Penitentes believe atonement comes by personal bloodshed rather than Christ's death and suffering.

Background Sources: *National Courier,* 16 April 1976, 5; "Guarded Secrets of the Penitentes," *Denver Monthly,* May 1980, 24-33; *Dallas Times Herald,* 12 April 1981, 20-27.

Address/Location: Ceremonies are practiced in the Philippines, Brazil, and the southwestern United States.

RAM DASS

What Harvard student in the sixties would have suspected that his bespectacled psychiatry professor, Dr. Richard Alpert, would someday become a Hindu guru?

The year was 1961 and a fellow professor named Timothy Leary had started dropping LSD. Alpert literally joined the trip. After six years of getting high, only to come back down to the same problems, Alpert decided to visit India. There he met a 23-year-old man named Bhagwan Dass. Alpert was so profoundly impressed with Dass that he took up fasting, yoga, and meditation. Eventually, Alpert was taken to Dass's guru, Maharaji, who lived in the foothills of the Himalayas. Dr. Alpert changed his name to Ram Dass, returned to America, and wrote a book entitled *Be Here Now.* It emphasized his philosophy of "living each moment meaningfully."

Ram Dass believes that everyone is on the same spiritual journey to recognize the oneness of all religions and the "truth" that God's spirit resides in each person. A guru is needed to reveal this "truth." A spiritual teacher will suggest the seeker's most expedient way to experience being "here now." Some might be recommended to indulge in yoga or sex while others are encouraged to meditate or chant mantras. Certain disciples are even given the same psychedelic drugs that failed to satisfy Alpert. Ram doesn't exactly eschew drugs. He credits their role in his own spiritual enlightenment by providing hallucinogenic experiences that paralleled spiritistic descriptions in *The Tibetan Book of the Dead.* As Ram Dass, Richard Alpert forsook his Jewish upbringing in Boston. (This estranged him from his family, although he tried to change this; in fact, when his father became terminally ill with cancer, Ram Dass served as his caretaker.) Ram Dass left Dr. Alpert far behind, as if his former vocation took place in another incarnation. He returns to India every other year for a spiritual recharging, and often travels the lecture circuit exuding an apparent happiness he never had during his Mercedes-Benz/private airplane/materialistic days at Harvard. He has even become an activist for the Seva Foundation, a charitable organization he helped found. As a father figure from the turbulent days of flower power, Ram Dass brings a message that meshes well into the Eastern/mystical mainstream of contemporary thought.

Founder: Dr. Richard Alpert, whose following developed in the early seventies with the publication of *Be Here Now.*

Text: Hindu scriptures.

Symbols: None known.

Appeal: Those who look to drugs as a means of transcending reality see Ram Dass as a psychedelic pioneer who has "been there" and knows what he is talking about. His views on religion, even though they are warmed-over *Raja Yoga* beliefs, are perceived as authoritative because of Dass's past.

Purpose: Baba Ram Dass teaches that fulfillment comes from avoiding introspection about the past and future. Instead, his disciples are encouraged to acknowledge their inner divinity and oneness with the universal deity. He claims the result is a nonhedonistic compulsion to explore momentary satisfaction.

Errors: The Hinduistic roots of his teachings are incompatible with a Christian worldview. Moral restrictions are ignored in favor of a pleasure principal, which assumes that reveling in "now" is a desirable way to work out one's karma. The biblical concept of future accountability for sin is replaced by the assumption that inner peace today is more important than preparing for judgment tomorrow.

Background Sources: Ram Dass, *Be Here Now* (San Cristobal, N.M.: Lama Foundation, 1971); *Circus,* July 1971, 40; *The Denver Post,* 15 May 1981, 35; Jane Sugden, "Ram Dass, Veteran Guru," *People,* 28 September 1987, 79.

Address/Location: The Sun, 412 W. Rosemary St., Chapel Hill, NC 27514.

RASTAFARIANISM

He popularized sacramental pot smoking and a king/god named Ras Tafari. He used reggae music, also known as "Jah Music," "Roots Music," and "Zion Rock," to introduce his Rastafarian religion to the masses. Wafting on stage in a swirl of Jamaican ganja (pot), Bob Marley would display a portrait of the late Ethiopian emperor, Ras Tafari (Haile Selassie). While fans cheered, the black musician would shout a dedication to his god.

Together with his group, the Wailers, Robert Nesta Marley introduced roots-rock-reggae to delighted global audiences in the early 1970s. The word *reggae* is Latin for "to the King." Interwoven in Marley's music were strong Rastafarianism messages to encourage worship of Haile Selassie, smoking of holy herbs, and wearing one's hair in unwashed corkscrew curls called "dreadlocks." Marley believed himself a spiritual leader, chosen to share Rastafarianism with the world. He sang, "Some are leaves, some are branches, I and I [Ras Tafari] are the roots."

Rastafarians believe they are reincarnated Hebrews, sons and daughters of Jah, and descendants of the biblical Israelites. They feel they are exiled Ethiopians who must struggle to free themselves from the West's capitalistic grasp. Rastafarians operate under the pretext of peace, love, and brotherhood. The world accepts their reggae music and movies (such as *The Harder They Come,* starring Rastamen Jimmy Cliff and Carl Bradshaw) as harmless entertainment, unaware of who Rastafarians are and the significance of their reggae music.

Because of drug usage and the black liberation political messages con-

342

veyed in its reggae music, the Rastafarian cult has also inspired crime. Murders have been committed by ganja-greedy thieves in homes where Haile Selassie is worshiped. Large quantities of "herb" are usually stashed in Rasta homes for the religious ritual of smoking "the wisdom weed," tempting Rasta gunmen and "wolves in sheepskin," non-Rastafarian men who wear dreadlocks, to steal and assault for the valued drug.

Bob Marley was an outspoken advocate of the Jamaica-based political religious cult, and in 1976 an attempt was made on his life by political opponents. The gunmen failed to kill Marley, who died in 1981 of brain cancer at age 36. The adulterous musician fathered eleven children by seven different women. He's still considered a prophet and is worshiped by many Rastas, some of whom believe Bob Marley's spirit inhabits other reggae singers or that his son Ziggy, by wife Rita Marley, is his reincarnation.

Born in a poor part of Jamaica, Marley gained worldwide recognition and wealth for his reggae music, whose rhythmic roots originated in Africa. Marley was introduced to Kingston record producers by Jimmy Cliff in 1962. A year later, he formed the group Bob Marley and the Wailers with Peter Tosh and Bunny Wailer. The group embraced Rastafarianism as their religion after Marley claimed Haile Selassie appeared to him in a vision. He then adopted Rastafarian beliefs and used his reggae music as a vehicle for spiritual, cultural, and political expression. Bob Marley and the Wailers merged reggae and Rasta in the minds of modern listeners.

Since Marley's death, the Jamaican reggae world has awaited a new musical messiah to provide hope in a poverty-ridden, restless world. Reggae artists such as Toots and the Maytals, Jimmy Cliff, Sly and Robbie, Black Uhuru, Steel Pulse, Burning Spear, Bad Brains, Ziggy Marley and the Melody Makers, Bunny Wailer, the late Peter Tosh, and of course, Bob Marley, continue to influence reggae fans with Rastafarian messages. Musicians like Sly Dunbar, Robbie Shakespeare, Judy Mowatt, and Yelloman have inspired cult followings since Bob Marley's death. Many contend that Ziggy Marley will be the next musical messiah.

Peter Tosh, a musician with Bob Marley and the Wailers, did not escape his murderers. Shot to death in September 1987, his murder appeared to be committed by robbers. But it is much more likely his death was related to the drug trafficking he helped generate. Tosh's female bookkeeper and lover had her own theory, claiming Satan killed Tosh because they planned to conceive a baby, who would be "a powerful boy with the Star of David on his forehead."

Many Rastafarians promote violent revolution and hatred toward whites. On the Caribbean island of Dominica in 1975 a group of young black guerrillas known as the Dreads modeled themselves after dreadlocked Rastafarians. They killed two Canadian residents, slaughtered an American tourist, and attacked local people. Such actions damaged Dominica's tourism, an economic disruption that forced the Dreads underground. In the West Indies, waves of robbery, rape, and an occasional murder by men with dreadlocks were committed after the Dreads devastated Dominica.

The founder of Rastafarianism was Jamaica-born Marcus Garvey, a well-known black movement leader in the early 1900s. The separatist taught blacks that Ethiopia was their promised land and urged them to identify with the wandering tribes of Israel. His teachings quickly became popular in Jamaica and later in America.

Garvey also prophesied that an African king would be crowned the black messiah-redeemer. In 1930, Prime Regent Ras Tafari announced his lineage to King Solomon and the Queen of Sheba. He was crowned King of Ethiopia and took the name Haile Selassie, which means "Power of the Holy Trinity." Marcus Garvey and his followers hailed him as the long-awaited messiah. Worshiping Ras Tafari, they called themselves Rastafarians or Rastamen.

The Rastafarian cult is a religious blend of Ethiopian Christianity, Old Testament Judaism, African animism, and spiritualism. The religion has no consistent dogma, nor does it have a spokesperson other than reggae musicians. To smoke marijuana is considered a biblical mandate and a way of reaching God. Rastas take this idea from 2 Samuel 22:9, which says "There went up a smoke out of his nostrils, and fire out of his mouth devoured: Coals were kindled by it" (KJV). For the Rastas, marijuana yields spiritual inspiration and a "reasoning of minds" between those who smoke it.

Rastas believe Haile Selassie is the lamb or sacred god of black people. Their dreadlocks are the "lamb's wool" or spiritual symbol of devotion to their creator, Jah. Rastas wear dirty, tattered clothing and live in communelike dwellings. They practice polygamy and often steal because they don't work. They've been known to attack police officers, refusing to accept them as authority figures.

According to Rastafarian interpretation of the Scriptures, the Western world will be destroyed in the near future. Their god, Haile Selassie, whom they refer to as "Jah," the "King of Kings," and the "Lord of

Lords," is the returned messiah. Though Selassie has been dead for more than a decade, Rastas believe he will rise from the dead.

Founder: Marcus Garvey, a black movement leader in the early 1900s, who stressed black pride, unity, and independence. Garvey urged blacks to accept Ethiopia as their promised land and to recognize their identity with the wandering tribes of Israel.

Texts: Rastafarians draw ideology from Marcus Garvey's back-to-Africa admonishments during the 1920s and 1930s, as well as from the Coptic and King James Bibles.

Symbols: Rastas wear dreadlocks, symbolizing the lamb's wool of their god, Haile Selassie. Dreadlocks are also worn to instill fear in white men. Rastafarians and reggae fans often wear red, green, and gold—the colors of the Ethiopian flag, which Marley used as a stage prop in his concerts. Many Rastas are strict vegetarians. Seeing themselves as Jews, they frequently wear yellow Stars of David or lion heads (for the Lions of Judah). Haile Selassie's portrait often adorns the backdrop at reggae concerts.

Appeal: Rastas believe the Rastafarian ideals of peace, love, and brotherhood will improve Jamaica. Bob Marley once said, "Conditions [in Jamaica] will only improve when the Rastas have the government there." The religion appeals to blacks frustrated with white civilization. Rastafarianism also provides religious justification for smoking pot. Reggae music is passive, vaguely spiritual, and frequently laments injustice and oppression.

Purpose: The purpose of Rastafarianism is to overturn capitalist privileges. Said Marley, "Until the philosophy wherein one race is superior and one inferior is permanently abandoned and discredited, there is war." Jamaicans are serious about their music and message. Reggae lyrics are sung to address political tensions and social grievances. Reggae music is filled with distorted biblical references to extend the Rasta message of black revolution.

Errors: Rastafarians revere Haile Selassie as Christ and claim Selassie lives and rules, since no trace of his body, grave, or ashes has ever been found. Bob Marley once expressed disgust over materialism and possessions. Said Marley, "God created the earth for us, but people wonder 'who owns the tree, who owns the ladder, who owns the ganja pipe?' " Yet, when asked about his $15,000 silver BMW, he replied, "BMW? That stands for Bob Marley and the Wailers. It seemed like the car we were supposed to have." Those who saw Bob Marley as the Rastafarian prophet now believe his son Ziggy is his incarnation. Says Ziggy, "My father was like the Old Testament. I'm the New Testament." Reggae music conveys messages about a false god, black revolution, and the legalization of marijuana.

Background Sources: *The Philadelphia Inquirer,* 27 September 1981, 1A-24A; *To the Point,* 21 July 1978, 22-23; *Media Update,* 8 July 1988, 12-13; *Billboard,* 1 August 1987, R6, R32-R33; *Rolling Stone,* 25 June 1981, 26-27; Ibid., 24 March 1988, 92.

Address/Location: Rastafarians are headquartered on Marcus Garvey Drive in Kingston, Jamaica.

REORGANIZED CHURCH OF JESUS CHRIST OF LATTER DAY SAINTS

In 1985, Emily Fern "Bunny" Spillman, a 73-year-old grandmother from Denver, Colorado, was among the first group of women to be ordained as elders by the Reorganized Church of Latter Day Saints, also called the "Saints" church or the RLDS. Spillman and her companions are empowered to preach, administer sacraments, and counsel fellow members, activities previously reserved for male elders.

The RLDS decision to break with tradition came after the church's president, Wallace B. Smith, presented a written revelation to delegates at a conference in Independence, Missouri. Accepting the document as the mind and will of God, the delegates voted to accept women into the priesthood. (Some observers have cynically suggested the real reason behind Smith's revelation is that the headship of the RLDS has always been hereditary, and the current prophet-president has no sons, only daughters.) This event accentuates the doctrinal differences between the RLDS and the better known Church of Jesus Christ of Latter-day Saints—also called the Mormons—which still bars women from ordination. (See separate section on the Mormons.)

Wallace B. Smith traces his ancestry to Joseph Smith, Jr., founder of both the RLDS and Mormon churches. The textual basis of both faiths is the work known as *The Book of Mormon,* which Joseph Smith, Jr. claimed to have translated from golden plates given to him by the angel Moroni. Several years earlier the teenage Smith had seen a vision during which Jesus Christ told him all churches were an abomination and that Smith should join none of them. Smith was directed to wait until God chose to use him to "restore the fullness of the everlasting Gospel of Christ again to the earth." Smith may have seemed an unlikely prophet for the latter days, and his *Book of Mormon* may be nothing more than a preposterous compilation of fiction and plagiarized Bible quotes. But today, Smith and his book are revered by the Mormons and the RLDS as foundations of their respective faiths.

The history of the two churches diverged during the early nineteenth century when a schism occurred within the Latter-day Saints over such doctrines as plural marriage for Mormon men, baptism of the dead, and the plurality of gods. In 1844, after Joseph Smith and his brother Hyrum were killed by a mob while in jail in Carthage, Illinois, the Latter-day Saints divided into factions. About 10,000 members followed Brigham Young westward, eventually settling in Salt Lake City, Utah. The majority of the Saints scattered, waiting until Smith's young son, also named Joseph, could fulfill the prophecy that named him to succeed his father.

In 1860, Joseph Smith III assumed leadership of the Latter-day Saints at age 27. The church added the word *Reorganized* to its name, further distinguishing it from the sect in Utah. According to an RLDS pamphlet, the church set about "regathering its scattered members, without 'adding to' or 'taking from' any of the original tenets established by the church when it was organized in 1830" in Fayette, New York.

Today, the Reorganized Church of Jesus Christ of Latter Day Saints has a nationwide membership of about 200,000 and is established in many foreign countries. Church headquarters are located in Independence, Missouri. The RLDS proclaims itself the true Latter Day Saints church, rejecting as heresy many of the more flamboyant tenets of Mormonism. Members profess Christianity, affirming "a belief in God and more particularly in Jesus Christ, the Son who came to earth for the purpose of redeeming humankind." The Holy Spirit is described as "the living power and presence of God, which has been experienced in the lives of persons and of the church down through the ages."

God is seen as personal, "the creator and sustainer of the universe," who nevertheless takes time to intervene in history and to reveal himself to his followers. The Saints member reasons that, while he cannot fully comprehend God, "the fact that God has been experienced in various ways is evidence of God's desire to be known." Ways in which God has revealed himself include "miracles," as well as spiritual experiences of individuals and groups.

Written records of spiritual experiences of the RLDS president-prophets become part of *The Doctrine and Covenants.* This text dates back to 1828 and is a compilation of documents that the church accepts as inspired statements representing "the mind and will of God" and as a standard of church laws and practice. Each new president-prophet is obligated to write down what he considers to be God's will for the church. After various RLDS councils and quorums have read these documents, a vote is taken and approved sections are added to The Doctrine and Covenants.

The Bible, *The Book of Mormon,* and *The Doctrine and Covenants* are the three standard books on which the church is founded. All are considered inspired scriptures. But since God's process of self-revelation continues even today, man's discernment of the scriptures is never quite complete or final.

The RLDS emphasizes its two priesthoods. The Aaronic priesthood is concerned with temporal activities, such as those attended by priests, deacons, and teachers. The more exalted Melchizedec priesthood consists of the elders and the high priests. Examples of its duties are ministering to others, preaching, teaching, administering church laws, and directing church affairs. Members are called to serve in either priesthood by "church officials responding to the spirit of inspiration and discernment."

Sacraments among the Latter Day Saints consist of baptism, for children aged eight; confirmation, by the laying on of hands; the blessing of infants; "The Lord's Supper" or Communion service; marriage; administration or anointing of the sick; ordination to the priesthood; and patriarchal blessing, given privately by the laying on of hands.

The RLDS church believes it is destined to do God's work among his people. Part of this conception is expressed by the ideal of Zion. According to the Saints, their church "is called to gather the covenant people into signal communities where they live out the will of God in the total life of society." The Saints recognize the potential partnership between the church and government agencies, community organizations and businesses. They work with these groups in cooperative ventures to improve the quality of life.

The Reorganized Church of Jesus Christ of Latter Day Saints may be a much more palatable faith than its larger sister church headquartered in Utah. Many of Mormonism's best qualities are present with few of the fanciful rites. But the RLDS is still based upon Joseph Smith and *The Book of Mormon* and still relies upon divine revelations bestowed upon leaders for its direction and growth. The possibility that these revelations may be human fabrications or demonic deceptions is undeniable.

Founder: Joseph Smith III, in 1860, based upon the church founded by his father, Joseph Smith, Jr., in 1830.

Texts: The Bible, *The Book of Mormon, The Doctrine and Covenants.*

Symbol: Logo is a stylized oval globe, the center circle depicting the Christ child standing between a reclining lion and a small lamb, captioned "Peace."

Appeal: Saints members believe in the importance of their work and the uniqueness of their history and calling. Their emphasis on human-oriented service and their hopeful vision of the future, as expressed in the Zion ideal for a future utopia, is attractive.

Purpose: The six objectives for the RLDS, adopted in 1966 and restated in 1973, refer to the interpretation of the "Zionic concept" in world terms. Other concerns included evangelism, emphasis on the value of individuals, and the growth of world understanding.

Errors: The RLDS reveres Joseph Smith, Jr., and his direct descendants as their prophet-presidents. They accept the scriptural validity of *The Book of Mormon* and *The Doctrine and Covenants* and deny biblical inerrancy, saying it has lost certain passages through human editing. The incarnation of Jesus is minimized by seeing man as an eternal and pre-existent being. RLDS has established an unbiblical priesthood that claims access to divine mysteries. Salvation is based on good works. Spiritual experiences and divine revelations are ways to know the Word of God, leaving open the possibility of evolving spiritual truth.

Background Sources: *The Rocky Mountain News,* 18 November 1985; *An Introduction to the Reorganized Church of Jesus Christ of Latter-day Saints* (Independence, Mo.: Herald Publishing House, n.d.); *Who Are the Saints?* (Independence, Mo.: Herald Publishing House, n.d.).

Address/Location: Evangelism Commission, Saints Auditorium, Box 1059, Independence, MO 64501.

See also Mormonism.

REV. IKE

"The lack of money is the root of all evil." So says black preacher Rev. Frederick Eikerenkoetter, better known as Rev. Ike. This distortion of 1 Timothy 6:10 is representative of Ike's Science of Living philosophy, a mixture of black Pentecostalism and Christian Science, laced with evangelical terminology. "Forget about the pie in the sky," this monetary messiah proclaims, "Get yours here and now. You can't lose with the 'stuff' I use."

What is Ike's "stuff"? While some cult leaders obscure their true doctrines with a veneer of orthodox Christian theology, Ike's aberrant beliefs are openly expressed. He sees the Bible as "a book of psychology rather than a book of theology." Satan is "the negative thoughts of lack and limitation" and Deity is "the Presence of God in you." Ike says the purpose of his preaching is to "teach the individual to be master of his own affairs by manipulating his own self-image." Heaven is replaced by "the eternal now" since there are no literal, spiritual realities. Sounding like Mary Baker Eddy, Ike declares, "Everything is a condition of the mind."

The cornerstone of Ike's appeal is rooted in an admittedly materialistic view of success and happiness. He makes no apologies for insisting that those who give generously to finance his own extravagant life-style will, in turn, receive similar benefits from the God-who-is-in-them. Ike's audiences at his Joy of Living meetings empty their pocketbooks in the hope of getting rich quick. Ghetto blacks who see little chance of upward economic mobility are easy prey for Ike's promises. As a result, the biblical concept of receiving from God by giving to God is set aside in favor of unadulterated greed. "The Bible says that Jesus rode on a borrowed ass," Ike explains. "But I would rather ride in a Rolls Royce than to ride somebody's ass!" Ike's blatant materialism is typified in a 1987 mailing, which included this request: "As a man of God I feel that I am to ask you to give God exactly $18.02"—a small amount, it seems, but apparently the accumulation of such amounts have helped fill Ike's coffers for many years. Ike also made this statement regarding poverty: "If it's that difficult for a rich man to get into heaven, think how terrible it must be for a poor man to get in. He doesn't even have a bribe for the gatekeeper."

The fallacy of such unbiblical motives may be easily recognized by the evangelical Christian. But for those who are biblically illiterate, Ike has cleverly filled a vacuum that may have been unwittingly left by the church. Some segments of Christianity have experienced a dearth of strong biblical preaching coupled with an emphasis on the so-called "prosperity gospel." Consequently, some nominal church members feel justified in seeking financial gain in the name of religion. Marginal Christians infected with this "disease" may be concerned very little that Ike's doctrines are nothing more than a rehashed Science of Mind approach. It might be argued that the appeal of the Rev. Eikerenkoetter would be greatly diminished if Christians sincerely reflected God's concern for the poor and lived like they truly believe that "a man's life consisteth not in the abundance of the things which he possesseth" (Luke 12:15).

Founder: Rev. Frederick Eikerenkoetter, born 1935.

Text: "The lack of money is the root of all evil," a misstatement of 1 Timothy 6:10. Rev. Ike also restates John 3:16 to read, "God so loved all of mankind that he gave every man Divine Sonship. And whoever believes in his Divine Sonship, whoever believes in his relationship to God, shall not perish but shall have everlasting life."

Symbol: None.

Appeal: Ike's goal is self-improvement and financial advancement by visualizing oneself in a positive frame of mind. Since all reality is a mental state, those who may not have natural or educational abilities to improve their socio-economic standing are told that by a developed pattern of giving to Rev. Ike they release some inner potential for wealth.

Purpose: Ostensibly, Ike proposes to abolish negative thoughts that induce poverty and replace them with positive mind power, which produces unearned wealth. In reality, it is Ike's financial status that is most directly enhanced, as evidenced by his unabashed and ostentatious display of diamonds and 16 Rolls Royces.

Errors: Orthodox Christian beliefs in self-sacrifice, denial, a personal devil, a transcendent God, the hereafter, and the importance of spiritual values more than material concerns are all negated. These doctrines are replaced by a mind-science approach that emphasizes immediate financial gain over future moral considerations. Ike says, "There is no God outside of you to do a d--- thing for you. Your only savior is your own realization that you are the Christ, the Son of the Living God." His entire system is in contrast to the command of Christ in Matthew 6:33: "Seek ye first the kingdom of God."

Background Sources: Miscellaneous issues of *Action* magazine, published by United Christian Evangelistic Association; *People,* 1 November 1976, 101-103; *US,* 21 October 1985, 60.

Address/Location: United Christian Evangelistic Association, 910 Commonwealth Ave., Boston, MA 02215.

ROSICRUCIANISM

Who they are, where they come from, and what they really believe is a matter of controversy with regard to most secret organizations. With Rosicrucians, these uncertainties are amplified by the volumes of undocumented literature they distribute. They insist that their belief is not a religion, not an occult organization, has no relationship with Freemasonry, and has nothing to do with spiritism. Though there is ample evidence to refute these assertions, Rosicrucians still claim they are nothing more than a "fraternal order" with the intent of awakening "the dormant, latent facilities of the individual whereby he may utilize to a better advantage his natural talents and lead a happier and more useful life."

This statement of purpose seems laudable, but it obscures the somewhat tainted history and esoteric practices that dominate Rosicrucian beliefs. If, in Webster's view, religion is a system of "faith and worship," then the Rosicrucians surely qualify. Those who begin a study of its teachings soon discover that self-advancement is no mere psychological goal. It is dependent upon a complex system of doctrines, rituals, and ceremonies laced with Judaic and Christian concepts, based on pagan mythology and occult practices.

In the seventeenth century, a work entitled *Fama Fraternitatis* appeared in Germany. The book described the religious discoveries of Christian Rosenkreuz, who claimed to have traveled to Egypt and uncovered the mystery of the "rose cross." Though historical dates for his existence are available (1378-1484), Rosicrucians claim the name Christian Rosenkreuz was symbolic, enabling them to assert a much earlier origin for their Order. Wherever their prior historical roots may lie, Rosicrucian Societies flourished in seventeenth- and eighteenth-century Europe. Some evidence indicates they exchanged ideas with Freemasonry. Current-day Rosicrucians deny this philosophical cross-pollination. Freemasonry does include a Rose Croix degree, and there appears to be a historical link between these two closed societies.

Rosicrucians claim that their Order first came to the United States in 1694 under the leadership of Grand Master Kelpius, who was connected with a European lodge. After a time of flourishing activity (Benjamin Franklin and Thomas Jefferson are said to have been Rosicrucians), the Order went into a self-proclaimed period of "outer silence" lasting 108 years. Secret work continued, but overt knowledge of the organization awaited a twentieth-century resurrection. In 1909 Order literature states that Dr. H. Spencer Lewis met with officials of the French Rosicrucian Order. Dr. Lewis was initiated and returned to spark a revival of the Order in America. His efforts continued until his "transition" (the Rosicrucian term for death) in 1939 when his son, Ralph, took over.

What Rosicrucian literature fails to mention is Lewis's contact with the occult group Ordo Templi Orientis (OTO) and the infamous British spiritualist Aleister Crowley. (Crowley was a homosexual, murderer, and practitioner of black sex magic. He sought to violate every moral law possible and actually renamed himself "Beast 666.") Lewis founded the Ancient and Mystical Order of Rosae Crucis (AMORC for short) in 1915. Apparently he was not at all embarrassed to receive the endorsement of the OTO, in spite of its unsavory practices. Religious researcher J. Gordon Melton claims that various emblems of the AMORC, including the Rose Cross symbol, were actually borrowed from Crowley's periodicals. Such information makes even more suspect AMORC's statement that it does not endorse any occult or superstitious beliefs. (Several other Rosicrucian Orders exist: for example, the Rosicrucian Fellowship, founded by Max Heindel, and the Societas Rosicruciana, an American variant, which requires its members to be Masons. Since AMORC is the largest and most visible representative, further discussion will be limited to it.)

To validate its authenticity (and perhaps obscure its more recent checkered history), the AMORC insists its roots extend back to ancient Egypt. In 1500 B.C., Pharaoh Thutmose III is said to have established certain "mystery schools" of the Great White Lodge. His successor, Amenhotep

IV, is claimed to be the "most enlightened man of his time" and the object of much AMORC reverence. No substantial evidence exists to connect these ancient rituals with a continuing observance leading to modern Rosicrucian practices. AMORC justifies this link by declaring that during certain periods of inactive cycles of "outer silence," Rosicrucian ceremonies and rituals were kept alive by secret practices. Therefore, with or without historical evidence, one cannot test the belief system. Its validity is asserted regardless of reason or proof.

Modern AMORC beliefs are a mixture of Egyptian religious tenets, paranormal and psychic interests, and pseudo-scientific pursuits based on alchemy. Members attempt soul travel, development of inner "intuition," healing, and also conduct chemical experiments. The absorbing nature of this approach permits Rosicrucians to encompass almost every form of mystical-transcendent experience, from water witching to mind control. Training for members takes place primarily by correspondence through a series of mail-order *Mandamus,* which are secret, sealed instructions. Neophytes are warned to never reveal the content of such literature nor to explain to outsiders their clandestine ceremonies. "Simply tell them you study one night a week," new members are instructed. "Always emphasize that AMORC is *not* a religion."

The facts indicate otherwise. Members are encouraged to construct what is essentially an altar (they call it a *telesterion*) in their homes. Emblems may include incense, an ankh, candles, and idols of Egyptian deities and rulers. They may hang on their walls a document entitled "Confession to Maat." *(Maat* is supposed to be Egyptian for "truth.") The affirmation begins, "Homage to thee, Great God, Thou Master of all Truth, I am pure." Neophytes are told they are petitioning the "forty-two principal gods . . . expressions of the principal god, the Sun-God, AMEN-RA."

Each lesson gradually introduces more AMORC theology. Since the neophyte affirms he is pure, there is no need for sins to be forgiven. Only "psychological obstacles" are acknowledged, and these are "confessed" to oneself. Prayers are made to "the God of your heart." The penalty for bad *karma* one has accumulated can be expiated by the law of *AMRA.* (A check donated to AMORC is suggested.) God is defined as the "Supreme Intelligence," a form of "pure energy," "The First Cause of All." This Brahmanistic-type deity is totally impersonal and is also said to be a "number endowed with motion."

The Bible takes a special drubbing from AMORC. Genesis is dismissed as "a beautiful poem." The New Testament is said to be devoid of the most important, private teachings of Jesus. Several books are recommended in the stead of Holy Scripture, such as *The Secret Doctrines of Jesus, The Book of Jasher,* and other volumes supporting reincarnation. Bible beliefs are replaced with a concoction of teachings about the lost continent of Atlantis and a race of Negroes called Lemurans. Jesus is said to be the highest initiate of the sun period, and the Holy Spirit is the foremost initiate of the moon period.

Though the AMORC officially denigrates spiritism, the sealed instructions encourage members to contact departed spirit Masters. These are called "psychic contacts with soul personalities" who are now part of "the Universal Soul." These "personalities" are said to be in need of an "identity" to find expression; therefore, the neophyte becomes that "physical medium." Christian theology would view this phenomenon as an example of demonic control when the "personality" (evil spirit) enters (possesses) the "physical medium" (body) of the unsuspecting initiate. In this perspective it is perhaps appropriate that AMORC denies that its "Rosy Cross" represents the Christian crucifix, since the cross of Christ symbolizes the defeat of Satan's kingdom.

Founder: According to the movement's tradition, Christian Rosenkreuz (1374-1484); the AMORC claims its origins are found in ancient Egyptian "mystery schools"; modern American Rosicrucianism dates from its founding in 1915 by Dr. H. Spencer Lewis.

Text: Various geometric and hieroglyphic symbols along with the hidden, esoteric knowledge of the Kher-Hebs, who are said to be the Masters of ancient Egyptian mystery schools.

Symbols: Foremost among their symbols is the "Rosy Cross" (a Christian cross with a rose in the center). Rosicrucians claim that Christians chose the cross as an "arbitrary symbol." To the AMORC, the cross represents "the body of man" with the rose symbolizing "man's soul unfolding and evolving."

Appeal: Extensive use of advertising entices the prospect to "develop your psychic power of attraction." Ads proclaim that great thinkers like Isaac Newton, Francis Bacon, and René Descartes were Rosicrucians and suggest "they were inspired and moved by the teachings and knowledge of Rosicrucianism."

Purpose: The exoteric aim is to help people achieve "an understanding of natural, cosmic laws as the only means of mastership of life."

Error: The esoteric ceremonies of Rosicrucianism lead its followers into ancient Egyptian secret rites that may result in demonic phenomena, including possession and spirit conjuration. (Initiation rituals are verbally affirmed with the words, "So mote it be," a standard oral oath of witchcraft cults.)

Background Sources: Miscellaneous AMORC literature, including *Master of Life, Who and What Are the Rosicrucians? Rosicrucian Digest* (March 1975), *History of the AMORC, Rosicrucian Initiation — Neophyte Guide, Recognition,* various issues of *Master Monograph, The Celestial Sanctum*; Walter Martin, *The Kingdom of the Cults* (Minneapolis: Bethany Fellowship, 1977); J. Gordon Melton, *The Encyclopedia of American Religions* (Wilmington, N.C.: McGrath, 1978), 177-184.

Address/Location: Rosicrucian Park, San Jose, CA 95191.

See also Freemasonry.

SATHYA SAI BABA

We've all seen the magician who gestures with his hands and out pops a bird. But he generally has on a coat, and you wonder just what he had up his sleeve. What would you think of a man with no sleeves who waves his hand and produces a U.S. gold coin (the feat took place in India) minted in the year of your birth? That's just one officially recorded "miracle" of Sathya Sai Baba, perhaps the most phenomenal guru of this century. Since his own sympathetic biographers provide the major source of information regarding Sai Baba, much of this chapter is based on their account. Consequently, what is known about his background is undocumented, leaving some of his claims open to the possibility they are based more on legend than fact.

The forerunner of Sathya Sai Baba, Sai Baba of Shirdi, was born in the middle 1880s in Hyderabad State, India. Before his death in 1918, he had convinced area devotees and skeptics alike that he was an incarnation of God, an *avatar*. Legends declare that he cured leprosy, cast out spirits, appeared in animal as well as human forms, and was especially fond of holy ash, which he produced out of thin air by a gesture of his hand. The ash, called *udhi,* was used for curing ailments and miraculous purposes. When he died, mourners wondered whose body would be the recipient of his next incarnation. Though countless Indian gurus lay claim to the office of an avatar, Hindu theology clearly states that only one incarnation of God may exist at one time.

Entering on the stage of potential avatars, Sathya Sai Baba was born in 1926 in Prasanti Nilayam, India. Even before his birth as Satyanarayana Raju (his given name), strange things happened in his home. Musical instruments would twang unaided in the night, and unseen hands would pound rhythms on a *maddala* (drum). On a certain occasion after his birth, he was laid on top of some bedclothes on the floor. His parents noticed movement in the cloth and looked to see a cobra entwined about the baby's body. Incredibly, no harm came to the child. (Later, devotees took this to mean that his incarnation also included the role of Sheshiara, Lord of Serpents.)

As a youngster, Satyanarayana would produce candy and fruit for his friends—out of an empty bag. When asked how these and other paranormal feats were performed, he explained that an invisible helper named Grama Sakti obeyed his will to give him whatever he wanted. At age 13 he suffered a scorpion bite (though no one could find the culprit) and lapsed into a coma. Shortly after this he exhibited different personalities, and various voices spoke from his body. Some of these entities quoted lengthy portions of Hindu scriptures the boy had never learned. His parents consulted a witch doctor, who failed in an attempt to exorcise any evil spirits from the lad. Two months and 15 days after the bite, he suddenly started producing objects out of the air with a mere flick of his hands. "I am Sai Baba," he declared. No one knew who he was talking about.

Eventually, people in the village of Prasanti Nilayam learned of Sai Baba of Shirdi and became convinced that Satyanarayana Ruja was an incarnation of the late Hindu saint. From then on, Satyanarayana became known as Sathya Sai Baba. (*Sa* means "divine," *ai* means "mother" and *Baba* means "father"—"the Divine Mother/Father.") Tales of Sai Baba's miracles began to abound. To convince men of his reincarnation as Sai Baba of Shirdi, he related conversations that were known only to the departed guru's disciples. He also supernaturally produced articles of devotion that had been placed at the shrine of the Shirdi tomb many miles away.

Whether or not any or all of the supposed miracles attributed to Sai Baba are true is open to question. Such claims either represent exaggerated legends or phenomenal psychic feats. Consider these examples of Sai Baba's powers: Flower petals thrown on the floor fall in the pattern of his name. Pendants, chains, rings, necklaces, and photographs can be plucked from the air by his bare hands and are then dispensed as gifts to devotees. Disciples name a fruit, and it instantly appears on a tree.

Food supply is multiplied. A blinding jet of light streams from his forehead. Cancer is cured. *Devas* (Hindi for "angels") hand him a carved glass bowl that materializes out of nothing. Idol statuettes suddenly appear. Psychic surgery is performed. Rocks turn into candy. A flower bud is transformed into a diamond. Demons are driven out. And a man is raised from the "dead" in a fashion that bears striking similarity to Christ's miracle in Luke 8.

His favorite "miracle" is to produce sacred ash from his waving hand. The ash (*vibhuti,* he calls it) is said to represent the regenerative aspect of the Hindu god Shiva. When given to devotees it becomes a curative powder for all sorts of ailments. At Shiva's annual festival, Baba always performs two miracles. One is the creation of a mound of ash from a small urn. The other is more repulsive to the Western mind.

Hindus sometimes worship Shiva in the form of a *lingam.* Though intellectual Hindus have elaborate explanations about the philosophy of *lingams,* these objects actually represent fertility symbols. The most common form is that of an elongated oval, effecting the shape of a male phallus. During the annual Shiva observance, Sai Baba may speak for an hour or more, and then writhes and twists in apparent pain. His temperature rises to 104 degrees. Suddenly he ejects an object from his mouth—a five-by-three-inch solid *lingam.* He has been known to spit out as many as nine *lingams* on one occasion.

What is the purpose of such paranormal phenomena? A chronicler of Sai Baba's life put it this way: "The miracles of Christ must be taken on faith; those of Sai Baba you can see for yourself." In other words, Sai Baba's miracles are the pudding-proof of the "truths" he teaches. As one writer explained, "They [Baba's miracles] build our faith . . . toward the production of a divine edition of ourselves."

Sai Baba's theology is classical Hinduism. Man is essentially *atma* (soul/spirit), an entity that is formless. It is manifested in five sheaths (spiritual essences) of man, who is divine but has forgotten his god-nature. "Man is not born in sin," Baba declares. Eternal bliss is only possible by conquering earthly desires to reveal the spark of divinity. "If you realize the atma-principle, you become God himself," according to Baba. There are three ways to attain this: karma (action), *jnana* (knowledge) and *bhakti* (devotion to a guru). The latter is Sai Baba's preference. In his perception, the *Sadguru* (God-realized guru) *is* God to the disciple. Only by putting himself completely in the hands of Baba may the devotee be guided to the knowledge of God-love. But who guides the hands of Sai Baba?

As he stands before his disciples, red silk robe flowing and Afro crinkled like a circular mop, he evokes tears and sighs of awe. The contrast between Jesus and Sai Baba is apparent. Though the latter lays claim to being Christ, the avatar for our age, the proofs of divinity both offer are distinctly dichotomous. Sai Baba's feats may not need an element of faith. But a man who claims to be God and then regurgitates replicas of sex organs brings into question the motive of his miracles. Charlatan or psychic, Sai Baba will need more than holy ash to cure what ails him.

Founder: Sathya Sai Baba, born 1926 as Satyanarayana Raju Pratsanti Nilayam, India.

Text: Hindu scriptures.

Symbols: None known.

Appeal: Unlike most Indian gurus who claim to have achieved God-realization, Sai Baba produces apparent miracles as a proof of his avataristic claims. His powers are seemingly greater than those of other *siddhis,* and he performs his feats more frequently. Those who do not believe in the Devil or are unaware of the extent to which his powers may be manifested will be impressed by Sai Baba. They must decide if the source of his phenomena is satanic, psychic, divine, or mere trickery.

Purpose: Baba's miracles are intended to validate his claims of divinity and cause devotees to submit to his wishes and teachings. By thus concentrating on their guru (Baba), who is the form of God, disciples are said to become more placid and thus realize their own oneness with the Supreme. Baba teaches that scriptures are partially effective spiritual guide books, but devotion to the *Sadguru* is the easiest and quickest way to the knowledge of God.

Errors: Sai Baba's miracles, though impressive, are limited in scope and degree. When confronted with this inconsistency of his presumed omnipotent nature, he argues that man has accumulated too much *karmic* sin to heal all those who seek relief. When Christ's resurrection and power over death is compared to his own eventual demise, Baba insists he has conquered death, too. By this he means that he has the power to choose his time and manner of death as well as his next incarnation. The fallacy of these rationales is self-evident.

363

Background Sources: Miscellaneous materials published by Sai Baba Center and Book Store, including "Who Is Sai Baba?" "Sathya Sai Baba Speaks"; Arnold Schulman, *Baba* (New York: Pocket Books, 1975); H. Murphett, *Sai Baba, Man of Miracles* (York Beach, Me.: Weisser, 1977).

Address/Location: India: Prasanti Nilayam (Home of the Supreme), Anantapur District, Andhra Pradesh; "Brindavan," Kadugodi, Near Whitefield, Bangalore, Karnataka State. U.S.: Tacete, California, and Sathya Sai Baba Center and Book Store, 7911 Willoughby Ave., Los Angeles, CA 90046.

SCIENTOLOGY

Make it past the Hare Krishna chanters on the streets of any large city, and you're likely to run into a more conventionally dressed, clean-cut young man or woman offering you a "free personality analysis." Who would suspect that the 200 questions to be posed are part of the recruiting program for the Church of Scientology? Why be skeptical of "an applied religious philosophy" that offers "a clear, bright insight to help you blaze toward your mind's full potential"? After all, Dianetics (meaning "through the soul") promises to reveal "the single source of all man's insanities, psychosomatic illnesses, and neuroses."

Scientology attempts to give the appearance that it is both a science and a religion. Whatever it is, it isn't cheap. An hour of Scientology counseling can cost $300. Some former members say they invested up to $30,000, and one man spent over $250,000, which may explain some claims that the organization's take is over $1 million per week. With guru-like control, its founder and mentor, L. Ron Hubbard, oversaw all Scientology activities from an offshore fleet of ships.

Lafayette Ronald Hubbard published his book, *Dianetics: The Modern Science of Mental Health,* in 1950. It was originally intended to be his psychotherapeutic answer to the techniques of modern psychiatry. The medical community responded with alarm, forcing Hubbard to formalize his theories into a religion and thus seek tax-exempt status and freedom from governmental interference for some of his organizations. Since then, it has blossomed to command the attention of an estimated

600,000+ followers and 4 million sympathizers. In 1986 the church stated it had 6 million members in 35 countries (though some defectors claim that current membership may be less than 700,000). The church reports that more than 7 million copies of *Dianetics* have been sold. Hubbard's reputation as an explorer, science fiction writer, and parabotanist (he was one of the first to expound the idea of communicating with plants) enlarged to make him the worldwide spokesman for this fast-growing cult.

It's difficult to understand Hubbard's teachings without a crash course in Scientology nomenclature. (The church has found it necessary to publish a dictionary with 7,000 definitions for the use of over 3,000 Dianetic words.) Hubbard taught that mankind is descended from a race of uncreated, omnipotent gods called *thetans,* who gave up their powers to enter the Material-Energy-Space-Time (MEST) world of Earth. Gradually, they evolved upward by reincarnation to become humans who could not remember their deified state. Scientologists are encouraged to awaken their dormant thetan potential by removing all mental blocks called *engrams.* Engrams are best described as emotional hang-ups, comparable to repressed memories stored in the subconscious. By removing these, persons can realize their true personhood, achieving total power and control over MEST.

Engrams are said to be traumatic experiences in past lives. The "analytical mind" reasons, but the "reactive mind" simply records engrams, which impede spiritual progress. Dianetics teaches the techniques for removing (*clearing*) all engrams. The one who joins Scientology, a *preclear* (PC), is said to be in need of *auditing* to discover his engrams. This is done by using a galvanometer called an E-Meter, which measures the resistance to electric current by recording galvanic skin responses. As with a polygraph (lie detector), the instructor (auditor) asks a series of questions while the student holds the two tin cans of the E-Meter in his hands. (More elaborate models are available for a "donation" of $215.) Scientologists insist the auditing procedure is like a church confessional. Those who have removed the psychic hindrances of their engrams are said to be *clear.* The clear one is a thetan who has audited out his reactive mind responses.

While *Today's Health* contends that Scientology attracts the "weak, confused, lonely, and emotionally ill," there are others who genuinely look to Dianetics for altruistic reasons. Scientologists have tried to keep a clean image, publicly eschewing drugs, adultery, and premarital sex. Members are usually well-scrubbed, respectable, middle-class types.

Church ministers wear the conventional black clerical clothing and white collar and even sport crosses, though they point out it isn't representative of Christ's crucifix. Scientologists talk at length about their anti-drug abuse program, called Narcanon, and their efforts with prisoners and the mentally retarded.

When their teachings and tactics are questioned, Scientologists are not prone to turn the other cheek. "Ron [Hubbard] says you only get hurt when you duck," explains Jeff Dubron, a church leader. Reports have continually surfaced regarding the church's alleged tactics of harassment, intimidation, and defamation of critics. An FBI raid on church headquarters revealed a hit list of enemies. Included were the mayor of Clearwater, Florida, who exposed their clandestine activities regarding a hotel purchase, and Paulette Cooper, who wrote *The Scandal of Scientology*. The government finally charged church officials with spearheading break-ins at several government offices. The purpose was to acquire documents that might embarrass and silence certain opponents. Seven Scientologists, including Mary Sue Hubbard, L. Ron's wife, were found guilty of conspiring to obstruct justice.

But ethics and legality of conduct are not the foremost criteria for evaluating any system of belief. Christians are concerned with Scientology's relationship to the Bible. A major creed of L. Ron Hubbard is that "man is good." This tenet is consistent with the Dianetic belief that man is descended from the gods and may someday evolve to reclaim his thetan potential. Other doctrines and practices include astral travel, regression to past lives, and the "urge toward existence as spirits" (Scientology Dynamic number seven).

Hubbard claimed that his teachings were "the road to spiritual freedom." Those who question the compatibility of Scientology and Christianity need to be reminded that Hubbard declared Dianetics to be "the spiritual heir of Buddhism in the Western world." The regal 30-room mansion and 57-acre estate the church occupies in England symbolize Scientology's success on earth. But Christians who are preparing for life after death feel a sense of compassionate concern for those who fruitlessly search for meaning in nonexistent past lives.

L. Ron Hubbard died January 24, 1986, at age 74. He had spent the last two years of his life on a remote and meticulously manicured 160-acre ranch site in California. Heber C. Jentzsch assumed leadership of the movement.

One of Hubbard's survivors was his eldest son, Ronald E. DeWolf, who changed his last name to remove any associations with his father. Even before Hubbard's death, DeWolf referred to him as "one of the biggest con men of this century," a black magic practitioner who concocted his theories while under the influence of drugs. DeWolf, now a Christian, also says his father had many mistresses and was plagued by venereal disease.

Founder: L. Ron Hubbard, 1911-1986; Church of Scientology founded in Washington, D.C., 1955.

Symbols: A cross, believed to have ancient religious connotations with the bar denoting matter and the vertical symbolizing spirit.

Appeal: Among those drawn to Scientology are disaffected youth looking for a simple, structured view of life; emotionally distraught individuals who shun traditional psychiatric techniques because they are too complex; and seekers of truth who are impressed with the dramatic claims of physical well-being and positive mental development promised by Dianetics.

Purpose: Scientology purports to explain all of life's difficulties and contradictions in terms of occurrences in past lives. These mental blocks are removed so the individual can return to the deified state from which he came many incarnations ago.

Errors: Occult practices of age regression and astral travel are based on theories of reincarnation. Extrabiblical information regarding man's origin (as a god called thetan) and mystical beliefs regarding the relationship of spirit and matter are essential to Dianetics. Man is good, Christ was merely a "cleared" individual, and the existence of an eternal heaven and hell is denied.

Background Sources: *The Denver Post,* 7 September 1976, 2BB; *The Kansas City Times,* 14 July 1977, 2B; "Scientology," a cassette recording by Walter Martin; *Newsweek,* 23 September 1974, 84; *Dianetics,* Scientology introductory pamphlet; L. Ron Hubbard, *Dianetics: The Modern Science of Mental Health* (New York: Church of Scientology, 1950); *People,* 17 August 1978, 20-24; *Christianity Today,* 7 December 1979, 54-55; *Celebrity,* no. 19, Scientology publication; *Christianity Today,* 7 March 1986, 52; *Newsweek,* 6 December 1982, 125.

Address/Location: Various world locations, including Washington, D.C., and Sussex, England; 1306 N. Berendo St., Los Angeles, CA 90027; P. O. Box 31751, Tampa, FL 33633.

S E L F -
R E A L I Z A T I O N
F E L L O W S H I P

(Paramahansa Yogananda)

If Paramahansa ("highest swan") Yogananda ("bliss through divine union") were alive today with access to the media, Eastern gurus such as Guru Maharaj Ji and Maharishi Mahesh Yogi would find themselves facing some stiff competition. Had he not died in 1952 after founding the Self-Realization Fellowship (SRF), the estimated 500,000 worldwide adherents of the SRF might be part of a much larger company of devotees.

Yogananda came to the United States in 1920 to address the International Congress of Religious Liberals. His subsequent lectures across America attracted a wide following out of which in 1935 he formed the SRF (current headquarters in Los Angeles). The appeal of SRF teaching is essentially Hindu, with the "realization" of God coming when one achieves "cosmic consciousness." To arrive at this state, one must pursue yogic disciplines, including exercises, daily meditation, and abstinence from meat and alcohol.

The foremost practice facilitating transcendence beyond the illusory material world is *Kriya Yoga,* described as a "highly scientific technique for the control of subtle life currents." As a Hindu, Yogananda taught that "cosmic consciousness" could ordinarily be attained only after a million years of reincarnations. With Kriya Yoga, the same results can be obtained in only three years with "intelligent self-effort." As a benefit, the SRF devotee "is gradually freed from *karma* or the lawful chain of cause-effects equilibriums." Yogananda boasted that 30 seconds of Kriya Yoga "equals one year of natural spiritual unfoldment." In addition, this esoteric mastery of breath control promises "continuous oxygenation of the blood . . . enabling the heart to become quiet." As a testimony to the application of Kriya Yoga, SRF officials report that "even 20 days after death, Paramahansa Yogananda's body was apparently devoid of impurities." Whatever the state of his corpse, his teaching did not alter the finality of death.

Background Sources: Paramahansa Yogananda, *Autobiography of a Yogi* (Los Angeles, Calif.: Self-Realization Fellowship, 1972); *People,* 6 October 1975; *Undreamed-of Possibilities* (Los Angeles, Calif.: Self-Realization Fellowship, 1971).

SHREE

RAJNEESH

(Bhagwan Shree Rajneesh)

To most mystical gurus, sex, drugs, and hedonism are impediments on the path to enlightenment. Not to Bhagwan Shree Rajneesh. "I don't profess anything," he declared, and his disciples acted accordingly. For students of Eastern religions who consider asceticism too confining, this was it.

At first, all one had to do was grab the next plane to Poona, India (a route taken by notables such as Diana Ross, Ruth Carter Stapleton, and 50,000 others). Once there, all clothes were shed for orange robes. Candidates for Rajneesh's brand of spirituality prostrated themselves the moment Rajneesh entered the room. The seekers then received a new Hindi name and a beaded necklace with Rajneesh's face in a locket. One important warning: devotees had to wash thoroughly—especially their hair. Guards stood ready to sniff the hair of each entrant, whose every lock had to be clean and free from oil before being allowed into his divine presence. Though he lays claim to being a "living God beyond time in a state of continuous bliss," Rajneesh has diabetes and a horrible case of asthma.

Bhagwan's teachings abound in 80 books and more than 500 tapes. The message is simple: Anything goes. He preaches indiscriminate premarital sex, open marriages, and the abolition of the family, which he says is "the biggest threat to human progress." In his perception of religion, Christianity is a "cult," and even the pope and Mother Teresa receive his castigation. Traditional *sanyasis* (holy men who meditate and renounce the world) may pursue the path to God for years. The Poona guru offers the state of *sanyas,* with all of its bliss, immediately. *Neosanyas* he calls it. "Westerners want things quickly, so we give it to them right away." He promises nothing less than "freedom from everything!"

For years, the bald and bearded Rajneesh was referred to as India's sex guru. At his resort in Rajasthan State he dispensed *tantric* (sexual) yoga and meditation. Western pilgrims at his Poona *ashram* received more of the same. Adhering to his admonition that "the path to desirelessness is through desire," they would smoke pot, disrobe, dance, jump up and down, and pursue sex however and with whomever they wished. The sterilization of female members avoided having to cope with one possible consequence of such libertine ways. Such antics attracted followers in 500 centers worldwide (100 of them in the U.S.). At one point Rajneesh claimed to have half a million followers, although at most he had about 40,000 devoted *sannyasins.* The estimated income totaled between $5 million to $7 million a year, with Rajneesh being chauffeured about in a Rolls-Royce Silver Shadow.

Born in 1931 as Mohan Chandra Rajneesh, he was raised as a Jain in a small village in Madhya Pradesh province. (Jainism is an Indian religion emphasizing extreme asceticism.) After receiving a master's degree in philosophy, he served for a while as a professor. In 1966 he left the teaching profession to fulfill what he saw as God's plan for his life — spiritually transforming humanity. In 1971 he took the title Bhagwan Shree Rajneesh, meaning, "The Blessed One Who Has Recognized Himself as God." He established his first *ashram* at Poona, India, in 1974.

The Poona *ashram* usually had approximately 5,000 to 7,000 devotees in residence at any given time. As Rajneesh attempted to create a communal theocratic state, area citizens were offended by the way his followers displayed uninhibited sexual affections in public. Circulated stories about erotic licentiousness and physical violence inside the *ashram* walls eventually provoked harassment from the townspeople. To escape the criticism (and avoid a crackdown from Indian tax officials), Rajneesh packed up his collector's 150,000-volume library and, claiming medical problems, entered the United States — along with twelve tons of luggage.

For years, he had been seeking "a new site, isolated from the outside world." As the dismantling of the Poona *ashram* was taking place, word surfaced that officials of the Chidvilas Rajneesh Meditation Center had already purchased (with $1.5 million in cash) more than 100 square miles of ranch land near Antelope, Oregon (120 miles southeast of Portland). Disciples attending his meditation sessions would observe the sex-guru sitting motionless for long periods of time as he entered a self-proclaimed period of "speaking through silence." It is now apparent that Rajneesh was formulating plans to establish the world's largest spiritual community on these shores—much to the chagrin of many solid Oregonians!

In August 1981 Rajneesh moved his sect to Rajneeshpuram, a commune built for his followers at a cost of $35 to $40 million. At its peak, the 64,000-acre commune was home to around 4,000 people and included a productive truck and dairy farm. Rajneesh owned 93 Rolls-Royces. Large weekly ads in *Time* magazine proclaimed messages such as, "*Repression* should not be a word in the vocabulary of a *sannyasin* [seeker]." A majority of Rajneesh's followers at this point were well-educated—64 percent had bachelor's degrees and 36 percent had advanced degrees; 22 percent were professionals in psychiatry or psychology.

The guru's teachings were an amalgam of Western psychotherapeutic techniques and Eastern religion. His devotees attended group therapy and practiced meditation. Courses offered at the Rajneesh International University in Rajneeshpuram included "Breath Energy Ecstasy" and "Rajneeshercize."

Meditation at Rajneesh's *ashram* went through five stages, from hyperventilative breathing to Sufi dancing. Participants were often required to wear blindfolds, and many discarded their clothing. Since Rajneesh saw the logical mind as a barrier to spiritual progress, it was stilled by such exercises as staring at his picture without blinking for an hour. Even his endless list of irrelevant rules was designed to rid one's thinking of questioning processes. He also encouraged "rebirthing," a state of returning mentally and emotionally to mother's womb before the trauma of birth. Ultimate illumination came when Rajneesh pressed his thumb into the center of the initiate's forehead to awaken the mystical third eye.

Rajneesh's kingdom began to fall apart in the early 1980s. Enraged citizens in nearby Antelope were doing all they could to get rid of the cult, which had gained control of the city council and renamed the town "Rajneeshpuram" in 1983. In November that year the State of Oregon sued, claiming the city of Rajneeshpuram was a theocracy and violated the U.S. Constitution. Although one court ruled the city's incorporation legal in July 1985, a host of other problems overcame the organization. The Indian government still sought $3 million in back taxes from Rajneesh's residence in Poona. Closer to home, suits and counter-suits filed by Oregon and even former followers resulted in increasingly negative publicity. In September 1984 his followers rounded up about 2,000 homeless people in major cities across the U.S. and shipped them to the commune. Local citizens accused them of attempting to take over the county under the guise of humanitarianism. The final blow fell when Rajneesh himself, arrested as a fugitive in North Carolina, pleaded guilty to illegal immigration charges in 1985 and was ordered out of the United States.

The movement collapsed amid rumors of wiretapping, arson, poisoning, assault, and shady fortunes in Swiss bank accounts. In September 1985 the guru announced his religion was dead, going so far as to claim that "Rajneeshism" had been created by his top aides, who had also tried to poison him. The people of Antelope got their town back, and Rajneesh's thousands of followers scattered, only a few staying at what remained of the nearby commune.

After leaving the United States, Rajneesh was turned away from several other countries. In November 1985 he returned to his original *ashram* in Poona, India, although his current personal secretary said that his followers would try to overturn the court ruling that ordered him to leave the U.S.

In the wake of AIDS, even before he left the U.S., his message shifted from the advocacy of free sex to discouraging such behavior, providing condoms and rubber gloves to those followers "who cannot or will not abstain from sex." An article in *The Rajneesh Times,* the movement's newspaper, even discouraged kissing.

Addicted to the pleasures of wealth and adulation, Rajneesh has been heard to admit his relief at not having to pretend he is enlightened anymore. In December 1988 he told 10,000 followers in India that his body had become host to the soul of the ascetic Gautama Buddha, which name he preferred over "Bhagwan." Several days later Rajneesh exorcised himself of that spirit when Gautama disapproved of his use of a Jacuzzi. His new name, he said, was "Zorba the Buddha." In January 1989 he announced that he had changed his mind about being Buddha and preferred to be called simply "Shree Rajneesh."

Founder: Shree Rajneesh, born 1931 as Mohan Chandra Rajneesh (also known as Acharya Rajneesh, Bhagwan Shree Rajneesh, Gautama the Buddha, Zorba the Buddha).

Texts: Hindu scriptures and Rajneesh's books, including *Beyond and Beyond, Above All, Don't Wobble,* and *Meditation: The Art of Ecstasy.*

Symbols: None.

Appeal: Graduates of consciousness-raising cults in the Human Potential Movement are often looking for a new discipline or experience beyond what they have already encountered. Rajneesh gives them a spiritual rationale for uninhibited self-gratification, especially of the sexual variety. To one unfamiliar with biblical guidelines regarding meditation and self-expression, his therapeutic approach of negating all hang-ups may sound like good advice.

Purpose: The goal of God-realization is accomplished when thinking and knowledge have been circumvented. One can live in a constant meditative state, an existence of innate responses to Rajneesh's programmed precepts. Each *sannyasin* is encouraged to live a sexually vigorous life with spiritual sanction.

Errors: Shree Rajneesh departs from traditional Hindu morality as well as biblical standards of sexuality. God is the universal consciousness, not a person. Man is the center of determining what conduct is permissible. Christianity enhances self-identity in contrast to Rajneesh's attempt to destroy one's emotionally protective barriers of self-worth. Meditation should be a concentrative act of the will, not a chaotic, mindless, druglike state of emptying out the consciousness.

Background Sources: *Time,* 16 January 1978, 59; *People,* 16 February 1981, 36-38; *People,* 23 March 1981, 78; "A Journey Towards Faith," *Radix,* n.d.; Paul Barrett, "Leader," *Gallery,* n.d., 21; Frank Zoretich, "Oregon County Fears," *USA Today,* 18 September 1984; Neal Karlen, "The Homeless and the Guru," *Newsweek,* 24 September 1984, 35; Roberta Green, "The Rolls Royce of False Prophets," *Eternity,* December 1985, 10; George Lurie, "Antelope, Ore., Makes a Return," *USA Today,* 30 January 1986, 3A; "Rajneeshee Leader's Spirit Fiery," *Rocky Mountain News,* 7 September 1987, 166; "Guru Wants to Return," *Rocky Mountain News,* 9 February 1988, 110; Howard G. Chua-Eoan, "People: Butt Out, Buddha!" *Time,* 16 January 1989, 78; "What's in a Few Name Changes?" *The Denver Post,* 16 January 1989, 10.

Address/Location: Main Rajneesh Meditation Center, formerly in Poona, India. Primary U.S. Centers: Chidvilas, 154 Valley Road, Montclair, NJ 07042; Geetam Rajneesh Sannyas Ashram, Box 576 E, Lucerne, CA 92356; Antelope, OR.

SIKH

FOUNDATION/

3HO

FOUNDATION

(Yogi Bhajan)

Yogi Bhajan has been accused of being a womanizer who demands group massages from female attendants with whom he takes turns sleeping. The charges stem in part from his mystical view of sex, which he teaches in the *tantric* tradition. In fact, Yogi Bhajan claims to be the "only living master of *tantrism.*" More than 5,000 followers (he claims 250,000) have joined his 150 Sikh Dharma U. S. *ashrams.* Bhajan's disciples arise at 3:30 A.M. for a day of meditation and to practice *Kundalini Yoga.* This system of yoga is supposed to be a simplified way of attaining spiritual enlightenment by releasing energy that travels up the spine.

Another title claimed by Bhajan is Supreme Religious and Administrative Authority of the Sikh Religion in the Western Hemisphere. Sikhism (discussed earlier in this book) is a monotheistic system of Hinduism and Islam that seeks God-realization through meditation. Indian Sikh officials aren't so certain that the once obscure Delhi airport customs officer deserves to be the leader of Western Sikhism, "the holiest man of this era." They view with suspicion his luxurious ways (over $100,000 a year in lecture fees). The manner in which the democratic principles of Sikhism are merged with the autocratic, sexually explicit style of Bhajan's 3HO (Healthy, Happy, Holy) Foundation is looked upon with equal skepticism.

In addition to indulging in nude massages and rapid breathing techniques, couples are instructed to stare into each other's eyes (or at a picture of Bhajan) while chanting *Ek Ong Kar Sat Nam Siri Wha Guru,* the repetition of God's name in a "sacred" language. Though yoga has never been an essential practice of Sikhism, Bhajan insists that in order for his disciples to experience the "infinity of God," they must position their arms and fingers in precisely patterned angles.

"The man who ties a turban on his head must live up to the purity of the whiteness and radiance of his soul," Bhajan proclaims from his 40-acre ranch near Espanola, New Mexico. The traditional Sikh symbols are uncut hair, symbolic daggers, combs, bracelets, and special chastity underwear (the "five Ks" – discussed earlier in the chapter on Hinduism). Critics wonder if Bhajan may have eliminated this special garment ensuring moral purity in his zealous pursuit of *tantrism*.

Background Sources: *Newsweek*, 21 April 1975; *Time*, 5 September 1977, 34-35; *Columbus* (Ohio) *Dispatch*, 12 December 1978; J. Gordon Melton, *The Encyclopedia of American Religions*, vol. 2 (Wilmington, N.C.: McGrath, 1978).

S I L V A

M I N D

C O N T R O L

The introductory lectures certainly seem harmless enough. And the come-on is directly to the point: "In 48 hours you can learn to use your mind to do *anything* you wish." That "anything" presumably includes waking up without clocks, increasing powers of memory, improving creativity, solving problems, and developing ESP. Silva Mind Control (SMC—also called Psychorientology) is the brainchild of José Silva, a Laredo, Texas, hypnotist who began mental experiments in 1944. His investigations were based on the assumption that the mind can generate more energy and function more effectively at a lower "subjective" state of brain wave frequency. Silva proposes to teach the student how to maintain alert consciousness while deriving the supposed benefits of deeper states of consciousness.

Alphagenics, the science of investigating and measuring brain waves, has classified four levels of consciousness: *beta*—the waking state of conscious actions; *alpha*—the state of relaxation and meditation; *delta* and *theta*—subtler levels of the mind that Silva Mind Control purports to unlock. At the delta level one has the capacity to achieve "cosmic awareness, enlightenment . . . Christ awareness," proponents of SMC contend. Such religious overtones are just part of the occult/mystical nature of José Silva's techniques.

In the past few years much attention has been given to the differences between the left and right sides of the brain. Silva, like other New Age cultists, claims that the right brain—the intuitive, "spiritual," feeling side—is too often neglected as we favor the left side, which is more rational and logical. According to Silva, Jesus came to free us from our left-brain fixation and teach us the value of our God-given right-brain abilities. Silva sees himself as one of the fortunate "10 percenters," the 10 percent of the population who can effectively use both brain hemispheres. (This is an interesting example of combining recent scientific findings—although the left-brain/right-brain dichotomy is still questioned by many scientists—with religious teaching to give SMC the flavor of being hip and relevant.)

Most people who are attracted by its glowing prospects see no harm in quietly listening to a prerecorded cassette that features a soothing voice giving instructions on how to relax. I have had the opportunity to attend public presentations promoting SMC. These sessions make no attempt to obscure the close association that "psychorientology" has with practices such as hypnosis, yoga, TM, biofeedback, and various paranormal phenomena. At one such meeting I watched an SMC promotional film that likened Silva's techniques to the powers exercised by spiritualistic mediums. Most people are apparently more fascinated than frightened by such associations. About 6 million people in more than 71 countries have plunked down approximately $200 each to embark on the 48-hour-long course. Advanced courses offer intense involvement in occult practices.

Silva Mind Control openly courts the development of extrasensory and clairvoyant powers. Students are also taught that dilemmas in life can be solved by mentally visualizing a "laboratory." Once this fantasized room has been "furnished," the subject is told to mentally solicit "laboratory technicians (counselors)." Sometimes SMC parlance refers to these assistants as "spirit guides" or "guardian angels." The evangelical Christian can hardly feel comfortable with the close parallel such "counselors" have to the spiritistic phenomenon of demonic manifestations.

SMC also takes over where positive thinker Norman Vincent Peale leaves off, and adds a dash of Christian Science as the clincher. Negative thoughts are forbidden in favor of positive perceptions, which, according to Silva, actually have the power to alter reality. But these "positive beneficial phrases" may become a system of salvation by works, since the illusion of evil need only be negated by merely pronouncing it out of existence. Thus, the methodology of SMC becomes a mental exercise more suited for manipulation by visualized "counselors" than by a suffering Savior.

Background Sources: José Silva and Philip Miele, *The Silva Mind Control Method* (New York: Simon and Schuster, 1977); Various SMC publications and promotional literature; Walter Martin, *The New Cults* (Santa Ana, Calif.: Vision House, 1980).

See also New Age Cults.

S N A K E

H A N D L E R S

Bearing a deadly diamondback rattlesnake on his shoulders, a 46-year-old man known as Prince performs a religious dance at the Holiness Church of God in Jesus' Name. He steps on a second dangerous snake with his bare right foot. With his other foot, he rakes the squirming ends of the snake as the clatter of the creature ensues. Oblivious to the bleeding wound on his hand, Prince steadily chants, "Praise the Lord" with mounting fervor.

Prince then returns the snakes to their boxes and walks behind the church's pulpit. He lifts a jar of liquid he claims is laced with strychnine to his lips and takes a gulp. Next he picks up a soft drink bottle filled with flammable liquid. The wick is lit, and Prince deliberately holds its fiery flames under his chin. Like other snake handlers, Prince believes dancing with snakes, drinking poisonous substances, and exposing his flesh to fire will provide eternal life.

But Prince found an early death instead of everlasting life. He was arrested for violating a North Carolina law against handling snakes. He defied authorities and continued to conduct religious services with the slithering serpents. Bitten on the thumb by a rattlesnake in Tennessee, Prince refused medical attention and died two days later.

Other snake handlers have died as a result of their dangerous practices. The Reverend Liston Pack witnessed two deaths in his church. Pack and his fellow Holiness Church of God members meet each week to pray, handle snakes, and drink strychnine. Known as the "Snake Man" in eastern Tennessee, Pack claims his faith in his religion was shaken only once. That was in 1973 when he watched his brother, Buford Pack, and the church's founder, Jimmy Williams, die writhing deaths after drinking strychnine. The incident only temporarily shook his faith, however, and he continued to handle snakes and drink strychnine.

Snake handling is primarily practiced in rural areas from Georgia to Ohio. The cult is made up of congregations of independent, fundamentalist churches often adhering to Jesus Only doctrines. The cult is prevalent in the Appalachian hills of West Virginia and had its start in 1909, when George Hensley, a Holiness circuit preacher, began the practice of snake handling in Tennessee. Hensley died in 1955 of snakebite, but the ritual of snake handling lives on.

The Jesus Church at Micco, West Virginia, is the center for snake handling, strychnine-drinking worshipers, who take their text from Mark 16:17-18 of the King James Version of the Bible. Their faith is based on a stone-cold reading of the words, "If they drink any harmful thing, it shall not hurt them," which is why the group drinks strychnine. They also interpret the words "They shall take up serpents" to mean they must handle poisonous snakes.

Snake handlers sing a song called "I Know the Bible's Right, Somebody's Wrong" as live rattlesnakes clatter in their clutches. These mountain people engage in ceremonies that last for hours and intensify in volume and emotion. The music and rhythmic clapping of hundreds of hands creates a religious fervor of enormous magnitude. The people jerk involuntarily, as if possessed.

Snake handlers raise their arms high and cry out Jesus' name as serpents glide everywhere. Then they pick up Eastern diamondbacks and timber rattlers and copperheads and dance with them. The idea of the practice is that true faith in God protects believers from harm. A middle-aged man with neatly combed hair holding two thick rattlesnakes in his hand explained, "The Lord told us what we could do, and that's exactly what we're doing." He and others believe snakes won't bite them and that successfully handling the venomous reptiles yields religious power and the approval of God. After the ceremony, the congregation gathers around a table spread with food.

Beyond handling serpents and fire and drinking harmful substances, snake handlers believe in casting out devils, speaking in tongues, and laying hands on the sick. An anointing or blessing ceremony is performed during religious services to protect the snake handlers from being bitten.

Says one snake handler of the blessing, "When I get anointed, I get numb all over." When members feel the anointing start to break, they put the snakes down. Anointment doesn't always work. One snake handler, Dewey Chafin, has been bitten 91 times. Most other snake handlers have been bitten several times. Those who are bitten refuse medical treatment, believing the matter is in God's hands. They maintain that God has more power to heal than doctors. Sometimes they triumph over the poison. Other times they die.

A snakebite is not viewed as a sign of sin or punishment. According to one advocate, "That's just the way God wants it. This is a suffering life, and you have to suffer if you want to reign with him." This philosophy conflicts with the Christian belief that God can work through people in the medical profession. Self-inflicted suffering is not commanded by God, as snake handlers believe. Snake handlers play with life and death, a game that leads to disillusionment and self-defeat.

Snake handlers may turn to their strange worship to offset their austere lives, many of which were economically devastated by the coal industry demise. Their church provides the guidelines and structure by which they live their lives. The church strictly forbids seeing movies, smoking or chewing tobacco, wearing makeup, or growing beards or long hair on men. The monotony of their lives can be broken by flirting with death under the guise of religion. Handling poisonous snakes permits them to release energy and feel alive.

Snake handlers claim they don't worship serpents. Yet the poisonous snakes are treated with the utmost reverence and respect, housed in the homes of church members and well fed. The snakes are carefully returned to their natural habitats in the fall. Explains Bishop Kelly Williams of the Micco Jesus Church, "Snakes, too, have the right to live. God gave it to them."

The pastor of a Tennessee snake-handling church also denies reverence for the reptiles. He speaks of God's role in the practice. Says the reverend, "I never test my faith. I am as afraid as you are of snakes, but perfect love casts out fear, and when you overcome fear you can pick up the serpent." His philosophy strays from Christian theology because God does not ask man to jeopardize his life in order to obtain his love.

Dancing with poisonous snakes and drinking strychnine is no way to worship God. It's radical cult behavior that can result in a death that parallels suicide. Some snake maneuverers allow their young children to handle snakes, which can end in fatality. In such cases, the snake handlers are committing murder. Junior Church, a snake handler, permits his children to handle snakes. He asserts, "I'd rather lose a child now and have it go to heaven than keep it 100 years and have it go to hell."

Founder: George Hensley, Holiness circuit preacher who in 1909 started snake handling in Tennessee and died of a snakebite in 1955.

Text: Snake-handlers' faith is based on Mark 16:17-18 of the King James Bible, which reads, "These signs shall follow them that believe; In my name they cast out devils. . . . They shall take up serpents; and if they drink any deadly thing, it shall not hurt them."

Symbols: Snakes symbolize danger, which, when conquered, earns approval from God. Strychnine symbolizes the harmful drink spoken of in Scripture. If successfully drunk, the favor of God is bestowed on the drinker.

Appeal: The snake-handling cult appeals to people living in austere rural areas, people who are forbidden outside entertainment or glamor. Those attracted to snake handling are the devout who feel the need to publicly demonstrate their faith by participating in a dangerous ceremony held several times weekly.

Purpose: The purpose of the religion is for struggling rural people to manipulate deadly serpents by biblical mandate. If they can handle the snakes, they've overcome the weakness of fear and find favor in God's eyes.

Errors: God doesn't ask us to endure self-inflicted suffering to win his approval. Snake handlers misinterpret the Bible to create danger and excitement in their lives. Jesus told the Devil, "Thou shalt not tempt the Lord thy God" (Matt. 4:7), a prohibition against Christians entertaining such presumptuous, life-threatening activities.

Background Sources: *The Denver Post,* 15 July 1977, 8BB; *The Rocky Mountain News,* 27 October 1982, 50; *US,* 18 July 1983, 35; *Christianity Today,* 12 July 1985, 56; *The Phoenix Gazette,* 29 December 1984, D3; *Charisma,* October 1985, 102.

Address/Location: Remote mountainous regions of eastern Appalachia.

SPIRITUALISM / SPIRITISM

"But it is Elvis!" she declared emphatically. "I was his fan for years. I know his voice and mannerisms. I'm telling you, it is Elvis Presley who comes to see me at night."

The lady speaking to me claimed to be an evangelical Christian. Before his death in 1977, she had idolized Elvis Presley. When he died, it was as though a loved one had passed away. Now, she felt comforted thinking that his spirit was reappearing to console her grief.

"I don't believe it's a masquerading demon," she insisted. "Elvis always tells me to worship God. He just talks to me, touches me, and assures me that he's gone to be with Jesus."

It was no small task to convince her that whatever had appeared to her had nothing to do with the person or spirit of Elvis Presley. Though her situation was unique, I have counseled scores of individuals who feel they are communicating with the actual presence of a departed friend or relative. Not only do such occurrences "confirm" an eventual reunion with loved ones, they also provide information about life beyond the grave. In a time of sorrow, many are tempted to look past death's veil for some seemingly objective "proof" that those for whom they grieve continue their existence in some other realm.

After a period of decline due to the onslaught of scientific rationalism, Spiritualism is once again on the rise. Our post-Christian age has produced a biblically illiterate populace unaware of Scripture's stern denunciations of any who attempt to seek knowledge or comfort by contacting the spirit world. Such conduct in Old Testament times was punishable by death (Lev. 20:6, 27). Today, these laws are seen only as the unenlightened injunctions of a theocratic state.

In recent times, the late Arthur Ford, a Disciples of Christ minister, served as a medium to perform séances on live television. Episcopal Bishop James A. Pike endorsed Ford's blasphemy by seeking to contact his son, who had committed suicide while on LSD. A best-selling book, *The Other Side,* explored Pike's burgeoning fascination with paranormal realities. Pike's ecclesiastical superiors neither censored nor defrocked the bishop for daring to attempt what cost King Saul his kingdom and his life (1 Chr. 10:13)!

Spiritualism / Spiritism may be mankind's oldest religion. From the shamans of primitive cultures and the seers of ancient paganism to the psychics who frequent today's TV talk shows, Spiritualism has an unbroken history in almost every culture. In the strictest sense of the term, Spiritism is the overt worship of spirit beings, exemplified by voodoo practitioners in Haiti, macumba devotees in Brazil, and black magic advocates in Africa. However, since any form of contact with spirit beings results in a deeply felt sense of devotion, obeisance, and honor for these entities, there is little real difference between Spiritism and Spiritualism. For practical purposes, any technical semantic distinctions will be ignored in this chapter. The term *Spiritualism* will be understood to also encompass the activities of most Spiritists, with our major focus being directed toward organized Spiritualism as it exists in Western culture.

Psychic activity in the eighteenth century centered on the life and work of Emanuel Swedenborg (discussed under Swedenborgianism in this book), as well as the experiments of Franz Anton Mesmer. Mesmer's investigations into hypnotism and magnetic healing sparked the interest of a shoemaker named Andrew Jackson Davis. In 1843 Davis was hypnotized, and while in a trance he displayed clairvoyant abilities and experienced visions. He philosophized about a system containing six spheres of existence in the afterlife by which man spiritually progresses upward. Davis's theories were explained in *Principles of Nature: A Divine Revelation* and *The Voice of Mankind,* books still revered by Spiritualists.

A more precise birthday of modern Spiritualism is March 31, 1848. The scene was the Hydesville, New York, residence of John Fox. Mrs. Fox became aware of some strange rapping sounds emanating from her upstairs and cellar. Margaretta, 15 years old, and Kate, 12, her two daughters, claimed they were communicating with a disincarnate entity they called Mr. Splitfoot. Splitfoot informed them he was actually Charles

B. Roena, a peddler who had been murdered in the house some years previously. The sisters worked out a code (one tap—no; three taps—yes) with Splitfoot.

Newspaperman Horace Greeley endorsed the "Rochester rappings," and hundreds of curiosity-seekers descended on the Fox home. All across the country, other mediums began making similar claims, and Spiritualism entered its golden age. Advocates included such renowned figures as James Fenimore Cooper, Sir Arthur Conan Doyle, Elizabeth Barrett Browning, Daniel Webster, and William Cullen Bryant. It was even rumored that Abraham Lincoln's wife was holding séances in the White House.

In 1888 the Fox sisters confessed that the rappings were accomplished by a method of cracking their toes. (Margaretta, who had become an alcoholic and a convert to Roman Catholicism, later retracted her confession and was readmitted into Spiritualism's good graces.) Despite this damaging admission, the Fox home in modern Lilydale, New York, is still considered a mecca of Spiritualism and bears a shrine marker declaring, "There is no death."

Spiritualism was introduced to England and Germany in the 1850s, and in the United States mediums flourished during the years 1880-1920. According to the National Spiritualistic Association, its ranks have increased to 160 member churches in America today.

The essence of Spiritualism is talking with or receiving information from beings who have departed this life. Communication with the beyond takes place at a séance. Interested parties gather in a darkened setting, since the entities are said to be less likely to appear in the full gaze of either too much light or too many people, especially if some are nonbelievers. Ectoplasm, the foul-smelling, milky-white substance that exudes as an "umbilical cord" from the medium's mouth, is said to be an energy form that will not function properly without darkness. Since ectoplasm may be the essence out of which the apparition and/or voice trumpet (the video and audio of the spirit world) emanates, séances are always held in dimly lit surroundings.

What goes on at a séance is unpredictable, though certain occurrences are standard fare. As the participants sit quietly in a circle, lights may appear, ghosts may materialize, a trumpet may convey the message of disembodied speech, objects may levitate, and the medium may be taken over by a spirit *control* who answers the inquiries of those who have gathered. The spirit guide, who generally is already known (*familiar*) to the medium, may control his subject's mind or subject the medium to a trance state. The voice and personality of the medium then change as the spirit imposes his will and character upon his vehicle of communication.

Mediums usually specialize in a particular type of spiritistic phenomenon. While a trance state is the type most commonly effected, others may use automatic handwriting, table tipping, or actual materializations. In the latter case, the spirit is often recognizable (either facial or full bodily dimensions appear) to someone present at the séance. This presumed visitation by a loved one seems incontrovertible proof of life after death, especially if the spirit relates information known only to the grieving participant.

What is the source of such eerie events? Some are unquestionably fraudulent. The contrived activities of magicians and hucksters have long been the nemesis of "respectable" Spiritualists. Swindlers have often preyed upon the grief of those who are bereaved and have staged séances for handsome fees. Henry Sedgwick, founder of the Psychical Research Society, which investigates the claims of supernaturalism, remained a skeptic until his death. However, the history of Spiritualism presents too many bona fide claims to dismiss such evidence outright. Only the nonbiblicist who ignores the sorcery of Pharaoh's magicians (Exod. 7:11) and the "signs and wonders" of the Antichrist (Rev. 13) would conclude that the feats described by the Spiritualists are beyond the realm of possibility.

Some researchers and certain Christian writers (myself excepted) feel that some paranormal happenings at séances may be attributed to the extraordinary psychic abilities of the medium. It has been speculated that a universal subconscious mind exists and that certain highly skilled experts can plug into the information it contains, much like getting information out of a computer. Such nonsupernatural ESP and telepathy may enable some mediums to draw knowledge out of the seeker's subconscious. However, certain documented cases of séances exist where the information interchanged was beyond the realm of any conscious or unconscious ideation of those present. While it may be arguable that the spirit of man possesses latent, untapped powers, two things seem certain. First, God never condones or promotes the exploration of these powers, especially when telepathic phenomena violate the moral sovereignty of another person's mind. Second, most phenomena of Spiritualism seem to exist in a realm that defies naturalistic explanation and confounds the investigations made by scientists and parapsychologists. Most evangelical observers would acknowledge that some Spiritualists genuinely communicate with spirit beings. The serious student of the

Bible believes such entities are fallen angels, the demonic emissaries of Satan's kingdom of darkness.

It should be noted that some Spiritualists claim there are biblical pretexts for their activities. The Transfiguration in Matthew 17 is viewed as an example of spirit materialization. Pentecost is said to have been the "greatest séance in history." In fact, Spiritualists believe that Jesus was the master medium of all time. They hold that the stone was levitated from his tomb and that his own disincarnate entity materialized before the gaze of the disciples. One Spiritualistic writer suggests that "by a slight change of name, 'medium' for 'prophet,' 'clairvoyant' for 'discernment of spirits,' 'psychic phenomena' for 'miracles,' 'spirit lights' for 'tongues of fire,' the close affinity of the two systems [Spiritualism and biblical Christianity] becomes apparent to all sincere investigators and students."

Gordon Lewis, Christian apologist and cult expert, has observed that this word game "makes the Bible endorse what its writers emphatically opposed! The prophets received their messages, not from the spirits of the dead, but from God. Spirits were discerned (1 Cor. 12:10), not by clairvoyant apprehension, but by their teaching of Jesus Christ (1 John 4:1-3). Biblical miracles, unlike Spiritualistic phenomena, took place in nature and in broad daylight. They served not to entertain nor comfort individuals, but to establish God's redemptive program."

Having discarded objective biblical truth on the basis of subjective, speculative spirit communication, Spiritualism has developed its own belief structure. Though many Spiritualists prefer to consider themselves Christians, The National Spiritualistic Association of Churches officially affirms that Spiritualists are not Christians. (They also disavow any endorsement of belief in reincarnation.) That is to be expected since one of their spokesmen has declared, "Advanced spirits do not teach the atonement of Christ."

Seeking to mimic Christian forms of worship, Spiritualistic churches conduct services that resemble the church gatherings of most denominations. There are, however, some significant differences. Though furnishings may include a pulpit, pews, crucifix, and organ to accompany singing, members receive "spirit greetings" in place of the pastoral blessing. The presiding minister's sermon may be delivered while in a trance. Psychic readings replace prayer, and familiar hymns such as "Just As I Am" and "Holy, Holy, Holy," have subtle lyric changes to avoid affirming Christian doctrine.

Spiritualism is a system of theories based on whatever information has been supplied by spirit beings who range from the profane and blasphemous to the refined and intellectual. Over the years, organized Spiritualistic churches have codified their beliefs into "Seven Principles" and "Nine Articles." These doctrines are listed below, allowing Spiritualists to speak for themselves as to their view of God and spiritual realities:

Seven Principles
1. The Fatherhood of God;
2. The Brotherhood of Man;
3. Continuous Existence;
4. Communion of Spirits and Ministry of Angels;
5. Personal Responsibility;
6. Compensation and Retribution Hereafter for Good or Evil Done on Earth; and
7. A Path of Endless Progression.

Nine Articles
1. We believe in Infinite Intelligence.
2. We believe that the phenomena of Nature, both physical and spiritual, are the expression of Infinite Intelligence.
3. We affirm that a correct understanding of such expression and living in accordance therewith constitute true religion.
4. We affirm that the existence and personal identity of the individual continues after the change called death.
5. We affirm that communication with the so-called dead is a fact scientifically proven by the phenomena of Spiritualism.
6. We believe that the highest morality is contained in the Golden Rule: "Whatever ye would that others should do unto you, do ye unto them."
7. We affirm the moral responsibility of the individual and that he makes his own happiness or unhappiness as he obeys or disobeys Nature's physical and spiritual laws.
8. We affirm that the doorway to reformation is never closed against any human soul here or hereafter.
9. We affirm that the precept of Prophecy contained in the Bible is a divine attribute proven through Mediumship.

What the Articles and Principles do not tell about Spiritualist beliefs may be summarized in the following statements: Every human is a divine child of God, no less a part of the Infinite Intelligence than was Christ. There is no actual hell, no ultimate judgment of man's life. The crucifixion of Jesus was no more than "an illustration of the martyr spirit."

Original sin, miracles, and the Virgin Birth have no place in Spiritualism.

In recent years the older forms of Spiritualism—such as séances—have declined in favor of the "newer" forms—trance channeling, for example—advocated by such notables as Oscar-winning actress Shirley MacLaine. Entertainers, never noted for their orthodox beliefs, have jumped on the New Age bandwagon, with Shirley MacLaine in the driver's seat. New Age beliefs are discussed elsewhere in this book, but it should be mentioned here that an important part of MacLaine's and others' beliefs is the concept of *spirit guides,* usually (but not always) spoken of as departed human beings who speak through *channelers,* who are like human telephones connecting the living to the spirit world. MacLaine's favorite channeler, Kevin Ryerson, is a prominent figure in her many best-selling books. According to MacLaine, her spirit guides communicate to her using the electromagnetic frequencies of Ryerson's body. (Note the scientific flavor of this statement. Note also that the old word *medium* is abandoned in favor of the more contemporary, scientific-sounding *channeler.*) MacLaine's spirit guides also have spoken to her without using a channeler. On one occasion they—at her request—took possession of her so she could give an electrifying stage performance. MacLaine also claims that her guides have validated their authenticity by revealing intimate details about her life, details no living being could know.

As with the New Age movement in general, MacLaine's belief system is a hodge podge of various cult and occult practices. While she claims that some spirit guides are departed human beings, she says that other entities have never been incarnated. (The older forms of Spiritualism usually had no interest in spirits that had not at one time been human beings.) MacLaine also rather uneasily combines her Spiritualism with her now-famous belief in reincarnation. (Some of her guides are, she says, people she has known in her past lives.) Classical Spiritualism—fairly conventional people who sought to contact the spirit of a departed loved one—may be waning, but the New Age movement with its "any belief may be valid" attitude encourages a new form of Spiritualism, a form that focuses on obtaining power. MacLaine's account of her mesmerizing stage performance, in which her guides "permeated" her legs and arms during her dance numbers, is an encouragement to many people to seek out these benevolent guides and the power they can provide. The Elvis devotee mentioned at the beginning of this section may have merely wanted assurance that the much-loved Elvis was indeed still alive in some way.

Most New Age-influenced people are not seeking comfort, but power.

What may be concluded about channelers and mediums whose receptivity to vibrations from the spirit world welcomes poltergeists (ghosts), apports (movements of objects by psychokinetic means), and clairvoyant powers to see beyond the five senses? Their search for secretive knowledge violates God's prohibitions on such behavior ("The secret things belong unto the Lord"—Deut. 29:29). Luke 16 clearly illustrates that an impassable gulf separates the dead from the living. And if they could return, Jesus declared that anything the dead might say would have no ultimate moral consequences on the living (Luke 16:31). Jesus himself came back from the dead, and yet the undeniable proof of his resurrection is not accepted by many.

There is nothing the "initiates of a higher order" have to offer by way of comfort that has not already been offered by the Holy Spirit, the Comforter. The capricious messages of ghostly apparitions at mysterious séances can hardly promise more than the certainty of life after death assured to Christians by the One who conquered the grave. Spiritualists are generally not devious individuals, though many are enticed into the darker realms of black magic. They are often kindly people, who make warm friends and vow to promote morality for the common good. But their good intentions cannot remove the sting of death. Death is the result of sin, and only by facing that fact squarely through repentance can the resurrection promise of Christ offer hope.

Founder: Spiritualism is the outgrowth of Spiritism, a universal pagan practice of fallen man outside the Judeo-Christian tradition. The National Spiritualistic Association of Churches, the oldest and largest of Spiritualistic bodies, was formed in 1893. Also prominent among the nearly 20 Spiritualist denominations are the International General Assembly of Spiritualists and the National Spiritual Alliance of the USA. Hardcore membership of Spiritualist churches probably numbers less than 10,000, though church officials estimate there are more than one-half million adherents.

Texts: Books by Andrew Jackson Davis, as well as *Oahspe* by John Newbrough, and the *Aquarian Gospel of the Jesus Christ* by Levi Dowling. Shirley MacLaine's many best-sellers, including *Dancing in the Light, It's All in the Playing,* and *Going Within* are popular examples of how Spiritualism finds expression in the New Age movement.

Symbol: The Spiritualist creed, affirming "the belief in personal survival of death, which can be demonstrated by mediumship."

Appeal: Spiritualism capitalizes on the distraught emotions of those who have suffered the loss of loved ones and desire to communicate with them after death. The spirits that are contacted may offer to reveal the past, prophesy the future, and divulge spiritual "truths." The bereaved, the curious, and those fascinated by the paranormal may be enticed to experience the apparent proof of an "afterlife."

Purpose: Spiritualism is defined by the National Spiritualistic Association of Churches as "the Science, Philosophy, and Religion of a continuous life, based upon the demonstrable fact of communication by means of a mediumship, with those who live in the Spirit World." Contact with the dead is presumed to bring consolation to the living. The information obtained from departed spirits is said to produce spiritual growth and moral advancement. In this way sin and wrong conduct will be overcome by personal effort.

Errors: The key test of any spirit's validity has nothing to do with the accurateness of its information but rather its views regarding Jesus Christ. Prayer is the only spirit world contact sanctioned by God, and the Holy Spirit is to be the only guiding source of spiritual information. Scripture abounds with prohibitions regarding the practices of Spiritualism (Lev. 19:31; Deut. 18:10-11; 1 Chron. 10:13; 2 Chron. 33:6; Isa. 8:19; Gal. 5:19-31; 1 Tim. 4:1). The Bible warns of "lying spirits," and the Spiritualist has no gauge to objectively determine the credibility of his sources, since the biblical standards for discerning spirits have been discarded. The hope of reformation in the hereafter removes the urgency of correct moral choice in this life. Messages from subjectively identified spirits takes precedence over the revelation of Christ's gospel. Spiritualism's main tenet is but the paraphrase of Eden's serpent, "Ye shall not surely die," a spokesman whom Christ identified as a liar and a murderer (John 8:44). The Apostle Paul clearly condemned the mediumship of Barjesus (Acts 13), declaring that one who participates in such sorceries is a "child of the Devil."

Background Sources: Edmund Gruss, *Cults and the Occult* (Grand Rapids: Baker, 1980); Gordon Lewis, *Confronting the Cults* (Nutley, N.J.: Presbyterian and Reformed, 1966); Walter Martin, *Kingdom of the*

Cults (Minneapolis: Bethany Fellowship, 1977); J. Gordon Melton, *The Encyclopedia of American Religions,* vol. 2, (Wilmington, N.C.: McGrath, 1978); William Petersen, *Those Curious New Cults* (New Canaan, Ct.: Keats, 1977).

Address/Location: The National Spiritualist Association offices are in Washington, D.C. Those training for ordination as a Spiritualist minister attend the Morris Pratt Spiritualist Institute in Whitewater, Wisconsin. Spiritualism is more prevalent in Europe than in the United States, especially in France and the United Kingdom. It also has a stronghold in South America, particularly in Brazil, which probably has more practitioners of Spiritualism than any nation in the world.

See also Ascended Masters, New Age Cults, Trance Channeling, Voodoo/Santeria.

S R I

C H I N M O Y

At one point in his musical career he adopted the name *Devadip,* a Hindu word meaning "the lamp of the light of the Supreme." Rock fans know him better as Carlos Santana, lead guitarist and guiding force of the rock group Santana. The name Devadip was given to him by his guru, Sri Chinmoy, the son of a West Bengal, India, railroad inspector. (Santana later converted to Christianity.)

Carlos is joined in his devotion by another famed guitar player, John McLaughlin. McLaughlin calls Sri Chinmoy "Perfection . . . a Divine Being." McLaughlin begins his concerts with meditation and proceeds to sing metaphysical lyrics that sometimes praise Chinmoy with unabashed devotion. (*Sri,* incidentally, is not a proper name but an Indian title of honor bestowed on revered men.) Though Chinmoy's actual following consists of less than a thousand fully committed disciples, his influence is far-ranging. He has talked with the pope and lectured at Yale. In a stroke of "enlightened" genius, Chinmoy has established a headquarters at the United Nations, where he supervises the bimonthly U.N. meditation program.

The Hindu doctrine of yoga is at the heart of Chinmoy's system of salvation. Students go through a process that may include *Hatha Yoga,* vegetarianism, and meditation. Chinmoy's way to God is by devotion and surrender to one's guru. Though such a mentor may not be absolutely essential, Chinmoy tells followers that having such a private tutor is certainly the quickest way to achieve the enlightenment he has known since age twelve.

It is crucial that a guru take a disciple through *Siksha,* the yielding of one's life to this teacher. Chinmoy's ritual of Siksha begins with a trance state during which his eyes roll back into their sockets, leaving only the whites visible. This state of meditative bliss (known in Hinduism as *samadhi*) has a powerful effect on the disciple who kneels before Chinmoy. Finally, the devotee receives a portion of Chinmoy's soul in exchange for unswerving service from that day forth. Those who have undergone Siksha claim the experience is so overwhelming they never again doubt Chinmoy's authenticity as a spiritual leader.

Chinmoy claims to have prolific creative talents. He says he has completed over 16,000 paintings in a single day, though such a pace would mean an incredible two per second! (Altogether, Sri Chinmoy has exhibited 132,000 paintings and drawings around the world.) Another phenomenal output was his record of 843 poems during a 24-hour period. He has published 700 books and pamphlets as well as two periodicals, *Chinmoy Family* and *Aum.*

His athletic accomplishments have also been phenomenal. Trying to show people how to push themselves to the limit, he has participated in triathlons, marathons, and the very strenuous ultra-marathons. Many of his followers are long-distance runners. More circus-like in nature are his amazing feats of weight lifting, including an elephant. Not bad for a 57-year-old who is only five-foot-seven.

Unlike many other gurus, Chinmoy does not promise instantaneous enlightenment. Potential followers are warned that they may spend a dozen or more years before they experience their oneness with the Supreme (Chinmoy's designation of God). His mission to America since 1964 is the result of a deliberate attempt to blend the East and West. "There are two aspects of God," he declares. "One is realization and the other is manifestation." To him, Eastern disciples bring the realization of God, while the Supreme's manifestation is seen in Western approaches to spirituality.

Founder: Sri Chinmoy, born 1931, West Bengal, India. Came to the United States in 1964.

Symbols: None known.

Text: Hindu scriptures.

Appeal: Since Chinmoy's personal life-style is less extravagant than that of most imported gurus, his following (though small) is more fervent. The laid-back image gives him the appearance of being more genuine.

Purpose: The guru-student relationship is central to his teachings. Total submission to one's guru facilitates the process of God-realization. His spiritual path is more in line with traditional Hinduism than some other yoga masters, lending emphasis to his selective approach of quality over quantity of disciples.

Errors: Jesus plainly stated that he was the only way to God (John 14:6), and this access is through his redemptive death. Chinmoy seeks to replace the mediatory status of Christ by putting a human channel (himself) between God and man. Chinmoy's doctrine of submission to a guru is the same lie of self-deification the serpent in Eden expounded.

Background Sources: *The Denver Post,* 6 May 1977, 3BB; *People,* 2 December 1976, 50; J. Gordon Melton, *The Encyclopedia of American Religions,* vol. 2 (Wilmington, N.C.: McGrath, 1978), 376; "Celebrities Uplifted by Inner Strength," *Toronto Globe and Mail,* 28 October 1988, A18.

Address/Location: Centers in the U.S., Canada, Europe, and Australia.

See also Yoga.

S W A M I
K R I Y A N A N D A

A former disciple of Paramahansa Yogananda, Swami Kriyananda's mystical name was conferred upon him by his spiritual mentor. It literally means "to do" (*kriya*) the way of "bliss" (*ananda*), or "to pursue and act upon the joyful path of yoga." Kriyananda was born in Rumania of American parents and was named Donald Walters. As an eloquent spokesman for Eastern mysticism, he has been called "the most respected non-Indian yoga exponent in the world."

Kriyananda was a vice-president of the Self-Realization Fellowship until he left to form his own 650-acre commune near Nevada City, California. Commune members meditate at least three times daily and refer to each other by newly designated Indian names. Related business ventures of the commune's Yoga Fellowship, Inc. gross $2 million annually. Devotees are attracted by his Practice of Joy seminars that emphasize the attainment of outward boundless energy and inward fulfillment. "Joy," declares Kriyananda, "is the central fact of your existence." To develop the state of *ananda*, groups are coached in chanting, meditation, "energization exercises," secret sacred yoga techniques, and Kriyananda's "Songs of Divine Joy."

"Belief is no barrier," he emphasizes. "Anyone can benefit: Christian, Jew, Hindu, believer, and agnostic." A closer inspection of *THE PATH, Autobiography of a Western Yogi,* Kriyananda's definitive work, reveals that his entire system presupposes a Hinduistic interpretation of life. These pagan concepts are considered to be the "original, pure essence" of the "ancient teachings." *Raja Yoga* is emphasized as a "science" to uncover the "truth" that man is an integral part of a greater Reality: "this Reality is conscious . . . infinite." Pursuing Kriyananda's path supposedly neutralizes bad *karma* and enables one to "tune in to higher knowledge and guidance."

Background Sources: Miscellaneous Ananda publications and promotional literature.

S U B U D /

R E N A I S S A N C E

(George Gurdjieff)

George Ivanovitch Gurdjieff didn't have the kind of household name that ensures popularity as a cult leader. His personality traits weren't any more endearing. Gurdjieff was a despot with a habit of unpredictability. He was known often to drive down the wrong side of the road at high speeds, accelerating until he ran out of gas. Even his death in 1949 didn't bring an end to his uncanny influence over men's lives. Today, an estimated 5,000 disciples follow his teachings. They are organized into secret societies located all across the United States, from California to Washington, D.C. The life of Gurdjieff was an enigma, but his teachings endure as the number of his followers continues to grow.

The birth and background of Gurdjieff are shrouded in the same mystery that characterized his life. It is likely that he was of Armenian origin. His father first interested him in the occult, and this fascination with the supernatural continued throughout his life. *Meetings with Remarkable Men,* his most widely read book, was made into a motion picture. The volume recounts his travels throughout central Asia, from Tibet to Russia and on to France, where he settled in 1922. It was there that his investigations into secret Sufi brotherhoods and Asian mystery schools prompted him to form the Institute for the Development of Man.

The actual teachings of Gurdjieff, which came to be called "esoteric Christianity," are hard to decipher. G-O groups (*G* for Gurdjieff and *O* for Peter Demianovich Ouspensky, his foremost contemporary disciple) don't advertise their gatherings. Disciples meet for the purpose of discussing Gurdjieff's books and indulging in whirling dervish-type dances, known as "spiritual gymnastics." Their intent is to embark upon "the great adventure of the search for self."

Gurdjieff sought to open up man's consciousness to higher planes of awareness. He believed that most people are "asleep," but they can be "awakened" by having a greater sense of self-awareness. Then they will be able to see their various egos and proceed to seek out which part of them is the real "I." This "Fourth Way," as it is called, is the path to self-transformation. Seekers are encouraged to begin each morning concentrating on putting their real "self" into each part of their bodies, beginning with the toes and so on. Eventually such "self-consciousness" enables one constantly to observe his body and become aware of unconscious mannerisms.

The purpose of such exercises is to shatter the illusion that reactions and intentions are a choice of free will. The next goal is attaining "objective consciousness," by which a person finally discovers his true self. Human effort thus enables one to "save" his own soul.

There is definite value in recognizing that man's heart and his spiritual aims are in a state of disequilibrium. But looking to human merit as a source of right thinking overlooks the fallen nature of man, which clouds any attempt to achieve a truly objective state of mind.

Gurdjieff's teachings are found in books such as *All Is Everything* (sometimes known as *Beelzebub's Tales to His Grandson*), *Meetings with Remarkable Men*, *The Fourth Way*, and *Life Is Only Real When I Am*. In the first of these he speaks of a future prophet of consciousness. Many believe that Muhammed Subuh, a Javanese government official, fulfilled that role. In 1925 a ball of light descended on Subuh and overwhelmed him, an event he called a *latihan* (God's power purifying the soul). Subuh combined three Sanskrit words to come up with the name of his movement—Subud.

Subuh went to England in 1956 and gained a following among former disciples of the late Gurdjieff. He developed a process for surrendering to God's power *(latihan)*. Prospective recipients enter a darkened room and await contact with someone who has already experienced *latihan*. When the power enters, participants exhibit body contortions and vocal utterances. Healing may occur (along with moans and screams) as the goal of an altered consciousness is achieved.

One of the most visible and controversial offshoots of Gurdjieff's philosophy is the Fellowship of Friends. This monastic, well-educated group (generally called "Renaissance") is led by a former grade school teacher named Robert Burton. Burton, who intimates he may be the embodiment of the Second Coming of Christ, lives with a portion of his followers (there are about 1,400 worldwide) in affluent splendor on a northern California ranch.

Gurdjieff's ideals of self-improvement receive a special application from Burton. He contends that the quality of life is enhanced by a worship of beauty and materialism. Higher consciousness is possible by filling one's environment with beauty and comfort. As a result, his disciples provided Burton with a Mercedes Benz and a lavish mansion filled with priceless works of art. Followers attend his bidding and provide free labor for the ongoing construction of cult facilities. Most of Burton's time is consumed in world travel, a task he undertakes to scout for new paintings and porcelains to be added to Renaissance's growing collection of artifacts. He explains to critics that it is his duty to elevate the culture and tastes of those who surround him.

Burton also prophesies a worldwide economic collapse and nuclear holocaust. His hideaway in the Sierra foothills will escape this disaster. The priceless art objects he has purchased will allow him and his group to be surviving apostles of an advanced culture and civilization.

Such refined ideals seem hollow when compared with Burton's moral flaws. When his mother was dying in the hospital, he was practicing a period of self-imposed silence. In spite of her suffering, he refused to speak, an act he sees as exemplifying virtuous self-denial.

Founder: George Ivanovitch Gurdjieff, born 1872, died 1949. Teachings established in Fontainbleau, France, 1922.

Texts: Books of Gurdjieff and P. D. Ouspensky.

Symbol: None.

Appeal: Gurdjieff's teachings represent a thinking man's cult. Philosophical speculation and the potential for self-discovery attract some. Others are intrigued by the clandestine nature of Gurdjieff groups, which give the illusion of being an elitist corps possessing superior knowledge about the mysteries of life.

Purpose: It is obvious that true happiness consists of that which is beyond immediate conscious perception (Gurdjieff called it the "something else"). Gurdjieff followed in the tradition of the ancient admonition to "first know thyself." The Work, as it is now called, believes that humans can evolve to spiritual understanding once they become aware of their own imperfections.

Errors: Gurdjieff taught that the highest goal is to have self-knowledge. Proverbs 1:7 states, "The fear of the Lord is the beginning of knowledge." The quest for higher consciousness always portends the danger of invasion by an alien spiritual intelligence. That "something else" Gurdjieff sought with his blend of Gnostic and occult philosophy is found in Christ, who transforms and regenerates the "I" to be a recipient of "abundant life."

Background Sources: William J. Petersen, *Those Curious New Cults* (New Canaan, Conn.: Keats, 1975); *The Denver Post,* 9 December 1977, *SCP Newsletter,* vol. 5, no. 4, June 1979, 8BB; *San Francisco Chronicle,* 20 April 1981.

Address/Location: Headquarters in New York City. Affiliated groups in major U.S. cities. Published locations and addresses not available. Prospective members often learn of the groups through advertising bookmarks, which have been inserted in the pages of works by Ouspensky. The bookmarks have phone numbers of local centers.

S U F I S M

R E O R I E N T E D,

I N C.

(Meher Baba)

Have you ever been kissed on the forehead? Probably lots of times, especially as a child. Most likely your reaction was to respond with affection or embarrassment. Meher Baba was kissed on the forehead, and he became God—or at least he thought so.

The fame of Jesus spread after his death because of the Resurrection. When Meher Baba "dropped his body" (Baba's term for death) on January 31, 1969, it remained in the grave. Ironically, his fame too has grown, but not because of any miracles he performed. In fact, Baba was prone to catch colds. He rationalized the seeming contradiction of being God yet not being disease-resistant by saying, "The physical body of even a God-realized Perfect Master is subject to ordinary contagion."

There certainly is no dearth of Baba-lovers (as they are called) more than a decade after his passing. They range from sophisticated socialites to college students on the latest Eastern-consciousness trip. Peter Townshend, leader of the British rock group The Who, has been an unabashed Baba-lover since his doper days of the sixties. "Baba is Christ," Townshend declared, because being a Christian is "just like being a Baba-lover." He dedicated a solo album to Baba; it featured songs extolling reincarnation and a final tune adopted from Baba's Hindu prayer, "Parvardigar."

Townshend's devotion exemplifies the status of deity accorded Baba by his followers. "A mere twitch of his nose could split the planet,"

Townshend said, "and a twiddle of his finger could save your life. Luckily his infinite power is used with compassion." If he were God, then why was there not more evidence of his omnipotence? Townshend explained: "Baba rarely interferes. He said, 'Why alter events that occur in a system that is self-perpetrating, self-correcting, and self-destructive when it goes too far?' "

Who is Baba and how did he come to be worshiped as an incarnation of Jesus Christ? Meher Baba was born in 1894 in Poona, India, near Bombay. His parents were Zoroastrians and named him Merwan Sheriar Irani. While attending college he developed an affection for an old Muhammadan woman believed to be a Sufi saint, one of the five Perfect Masters of the Age. One day she kissed him on the forehead, an event that Baba claimed triggered an instantaneous God-realization. From that moment on, Baba was never the same.

He proceeded to spend seven years studying with the Perfect Masters of his time. One of them, Upasni Maharaj, threw a stone at Baba, hitting him in the exact spot where the old woman had planted her kiss. Presto! The event triggered Baba's instantaneous God-realization, and he became aware of his new destiny as the Perfect Master. From then on he became known to his followers as Meher Baba (the "Compassionate Father"), the *avatar* (incarnation of God) for this age, in the lineage of Zoroaster, Krishna, Rama, Buddha, Jesus, and Muhammad. More than that, he claimed to be the final incarnation of the godhead.

In 1921 he gathered a group of disciples and established a colony, including a hospital and school. The unique distinction that set him apart from other *sadhus* and holy men of the East was the self-imposed silence he declared on July 10, 1925. "You have had enough of my words, now is the time to live by them," he declared. By "my words" he meant the precepts of all the religious leaders of his previous incarnations. As Jesus et al., he had said enough. Now was the time to act.

His communications continued by means of an alphabet board and hand gestures. Baba promised this self-imposed silence would someday be broken before he dropped his body. He predicted the words he would speak would bring a surge of spirituality throughout humanity. Needless to say, Baba-lovers waited breathlessly at every public appearance, thinking each occasion might be the time for Baba's anticipated utterance. The Compassionate Father had indicated over and over, "I love you more than you can ever love me or yourself." This intensity of devotion to his disciples made them eagerly await his final words as if they were tantamount to the Second Coming of Christ.

In the meantime, Baba crystallized his teachings by issuing the five-volume *Discourses*. He also published a document entitled "Chartered Guidance from Meher Baba for the Reorientation of Sufism as the Highway to the Ultimate Universalized." His theology was rooted in the Hindu tradition of *Bhakti Yoga*, which teaches that the pathway to God is facilitated by devotion to an earthly yogi. All the better if this yogi claims to be the ultimate avatar. And Baba was not shy about demanding that followers yield totally to him. He pompously declared, "I am neither a mahatma, nor a saint, neither a sadhu or a yogi. I am the Ancient One. The Highest of the High."

What truths then did "God" expound? Basically, Baba introduced Western minds to a warmed-over, syncretistic combination of Hinduism, Buddhism, Zoroastrianism, and Islam. Souls come to earth, he taught, from two sister planets. These souls begin their evolutionary journey upward by incarnating first in stones, then to metals, then onward through vegetables, insects, reptiles, spiders, fish, birds, kangaroos, monkeys, and humans. The human form may dwell on one of seven planes of existence, decided by man's degree of adherence to what Baba called the "seven realities." The final plane is nirvana, where one's consciousness merges with God. But Baba-lovers must be careful. One false step of failed devotion to Baba, and it's right back down to the lowly rocks to start all over again.

But was Baba's silence ever broken? What were those divine words he promised would transform mankind? No one knows, and it seems that Baba died before being able to utter the truths for which his "lovers" had longed. The reader may reach his own conclusions about this man who claimed divinity and yet was smitten by death before being able to fulfill his most heralded prophecy.

Founder: Meher Baba, born Merwan Sheriar Irani, in 1894, Poona, India. Died January 31, 1969.

Texts: Hindu scriptures; *Discourses, God Speaks,* and *Listen Humanity* (books by Baba).

Symbols: None.

Appeal: Baba's claim of divinity must be accepted or ignored. He either was the Christ, an incarnation of God, or a deluded sham. For certain people who have an authority vacuum in their lives, Baba provides a father figure as well as a deified object to worship. Devotees can thus immerse themselves in Baba, tossing reason aside, and heed his call, "Come unto me."

Purpose: "All religions are basically dear to me," Baba taught. "It is not so much what you believe that counts, but what you are." In other words, happiness in this life and preferential reincarnations in the next life are not dependent upon doctrine, but rather on devotion—to Baba. Baba claimed to be God, and his religious philosophy is rooted in the impersonal concepts of divinity explicit in Hinduism; therefore, the goal of his disciples is to become at one with their avatar.

Errors: Baba was a created being, and thus his desire to be worshiped as God falls under the judgment of Romans 1. Jesus warned of false Christs and declared, "Go ye not therefore after them" (Luke 21:8). Romans 12:1 implores men to present themselves as a "living sacrifice" to God, not to a mustachioed Indian whose most important prophecy (breaking silence) was unfulfilled.

Background Sources: *Rolling Stone,* 26 November 1970, 25-27; William J. Petersen, *Those Curious New Cults* (New Canaan, Conn.: Keats, 1975); Meher Baba, *God Speaks, Discourses,* vols. 1-5 (New York: Dodd, Mead, 1955).

Address/Location: Former U.S. headquarters, Myrtle Beach, S.C.; Sufism Reoriented, Inc., 1300 Boulevard Way, Walnut Creek, CA 94595.

SWEDEN-
BORGIANISM

His body had been laid to rest for more than 200 years in Sweden's Uppsala Cathedral, but only recently did his skull join the rest of his bones. The Swedish Royal Academy of Science paid $3,000 at Sotheby's London auction to purchase the head of Emanuel Swedenborg, an eighteenth-century mystic, scientist, and religious philosopher. Swedenborg's remains were considered so valuable that an official diplomatic pouch was dispatched to return the skull to his Swedish homeland.

Emanuel Swedenborg (1688-1772) was born the son of a pious Lutheran minister. He grew up to be a dynamic intellectual who circulated in the highest echelons of government and academia. His expertise in the field of geology earned an appointment as a college professor and membership in the Swedish Diet. Swedenborg traveled widely and gained a reputation as an expert in the field of metallurgy and crystallography. At the age of 52 his life changed abruptly when he answered what he felt was a divine calling to become a revelator of the symbolic meanings in Scripture.

Swedenborg developed mediumistic abilities (automatic handwriting and clairaudience—hearing something not actually audible to others) and practiced astral travel, journeying to the spirit world to communicate with good and evil angels (deceased humans). The messages from these beings convinced him that the Bible needed special interpretation. This led him to write a commentary on the Bible and several lengthy treatises, including *Arcana Coelestia: The Earths in the Universe.* His visions included conversations with persons whom he identified as Luther, Calvin, St. Augustine, and the Apostle Paul. (The latter would not have taken kindly to him because Swedenborg's theology proposed eliminating the Pauline Epistles from the Bible, along with much of the Old Testament.)

Today, Swedenborgian ministers, who represent one of the three main branches of the Church of the New Jerusalem, generally consider Swedenborg's writings to be "divinely inspired." The "truth" he brought is said to represent "the second coming of Christ." In Swedenborg's theological system, those who die enter an intermediate state where they prepare for heaven or hell. In hell, one becomes an evil spirit, but in heaven an angelic status awaits. Either existence is a spiritual state since there is no bodily resurrection. In this life after death, each soul retains the physical appearance of early adulthood as it was lived on earth.

The historic Christian concept of the Trinity is discarded, along with the vicarious atonement—an "abomination" and "mere human invention," according to Swedenborg. Christ's death on the Cross is described as "a climax of a life of service," not "a debt of blood." The personality of the Holy Spirit is specifically denied, and Jesus Christ is God alone, an "indivisible . . . Divine Essence" manifested as three principles. This unique form of Spiritualism is followed by approximately 20,000 Americans and at least 100,000 others worldwide, with the largest concentrations in England. (Headquarters of the U.S. branches are: General Convention of the New Jerusalem in the U.S.A. [The Convention]—Newton, MA; General Church of the New Jerusalem—Bryn Athyn, PA. Also, the Swedenborg Foundation, Dept. EW, 139 E. 23rd St., New York, NY 10010.)

Background Sources: *Eternity,* May 1981 44-45; *The Denver Post,* 16 January 1976, 3BB; Walter Martin, *Kingdom of the Cults* (Minneapolis, Minn.: Bethany Fellowship, 1977); J. Gordon Melton, *The Encyclopedia of American Religions,* vol. 2 (Wilmington, N.C.: McGrath, 1978).

THEOSOPHY

Robert Kennedy lay dead on the floor of a Los Angeles ballroom. Another Kennedy had been assassinated! What was the motive this time? There was no doubt who did it. The gun had been wielded by a young Middle Eastern fanatic named Sirhan Sirhan. Why did he pull the trigger? Investigators might have found the answer if they had bothered to thumb through the pages of the first book Sirhan requested after he was jailed—*The Secret Doctrine* by Helena Petrovna Blavatsky. The principles of Blavatsky's Theosophical doctrines may well have guided the murderous thoughts of Sirhan Sirhan. Sirhan's expedient philosophy of superior spiritual knowledge (which was inspired by Blavatsky's Theosophical teachings) may have made Sirhan feel he had the right to take matters into his own hands.

Helena Petrovna Blavatsky was born in 1831 of an aristocratic Russian family. She exhibited psychic tendencies at an early age, a portent of things to come. Her marriage at the age of 17 to a much older Czarist general lasted only three months. Her perfidious marriage vows were symptomatic of her basic lack of moral character. Biographers report that she swore fluently in several languages, went through two marriages and many lovers, and gave birth to an illegitimate child. Mrs. Blavatsky exhibited a violent temper and was addicted to hashish. Of her ability to sway masses to accept her teachings, she once declared that people "in every part of the world have turned into asses at my whistle and have obediently wagged their long ears as I piped the tune."

Blavatsky's corrupt character hardly qualified her to inaugurate a global religious movement with the motto: "There is no religion higher than truth." Yet the Theosophical Society owes its conception to her guiding hand.

Through the years, her mix of Hinduism and Spiritualism attracted the likes of George Bernard Shaw, Thomas Edison, William Butler Yeats, and Jawaharlal Nehru. Such access to influential people gave Theosophists power beyond their numbers, an estimated 25,000 in 60 countries, including 6,000 in the United States. Recent interest in the occult has swelled the ranks of this organization, which was once dwindling in size partly due to strife from internal dissension.

After her divorce from the elder Mr. Blavatsky, Helena Petrovna proceeded to travel widely. While visiting the United States, she became intensely involved in Spiritualism. She claimed that during her journeys to Tibet she had made contact with disembodied higher spiritual beings whom she called *mahatmas*. Blavatsky told how these masters of the spirit-world had guided her entire life through letters and messages, with even her home containing an altar to the *mahatmas*. In New York she met Col. Henry Steel Olcott, who shared her occult interests. Along with another of her admirers, William Quan Judge, the three formed the Theosophical Society in 1875. Her first book, *Isis Unveiled,* became the Society's central document, and a year later *The Secret Doctrine* was added to the Theosophical "canon."

To outsiders, Theosophy presents a benign image of religious liberals intent only on fulfilling three major tenets: (1) forming a universal brotherhood of mankind; (2) investigating the unexplained laws of nature and the latent powers of man; and (3) encouraging a comparative study of religion, science, and philosophy. A closer look at Theosophical thought reveals a complicated system of cosmological theories based on Hindu doctrine. Blavatsky's universe contains a pantheistic plethora of gods, lesser deities, and *devas* ("angels" in Hinduism), arranged in a hierarchical pattern based on numerological symmetry.

Both man and earth are destined to evolve through seven stages. Earth is in its fourth cycle and man is in his Fifth Root Race, from which point he will evolve upward spiritually. The human body is composed of seven qualities: divine, monadic, spiritual, intuitional, mental, astral, and physical. To evolve spiritually, man must raise his consciousness beyond earth's material plane with the aid of occult phenomena and the *mahatmas.* Though Blavatsky owed a debt of gratitude to Spiritualism for sparking her early endeavors, she eventually became an ardent foe. According to her, Spiritualists were erroneously engaged in contacting the lower levels of psychic entities. Helena Petrovna was more concerned with directives from the ruling masters of the spirit world.

Foremost among these deities is a being known as the Lord of the World. Under his authority are a trinity of Buddhas and a variety of "rays" and emanating spirits, including Master Morya and Master Koot Hoomi. Master Jesus is considered to be a reincarnation of Lord Krishna, the Hindu deity. The cosmological status now held by Christ had once been filled by the Greek god Apollonius. The desired destination of man's soul is *devachan*, "heaven" to Theosophists. "Hell" is known as *kamaloka*, a purgatory type of existence where souls await another chance in a new reincarnation. Even the most evil offender need not fear a permanent, final divine judgment. "Man is a god in the making," wrote one leading Theosophist.

Blavatsky traveled to India in 1879 and declared that the Theosophists' headquarters would be in Adyar, a suburb of Madras. It was there that the vocal and written communications from the *mahatmas* became more frequent. However, during a return visit to England in 1884, Blavatsky's spiritualistic messages came under closer scrutiny. She was accused of being a magician, hypnotist, and charlatan. The prestigious Society of Psychical Research investigated her claims and found them to be considerably lacking in credibility. This blow to Blavatsky's veracity nearly destroyed Theosophy.

One major accomplishment of her stay in London was meeting Annie Besant, a radical activist. Upon joining the Society, Besant's oratorical skills brought about a resurgence in Theosophy's growth. She eventually became head of the Society after Blavatsky's death in 1891. Though Helena Petrovna had once been toasted as a "world traveler, multilinguist, psychic, knowledgeable occultist, and altruist," she died as a lonely, obese, and miserably sick woman who was considered a fake and deserted by most of her followers.

With Blavatsky gone, Henry Olcott and William Quan Judge struggled for control of the U.S. Society. They eventually split into two factions, with Olcott, who was more interested in Eastern occultism, directing the European group. Before his death in 1907, Olcott claimed to receive messages from the *mahatmas* indicating Besant was next in line to lead the flock. In the United States, Judge tried to synthesize Western philosophy with occult theories and openly split with the London/Adyar division in 1895. Shortly after Judge died in 1896, Katherine August Westcott Tingley (she had been thrice married), a Spiritualist with amazing occult powers, took over the American branch of Theosophy.

Most of today's Theosophists belong to the Olcott/Besant wing, though a smaller group faithful to Judge and Tingley continues with headquarters in Altadena, California. The Theosophical Society of America, with headquarters in Wheaton, Illinois, keeps close ties with the British Theosophical Society. Current president is Dorothy Appenhouse. Remaining true to the vision of Blavatsky, she has encouraged modern Theosophists to dabble in contemporary occult phenomena such as Kirlian photography, and in paranormal practices like psychokinesis. Coates cautions those who look to Theosophy as a spiritual lodestone by saying, "We have more questions than we have answers."

Though Theosophy seeks to encompass all religions, the Christian message understandably comes in for considerable drubbing. Theosophists have no need for the cross since *karma* and reincarnation guide their search for redemption. The atonement of Christ is dismissed as a "pernicious doctrine" perpetuating the deplorable idea that "wrongdoing by one can be set right by the sacrifice of another." After all, the incarnation of Christ had no unique significance since, according to Theosophy, "christs and saviors of the age have been appearing at propitious times since humanity began existence."

Its foremost leaders have led undistinguished lives, its leadership has historically been rocked by scandal and internal dissent, and its teachings have been tinged by the dark, spiritistic arts. Yet Theosophy survives, and indeed thrives in the fertile soil of today's disenchantments with materialism. A leading Theosophist once declared, "Theosophy evokes a philosophy so profound and recondite, trying to explain it to someone is impossible. It takes years—lifetimes." And, it might be added, it also takes rosy-tinted glasses to overlook the foibles and fables of its founders.

Founder: Madame Helena Petrovna Blavatsky was born in Russia in 1831, the daughter of Peter Hahn, descendant of a noble German family. She died in 1891 while living in exile in Germany. The Occult Theosophical Society was founded in New York in 1875 by Blavatsky and Henry Olcott, aided by William Quan Judge.

Texts: Writings of Madame Blavatsky, including *The Secret Doctrine, Isis Unveiled, Cosmosgenesis,* and *Anthropogenesis.* Though Blavatsky's books are considered divinely inspired, other books and authors are also revered: Besant—*Ancient Wisdom*; Judge—*Ocean of Theosophy*; Leadbeater—*At the Feet of the Master*; L. W. Rogers—*Elementary Theosophy.* The religious philosophy of Theosophy is rooted in Hindu religious texts (*Vedas, Upanishads, Bhagavad-Gita*) and other occult sources.

Symbol: A combination of religious designations including Egyptian ankh fertility symbol, a backward swastika portraying energy, the Sanskrit word *om* meaning "oneness," and the Jewish Star of David.

Appeal: Its lack of official public dogma makes Theosophy attractive to religionists who take a universalist view. Many find its inclusion of mystical practices (vegetarianism, yoga, *mahatmas*) a way to incorporate Eastern ideas into a Western tradition without turning to more extreme cults such as Hare Krishna. Those enamored by psychic phenomena may be intrigued by stories regarding the supposed occult powers possessed by Blavatsky. (Theosophists proudly displayed at their centennial meeting a pair of sugar tongs she allegedly "called into existence through an effort of her will.")

Purpose: "We are seekers of truth," former leader Coates declares. Though the esoteric teachings of Theosophy constitute a complex system of doctrines based on Hinduism and various mystery cults, members insist their Society represents a philosophy and not a religion. Theosophy espouses goals of world peace, brotherhood without distinction of sex or creed, and investigation of occult and paranormal phenomena that presumes to reveal unexplained laws of the universe. Though Blavatsky officially denigrated Spiritualism in her later years, the realm of psychic powers is of special interest to Theosophists.

Error: Theosophy comes from the Greek *theosophia,* meaning "divine wisdom." In reality, theosophical thought is merely a modernized version of the pantheistic Gnostic teaching so sternly condemned by the Apostle Paul in his Letter to the Colossians. The supremacy of Christ as extolled in Colossians 2:10 ("the head of all principality and power") is reduced in Theosophy to a "Christ principle" apart from Jesus. This cosmic Christ-consciousness is claimed to be attainable by all men, since in Besant's words, "all men become Christs." By asserting that humanity is but "a spark of the divine fire," Theosophy deifies the created and denigrates the Creator. Instead of walking "in the light" to know "the blood of Jesus Christ his Son cleanseth us from all sin" (1 John 1:7), Theosophists flounder in the darkness of reincarnation beliefs, which they call "the religion of self-respect."

Background Sources: *Newsweek,* 24 November 1975, 10; *The Herald Weekend Magazine,* 7 December 1980, 16-20; Marian Meade, *Madame Blavatsky, The Woman Behind the Myth* (New York: Putnam, 1980); Walter Martin, *The Kingdom of the Cults* (Minneapolis: Bethany Fellowship, 1977); J. Gordon Melton, *Encyclopedia of American Religions,* vol. 2 (Wilmington, N.C.: McGrath, 1978).

Address/Location: International Headquarters are in Adyar (Madras), India. U.S. headquarters: The Theosophical Publishing House, P. O. Box 270, Wheaton, IL 60189. The address of the Blavatsky Foundation (dedicated to promoting her "life and works") is: P. O. Box 1543, Fresno, CA 93716.

See also Anthroposophical Society.

T R A N C E
C H A N N E L I N G

Why am I here? What is my purpose in life? To answer such questions, scores of Americans are resorting to trance channeling—communication with spirit entities through human contacts. Some seek material gain. Others want advice about marital situations, career changes, and spiritual growth. Still others, disillusioned with organized religion and seeking to fill a spiritual void, stretch imagination and credibility, trying to contact beings from other planes of existence.

Channelers assume a mythical quality for the purpose of communicating from other planes of existence. Apparently, channeling has been part of human history since recorded time. The enigmatic theory that the dead can communicate with the living across dimensions unknown to man has persisted in all cultures. Channelers have been known by other names: priests, gurus, prophets, saints, and holy ones.

The bodies of channels supposedly are commandeered by entities from the spirit world. The channeler often enters an altered conscious or unconscious state, which permits transformation of the personality into a spirit guide. Channelers claim such guides have a hotline to universal truth. Mediums usually predict the future, while channelers concentrate on the present.

Referred to as "pioneers of the psyche," trance channelers envision a world brimming with healthy, happy, enlightened people who have found the answer to an ancient dilemma—how to live peaceably together. Carl Raschke, professor of religious studies at the University of Denver, says of trance channeling, "It's a form of mass hypnosis that is leading to mass acceptance of the irrational." Marcello Truzzi, head of Eastern Michigan University's Center for Scientific Anomalies Research, says, "It's a democratization of the supernatural. Everyone is their own priest . . . their own god."

There is no shortage of channels for entities to employ. A Seattle Episcopal priest, the Reverend Laura Cameron-Fraser, was forced from her church for believing a spirit named Jonah spoke through her. She finds it illogical that God stopped talking to human beings and says, "I have reason to believe that Jesus Christ's voice is being heard today through channeling." Cameron-Fraser also claims the Bible was written by trance channelers and that Old Testament prophets were channelers.

Actress-author Shirley MacLaine was a forerunner of an army of popular mediums, who became channels to entities from the spirit world. In her book *Dancing in the Light,* MacLaine focused national attention on J. Z. Knight, a successful Washington state channel, who serves Ramtha, a 35,000-year-old male spirit. Knight goes into a deep, cataleptic trance, claiming to leave her body so the powerful spirit can enter. Ramtha calls himself the "Enlightened One" and says he once conquered Atlantis as a warrior. Claiming to hail from the lost continent of Lumeria, Ramtha talks for hours and marches around grandly when summoned by Knight.

Raised in a strict Christian household, J. Z. Knight admits to earning millions of dollars through Ramtha. She employs a staff of 14 to organize seminars and to publish tapes and brochures. Thousands have paid up to $1,700 each to hear Ramtha preach New Age self-reliance mingled with Eastern mysticism. Ramtha claims there is no right or wrong, just individual reality. He says, "The kingdom of God is within us all. Everyone has the power to master his destiny and achieve his desires through positive thinking."

A trance channeler known only as Susie communicates with a spirit called Enoch, who believes retarded children are reincarnated souls in a state of bliss who "choose to come and see the world through these blissful eyes . . . it is their choice." Susie, a recovered alcoholic and cocaine addict who shuns publicity, enters an altered, unconscious state that permits her personality to dissolve into one of seven "guides." She charges $45 for a private session and conducts free public seminars.

One well-publicized channeled entity, Seth, who speaks through Jane Roberts, described himself as "an energy personality essence no longer focused in physical reality." His primary message through trance channeler Roberts over a 20-year affiliation is that each of us creates our own reality by our beliefs and desires. Seth commands supplicants, "Enjoy yourself! Listen to your own inner wisdom." Seth proclaims that reality is self-created through beliefs; thus, changing one's belief alters reality. Each of us supposedly has counterparts, entities who once lived and others who live now, all of whom become facets of the personality and form a "greater self."

Barbara Rollinson-Huss of Broomfield, Colorado, wants to build a research center for spiritual training on 44 acres in Colorado Springs. The acreage is near the NORAD missile site. Rollinson-Huss is unconcerned. Her spirit guide told her NORAD won't be there much longer. She charges $85 per session and claims to channel information from dolphins. During one channeling session, Rollinson-Huss became an Oriental spirit, who spoke with a Chinese-American accent. The spirit of Jesus followed by Buddha, allegedly came upon the channeler.

Some critics think channeling results from self-hypnosis, which involves relaxation, concentration, turning inward, and focusing upon certain words, sounds, or images. The goal is to change one's state of consciousness. New Age advocates support the philosophy that each of us is part of a Universal Mind, which permits talking with departed spirits about mundane human matters.

No significant scientific understanding of channeling has verified its claims to transcend time and space. Still, Wall Street investors have consulted channels for stock market guidance, and even the United States Army reportedly has investigated the military implications of extrasensory perception (ESP). Communicating with spirits is lucrative. Shirley MacLaine charges $300 per person to attend her seminars called "Connecting with the Higher Self."

Founders: Various channelers, who claim to communicate with entities in the spirit world.

Text: None. Tradition of witchcraft, pagan oracles, and modern spiritualism all mingle. Shirley MacLaine's many books are among the most popular and influential works that focus on channeling.

Symbol: None.

Appeal: An estimated 23 percent of Americans believe in reincarnation, according to a *USA Today* poll, and 14 percent believe in mediums.

Communication with dead loved ones apparently proves that life exists after death. Receiving advice from spiritual mentors, who claim intellectual superiority and advanced knowledge, provides comfort for the confused and distressed.

Purpose: Trance channeling breaches the spiritual chasm between life on earth and life after death, providing spiritual, moral, and financial help from allegedly advanced entities.

Errors: Channelers adhere to the New Age idea that Jesus Christ was not divine, only one of many prophets who came to earth to educate mankind. God is within each person, who directs and controls his own destiny. Human channels can intervene in the spirit world and summon spirit entities to communicate with the living for mundane purposes. It was for such activities that God required the life of King Saul (1 Chron. 10:13). Known as necromancy in Scripture, trance channeling was considered an abomination by God (Deut. 18:11).

Background Sources: *The Denver Post,* 23 June 1985; *Time,* 15 December 1986; *New Age Journal,* November-December 1987; *New Realities,* March-April, 1988; *USA Today,* 28 January 1987.

Address/Location: Worldwide.

See also New Age Cults, Spiritualism.

TRANSCENDENTAL
MEDITATION

The words *transcendental* and *meditation* are not exclusively definitive. And even the Maharishi Mahesh Yogi acknowledges in his writings that some Hindus believe this ancient spiritual discipline was conveyed to man centuries ago by one of the Hindu gods, Lord Krishna.

Worse yet for the Maharishi (devout disciples insist "the" must be dropped when referring to him), the pretense that TM (as it is popularly known) "isn't a religion" is no longer defensible. On October 9, 1977, U.S. District Judge H. Curtis Meanor issued an extensive 82-page opinion upholding the plaintiff's claim regarding the religious nature of Transcendental Meditation. In Judge Meanor's words, "No inference was possible except that the teachings of SCI (Science of Creative Intelligence) and TM and the *puja* are religious in nature. No other inference is permissible or reasonable, especially because the court is dealing with the meaning of the constitutional term and not with a factual dispute." Seventeen months later, the United States Court of Appeals for the Third Circuit, sitting in Philadelphia, affirmed this ruling.

The legal opinion regarding TM is of value to those Christians concerned about its incursions into public schools, prisons, the military, and other government-funded institutions. Government grants (17 in all at one time, including $21,540 from the Department of Health, Education and Welfare destined to show 150 high school faculty members how to teach TM) have been halted. But with an estimated 1 million adherents in the United States alone, TM isn't going to fade away quickly. Senators, sports stars, movie idols, businessmen, and even doctors continue to tout its benefits. And Americans who are generally ignorant of religious traditions outside of the Judeo-Christian model usually dismiss references to Hindu gods as so much gobbledygook. But the old Yankee maxim "If it works . . . " has given impetus to the Maharishi's plans for the future.

To a generation raised on quick-relief commercials, expediency is all important. Thus, when an M.D. advises, "no technique of meditation is as effective as TM in producing deep rest and consequent psychophysiological integration," who really cares about the intrinsic pagan nature of such a practice? After all, the publicized benefits of TM include relief from insomnia, normalization of weight, beneficial effects on asthma, faster reaction time, broader comprehension, and improved ability to focus attention.

Maharishi Mahesh Yogi was born Mahesh Brasad Warma, 1911, in Jabalpur, Madhya Pradesh, India. At 31 years of age he graduated from Allahabad University with a degree in physics. He worked for a while in a factory until crossing paths with Swami Brahmananda Saraswati, Jagadguru, Bhagwan Shankaracharya of Jyotir Math (commonly known as Guru Dev—"Divine Teacher"). Guru Dev had left his home at age nine to seek enlightenment. Under the teachings of Swami Krishanand Saraswati he achieved his God-realization and became known as an *avatar*, a manifestation of the Divine.

Guru Dev had revived a technique of meditation that originated from the Hindu monastic tradition of Shankara, a philosopher who established the practice in the ninth century A.D. For twelve years, Maharishi ("Great Sage"—a name he adopted in 1956) was the favorite student of Guru Dev. When his spiritual mentor died in 1953, Maharishi retreated to a Himalayan cave for two years. In 1958 he ended up in Madras, where during a lecture he spontaneously announced a plan to spread TM all over the world. He formed the International Meditation Society and headed for the West. In Los Angeles, he chartered the Spiritual Regeneration movement in 1959. He finally settled in a London apartment, where nothing much happened until 1967.

Flower power was in bloom, but the sex- and drug-crazed ways of the Beatles had brought the Fab Four disillusionment and frustration. George Harrison met the Maharishi and persuaded John, Paul, and Ringo to join him on a pilgrimage to India. There the Beatles, with Mia Farrow in tow, sat at the Maharishi's feet to be schooled in the ancient Vedic practice of transcendental meditation. The Rolling Stones and the Beach Boys joined the bandwagon. Of the latter group, Mike Love and Al Jardine became TM teachers. Brian Wilson augmented the faith of his comrades by lyrically declaring, "Transcendental Meditation, it works real good/ More, much more than I thought it would." With such celebrity endorsements the Maharishi confidently boasted, "I shall bring fulfillment to the hippie movement."

The Maharishi pocketed a week's pay from his followers (a substantial sum for a Beatle!) and blitzed the United States with a lecture tour. The disarming smile of this giggly guru ubiquitously dominated magazine covers and TV talk shows. With flowers in hand he repeated the basic theme that the mind has a natural tendency to seek happiness. But peace and serenity are only possible if one passes beyond the normally experienced states of consciousness: sleep, dreaming, and wakefulness. Man must learn to "meditate" so he can "transcend" to the fourth state of "bliss consciousness," a condition of "pure awareness" where one is tuned-in to "creative intelligence."

The promises were euphoric. Maharishi confidently predicted that just one percent of the population practicing TM in any locality would reduce crime and empty the hospitals. Many victims of stress and hypertension gave glowing testimonials. Some argued that such relief was merely due to an anticipatory attitude aided by the 40 minutes of restful posture that TM required each day. But supporters seemed to far outnumber detractors until the bubble of optimism burst.

"We were wrong," the Beatles concluded, with John accusing the Maharishi of being a "lecherous womanizer." His following was nearly defunct, and crowds no longer seemed charmed by his Hinduistic platitudes. Though he had once hobnobbed with celebrity luminaries, the Maharishi headed home with the pronouncement, "I know that I have failed. My mission is over." His stay in his Rishikesh, India, *ashram* was cut short by a government-launched financial inquiry, so he set up shop in Fiuggi Fonte, an Italian resort community. There he decided to revamp his entire approach and vocabulary. His resplendent beard and hypnotically dark eyes disappeared from American TV screens. But not for long.

Religious terminology was dropped in favor of psychological and scientific language. The Spiritual Regeneration movement became the Science of Creative Intelligence (SCI), and the Maharishi presented an image of a friendly psychotherapist rather than a Hindu monk. His inner circle may have heard him call the *Bhagavad-Gita* "an anchor for the ship of life sailing on the turbulent waves of time." But outsiders only heard the oft-repeated litany, "It's not a religion."

The ruse worked. By the mid-1970s, more than a million Americans had tried TM. Seven thousand teachers were propagating the Maharishi's gospel in more than 100 U.S. centers. Income jumped to over $20 million a year as 30,000-40,000 followers a month joined the movement to meditation. For an introductory fee of $55 for college students and $125 for adults (now up to $85 and $165), anyone was guaranteed inner peace. Best of all, there was no renunciation of materialism or desire in the Buddhist tradition and no repentance of sin nor reformation of character in the Christian tradition. All around the world, in prison cells and military barracks, TMers gathered twice a day to chant their *mantras.* The Maharishi was virtually deified as a yogi who had achieved "a perpetual fourth state of consciousness" with an "awesome" clarity of mind.

Though TM has popularized the terms *meditation* and *mantra,* most people are still a little vague about their precise definitions. They mean more than "deep thinking" and "a funny-sounding word." To understand their usage in TM, it is necessary to decipher the religious framework of the Maharishi's entire system.

The religious philosophy of the Maharishi is rooted in Vedantic Hinduism. God is a pantheistic, pervasive Absolute Being (*Brahman*). Even man's inner self is part of this divine Being. In Christianity, man's dilemma is separation by sin from a transcendent Deity. The Maharishi sees man's foremost problem as alienation from his true Being. Salvation is derived by contacting this inner state of pure consciousness. Meditation is the key to transcending (going beyond) the three levels of normal consciousness (discussed earlier) to the fourth state, where one is cognizant of his soul's true nature.

Three additional levels exist: cosmic consciousness, complete God consciousness, and Unity consciousness. Beginners in TM hear only about the first two, but the Maharishi's ultimate goal is to lead all humanity to Unity consciousness. At that point, the meditator is liberated from the karmic cycles of reincarnation by achieving sinlessness.

For the present, the Maharishi is content with introducing adherents to the fourth level of consciousness. But what the meditator may not realize is that the interpretation of the process is based on assumptions that represent a systematic approach to Hindu theology. At the heart of this hypothesis is the mantra. Representatives of the Maharishi insist it is only a vibratory sound with "no denotive meaning." On the contrary, Hindu tradition believes that such words or syllables have supernatural powers, often invoking a deity who is believed to embody the sound.

TM as prescribed by the Maharishi requires the initiate to sit with eyes closed in a quiet, relaxed position, 20 minutes in the morning and again in the evening. All the while his mind repeats the Sanskrit word deemed to be his personal mantra. This mantra is the means of diving to the depths of the mind's ocean, delving into ever subtler recesses of thought. No mental discipline is necessary. The mantra does it all. Just let the mind go out of gear and coast to its desired destiny of fulfillment.

In the process, one's deepest thoughts emerge and dissipate like tiny champagne bubbles. As the incantation progresses, the meditator is supposed to be relieving tension and disposing of stress. When the source of all thought is reached, the chanter has available "a reservoir of energy, intelligence, and happiness." Only 73,500 minutes of meditation later, the faithful have hope of absolute union with Being, provided they never meditate before bed or after a meal.

Mantras aren't easy to acquire. The introductory fee is a mandatory requirement. Every meditator must also undergo an initiation ceremony that is distinctly idolatrous in nature. The initiate, with fruit, flowers, and a white handkerchief in hand, takes off his shoes and enters a candle-lit room. Then, the instructor directs the initiate to lay these items on a flower-banked altar that features a color portrait of Guru Dev. Incense pervades the atmosphere. Finally, the teacher kneels before the altar and begins to sing in Sanskrit. The initiate may stand or kneel, too, as he listens to this ten-minute recitation.

When TM first became popular, most people didn't question this part of the ceremony. They were told it was "not a religious observance" but merely an opportunity for the teacher to "express his gratitude to the tradition from which TM comes." Apprehensive students were said to be "witnessing" the ritual, "not participating." Christian researchers weren't placated by this innocuous tale, and persisted in their attempts to uncover the truth about the proceedings. What they discovered came as no shock.

The TM initiation song is actually a devotional Hindu hymn called a *puja*. Guru Dev's picture represents a *murti,* the literal embodiment of God in corporeal form. While singing the *puja* (which means "worship") the instructor first invokes the favor and presence of the Hindu gods. Then he presents 17 offerings to Guru Dev before finally praising him (personified by his picture-idol) as an incarnation of deity. Among the lines recited are: "To lotus-born Brahma the Creator, to Shakti, . . . I bow down. At whose door the whole galaxy of gods pray . . . Guru, I bow down . . . the teacher of the truth of the Absolute, to Shri Guru Dev, I bow down."

After this incantation, the teacher leans toward the initiate and whispers a mantra in his ear. The secret word is supposed to be his own specialized mantra, chosen for him by a Maharishi-trained instructor. The mantra must never be divulged to an outsider, even a spouse, or it will lose its magical powers. The meditator's own particular temperament, personality, and profession have presumably been analyzed to determine *the* mantra that will produce the appropriate psychic vibrations. In fact, recent investigation has shown that only 16 TM mantras actually exist, and these are dispensed according to age.

Does the mantra really work? Though the Maharishi's organizations publish volumes of information about research studies, most non-TM scientists are skeptical. No body of findings exists that has been subject to the proper objective controls that would substantiate the claims of TM. The American Association for the Advancement of Science evaluated TM as to its stress-reducing capabilities. Tests concluded that the Maharishi's meditation techniques "produced no measurable change whatever in the body's basic metabolism, and further, TM did not induce a unique state of consciousness."

Evangelical critics charge that even without provable positive effects, there are dangerous spiritual consequences. To begin with, TM conditions the meditator's view of reality and religion, predisposing him toward an Eastern concept of man and God. The guilt of sin can be neutralized by inducing a false sense of serenity, replacing the stress caused by conviction. Demonic phenomena may result because spiritual defense mechanisms become ineffective when the mind enters a state of passivity. Some meditators report a "blackout phenomenon," waking up hours after starting to chant, unable to remember what has happened. In addition, some advanced meditators exhibit neuroses and psychoses resulting from the practice of "unstressing," the procedure of shedding karma from one's present and past lives through prolonged meditation.

To counter such criticism and to legitimize his efforts, the Maharishi has tried to further refurbish his image. God-name mantras have been dropped and the organizational entity has been subdivided. The TM empire now includes: World Plan Executive Council, Student International Meditation Society, American Foundation for Creative Intelligence, American Meditation Society, Maharishi International University (in Fairfield, Iowa), Maharishi European Research University, Institute for Fitness and Athletic Excellence, and Affiliated Organizational Conglomerate. The Maharishi directs the activities of all these organs from his international headquarters in the Swiss village of Seelisberg.

As the number of new converts plunged to an estimated low of 4,000 per month in the late seventies, TM launched its most controversial aspect—the *Sidhi* program. (*Siddhi* is a Sanskrit term denoting supernatural, occult powers. The Maharishi has adopted the variant spelling *Sidhi* for trademark purposes.) A *Sidha* (one who has completed Sidhi training) spends from $3,000 to $5,000 to reach an enlightened state of infinite compassion. He is also supposed to have the ability to walk through walls, become invisible, and levitate.

Advanced meditators claim to have mastered dematerialization and flying, "just like Peter Pan." In mattress-filled rooms ("landings are unusually bumpy"), the Maharishi's most ardent followers say they begin by hopping, then floating, in preparation for flight. Leaders claim that nearly 4,000 have conquered the art, but offers by the press of up to $10,000 to witness a meditator on the wing have gone unclaimed. The validity of the Sidhi program is undercut by the Maharishi's preferred form of transportation—his two Rolls-Royces and private helicopter that await outside his residence.

By promoting such bizarre phenomena the Maharishi may have lost his hold on mainstream America. But he seems oblivious to any indication that his welcome has been outworn. From his head office in the "International Capital of the Age of Enlightenment," a decree recently went forth: "Society will soon be characterized by harmony and happiness. Through the Science of Creative Intelligence, education will be ideal, producing fully developed citizens. Through the Transcendental Meditation programme, health will be perfect. There will be peace in the family of nations." In 1984 a three-week "Taste of Utopia" conference gathered Maharishi disciples from 30 countries to infuse a troubled world with a force they called "positivity." The conference, held in TM's university in Fairfield, Iowa, gathered 7,000 meditators (seven thousand is approximately the square root of one percent of the world's population, supposedly a number of some significance). Devotees claimed that "positivity" was really effective during that period, since the U.S. stock market rose, three nations showed a decrease in traffic fatalities, and there were fewer war deaths. One wonders if the word *coincidence* ever occurred to the meditators.

Whether TM's vaunted relief from tension will enhance the moral virtue claimed by this pronouncement is yet to be proven. The mantras may give meditators an improved sense of well-being. But it remains to be seen whether such positive feelings will also produce individuals who act in accordance with sound ethics. TM's ethics may also be seriously questioned, since in 1987 a U.S. District Court found two TM organizations guilty of fraud and negligence and ordered them to pay damages to Robert Kropinsky, who said TM had not made good on the promises that chanting would reduce stress, improve his memory and health, and enable him to levitate and otherwise manipulate the laws of nature.

Founder: Maharishi Mahesh Yogi, born in 1911 as Mahesh Brasad Warma in Jabalpur, Madhya Pradesh, India.

Text: Hindu scriptures, including the *Bhagavad-Gita,* which the Maharishi views as an "indispensable" religious document.

Symbols: The letters *T* and *M,* capitalized and appearing together (TM) as an abbreviated reference to Transcendental Meditation.

Appeal: Most seekers do not turn to TM in a search to find religious truth. They are looking for a means of attaining inner peace and cessation of stress with little involvement of time or discipline. TM claims phenomenal psychophysiological benefits as well as release from guilt feelings.

Purpose: The public posture of TM insists that the Maharishi's mantras open the mind to a state of "bliss consciousness" that unleashes creative impulses and reduces stress. In the place of suffering and salvation, TM promotes health and happiness. Once there is one TM teacher for each 1,000 citizens on Earth, social ills and conflicts will cease. The esoteric aims are to introduce the meditator to the underlying Hinduistic theological precepts (i.e., "all is one" and man is a god). As for those who do not practice TM, the Maharishi says, "There will not be a place for the unfit . . . in the Age of Enlightenment." TM practitioners who go on to advanced stages will ultimately experience a merged unity with pure Being and may possibly become unwitting mediums for familiar spirits. (Though the Maharishi acknowledges the existence of demons, he cautions against any contact with them.)

Errors: The TM initiation ceremony violates the First Commandment. Matthew 6:7 denounces the chanting of mantras. Maharishi Mahesh Yogi's monist view of the universe is not compatible with the scriptural presentation of a personal God, who as Creator is distinct from his creation. Christian meditation is an outward concentration on the Word and ways of God, whereas TM is a passive, selfish, inward withdrawal from reality. The repetitious sensory stimulation dulls the conscious mind and makes it vulnerable to evil invasion. Christ's blood atonement is rejected in the Maharishi's statement, "[TM] is the only way to salvation and success in life: there is no other way."

Background Sources: Books by Maharishi Mahesh Yogi, including: *Science of Being and Art of Living* (Bergenfield, N.J.: New American Library, 1963); *On the Bhagavad-Gita: A New Translation and Commentary* (Baltimore: Penguin, 1967); *Meditations of Maharishi Mahesh Yogi* (New York: Bantam, 1968); *Transcendental Meditations* (New York: Delacorte, 1975); Pat Means, *The Mystical Maze* (San Bernardino, Calif.: Campus Crusade for Christ, 1976); Jack Sparks, *The Mind Benders* (Nashville: Thomas Nelson, 1977); *Liberty,* May-June 1979, 14-15; *The Province* (Vancouver, B.C.), 28 October 1978, 21; *The Junior Statesman* (Indian youth magazine published in Calcutta), 20 January 1968; *Rolling Stone,* 3 June 1976, 10; *SCP Newsletter,* November 1977; *Christianity Today,* 9 April 1976, 17; *Newsweek,* 7 January 1974, 73-75; Ibid., 13 June 1977, 98-100; *Time,* 23 October 1972, 102-105; Ibid., 13 October 1975, 71-74; Ibid., 8 August 1977, 75; *Right On,* November 1975, 8-14; *TM Newsletter,* July-August, 1976; miscellaneous TM promotional literature; "Utopian Thinking in Iowa," *Newsweek,* 2 January 1984, 31; "Manipulative Metaphysics," *Christianity Today,* 20 February 1987, 54; *USA Today,* 4 March 1985, 11A.

Address/Location: TM Centers in 140 countries and approximately 400 U.S. cities. U.S. office is Maharishi National Capital of the Age of Enlightenment for the U.S., 5000 14th St. NW, Washington, DC 20011. World headquarters is at Maharishi International Capital of the Age of Enlightenment, Arogyadham, Maharishi Nagar, Ghaziabad, U.P. 201304, India.

U F O S

Ken Arnold could hardly believe his eyes. There, just outside the window of the small aircraft he was piloting, were nine metallic discs floating in the air. They darted about with incredible speed and maneuverability. When Arnold landed, he immediately reported the incident. "What did they look like?" he was asked. More than three decades later his answer is still the descriptive preference of those who have had similar experiences—"flying saucers."

Though observations of UFOs (unidentified flying objects) have occurred at random times and locations, the phenomena do bear similarities. The craft are usually described as being circular, cylindrical, or spherical in shape, with flashing lights and luminous brilliance. They change color and shape, appear and disappear, and seemingly defy the laws of thermodynamics. In just a few seconds they can accelerate from a standing position to speeds clocked at several thousands of miles per hour, and then make a 90-degree turn in midair. In their wake are left vile odors, mutilated animals, radiation burns, charred landing spots, and various kinds of electrical interference.

Dr. J. Allen Hynek, considered by some to be the world's ranking expert on UFOs, has classified these appearances according to the following categories of "close encounters": (1) observation of a UFO within 500 feet; (2) physical traces left behind; (3) actual contact with the occupants; and (4) abduction or examination by these beings. The evidence concerning all four kinds of encounters is overwhelming, and in some cases, irrefutable. Number 3 is the "close encounter" referred to in the film titled *Close Encounters of the Third Kind*. This was just one of many immensely popular movies focusing on extraterrestrial beings. Others include the top-grossing film of all time, *E.T.* Time-Life Books, generally considered a respectable publishing firm, bombarded TV screens in 1989 with titillating ads promoting their new books dealing with the occult, ESP, and extraterrestrials. Where the media are concerned, belief in UFOs is quite respectable, as evidenced by the Carpenters—for many years the squeaky clean darlings of American pop music—recording the song "Calling Occupants of Interplanetary Craft."

With all the talk these days about UFOs and the widely circulated stories of people who claim to have communicated with the pilots of such craft, modern man is being forced to take these strange events seriously. UFO tales must either be explained, or explained away. If they are not real phenomena, then they should be dismissed without further consideration. If such occurrences are legitimate, then the nature and origin of UFOs need to be determined. Furthermore, Christians have an additional concern as to how these appearances may affect the spiritual future of mankind.

Are UFOs for real? Most are not and are easily dismissed as mistakenly identified planets, rocket launchings, weather balloons, and atmospheric phenomena. The Air Force Project Blue Book was able to provide a rationale for all but 700 out of 12,600 cases of sightings between 1947 and 1969.

Other reports are not so easy to dismiss. What of the cases where UFOs have torn off treetops, ricocheted bullets, and razed thousands of acres of forest (in the Soviet Union)? What about the hundreds of reports from responsible citizens claiming to have seen and heard unexplainable objects zooming across the sky? Why do these flying machines often hover near power lines, bodies of water, and military installations? Can such a diversity of situations with striking similarities all be dismissed as hallucinatory speculations or imaginations run wild?

If UFOs are from some unknown human source, who is responsible for them? The Russians are as puzzled as anyone. Only the industrialized nations could possibly have access to the kind of antigravitational technology necessary for such phenomena. If any advanced nation does have knowledge of such secrets, how has such information been so well hidden for so long? Supposing that such expertise does exist, only satanic influence would lead men to wreak such havoc and terror on their own unsuspecting countrymen.

The most commonly accepted theory regarding the origin of UFOs is that of ETI's (extraterrestrial intelligences). Unofficially, the U.S. government presumes that such craft must come from other planets. NASA has asked Congress for $2.1 million to begin what it calls a "Search for Extraterrestrial Intelligence." When the Voyager spacecraft rose beyond earth's gravity, it carried aboard a twelve-inch copper LP title, "Sounds of Earth." The record contained 90 minutes of playing time, including numerically coded explanations of our geology, chemistry, and mathematics.

Psychologist Leo Sprinkle of the University of Wyoming Division of Counseling and Testing, who is also a consultant for the Aerial Phenomena Research Organization, claims that he has hypnotized over 50 people who say they have been aboard UFOs. Professor Sprinkle reports that these subjects are able to recall their stellar voyages in minute detail.

The accounts of ETI contacts seem to fit a pattern. The person is normally engaged in some ordinary activity when suddenly a UFO is sighted and then curiously investigated. As the humanoid occupant approaches, the contactee usually is frightened at first. Then the creature gives reassuring gestures to calm the earthling and proceeds to give him a physical examination by passing a probe over his body. Some victims tell of sexual encounters with their captors. Contactees usually report that communication with the ETI takes place nonverbally by telepathy. The humanoids insist they are benevolent agents sent to help mankind and assist us in understanding the deeper nature of spiritual truth. A brief summary of something approximating occult philosophy is conveyed, and then the contactee may be hypnotized or placed in a trance to forget the abduction.

Accepting the existence of extraterrestrial beings necessitates subscribing to one of two explanations for their origin: the evolutionary hypothesis or a belief in other God-created stellar civilizations. The option of evolution is not available to the Christian. The simplest, single cellular organism known to man is still far too complex to have spontaneously evolved by chance anywhere in the universe. The Bible teaches that God alone is the Creator of life, and the feasibility of conscious beings springing forth from nonorganic life is not scripturally supportable.

On the other hand, since there is no specific Bible verse prohibiting the possibility of extraterrestrial life, some argue that this omission leaves open the option that God may have created beings on other planets. Proponents of this theory insist that in the vastness of space there must surely be other races of creatures to whom God has given life. "We're so small and insignificant compared to the infinite realm of the universe," the argument goes, "how dare we be so egotistical as to assume we are alone?"

In his book *The High Frontier: Human Colonies in Space,* Princeton physicist Gerald K. O'Neill put it this way: "The idea that we as intelligent life are unique is of course absurd. The more we learn about the origins of life, the more we realize that the conditions under which life first began on earth must have been duplicated many times over in other parts of the galaxy."

If God did choose to create intelligent beings on other planets, they too would be tainted by Adam's sin, which affected the entire cosmos. They would be fallen creatures like mankind and thus have the same technological limitations that we do. If sin's retrogressive impact on man's advancement has prevented us from going to visit them, how could they possibly come to us? If for some reason sin has not invaded their race, would God permit such an unfallen civilization to contact us and thus be contaminated by our sin? The answer to both of these questions is decidedly negative. If extraterrestrial beings do exist, surely the Lord would have told us without equivocation. It seems that such a crucial matter would be discussed somewhere in the Word of God.

Since it appears likely that neither human agencies nor extraterrestrial creatures are the source of UFOs, we are left to consider whether they are of supernatural origin. Robert Achzenner (author, lecturer, and UFO expert) has put it this way: "I have come to these conclusions. The unknown objects and their manifestations are real; they are intelligently controlled; and no government authority or scientific agency knows what they are, where they are from, or why they are here."

One thing appears certain: We are not alone. Something or someone is out there. Professor Leo Sprinkle (mentioned earlier) expressed his view of the situation like this: "My guess is that they're more than just a physical phenomenon, that they're a psychic or spiritual phenomenon too."

J. Allen Hynek said these aliens may come from a "parallel reality." He concluded, "I suspect that a very advanced civilization might know something about the connections between mind and matter that we don't."

Is it possible that this "parallel reality" is angelic in origin? Such a presumption cannot be excluded, since the Bible does warn us that in the end times "great signs shall there be from heaven" (Luke 21:11). Likewise, the prophet Joel declared that God would "show wonders in the heavens." There are some committed believers who suggest that a percentage of UFOs are "chariots" of the Lord's "hosts." Others wonder if perhaps the rapture of the saints will take place when living Christians board flying saucers and are whisked away to be with the Lord. Another possibility often stated is that UFOs are evidences of God's angelic army amassing for the war in heaven prophesied for the Last Days.

To discuss whether or not UFOs are of godly origin, we need to divide the phenomena into two categories: encounters of the first kind (sightings), and encounters of the third kind (contact). Third stage encounters do not appear to be angelic. The conduct of UFO occupants (for example, sexual assaults and induced trance states) and the metaphysical message they bring is contrary to the activity that would be expected of unfallen angels. Whenever they appear in Scripture, angels of the Lord always carry out specific, divine missions. Their purpose is to convey a glorious revelation of God's plan (for example, the announcement of Christ's birth—Luke 2:9-14) or executing the Lord's wrath and judgment (the destruction of Jehoshaphat's enemies—2 Chron. 20:22; the overthrow of Sodom and Gomorrah—Gen. 19:22-25). Above all, as evidenced by Revelation 22:8-9, they never draw attention to themselves. True angels of the Lord speak only when divinely commissioned to do so, with the intent of directing man's attention heavenward to God.

Having ruled out the probability of angelic encounters of the third kind, what may be said of UFO encounters of the first kind (sightings)? Obviously, if no direct, personal contact is made with the occupants of such craft, no objectively conclusive statements can be made. But inferences can be drawn from the nature of such visitations. The occurrences of poltergeist phenomena and the terror brought upon observers are indications of a demonic visitation. When God intervenes supernaturally, it is to bring comfort and peace, unless there is a clear reason for his wrath to be exhibited. What can be said of blips disappearing from radar screens and flashing oval objects floating through distant skies? While neither God nor Satan can be positively identified as the source, the latter seems a far more likely culprit.

The descriptions given of UFO occupants usually include grotesque features and oddly shaped structures. They may have enlarged heads, slits for eyes, ethereal forms, and antennae sticking out of their skulls. Most accounts are of beings that bear a distinct resemblance to the "familiar spirits" described in classical spiritualism.

When UFO visitors speak, their message brings neither solace nor information in conformity with God's Word. They talk of cosmic awareness and transcendence to higher spiritual planes. Their discourses never glorify Christ as God and Creator. Instead, contactees are told to prepare for an age of peace that will be ushered in by these unidentified aliens. UFO occupants also encourage participation in a variety of psychic practices: astral projection, psychokinesis, automatic handwriting, clairvoyance, and levitation. Sin, judgment, and the redemptive work of Christ are never mentioned. Their words, their actions, and their appearances betray the concealed satanic origin of these beings.

If it can be concluded that the majority of UFOs are of demonic origin, then what is their ultimate purpose? Couldn't the devil just as easily accomplish his ends by another means, or do UFOs serve a unique role in the master plan of Satan to deceive mankind?

An interesting insight is provided by Jacques Vallee, a Frenchman with a master's degree in astrophysics and a doctorate in computer science. As an exponent of UFO investigations, he concluded that such phenomena are creating "a willingness to believe in extraterrestrial life." He goes on to point out that "attitudes on the subject among scientists, the media, and the public have totally changed in twenty years. We can rationalize this change or we can recognize it for what it is—the result of a shifting of our mythological structure."

It may be that UFOs are reeducating mankind to accept a casual familiarity with paranormal activity. This conditioning process will be completed under the reign of the Antichrist. During that time an inanimate image will live and speak (Rev. 13:15), a fatal wound will be healed (Rev. 13:14), and fire will fall from heaven (Rev. 13:13). The Apostle John explains that such miracles will be used to deceive humanity into following the Antichrist (Rev. 13:14; 16:14).

Modern man would like to think he is more advanced than the primitive pagans of antiquity. But is their mythology of gods, goddesses, and superbeings really any different from the twentieth-century mind's fascination with contacting humanoids from distant planets? The Greeks built their altar to the unknown god, while we erect giant dish antennae to probe the heavens in search of some distant trace of extraterrestrial life indicated by a pulsing radio wave. Perhaps the persistent Old Testament warnings against any communication with "familiar spirits" applies to modern interest in UFOs as well.

Founder: Not applicable.

Text: Various occult and pagan writings are cited, suggesting they are metaphoric references to UFOs. Some claim that Ezekiel 1 is a biblical account of UFOs.

Symbol: None.

Appeal: It is becoming increasingly obvious that mankind's dilemmas need an external solution. Those who refuse to seek a transcendent God may assume that extraterrestrials of higher technological and spiritual state may be able to save humanity. Man's curiosity with the unknown gives UFOs a mystical fascination.

Purpose: Man's intent is to discover if UFO occupants are of a higher state of evolution. If so, communications with them may reap certain scientific benefits. From Satan's standpoint, UFOs may be preparing the modern mind to accept a casual familiarity with supernatural phenomena. This would facilitate the Antichrist's reign, and until then, create a milieu in which evil spirits may operate more freely.

Errors: The Bible does not give the slightest hint that extraterrestrials exist. Scripture indicates that God created only two kinds of beings — angels and men. In addition, Romans 8:19-23 indicates that Eden's fall was cosmological in its effect. Therefore, since the death of Christ at Calvary was distinctively for the sons of Adam's race, how many other times would he have needed to give his life to redeem other civilizations? Secular UFO interest fails to consider the possibility that such phenomena may be supernatural (demonic) in nature.

Background Sources: *To the Point* (South Africa), 15 September 1978; *Denver,* February 1978, 34, 38-39; *Newsweek,* 21 November 1977; *The Anchorage Times,* 1 January 1978, B5; *SCP Journal,* August 1977, vol. 1, no. 2; J. Allen Hynek, *The UFO Experience* (New York: Ballantine, 1972).

Address/Location: CE 3K Skywatchers, P. O. Box 2300, Grand Central Station, New York, NY 10017; Center for UFO Studies, 925 Chicago Ave., Evanston, IL 60202.

See also Aetherius Society.

UNIFICATION
CHURCH

(Rev. Sun Myung Moon)

"The Cross is the symbol of the defeat of Christianity." I was stunned at that statement and wondered if the speaker really meant what he said. The Rev. Sun Myung Moon had harangued the audience through his Korean interpreter for over two hours. His message was filled with many theological absurdities, but this last statement topped them all. "The Cross is the symbol of the defeat of Christianity," he repeated.

Full page newspaper ads had stirred this writer's curiosity. "Christianity in Crisis — New Hope for America," the headlines declared. The year was 1973, and few people had yet heard of this militant messiah. The word *Moonie* had not yet entered the average person's vocabulary. Today, the Rev. Moon, "Lord of the Second Advent" to his disciples, stirs international controversy.

Did he actually intend to ridicule the cross of Christ as representing the hallmark of Christianity's failures? Moon went on to explain the theology that hatched this conclusion. Before Adam had a conjugal relationship with Eve, she was sexually seduced by the serpent, none other than the Archangel Lucifer. The evil offspring of this union (Cain) became the seed from which Communism sprang. Abel, Adam's child, started the lineage resulting in the spiritual democracies of South Korea and the United States. With the blood line of humanity tainted by Eve's sexual sin, God's original purpose in creating Adam and Eve was thwarted. He had wanted them to procreate a perfect human family; therefore, Christ came to earth as a man to correct Adam's failure.

Moon says that Jesus of Nazareth was the bastard offspring of Zechariah and Mary. ("Jesus is not God himself," he states.) Since God intended for Christ spiritually and physically to redeem mankind, he needed to marry, father children, and begin rearing the perfect family. But before he could find the Eve he searched for, the Jews killed him. As a result, his death on the cross fulfilled only half of God's plan, the spiritual redemption of man. Since then, God has searched for 2,000 years to find someone who would redeem the human race by becoming the True Parent—the Third Adam, who must have a sinless life and be completely dedicated to God's will. If he qualifies, he will succeed where the First Adam (in Eden) and the Second Adam (Christ) have failed.

Such theological assertions are only a small part of the highly unorthodox worldview held by the Rev. Moon. He could easily be ignored as another Oriental fanatic were it not for the fact that over 2 million people worldwide (30,000 or more in the United States) take his doctrinal fantasies as their supreme spiritual authority. As a result, this millionaire industrialist from South Korea has enslaved the minds of thousands of young people, stripped them of their personal belongings, and pressed them into virtual servitude. In doing so, he has amassed a fortune for himself and his church.

Moon's bold denouncement of Christ's crucifixion is only one of his many notable and outlandish statements. He has also been quoted as follows:

"I will conquer and subjugate the world. I am your brain."

"He [God] is living in me. I am the incarnation of himself."

"I want to have members under me who are willing to obey me even though they may have to disobey their own parents."

"In restoring a man from evil sovereignty, we must cheat."

"Master [Moon] here is more than any of those people (saints and prophets) and greater than Jesus himself."

How did the Rev. Moon develop the egomania that led to such pretensions of self-deification? He was born in 1920 as Yong Myung Moon and was reared in a Presbyterian family. His childhood clairvoyant inclinations climaxed at the age of 16 when Moon claims he had a vision of Jesus. He claimed that Christ commissioned him to fulfill his interrupted task of physically saving humanity. Moon married his first wife in 1944 and began gathering a following. After meeting Park Moon Kim, a self-proclaimed messiah, Moon changed his name from Yong Myung Moon (Dragon Shining Moon) to Sun Myung Moon (Sun Shining Moon). The next few years were spent in prison. Moon says he was persecuted for opposing Communism, though his contemporary critics claimed that accusations of ritual sex practices were the real reason behind his incarceration. In 1954 his wife divorced him. Shortly after this he officially organized the Unification Church. Three years later he published his spiritual manifesto, *Divine Principle*. Meanwhile he searched for the perfect woman. His marriage to a fourth wife, Hak Ja Han (some say he never divorced number two before going on to number three), was proclaimed as the "marriage of the Lamb" prophesied in Revelation 19. Such eccentricities brought charges of moral improprieties and excommunication from the Presbyterian church.

This rebuke certainly didn't affect his business success. His Korean conglomerates of munitions, tea, and titanium accumulated an estimated worth of $20 million. His next target for money and Moonies was the United States, where he headed in 1972. The stage had already been set in 1959 when Young Oon Kim, an associate, brought Moon's message via an English translation of *Divine Principle*. Spiritualistic medium Arthur Ford extolled Moon as the New Age voice of religious thought.

Once he arrived in America, Moon wasted no time in getting on with his job in high style. He purchased a million-dollar headquarters complex and a $625,000 residence in upstate New York. The New Yorker Hotel and Tiffany Building were also added to his real estate portfolio, with rumors of overtures to buy the Empire State Building. A large circulation newspaper called *News World* was launched and nationwide tours heralded his message. Moon defended the beleaguered Richard Nixon and was photographed with Hubert Humphrey and Ted Kennedy. His political aspirations were as exaggerated as his spiritual goals. He wanted nothing less than to organize a religious party and institute a worldwide, theocratic rule.

As Moon and his followers gained the attention of a skeptical press, a national controversy erupted. Parents charged him with brainwashing and hired deprogrammers to rescue their children from his clutches. Questions were raised regarding the legality of immigrant status for his Korean followers. Moonies swarmed Capitol Hill to cajole members of Congress. Meanwhile, other followers invaded shopping centers and airports, hawking flowers and candles to the tune of millions of dollars every year.

Not so long ago, all this would have seemed like the plot line from a novel. In this case, fact is indeed stranger than fiction, providing an interesting commentary on the religious climate of America. It can't be denied that Moon's teachings strike a responsive chord with many. Young people disillusioned with the institutional church and yearning for security within an authoritarian structure have been the fuel for his spiritual fuselage. Invited to a weekend retreat of flattery, smiles, and "love bombing," initiates hear nothing of Moon or his claims. It is later that the cult tactics of sensory deprivation, physical exhaustion, and intense indoctrination are used to introduce neophytes to their "True Father and Mother" — Mr. and Mrs. Moon.

Moon's theological scheme is based on a scope of history divided into an Old Testament Age, a New Testament Age, and the present Completed Testament Age. The latter requires a new revelation of truth to supplant the Bible, and Moon's 536-page *Divine Principle* fills the bill. It was dictated, he explains, by God to him through the process of automatic handwriting. Its "truths" were compiled only after Moon had conferred in the spirit world with Buddha, Jesus, and other notable religious figures. All bowed in acquiescence to Moon, imploring him to bring humanity the unuttered revelations supposedly mentioned by Jesus in John 16:13. Moon also reserves the option of continuing to add supernatural revelation or adjusting his "divine principle" at a future date.

Central to his belief system is the concept of a Third Adam, Messiah and Lord of the Second Advent. Moon declares that this world savior will "appear in the East," that he will unify all religions, and that his birth date (determined by numerological calculation) was sometime about 1920. More specifically, this messiah must come from an Oriental land populated by Christians. He will be persecuted by the masses who reject him. Like John the Baptist who came as Elijah, this "lord" will appear in a physical body.

Though Unification Church leaders are careful publicly to avoid naming Moon as this messiah, the deductive conclusions are inescapable. The suffering, torture, and bloodshed he claims to have endured in Communist prisons are supposed to be further proof of his redemptive mission. Moon neither confirms nor denies that he is the Promised One but does purport to have personally conquered Satan. The present battle line between good and evil, God and the Devil, is the 38th parallel between North and South Korea. Since the Almighty has chosen the United Sates as the bulwark against satanic Communism, it is Moon's duty to reverse America's moral and spiritual decline.

Moon promises more than a message. It is his duty to take up where Christ left off. The union with his present wife is presumed to result in a new humanity, not polluted by Lucifer's bloodline. Do the failed marriages of Moon disqualify him to be a messiah? "No!" Moonies respond, emphatically. His mission to save humanity is so crucial that more than one perfect woman could have been the "True Mother." God prepared three "Eves," and they all failed. Hak Ja Han is *the* Mother of mankind who has finally been chosen of God. Sin, in Moon's estimation, is a matter of genetics, not moral choice. And salvation is a matter of being born of his physical bond or entering a marriage union chosen and blessed by him.

Knowledgeable critics charge that when the cult was small, the doctrine of "blood cleansing" (removing Lucifer's genetic interference) was accomplished by having female Unification members engage in sexual intercourse with the Rev. Moon. The dramatic growth of the cult necessitated that this premise be expanded to include purification for any male who has had relations with a woman "cleansed" by Moon. Now, those who totally submit to his authority may consider their devotion to be a spiritual kind of purification not requiring sexual cohabitation.

The absolution Moon offers may require members to turn over all their financial assets to the Unification Church. Any children may be removed from personal parental guidance and placed under the church's corporate care. Prior marriages have to be ended and resolemnized by Moon. Those who are single must wait until after seven years of service to Moon before he chooses a mate for them. Some do not meet their future marriage partner until the day of the wedding and are not allowed to consummate the union until 40 days thereafter. To conserve Moon's time and energy, mass wedding ceremonies are held where as many as 1,800 are joined in matrimony at one time.

There are many other strange beliefs held by Moon. In some cases, members are encouraged to isolate themselves from all contacts with parents and past associates. Mother and Father Moon are the True Parents (the term "heavenly Father" is reserved for God) and the only ones worthy of devotion. In exchange for this submission, all the necessities of life are provided. Food, clothing, and accommodations, everything from toothpaste to trousers, are served up communal-style for those members who forsake all to pound the streets selling wares to augment church income. A minimum quota is suggested (such as $100 or more per day), though some ex-members claim to have brought in as much as $1,600 in one outing. Estimated totals indicate this approach brings in about $1 million every five days. Deliberate misrepresentation ("heavenly deceit") is used when a customer inquires regarding the destination of the proceeds. People are far more inclined to give to a "drug rehabilitation program" or to "feed starving children" than to fill the coffers of a self-anointed messiah. Members have also been known to solicit from wheelchairs in order to enhance the sympathy motives of potential contributors.

Moon's theology is a mixture of Christian concepts and spiritistic practices. He teaches that heaven is a realm of the spirit world. Hell is inconsequential because it will "pass away as heaven expands." One's destination after death depends on his spirit's "quality of life on earth; by the degree of goodness we build into them through our actions." Unlike the Christian promise of immortal perfection, Moon insists that in the afterlife his followers will experience the same "desires, dislikes, and aspirations as before death." Any spot sprinkled with soil from Korea is considered to be holy ground. Evil spirits may be expelled by a sprinkling of Holy Salt. An application may be surreptitiously applied from behind whenever someone considered evil enters one of their centers.

Sunday mornings are set aside to pay homage to the True Parents. Rising at 5:00 A.M., the Church Family bows three times before a picture of the Rev. and Mrs. Moon. A pledge follows in which members vow to do whatever necessary to bring about Moon's will on earth. At times, prayer sessions (with petitions directed to Moon himself) become loud, frenzied affairs. Observers report seeing some devotees sob and wail, pounding their fists on the floor in explosive outpourings of grief and exclamations of victory. Moonies were described by one reporter as jerking spasmodically "in spiritual transport, like participants in a voodoo ceremony." Such traumas of self-evaluation are better than receiving a humiliating tirade from Moon. To those who fail his goals, the True Father is merciless. He scathingly attacks slothful members, accusing them of not helping to build the kingdom of heaven on earth.

From the beginning, occult practices have overshadowed Moon's approach. He admits communicating with familiar spirits by means of séances. Though the Christian ordinances of baptism and communion are avoided, the Unification Church accepts clairvoyance, automatic handwriting, and mediumistic trances. Moon confidently predicts, "As history approaches its end point, more and more people will have spiritual and psychic experiences." He promises followers that those who are completely surrendered to his precepts will witness spirit materialization of their Father (Moon). Certain members claim to have observed this phenomenon while others credit Moon with the ability to read their minds. Some initiates have been lured by dreams in which Moon and his wife have appeared to call them to service in the church. Ironically, those who consider forsaking Moon's teachings are warned that such actions may result in satanic possession.

Moon for a time fell out of grace with Seoul's new governmental leaders, and favorable mention of him in the press was barred in his homeland. Many Koreans seemed genuinely embarrassed by Moon's image. In the U.S., public consciousness of his unsavory tactics is better known than the tactics of most cults. This has created a plethora of problems. Some of his church-owned buildings in New York have been declared taxable. And the U.S. Immigration and Naturalization Service has recommended Moon's deportation based on the falsified credentials of his wife's application for permanent resident alien status. A federal grand jury in New York handed down a twelve-point indictment charging Moon and an aide with tax evasion. In 1982 a court found him guilty of conspiracy to avoid taxes on $162,000 in personal income. In 1984 Moon was sent to the Federal Correctional Institution in Danbury, Connecticut, for eleven months. (The Danbury facility has a reputation as a "country club" prison, more like a college dorm than a typical prison.) After release he was to serve for seven months at Brooklyn's Oxford Project Halfway House, but during this period he was allowed to conduct his church business. While Moon's detractors were and are many, it became clear with his short (and relatively painless) imprisonment that his political and financial clout had made him, at least to some degree, above the law. (A curious sidelight on the case: Many organizations—including the National Association of Evangelicals, the National Council of Churches, and the American Civil Liberties Union—filed amicus briefs with the court, voicing their sympathy with Moon. Jerry Falwell was one of many religious leaders who claimed that Moon's prosecution was an assault on religious freedom.)

Moon's aide, Mose Durst, claimed the publicity did not hurt the Unification Church. Rather, he says, membership jumped from 5 to 6 percent nationally. This seems essential, since the church must somehow make up for the estimated 50 percent attrition rate of disillusioned followers. But so long as America remains a society of rootless youth, Moon's vision of hope for the future will continue to attract a sizable following. In fact, Moon's disciples are so confident of the days ahead that Mose Durst now openly declares Moon to be the "second Messiah" succeeding Jesus.

The Moon empire is wider than anyone thinks. The Unification Church invested at least $70 million in Uruguay, and therefore gained considerable control in that country. Because of its anti-Communist stance, they made powerful friends. The Church purchased Banco de Credito, the third largest bank in Uruguay, plus the country's largest luxury hotel in Montevideo. Added to this impressive list of holdings, the Moonies also own three printing presses in Uruguay, a newspaper, and huge amounts of farmland.

Elsewhere in South America, Moonies had less success. Brazilian riots ousted them from that country, and the Church gained little power or influence in Bolivia, Chile, and Paraguay.

The Washington Times is owned by Moon, as are 83 fishing boats in Virginia and Massachusetts, and enormous real estate holdings throughout the U.S. (The boats were controversial for a time because, as "church boats," they were tax-exempt, even though they were clearly commercial in nature.) Paragon House, a book publishing firm in New York, was begun in 1984, with prominent scholars on its editorial board. And a number of front organizations help to channel church money toward various anti-Communist movements. This is not difficult to believe, given the estimated 3 million members worldwide. The phrase "power corrupts" comes to mind, and Christians rightly bewail the influence of this self-proclaimed messiah and his growing empire.

Founder: Sun Myung Moon, born January 6, 1920, in Kwangju Sangsa Ru, Korea, which is now controlled by Communist North Korea.

Text: *Divine Principle,* by the Rev. Moon. Moon's revelations are said to be the "things to come" referred to in John 16:13.

Symbol: A square surrounded by a circle. Four spokes radiate from the outer circle to the center where they meet a smaller darkened sphere inside the square. This inner circle radiates spokes to the edge of the square.

Appeal: Many Moonies are former evangelicals or frequent churchgoers. Their frustrations with hypocrisy and lack of dynamic leadership led them to Moon. In the Unification Church they discover authority, a nonjudgmental, accepting kind of love, and a vision for world unity and peace.

Purpose: Cult literature states, "In the work of restoration [mankind's salvation], God worked to find one individual who could overcome his evil nature, and on the foundation of that person's faith to find a family around him, a society, a nation, and finally to restore the whole world." Christianity holds no hope since God has discarded it as a corrupt and outdated religion. God is pictured as a sad creature, surrounded by evil and estranged from his creation. Moon is the man who will cheer God's heart by accomplishing what Christ failed to do: redeem man physically from the curse of the serpent's sexual seduction of Eve.

Errors: The God depicted in *Divine Principle* is neither omnipotent nor sovereign in earth's affairs. Assigning a female nature to the Holy Spirit and ridiculing Christ's resurrection are blasphemy of the highest order. Moon's doctrine of sinless perfection by "indemnity" (forgiveness of sin by works on Moon's behalf), which can apply even to deceased ancestors, is a denial of the salvation by grace offered through Christ (Gal. 1; Eph. 2:8-9). The warning in Matthew 24 regarding false prophets is clearly fulfilled in Moon's doctrines and claims to spiritual authority.

Background Sources: Sun Myung Moon, *Divine Principle* (New York: Unification Church, 1973); Sun Myung Moon, *New Hope* (New York: Unification Church, 1973); "The Unification Church—Who We Are," introductory pamphlet; *Psychology Today,* vol. 2, no. 8, August 1976, 16-21; *Circus,* 13 April 1976, 50-53; *Time,* 10 November 1975, 44; Ibid., 14 June 1976, 49; Ibid., 6 July 1981, 37; *Christianity Today,* 1 March 1974, 101; Ibid., 28 February 1975, 42; Ibid., 19 December 1975, 13-16; Ibid., 12 March 1976, 45; Ibid., 8 October 1976, 59-62; Ibid., 20 July 1979, 38-40; *People,* 20 October 1975, 7-9; Ronald Enroth, *The Lure of Cults* (Chappaqua, N.Y.: Christian Herald Books, 1979); Chris Elkins, *Heavenly Deception* (Wheaton, Ill.: Tyndale, 1980); *The Denver Post,* 1 February 1974, 6FF; Ibid., 5 December 1975, 5BB; Ibid., 18 February 1977, 8BB; Ibid., 3 March 1978, 4, 5BB; Ibid., 8 May 1981, 5BB; *Newsweek,* 26 March 1975, 63; Ibid., 14 June 1976, 60-66; Ibid., 19 May 1980, 27; *Media Spotlight,* January-March 1986, 1; Edward Schumacher, New York Times News Service, "Rev. Moon's Uruguay Ties," *The Dallas Morning News,* 26 February 1984.

Address/Location: The Holy Spirit Association for the Unification of World Christianity. U.S. Headquarters: 1365 Connecticut Ave., N.W., Washington, DC 20036; International Training Center, 723 South Broadway, Tarrytown, NY 10591.

U N I T A R I A N
U N I V E R S A L I S T
A S S O C I A T I O N

If religious movements could be classified psychologically, the label schizophrenic would certainly apply to the Unitarian Universalist Association. Members attempt to laud the selfless sacrifice of Christ's crucifixion and often quote Scripture in a feigned effort to validate its worth. On the other hand they repudiate the Virgin Birth and Atonement, as well as the Nicene, Chalcedonian, and Apostles' Creeds affirming the inerrancy of the Bible. They also reject the Trinity in favor of a Unitary God and subscribe to the doctrine that all souls will ultimately be saved.

In 1959 the Unitarian Church merged with the Universalist Church, and today the combined groups claim slightly fewer than 200,000 members in nearly 1,000 churches. There are no sacraments observed by the constituents, who hold Jesus to be no more than a great prophet. Their aim, according to the charter of the Universalist Church, is to "promote harmony among adherents of all religious faiths, whether Christian or otherwise." Such inclusivism has prevented the Association from being accorded official recognition by national Christian bodies (for example, the National Council of Churches), though some Unitarians do belong to local ministerial groups.

Since the truth of God is said to be revealed in the sacred writings of all great religions, the philosophy of Unitarians is reduced to little more than an ethical system of morality. Heaven and hell are anathema to Unitarians, and the doctrine of the Atonement is said to be "offensive" and "unbiblical." As an outgrowth of eighteenth-century Enlightenment, including rationalism and anti-supernaturalism, Unitarian thought has historically attracted leading intellectuals, such as poet-essayist Ralph Waldo Emerson. Present-day members differ as to whether they should classify themselves as being Christian. Their adherence to universal truth as declared in the teachings of all prophets of all ages renders the terms *Christian* and *Unitarian* to be mutually exclusive.

Background Sources: *Christianity Today,* 2 August 1972; Walter Martin, *Kingdom of the Cults* (Minneapolis: Bethany Fellowship, 1977); J. Gordon Melton, *The Encyclopedia of American Religions,* vol. 2 (Wilmington, N.C.: McGrath, 1978).

UNITY

SCHOOL

OF

CHRISTIANITY

"This has been a message from Unity," the announcer intones. It certainly sounds good. Who wouldn't want such a pleasant approach to life? Just think of it. No more guilt, disease, or financial worries. Every problem solved. Why not write the Missouri address and find out what it's all about?

This scenario is an example of the way thousands of people every year fall prey to Unity's slick advertising campaign. The Unity Village headquarters in Lee's Summit (near Kansas City), Missouri, enhance their radio and TV promotions with a slick, well-financed printing operation. Periodicals like *Wee Wisdom* appeal to Sunday school children, and Ernest Wilson's book *Have We Lived Before?* homes in on adults ripe for reincarnation teachings. Such media exposure has paid off. Unity's mail-order approach has reached an estimated 6 million "readers and followers" worldwide, with approximately 300 centers in several countries.

To the casual observer, Unity's beliefs may seem like nothing more than power-of-positive-thinking homilies. But those acquainted with the fertile ground of late nineteenth-century pantheistic philosophy will readily see Unity's similarity to Christian Science and New Thought. That is to be expected. A Belfast, Maine, clock-maker, Phineas Parkhurst Quimby, fathered all three cults. His theories of animal magnetism and mental healing were plagiarized by Mary Baker Eddy (Christian Science founder) and Julius and Annetta Dresser, along with Warren Felt Evans (New Thought creators). Charles and Myrtle Fillmore adopted their brand of Quimby's teachings to launch Unity in 1889. (The actual name *Unity* was designated in 1895.)

Myrtle claimed she was tubercular until she learned, "I am a child of God; therefore I do not inherit sickness." Charles, a cripple with tuberculosis of the hip, had explored Spiritualism and Hinduism. Both later testified that living by Christian Science and New Thought principles cured their ills. Eventually they split with the two groups on minor points of theology. The Fillmores dropped the Christian Science belief that matter is not real. They added a reverence for Jesus and the doctrine of reincarnation to New Thought philosophy. In fact, Charles Fillmore believed he was a reincarnation of the Apostle Paul.

Reincarnation is one of Unity's least publicized but most distinctive doctrines. Charles and Myrtle borrowed heavily from the Hinduistic teachings of Swami Vivekananda from India. But sensing that the idea of soul transmigration back to an animal form might not set well with Westerners, they insisted that reincarnation could only occur in human bodies. Several Bible references are used to justify this teaching, such as the instances where Christ is called the Son of David. (To Unity this is an indication that Jesus had been previously incarnated in King David.) Confronting such scriptural perversion with proper biblical exegesis would be pointless. Charles Fillmore declared that the Bible is only one of many sacred books to be revered. He went so far as to suggest that the Word of God is an inferior form of revelation for those "who are not themselves in direct communication with God."

It should, therefore, come as no surprise that the belief system of Unity severely departs from orthodox Christian doctrine. As in Christian Science, God is said to be a principle of love, and his Son is only an example of how we too can come to our own Christ-consciousness. Since, according to Fillmore, there are other "spiritually illuminated persons" who can "help one get started on the right path for finding God," Christ does not have an indispensable role in Unity's perception of salvation. Unity believes that "atonement means reconciliation between God and man through Christ." Such an evangelical-sounding statement is clarified by the qualification that "reconciliation means a reuniting of our consciousness with the God-consciousness." The traditional Christian position is that reconciliation should be based on forgiveness of sin and removing the barrier of rebellion between man and God. In Unity, redemption isn't necessary because evil and sin do not exist. Since God is in everything (including plants and inanimate objects), this premise of pantheism does away with both the devil and man's fallen unregenerate nature.

The average person who explores Unity probably never delves that deeply into its theology. Like many such cults, participants experience the benefits of its principles without necessarily adhering to its more refined doctrines. Initiates are discouraged from leaving their own churches, though they later encounter pressure to more closely align themselves with Unity Centers (some of which are called churches). Most inquirers are attracted by the core of the cult, Silent Unity. This group handles prayer requests and expresses apparently genuine concern for the problems brought to them. Each year Silent Unity receives an estimated 2.5 million requests for help. Letters from Silent Unity recommend "affirmation" or "meditations" to get inquirers' thinking back into the right mode to solve their problems. By thus adjusting their mind to the "divine mind," physical ills and difficulties will vanish.

Will they? For some the answer is decidedly, "Yes." Those with physiological or emotional symptoms resulting from mental stress are bound to experience some relief by adopting a positive outlook on life. Even organic disorders may have the healing process accelerated by the right frame of mind. But such a commonly accepted fact of medical science is a long way from Fillmore's belief that "thoughts of disease will produce microbes of destruction." Still, there is no doubt that many are impressed with the religious warmth by which Unity's emotional guidance is dispensed. Psychological aid is a worthy merit, but it should never take the place of adherence to spiritual truth rooted in objective revelation. The question is not whether Unity works, but how it works without having any biblical basis for its benefits.

Founders: Founded in 1889 by Charles and Myrtle Fillmore of Kansas City, Missouri. Myrtle died in 1931, Charles in 1948. His son, Lowell, is now the leader of Unity.

Text: The Bible, though passages are spiritualized and allegorized to fit Unity teachings. All sacred writings of world religions are accepted. Charles Fillmore wrote: "Unity believes there is good in every religion on earth and that we should keep our minds open."

Symbols: A number of them: a circle with wings on both sides and the word *Unity* across the front; the several-storied tower that rises above the Unity Village complex; a light shining at night from a lone window symbolizing "The Light that Shines for You," a reference to Silent Unity's constant prayer vigil.

Appeal: Christian terminology is used to promote syncretistic metaphysical beliefs. Some with a poor mental perspective on life may be uplifted by Unity's emphasis on love and positive emotions. Their restoration to psychological health would undoubtedly accrue certain physical benefits. In addition, Unity's optimistic attitude toward material prosperity may have compelled some toward greater financial gain.

Purpose: Charles Fillmore viewed physical ills and failure as an outgrowth of mental disequilibrium. One must overcome this by affirming that God is the source of all desirable values and that God and man are inseparable. The divine mind of God is in all men, and perfection (as attained by Jesus) is possible by acknowledging this inner divinity and removing the illusion of sin.

Errors: Unity's goal of harmony with the mind of God ignores the scriptural truth that union with God requires a penalty for sin and the shedding of blood. In the words of Charles Fillmore, "The number and seriousness of our past mistakes do not matter to God. He holds no grudges and has no account book." A mere affirmation denying the existence of evil does not eradicate its effect on man's soul. Fallen humanity bears guilt for transgression, and good thoughts and beneficent feelings will not suffice to remove the consequences of divine judgment.

Background Sources: *The Denver Post,* 29 November 1975, 5BB; writings of Charles Fillmore, including *Talks on Truth, Jesus Christ Heals, Prosperity,* et al.; Walter Martin, *The Kingdom of the Cults* (Minneapolis: Bethany, 1965); Kenneth Boa, *Cults, World Religions, and You* (Wheaton, Ill.: Victor, 1977); Charles R. Fillmore, "The Adventure Called Unity" (pamphlet); *Daily Word,* Unity devotional publication (various issues); *Unity—A Way of Life,* Unity periodical (various issues).

Address/Location: Unity School of Christianity, Unity Village, MO 64065.

See also New Age Cults.

URANTIA

When a book is described as "the finest worldview of religion available to contemporary man," it stands in judgment of its own endorsement. This claim of superiority made by the members of Urantia Societies is supported by their insistence that *The Urantia Book* was personally delivered by superhuman, extraterrestrial beings. The book's 2,097 pages are said to be the "finest major divine revelation since the coming of Christ to our planet." Is it any wonder Urantia followers devoutly believe they are "custodians of the greatest message ever given to man"?

Urantia teaches that all religious concepts are outdated for our age. (In contradiction, their promotional literature insists that membership in other churches or religious organizations is compatible with membership in Urantia.) Urantia proposes to augment established religious precepts with a new understanding of man's evolutionary ascent. To accomplish this end, the organization is structured around Societies (ten or more dedicated followers who study *The Urantia Book*) chartered by the Urantia Brotherhood. The Brotherhood is described as "a voluntary and fraternal association of believers in the teachings of *The Urantia Book.*"

The Urantia Foundation is the nonprofit, tax-exempt entity that is custodian of *The Urantia Book*. Since its publication, approximately 100,000 copies have been sold. (The current price is $34.) A five-member Board of Trustees who are appointed to life terms manages the Foundation. Thirty-six members of the General Council govern the affairs of the

Brotherhood. The Societies claim domestic and foreign active membership of about 1,000. Members I have met have been well-educated individuals of the upper socioeconomic strata. Since the Brotherhood
admittedly seeks quality rather than quantity it may be assumed that
Urantia's scope of influence exceeds its actual numbers.

First published in 1955, *The Urantia Book* expounds a strange psychic revelation based on the cosmological view of our universe as seen
from the perspective of beings from another world. The four parts of
the book include an analysis of our Earth (Urantia, as it is known by these
extraterrestrials) and its super-universe, *Havona*. In addition to descriptions of spirit entities, names of celestial designations are given, which
describe places such as Salvington, Nebadon, and the Isle of Paradise.
There are actually three Trinities—the *Paradise Trinity,* the *Ultimate
Trinity,* and the *Absolute Trinity.* The Paradise Trinity is supreme, consisting of the Universal Father, the Eternal Son, and the Infinite Spirit.
The book includes a discussion of the hidden years of Christ, from age
twelve to his public ministry. It purports to show the "religion of Jesus,"
not the "religion about Jesus."

The *Urantia Concordex,* a companion to the *Urantia Book,* claims that
the planet Urantia (Earth) is part of a local universe of 10,000,000 habit-
able worlds, known as Nebadon. Erect bipeds of neighboring planets
refer to Urantia as the "World of the Cross," a disturbed, disorderly planet
elevated by a great ruler, whom Earth inhabitants call Jesus Christ. The
Concordex claims Jesus of Nazareth was actually the mortal incarnation of Michael of Nebadon, who sacrificed himself to elevate Urantia
to a place of honor and interest and will one day reclaim leadership of
the cosmos of Nebadon. The *Urantia Concordex* also claims that an
8-foot-tall Adam was, like Jesus, sent to Urantia to uplift the human race
38,000 years ago. The *Concordex* contends that the Christian church is
"in the larval stage of the thwarted kingdom." The only hope for Earth
inhabitants is to tune into an energy source called the Thought Adjuster,
a fragment of God sent to inhabit the souls of Urantia mortals. Upon
death, one's Thought Adjuster and soul rejoin to ascend into eternity.

According to Urantia, Jesus is *a* son of God who perfected his divinity by seven incarnations among various creatures of the Universe. His
seventh incarnation on Urantia as Joshua ben Joseph (p. 1323) was intended to teach us that we, too, are sons of God. (Before that he was known
as Michael of Nebadon.) He is not to be equated with *the* Eternal Son
of the Paradise Trinity. Jesus is merely number 611,121 in the evolving
scheme of Creator Sons who form and rule local universes. His three

years of ministry ended by crucifixion, the cross being unnecessary since "the Father in Paradise did not decree, demand, or require the death of his Son. All of this was man's doing, not God's" (p. 2002).

Urantia may claim to welcome Christians into its membership, but *The Urantia Book* denies most cardinal doctrines of Christianity. In *The Urantia Book* all major world religions are said to have monotheistic compatibility (pp. 1442-1454). The Fall of man is dismissed as a "distorted story" (pp. 836-838), since Adam and Eve actually "carried on in the Garden for one hundred and seventeen years."

On pages 2020-2023 the bodily resurrection of Christ is refuted. ("His material or physical body was not part of the resurrected personality . . . the body of flesh in which he lived . . . was still lying there in the sepulchre" – p. 2021). Above all, the New Testament concepts of blood atonement and redemption from original sin are dismissed as the expression of a "primordial ghost fear" (p. 1005). In the place of these essential Christian beliefs, Urantia proposes a system of soul transmigration, with man gradually ascending from animal-to-human-to-God.

The Urantia Book is so expansive that an exhaustive analysis is impossible. Listed below are a few more areas where the *Book* departs from Christian belief:

1. Prayer is not to be attempted until one has "exhausted the human capacity for human adjustment." In addition, "words are irrelevant to prayer" (p. 1002).
2. Paul's doctrine regarding atonement (Heb. 9:22) "unnecessarily encumbered Christianity with teachings about blood and sacrifice" (p. 984).
3. The home is seen as a "sociologic institution" (p. 931), and the belief that marriage is a sacred state is called "unfortunate." "Deity is not a cojoining party" in marriages that dissolve (p. 929).
4. Mankind's parents were named Andon and Fonta, who procreated Sontad.
5. Adam, Solomon, and David were not in the direct line of ancestry of Joseph, the father of Jesus (p. 1344).
6. Jesus adopted the term "Son of Man" at age 15 after reading a passage in the so-called Book of Enoch (p. 1390).
7. During his twenty-eighth and twenty-ninth years on earth, Jesus toured the Roman world, accompanied by two natives from India (p. 1427).

8. The indwelling Christ is not essential to salvation, since "Jesus does not require his disciples to believe in *him* but rather to believe with him" (p. 2089).

Impersonal as well as personal concepts of deity are expounded without any acknowledgment of such an inconsistency. In some instances, both unitarian and trinitarian views seem to be considered acceptable. The only ultimate guide to faith is reliance on the "Indwelling Thought Adjuster" instead of consulting objective revelation. Thought Adjusters are said to be "undiluted . . . parts of Deity" who guide humans on the path of spiritual progress through countless lifetimes on other planets, "universe upon universe until [humans] actually attain the divine presence of [their] Paradise Father." Christians faced with such a philosophical outlook may find it difficult to present the unique claims of Christ, since the Urantia member's inclusive view will seem to accept any doctrinal viewpoint. But a careful study will clearly illustrate that *The Urantia Book* contains contradictory, extrabiblical information opposing the most crucial of Christian precepts.

Founder: Dr. Bill Sadler, to whom *The Urantia Book* was delivered by seven spirit beings in 1934. A group of 37 people, called the Forum, studied the original manuscripts before incorporating the Urantia Foundation in 1950. John Hales is the current president.

Text: *The Urantia Book,* a 2,097-page volume said to be written by celestial beings and communicated by automatic handwriting (an occult practice). It was first published in Chicago, 1958.

Symbols: Three concentric circles.

Appeal: For those who do not accept biblical infallibility, *The Urantia Book* provides a fascinating disclosure of esoteric and cosmological information. The curious or speculative mind not rooted in Christian doctrine can easily be drawn to it.

Purpose: Urantia literature says the Foundation aims to improve man's "comprehension of Cosmology and the realization of the planet on which we live to the universe of the genesis and destiny of man and his relation to God, and of the true teachings of Jesus Christ."

Error: Urantia revelation is held to be superior to Scripture. Man is not a unique creation by God but an evolving being, descended from the animal kingdom, destined to be an angelic spirit being, and eventually become a god. Man only needs to acknowledge that a portion of God's Spirit (the Thought Adjuster) dwells within him. Moral accountability is replaced with the Hinduistic idea of merging with God by soul transmigration. Paul's Epistle to the Colossians responds succinctly to such Gnostic-originated concepts, suggesting that Jesus is only one among many spirit beings who serve as intermediaries between God and man.

Background Sources: Urantia Foundation literature, including *Leavening our Religious Heritage, Our Task, The Urantia Book* and *Basic Concepts of the Urantia Book,* all published by the Urantia Foundation; Elliot Miller, "The Urantia Book," Christian Research Institute Inc., 1979; J. Gordon Melton, *The Encyclopedia of American Religions,* vol. 2 (Wilmington, N.C.: McGrath, 1978), 119; *SCP Newsletter,* vol. 7, no. 3, August 1981; Clyde Bedell, *Concordex of the Urantia Book* (Santa Barbara, Calif.: Clyde Bedell Estates, 1986); Karl Cates, *José D. Cepeda, The Iskander,* 11 May 1986.

Address/Location: The Urantia Foundation, 533 Diversey Parkway, Chicago, IL 60614; Center for Urantia Book Synergy, Inc., P. O. Box 3915, Santa Barbara, CA 93130.

VEDANTA
SOCIETY

(Swami Vivekananda)

The increasing influence of mystical thought on Western religious values owes a debt of gratitude to the first Hindu guru to be widely accepted as a legitimate spokesman for the East – Swami Vivekananda (1863-1902). In 1893 he addressed the Parliament of Religions in Chicago and took the conference by storm. His subsequent national exposure via lecture tours led to his founding of the Vedanta Society in 1894, which was the first official Hindu organization to be established in the United States. The proliferation of many current cults is but the fruition of this landmark event.

Named Narendranath Datta at the time of his birth, he later assumed the *swami* name of Vivekananda ("Bliss of Discrimination" between the real and the illusory) and became a devoted disciple of the Bengali holy man, Sri Ramakrishna, who served as a priest in Calcutta's Kali Temple. Ramakrishna often experienced *samadhi* (the bliss of altered trance consciousness) and concluded that all gods and religions were but multiple manifestations of the one Absolute. He then pursued the path of *Vedanta* (the goal of knowledge based on the *Vedas* – sacred Hindu scriptures) and developed an intellectual approach to Hinduism based in part on charitable works of mercy. Vivekananda viewed Ramakrishna as an *avatar* worthy of the kind of devotion shown Christ by his apostles, and upon the holy man's death, he founded the Ramakrishna Mission in Calcutta.

Through the Vedanta Society, Vivekananda was able to influence favorably many prominent figures, including authors Aldous Huxley and Gertrude Stein. While insisting on the primacy of Hinduism, Vivekananda told them, "We accept all religions as true." Those who favorably view Vivekananda's influence on Western religious thought might do well to visit personally (as has this author) both Kali Temple and the Ramakrishna Mission in Calcutta. Kali, the blackened goddess of death, stands draped in a necklace of human skulls and holds a bloody severed head in one hand. Near the entrance of Kali Temple I witnessed bloody goat sacrifices before a phallic *lingam* (genital replica). Not far away, at the Ramakrishna Mission Temple, I watched poor peasants bow before an idol, offering the deity the little money they had. The idol's favor meant more to them than obtaining food to sustain the lives of their children. Transporting this pagan spiritual heritage to the West is the Vedanta Society's ultimate goal. Such dehumanizing aims cannot be obscured by any intellectualized discourses regarding "existence of the One Cause" or "merging the self with Reality."

Background Sources: J. Gordon Melton, *The Encyclopedia of American Religions,* vol. 2 (Wilmington, N.C.: McGrath, 1978); *Spiritual Counterfeits Project Newsletter,* vol. 5, no. 3, April-May 1979.

VOODOO / SANTERIA

Haitians call it voodoo. Cubans and other Latinos refer to it as Santeria. Brazilians christen it Macumba, and Trinidadians call it Shango. Regardless of the name, all are derivatives of tribal African religious practices responsible for increasing violence, murder, and spiritual enslavement in the United States.

The dangerous cult of voodoo has been glorified by such movies as *The Serpent and the Rainbow* and *Angel Heart* and has become increasingly popular in this country. Some cities have pharmacies where customers can purchase snakeskin, dried bird claws, bones, roots, incense, statues, candles, and other paraphernalia to use in voodoo spells and potions. People use the crude drugs and voodoo magic to ward off evil spirits, gain control over other people, win lawsuits, and advance in the business world.

Voodoo thrives in many parts of America. A colony in South Carolina boasts of its return to old African ways and the practice of voodoo. While voodoo is popular in Mississippi and Louisiana, Santeria flourishes in Florida. Practicing voodoo is particularly popular in New Orleans and is growing in America among refugees. Police investigated the 1986 mutilation murder of a baby in Connecticut and linked it to the centuries-old Santeria religion. Surrounding the baby were pennies, fruit, and other trinkets, indicating involvement of the Caribbean religious cult.

Santeria is especially popular in Dade County, Florida, where a third-grade student skipped school to become a Santeria priestess. The Cuban form of voodoo traces its roots to Africa, calls for the sacrifice of animals to saints, and uses chanting and bathing in its initiation rites. The girl's initiation rites took three to four weeks, according to religious experts, and she was legitimately excused from school.

Santeria's ways are secretive, its size unknown. Devotees argue that they've been victimized by unequal law enforcement and religious persecution. Some feel they've been painted as bloodthirsty pagans. Says Gene Bailly, a Santerian priest, "Santeria has a bad name. People think it's witchcraft, think it's Satanism. It's misinformation." He calls Santeria a deep, ancient religion.

In Miami, religious stores in Cuban neighborhoods sell candles, Roman Catholic icons, and live animals for sacrificial rites. The Santeria cult originated among black slaves the Spanish brought to Cuba. Forced to embrace Catholicism, the slaves held on to their religious roots by transferring the characteristics of their own gods to Christian saints.

Law enforcement officials say animal sacrifice rituals in the Miami area are so common the river's clean-up boat picks up an average of 100 carcasses a week. *Santeros,* or priests, slaughter animals as an offering of blood to appease their gods. In exchange, they hope to be blessed with good fortune. Explains one Santeria advocate, "The saints have to be fed, and blood sacrifice is one of the ways you feed them." Palo Mayombe, a black magic offshoot of Santeria, is more malevolent, often using human skulls obtained by grave robbing.

Known to anthropologists as *vodoun,* voodoo is a system focusing on a distant god known as the Grand Master, who manifests through various rituals. He has a pantheon of spirits, such as benevolent ones invoked by *rada* rites and harsher spirits invoked by bloody *petro* rites. The harsh spirits supposedly are crude and malicious when possessing someone.

Voodoo has played a powerful role in Haitian politics. The notorious slave revolt of 1791 began at an August evening voodoo ceremony. Participants pledged allegiance to Satan if their nation were freed from the French. Nearly two centuries later, voodoo was a major factor in the rise and fall of the Haitian Duvalier dynasty. At first voodoo frightened and intimidated the people into submission, then it enraged them into violence and destruction.

"Papa Doc" Duvalier ruled Haiti for 14 years, dying in 1971. He used voodoo to instill fear in the Haitians and to strengthen his power. When he became president in 1957, many peasants believed him the incarnation of the voodoo god, Baron Samedi, the spirit of death and one of the malevolent spirits of the voodoo pantheon.

Duvalier often dressed in black suits and donned voodoo trappings to encourage that belief. Duvalier also named his security force *Tontons Macoutes* after the legendary Haitian bogeymen who snatched naughty children. To impress his followers with voodoo power, he changed the Haitian flag to red and black, the colors of voodoo secret ceremonies. During his reign, Duvalier's minions murdered thousands of Haitians. He claimed to sleep in a tomb once a year to commune with spirits. Jean-Claude inherited his father's dictatorship in 1971 and continued the vicious, despotic voodoo regime of demonism. As Jean-Claude "Baby Doc" Duvalier's dynasty disintegrated, he summoned in vain voodoo priests to help him control the unrest. He finally fled Haiti in 1986. Now that Baby Doc is gone, the new rulers have changed the black and red flag to red and blue.

Walter Serge King was a wiry, light brown voodoo visionary who lived in New York. The son of a follower of Marcus Garvey (an early 1900s black movement leader who taught blacks that Ethiopia was their promised land), King yearned to rediscover his cultural roots and became an African dancer in a traveling troupe. He studied ballet, wandered through black Africa, and roamed Haiti.

Upon returning to New York, Serge King became a well-known figure in black nationalist groups. When most black leaders were advocating political power, King pushed for a broader cultural nationalism, but knew he couldn't unite a deeply religious race of blacks without a powerful catalyst. He decided voodoo was that spiritual catalyst. King was initiated into a voodoo cult in Cuba in 1959, after which he returned to New York City. He then opened the first temple devoted to pure African voodoo and acted as "Chief Bab" (short for *babalawo,* or priest).

While differences exist between voodoo and Santeria, the two cults have several gods and rituals in common. Each sect also believes that all events in this world are shaped by divine forces outside it. A major voodoo philosophy is, "Take care of the gods and they will take care of you." For example, during their year in white, Santeria initiates learn their religion's secret ceremonies, study the Yoruba language so they can address their gods in the god's own tongue, and learn the favorite foods and drinks of their gods.

Ogun, the god of iron and war, supposedly likes roosters and male goats for dinner, and his favorite drink is rum. Erzulie, the voodoo god of life, craves desserts, especially decorated cakes and creme de menthe. Damballah desires champagne, whereas other voodoo gods settle for Coca-Cola.

When voodoo worshipers become possessed by the spirit that has descended and entered their bodies, they usually shriek or howl. Some violently shake or writhe, as if experiencing an epileptic fit. Suddenly the possessed person becomes entranced, passes out, and falls to the ground. While in the trance, some worshipers walk over broken glass or burning coals. Others place their hands in burning oil or alcohol. Voodoo advocates vow that if worshipers show no bodily harm after such ordeals, it means spirits have entered their bodies.

Voodoo may be partially accountable for the AIDS outbreak in Haiti. Because voodoo priests use cadaver components in various potions and powders and because human blood is used in sacrificial worship, some AIDS experts believe the disease has been spread by contact with these contaminated remains. It seems to be the reason why AIDS is so common in Haiti but not on other Caribbean islands.

Voodoo is an occult religion rooted in Satanism. Tempting possession is also tempting serious spiritual risk. The Bible teaches us to drive spirits out, not ask them in. God calls us to offer our bodies as holy, living sacrifices, not to appease spirits by making gifts of dead animals. An attempt to consort with spirits brought about King Saul's end, and perhaps the same judgment befell the Duvaliers in Haiti.

Founders: African slaves, who imported occult tribal beliefs.

Text: None. Oral tradition.

Symbols: Fetishes, icons, voodoo dolls. Other symbols protect the wearer against poisoning, death hexes, evil spirits, sickness, injury, and accidents.

Appeal: The statement is often made that voodoo helps Haitians face the crushing poverty in their country. While such religious eccentricities may attract illiterate masses in the Caribbean, the appeal in the United States is much different. Voodoo and Santeria lure a dark part of the human psyche that covertly craves uninhibited behavior and revenge.

Purpose: People practice voodoo to appease their gods and bring good fortune on themselves. Some practice voodoo to instill serious negative psychological effects on others.

Errors: The Bible teaches us to tread on demons, not invoke them (Luke 10:19). In occult voodoo practices, possession is invited. Voodoo offers blood sacrifices to appease spirits, but the Lord doesn't require us to kill for him. Also, voodoo malevolence to further one's position socially or professionally is evil and selfish behavior. While many practice both voodoo and Christianity, voodoo's distant "Grand Master" deity and its pantheon of spirits conflict with the biblical cosmology.

Background Sources: *Drug Topics,* 3 May 1982, 56; *The Press* (Atlantic City, New Jersey), 21 March 1986, 6; *The Rocky Mountain News,* 8 December 1984; *Dallas Life Magazine,* 15 July 1984, 29; *Newsweek,* 17 February 1986, 46; *USA Today,* 1 June 1987, 2A; *The Seattle Times/Seattle Post-Intelligence,* 25 November 1984, B14; *The Vancouver Sun,* 1 February 1980, 7L; *The National Observer,* 20 November 1975, 20; *The Stuart* (Fla.) *News,* 8 February 1981, A5; *The Rocky Mountain News,* 23 March 1986, 30; *Newsweek,* 22 June 1981, 44; *OMNI,* December 1987, 132-133.

Address/Location: Haiti; Southern United States where large colonies of Cuban Americans live; New Orleans, Louisiana.

See also Black Magic, Macumba, Witchcraft.

W I T C H C R A F T

An estimated 9 million women and girls met death by fire between the years of 1300 and 1700 for practicing witchcraft. In the eighteenth century, 19 suspected witches were killed in Salem, Massachusetts. Despite such extreme countermeasures, the occult rituals of witchcraft are widely practiced today around the world. No longer threatened with death, witches enjoy a degree of respectability in America's lenient New Age society. Witchcraft is officially recognized as a religion by the IRS, which has granted tax exemption to the Church and School of Wicca ("seekers of wisdom"). At one Midwestern university, 500 students enrolled in a course in witchcraft. Because some witches are reluctant to announce their pagan affiliations, estimates of those involved in organized witchcraft in the United States today range from 100,000 to 600,000.

The history of witchcraft is sketchy, since ceremonies and beliefs are orally communicated. Witchcraft rituals have been traced to worship of the Greek goddess Artemis, Diana of the Romans, the Egyptian moon goddess, and the fertility goddess of the Canaanites. Modern witches believe in two primary deities: Hecate, the Greek goddess of ghosts, and Pan (Lucifer), the god of the woods and shepherds. Witches insist their Pan, even though horned and cloven-hoofed, is not the same Lucifer condemned in Scripture.

Many cartoon images of witches are based on fact. Before Christianity, old women living on edges of villages were responsible for healing, midwifery, and counseling people. They kept cats to control mice-ridden medieval cottages and used broomsticks as weapons while gathering herbs in the forest. Dark cloaks were common dress. Toads provided a glandular secretion that was used as an anesthetic. Ancient recipes for "flying ointment" included belladonna and aconite, powerful hallucinogens.

No longer resembling the stereotypical hags in Shakespeare's *Macbeth,* today's witches are physicians, policemen, secretaries, merchants, mechanics — even ministers. Their credo is, "If it harms none, do as you will." Witches claim they don't practice evil magic, since they believe anything sent out will return threefold. They also adhere to tenets of reincarnation and karma.

Witches identify themselves as pagans, druids, and wiccans. Such terminology as earth or nature religion, positive magick, the craft, the craft of the wise, wisecraft, goddess worship, wimmin religion, and shamanism is also associated with witchcraft groups. Resurgence of neopagan witchcraft is partially traceable to the 1960s feminist and the environmental protection movements. Margot Adler, author of *Drawing Down the Moon,* an exhaustive study on witches and druids in America, says, "Neopaganism is partly a response to a planet in crisis. People today are looking for a religion that ties in with the natural world."

Meetings attended by 13 members (a *coven*) are held weekly at a *covenstead,* generally a leader's home. Larger meetings, called *esbats,* occur on special days of celebration (*sabats*). (The term was first used in 1662.) Each coven is usually autonomous, except for those groups that owe their initiation to another witch's assembly. Membership is by invitation, and progress occurs through degrees.

Some ceremonies begin with members shedding their clothing to become *skyclad,* believed to permit easier release of the body's energy. An imaginary circle is drawn around the coven with a ritualistic dagger called an *athame.* Candles are lit, and incense is burned on an altar. A priest or priestess moves to each point of the compass to summon the four guardians, symbolic of the elements of earth, air, fire, and water. Such rituals come from the *Black Book* or *Book of Shadows.* Witches intone:

> *Queen of heaven, Queen of hell,*
> *Horned Hunter of the night.*
> *Lend your power unto the spell,*
> *Work my will by magic rite.*

Ceremonial activities include hexes and healing by the laying on of hands. Love spells can be cast upon reluctant suitors. Spirits are called upon to answer questions and speak through mediums. Animal sacrifices may end the ceremonies, though most mainstream "respectable" witches deny such activity.

Gerald Gardner, who was born in England in 1884 and died in 1964, did more than any other modern individual to revive witchcraft. Gardner was an occultist, an initiate of the secretive Ordo Templi Orientis, and a friend of British Satanist Aleister Crowley, from whom he borrowed certain practices. Though poorly educated, Gardner pursued anthropology on his own and studied occultism with the daughter of Theosophist Annie Besant. Publication of his book *Witchcraft Today* led to a revival of interest in the craft in England.

Witchcraft in America was revived by Dr. Raymond Buckland, an anthropologist, and his wife, Rosemary, who studied under Gerald Gardner and brought his brand of Wicca to America in the 1960s. Witch Sybil Leek, who started with Gardnerian rituals, also came to America in the 1960s and established several covens. The Religious Order of Witchcraft was incorporated in 1972 in New Orleans, Louisiana, by Mary Oenida Toups, its high priestess.

In the early 1970s, Gavin and Yvonne Frost of New Bern, North Carolina, opened the Church and School of Wicca, one of the most visible and active witchcraft movements. Gavin and Yvonne pay less attention to traditional witchcraft deities, promoting instead the development of psychic powers. Their basic message is that any suppression of the body's desires is unnatural and unwise. The Frosts also promote the Gardnerian concept of astral sex with spirit partners (incubus or succubus).

Several other witchcraft groups have gone public. The Church of the Eternal Source centers on ancient Egyptian culture and occultism. Members have been attracted by the archeological significance of Egypt, leading them to spiritual encounters with Egyptian deities. The Church of All Worlds is nature-oriented and promotes a symbiotic relationship between humans and earth through a form of pantheism. The Radical Faerie Movement consists of gays and lesbians, who connect their sexual choices with aged pagan nature religions.

Most participants of the occult don't get involved with high-profile witchcraft. Instead, they read the books and study the ceremonies of organized witchcraft, then invent their own brand of the craft. Usually they combine elements of witchcraft with black magic and self-styled Satanism. The resulting mixture is dangerously combustible.

Founder: Ancient pagan religion predating Christianity.

Text: Oral tradition and individually compiled *Book of Shadows.*

Symbols: Pentagram, pentacle (five-pointed star), the ankh.

Appeal: Serious students of witchcraft are often people who feel man is out of control, unaligned with the cycles of nature. They turn to witchcraft for healing and to become one with their environment. They believe knowledge is power through which they can control their lives, destinies, and the world.

Purpose: Witches claim they seek to understand the connection between man and his environment. One witch has explained the craft as follows: "To obtain knowledge. To have the power and use it to achieve balance. To discover truths . . . possibly unleash the gods and goddesses within us all." Reincarnation is crucial to the witchcraft idea that good and evil are returned through karma.

Errors: Witchcraft denies biblical doctrines of heaven and hell, original sin, and the denunciation of demons. Scripture repeatedly denounces witchcraft (Lev. 19:26, 32; Deut. 18:10-11; Gal. 5:20). The elemental forces conjured are demons, and the horned deity revered is the devil. Though white witches claim to be benevolent, all such association with the spirit world is forbidden by the Bible.

Background Sources: *Insight Northwest,* October-November 1984; *Calgary Herald,* 22 October 1983; *Moody Monthly,* January 1983; *US,* 23 June 1981; *U.S. News & World Report,* 7 November 1983.

Address/Location: Worldwide.

See also Black Magic, Macumba, Voodoo/Santeria.

WORLDWIDE CHURCH OF GOD

(Armstrongism)

The orchestra swells, the music crescendos, and a deep-throated voice intones, "The World Tomorrow, with Garner Ted Armstrong." Or at least that's what used to be said before Garner Ted's philandering with money and women (a reported 200 consorts) resulted in a four-month exile in 1972 and final expulsion in 1978. Octogenarian Herbert W. Armstrong went back on the tube himself and reclaimed total autocratic control over the 68,000 members of the Worldwide Church of God (WCG).

His domain included Ambassador College campuses in Pasadena (California), Big Sandy (Texas), and St. Albans (England). H. W. was known for his frequent association with distinguished officials and world governmental leaders. He traveled aboard a private jet, a symbol of the opulent life-style for which he had been criticized. Armstrong fancied himself as an international statesman and had gained access to high offices (Egypt's Sadat, Israel's Begin, India's Gandhi) by bestowing philanthropic gifts. Critics charged him with having $30,000 worth of carpet in his office and lavishing $500,000 on the Vienna Symphony, which performed at the opening of his extravagant ($11 million) Ambassador Auditorium.

Armstrong, self-styled prophet of the "one true church," started out as an advertising salesman in Des Moines, Iowa. After being influenced by the teachings of an Adventist offshoot, his wife convinced him that salvation was only possible by keeping all of God's commandments. These injunctions were later to become an integral part of WCG doctrine: Sabbath-keeping, Old Testament kosher laws, and observance of

Jewish feasts. Other precepts adopted by Armstrong were: rejection of the Trinity, noninvolvement in governmental affairs, denial of hell, annihilation of the wicked, and Anglo-Israelism (a belief that caused him to split with the Church of God Seventh Day).

His background in promotion alerted him to the possibilities of media exposure. From an initial broadcast on a 100-watt station in 1934, the Armstrong empire grew to include scores of radio and TV outlets (500 in Garner Ted's heyday). In addition, *The Plain Truth,* a slick four-color monthly magazine (which once had a 2-million circulation in five languages), entices future church recruits. Its patriotic, morally concerned editorial slant caters to middle Americans. To those frustrated with crime, pornography, and political uncertainty, it promises a brighter "world tomorrow" without saying exactly how it is to be achieved and who is to lead the way. (*Quest* magazine, an expensive, glossy bimonthly, serves as a public relations vehicle dedicated to "the pursuit of excellence," and is published by Ambassador International Cultural Foundation, a WCG front organization. As of the writing of this book, *Quest* was rumored to be for sale.)

Almost never mentioned are the WCG beliefs that make this homegrown sect an enigma. Some of these strange doctrines have recently been modified to accommodate a more open, public image. Others remain intact. These teachings (which may or may not have been rescinded by the time this book reaches the reader) include: a form of triple-tithing to underwrite the Church, Church Festivals, and special funds; hesitation to seek physicians and surgery; implicit requirements that members dissolve post-divorce marriages (a dictum repealed in 1976), and condemnation of recognizing birthdays as well as Easter and Christmas. Future changes in doctrine are likely because the WCG holds to a view of progressive theology claiming "no final understanding of the Word of God" and asserting a "willingness to incorporate new understanding." Until recently, knowledge of any WCG teachings was scarce to come by. Church meetings were held in public buildings, services were unannounced, and uninvited visitors were politely ushered out.

It was Armstrong's belief in Anglo-Israelism that drew the most theological attention. Though Herbert denied it, his doctrine closely resembled the theory expounded by Canadian Richard Brothers, a psychic visionary who lived in London in the eighteenth century. (His ideas were later popularized in 1840 by Scotsman John Wilson.) Ignoring sound rules of linguistics and hermeneutics, the theory suggests that England (Ephraim) and the United States (Manasseh) are what is left of the so-called Ten Lost Tribes of Israel. Ancient Judah and Israel are believed to be two separate entities (the former are Jews as they are known today). After the Assyrian captivity, Israel migrated northward to eventually become the Anglo-Saxons of British heritage.

Armstrong taught that the promises of God due to his chosen people have been transferred to America and the United Kingdom. He also declared that Queen Elizabeth sits on the throne to which Christ will return. Although sound Bible scholarship questions whether or not Israel and Judah should be separated and debunks the idea that any tribes were ever lost, the WCG maintains that the British Coronation Stone of Scone was actually brought to the Emerald Isle by the prophet Jeremiah. Armstrong believed the war of Armageddon was near and that Germany (modern Assyria) would lead a ten-nation confederation into this battle.

Worldwide Church of God members need not fear the coming conflagration. God's "true church" (i.e., WCG) will be raptured to Petra (the ancient rock city south of the Dead Sea in Jordan). When will all of this take place? Armstrong variously set the dates for 1936, 1943, 1972, and 1975, though the WCG today officially refutes such date-setting. When the 1975 date passed without prophetic fulfillment, H. W. imposed a permanent silence on the issue. He had already erred in 1965 by declaring that Jerusalem would remain in Gentile hands until the return of Christ. Then came the Six Day War in 1967.

If a predisposed view of Jewish history and a predilection for expensive tastes had been his only shortcomings, Herbert W. Armstrong might have been dismissed as easily as any other religious zealot. However, his ubiquitous broadcasts and publications reached (by his estimates) 150 million people weekly. Therefore, closer scrutiny is in order to determine if his doctrines are merely fanciful or heretical. Those who were easily impressed by his railings against society's ills ought to explore the solutions offered by his system of theology. Identification with his moral viewpoint may cause one to accept uncritically a belief structure that doesn't mean what it appears to say.

Speaking of his "conversion," the elder Armstrong declared, "God called me . . . for the most important commission in 1900 years." That message, as he explained, teaches the born-again experience is a process, not an instantly imputed act. "We are not yet born of God—only heirs—only begotten," he emphasized. H. W. insisted one cannot be truly "saved" in this life, since redemption will not be completed until the resurrection. According to H.W., "salvation cannot be opened to humanity until Jesus unseats Satan and restores the government of God to this planet." In the meantime, some WCG followers live in fear of offending God and losing their salvation, careful not to miss a church feast or fall short of their financial obligations to the WCG.

Perhaps the most dangerous Armstrong doctrine is the contention that deity is an attainable goal of man. A recent WCG publication insists, "We are to be changed from physical to spiritual [a denial of the bodily resurrection] . . . into the spirit of God. We must be God. Blasphemy? No. Believe it or not, you are a potential omnipotent power. You were born to become God!" Note, the writer doesn't say *a* god. He says *God*. This view, of course, robs Christ of his unique position as eternal God. Man, who was created by Christ, is thus elevated from his finite position to a status equal with Infinity. (Armstrong also believes that man will someday join God in recreating the entire universe.)

Garner Ted's sexual misconduct drove away many members to splinter groups. The younger Armstrong said his father had rebuffed several attempts at reconciliation. Garner Ted presently heads the Church of God International, based in Tyler, Texas; this group has 5,000 members and annual revenues of $2 million. Top church leaders resigned, and the government for a time placed Herbert's purse strings in receivership, an action the California Courts later ruled was "ill-conceived litigation." In addition, his closest associate and heir-apparent, Stanley Rader, left his position as treasurer and board member. (In 1980, Rader reportedly drew a salary of $350,000 to serve as the church's executive manager.) In 1988, circulation of *The Plain Truth* had dropped by one million. Other scandals caused problems. At age 92, Herbert W. Armstrong was divorced after a seven-year marriage to his wife Ramona, aged 45. The litigation reportedly cost the church more than $5 million in legal fees. Transcripts of court proceedings reportedly indicated that Armstrong's sexual misconduct extended even to incest. It was also revealed that Ramona and Herbert had had a sexual relationship for three years prior to their marriage.

Herbert W. Armstrong died in 1986 at the age of 93. Just before he died he published his last book, *Mystery of the Ages,* which he claimed contained seven mysteries revealed to him by God. Armstrong's designated successor is Joseph Tkach, who now oversees the 92,000-member organization. Four spokesmen replaced Armstrong on "The World Tomorrow" telecast. Though the church has prospered since Armstrong's death—membership has grown by 7,000, and annual income grew from $140 million in 1985 to $163 million in 1988—Armstrong's legacy of misguided teaching continues to mislead the undiscerning.

Founder: Herbert W. Armstrong, born 1892, Des Moines, Iowa; cult founded in Eugene, Oregon, 1934; died in January 1986.

Text: Emphasis on Old Testament Scriptures regarding feasts, festivals, and dietary laws.

Symbols: Visual—none known; verbal—"The World Tomorrow," a theme of media broadcasts.

Appeal: Conservatively inclined people concerned about moral decay may be attracted by Armstrong's denunciation of social evils and calls for biblical allegiance. WCG broadcasts and publications contain a measure of truth that draws disaffected traditional church members. The absence of overt fund solicitation and the sobering style of their news commentaries give a respectability that belies the true nature of church activities and doctrines.

Purpose: Herbert W. Armstrong believed that the true church and its pure message had been underground for 1900 years. Now, just prior to the return of Christ, he had been called of God to bring a message that will dispel the confusion of all other false denominations who consider themselves Christians. The Worldwide Church of God is the only legitimate representative of the gospel of Christ.

Errors: Armstrong "Galatianized" the gospel by adding laws and commandments to the message of grace, a violation of the principles set forth in Colossians 2 and Romans 14. Ephesians refutes the ethnic and nationalistic superiority inherent in the unbiblical theory of Anglo-Israelism.

Background Sources: *The Good News,* July 1976, 28; various issues of *The Plain Truth,* especially April 1977, 3, and May 1977, 39; *Christianity Today,* 17 December 1971, 6-9; Ibid., 1 April 1977, 20-24; Ibid., 20 February 1981, 41; *Time,* 15 May 1972, 87; Ibid., 4 March 1974, 50; Ibid., 15 June 1978, 54; Ibid., 23 February 1981, 54; *Eternity,* May 1981, 15; *Christianity Today,* 15 January 1988; Dr. Roy Knuteson, "The Final Testimony of Herbert W. Armstrong," *The Discerner,* April-June 1986, 9; *Time,* 27 January 1986, 78.

Address/Location: Worldwide Church of God, Box 111, Pasadena, CA 91123; foreign offices in England, Australia, Canada, and South Africa.

Y O G A

Her face is fresh and her body is incredibly slim. She looks like the model for a health food ad. The calisthenics she has just led you through are guaranteed to knock off the pounds overnight. For an exercise instructor she certainly lives what she preaches. But how does she stay in such good shape?

Almost anticipating that question, she informs her students, "Now I want to show you how to *keep* those muscles toned and make sure the fat *stays* off. Sit on the floor and cross your legs. Now, put your shoulders back. Close your eyes. Take a deep breath, and as you let it out say, 'Om.' Let the *m* string out . . . like humming. This will help you to relax. Then we'll try some other yoga positions."

Yoga? Everyone thought this was a weight-loss class. Why doesn't the teacher have the students just sit in chairs to relax? Isn't yoga some kind of religion? Oh, well, there's really nothing "religious" about what she wants everyone to do. Might as well go along with it. Besides, the sound of that *m* is kind of soothing. Giving it a try can't hurt . . . or can it?

Yoga as it is practiced in the Western world certainly doesn't lack for advocates. Author Erica Jong says it has spurred her creativity. Artist Peter Max credits yoga with his success, as does Carol Burnett and gymnast Olga Korbut. Other practitioners include senators, nuns, ministers, and rock stars such as Ritchie Blackmore who wrote a song extolling its virtues. It is practiced in YWCAs and YMCAs, public schools, health spas, and churches. In an age of tranquilizers, cholesterol, cigarettes, booze, cocaine, and hypertension, yoga has become, for many, the American way to assuage neurosis and avoid physical neglect.

Most people have a naive openness to Eastern religions and have assumed yoga to be nothing more than an exotic way to achieve a beautiful body. Unfortunately, they presume that the exercises are harmless provided that they are not practiced with a spiritual intent. But yoga is much more than a series of muscular maneuvers designed to relieve tension. It is a Hindu tradition going back nearly 5,000 years and is based on mystical doctrines. Yoga, taken from the Sanskrit word *yuj* meaning "to join," literally means "union with God." Which God?

A major text on yoga states, "The aim of all yoga is realization of the Absolute Brahman." This abstract concept of God is difficult for the Western mind to understand. The Bible presents a personal, anthropomorphic God to whom we are personally, morally responsible. The God of yoga is an impersonal deity who pervades the universe as an energy force. Hindu belief teaches that God *(Brahman)* is unknowable, inexplicable, and at the same time present in all living things. Sometimes Brahman is referred to as the Universal Being, the Supreme Absolute, or Pure Consciousness. Whatever the name, his manifestation to men is known through the Hindu god *Shiva.* And it is Shiva, the Hindu divinity who is the manifestation of destruction, who plays an integral part in the practice of yoga.

One of the basic beliefs of yoga is the dichotomous view of a material (physical) body and a so-called subtle (spiritual) body. The Bible does teach that the flesh (the physical body) and the spirit are enemies (Rom. 7:18-19; Gal. 5:13-16). But Scripture does not say that the physical body is inherently evil. It only states that the flesh is more easily tempted to sin. Yoga, on the other hand, believes that the spiritual body is held in bondage by the physical body. Consequently, the positions are intended to manipulate the skeletal and muscle structure in such a way as to release the spiritual body for its goal of yoga, union with God.

The primary concern of yoga is to heighten God-consciousness by elevating the awareness of the spiritual body. At no time does it seek to convert the spirit of man, assuming that it is intrinsically good. Christ has promised to regenerate man's spirit (John 3:1-7) and give unto him the Holy Spirit, that he might have power and victory over flesh. This promise is fulfilled by placing trust in Jesus, not by contorting limbs.

Swami Vishnudevananda, a foremost exponent of yoga and author of *The Complete Illustrated Book of Yoga,* succinctly explains the purpose of yoga. He states, "It is the duty of each developed man to train his body to the highest degree of perfection so that it may be used to pursue the spiritual purposes. The expression of the spirit increases in proportion to the development of the body and mind in which it is encased. The aim of all yoga practice is to achieve truth wherein the individual soul identifies itself with the supreme soul of God." How is this accomplished?

Swami Vishnudevananda declares, "The supreme power of nature" is a coiled serpent lying at the base of the spine. She is the goddess *Shakti*, whom Hindus believe is "the giver of immortality and eternal happiness." But Shakti can only fulfill her promise by achieving union with Shiva, her consort. (Shiva is one member of the Hindu trinitarian godhead – Brahma, Vishnu, Shiva.) Shiva is said to reside at the center of the forehead between the eyebrows. The purpose of yoga is to arouse the serpent powers of Shakti (sometimes called *kundalini)* so that she rises through the *sushumma,* a hollow canal said to be running through the spinal cord. On the ascension, Shakti passes through six *chakras,* spiritual energy centers. The seventh *chakra,* her destination, is Shiva. Once Shakti merges with Shiva, union, or yoga, is achieved. The next goal is permanent union to become a liberated soul and be unlimited by time and space – at one with God. The person who accomplishes this goal then possesses all powers, psychic abilities, and sinless perfection.

How does all this affect the average housewife who stands on her head to lose weight, or the business executive who contorts his muscles to placate an ulcer? There are four forms of yoga: *Karma Yoga* (spiritual union through right conduct); *Bhakti Yoga* (union with the Absolute by devotion to a guru); *Juana (Gyana) Yoga* (access to God through knowledge); and *Raja Yoga* (God-realization through mental control). Raja Yoga has three subdivisions, one of which is *Hatha Yoga,* the practice most familiar to the general public. Hatha Yoga is in turn divided into eight stages: (1) body purification; (2) postures; (3) *mudras* (postures that produce psychic energy); (4) breath control; (5) stilling the mind; (6) concentration; (7) meditation; and (8) union with god (Shiva).

Body purification, for example, can involve belching air, vomiting water, swallowing a 15-foot-long cloth, or running a string up the nose, through the nasal cavity, and out the mouth. (These procedures are known as *kriyas.*) The meditative aspects of yoga are designed to still the senses by gazing at an object without blinking (referred to as *tratak).* Some yoga meditations involve the recitation of a *mantra* (the resident name of a Hindu deity) and Hindu prayers.

Most people who begin yoga assume that the positions are mere tech-

475

niques to calm the body and improve physical fitness. But yoga has distinctly religious purposes involved in every aspect. The postures *(asanas)* are sometimes designed with a devotional intent, such as the *soorya namaskar,* sun exercises. They are to be practiced by facing the rising sun and repeating the twelve names of the Lord Sun. Other positions are named after gods *(Baby Krishna, Lord Nataraja* poses) and animals (lion, scorpion, cobra, etc.). Western yoga instructors often de-emphasize these religious overtones, but such departure cannot lessen the ultimate result.

Swami Vishnudevananda states, "Hatha Yoga prescribes physical methods to begin with so that the student can manipulate the mind more easily as he advances, attaining communication with one's higher self." Some might argue that although Raja Yoga (the distinctly religious discipline of which Hatha Yoga is a part) has a spiritual intent, Hatha Yoga may be practiced free of these consequences. Again, the Swami warns, "Many people think Hatha Yoga is merely physical exercise. But in reality there is no difference between Hatha Yoga and Raja Yoga."

The postures of Hatha Yoga are designed to condition the mind to experience an altered state of consciousness. Each pose is presumed to be tuning the body, glands, and psychic nervous system to a level of spiritual susceptibility and altered awareness. Hindu yoga teachers have long defined this discipline as religious both in goal and practice. Can it then be casually disassociated from its pagan origins simply because a Western teacher redefines its intent?

Once the yoga novice has learned a few basic postures, he is quickly introduced to the breathing exercises *(pranayamas).* He may be told that these are for relaxation or clearing of the lungs. However, this aspect of yoga is actually designed for the purposes of controlling what is called *prana.* This so-called "vital breath" is said to be a form of soul energy that originates with the Universal Life Force (God, Brahman) and permeates all living matter. *Prana,* sometimes called *ki,* is supposed to be the source of psychic energy and the fount of all extrasensory phenomena experienced in advanced states of yoga. *Prana* is localized in the *chakras,* the spiritual energy centers through which Shakti rises on the way to her psychosexual union with the Shiva. The *chakras* regulate *prana* and thereby manipulate one's willpower and all bodily functions.

Yoga's breathing exercises control *prana,* a practice claimed to be beneficial in ridding the body of diseases. *Prana* may also be transmitted as a spiritualistic healing force by the laying on of hands and connecting one's mind with "the cosmic power of god." It should be obvious that Hatha Yoga promises more than supple limbs and relief from tension. Yoga's ultimate purpose is union with Brahman and acquiring the resultant peace and harmony which Hindus believe comes from such God-realization. The supposed consequence of this achievement is the complete cessation of sickness, evil, stress, and domination of the spirit by the body. In this state, perfect souls may then unite immortally with God.

Such goals are certainly admirable. But are they attainable? The answer is no when they are compared to a Bible-based view of God, man, and the concept of union with God. Scripture teaches that a chasm of sin separates man from his Creator. This gulf can only be spanned by an act of reconciliation to God through believing in the death of his Son. Any attempt to merge or unite one's consciousness with an "Ultimate Reality" would encounter the sin barrier and thus be thwarted. It is not the human merit of ascetic disciplines that brings one harmony with God. It is by the blood of Christ that the partition of Adam's disobedience is eradicated. Faith in the saving power of that blood can bring true union with God and his will.

Yoga advocates are certainly to be admired for their devotion to healthy bodies. Many who strenuously oppose the religious overtones of yoga are themselves gluttonous specimens of the junk-food syndrome. All too many people consume inordinate amounts of coffee, sweets, and soft drinks. These individuals are certainly going to find some immediate physical benefits in yoga. Care for one's physique is important, but not at the risk of aligning oneself with pagan principles. The popularity of yoga presents a formidable challenge to Christians who ought to make their bodies a welcome place for the Holy Spirit to reside (1 Cor. 3:16-17; 6:19-20).

Founder: No specific person can be designated. The principles and practices of yoga developed as ascetic and physical means to achieve the spiritual purposes of Hinduism.

Text: The Hindu *Vedic* scriptures provide the theological and philosophical basis for yoga's presuppositions.

Symbol: None.

Appeal: Man has become a victim of his modern diet. Obesity and a sedentary life-style have become an increasing focus of concern for those who value their health and physical appearance. Yoga seems like an exotic and less strenuous way of restoring youthful vigor.

Purpose: Its original intent as a variant of Hinduism was to achieve spiritual union with the impersonal Supreme Absolute deity. It may be argued that most Westerners derive its physical benefits without entanglement in such theological premises. However, there is always the possibility that one may be drawn to experiment with the deeper stages, which are distinctly religious in nature. The book *Yoga, Youth and Reincarnation* states, "Yoga is accomplished when the individual spirit merges with the Universal Spirit [God] in a spirit of oneness."

Errors: It is poor logic to assume that commitment to a religious system of approach to false gods may be excused by divorcing part of the system from its ultimate aim (i.e., doing yoga exercises for physical reasons independent of their intended integration into a methodology of spiritual merit by "works"). The Christian's concept of peace with God is based on reconciliation to the Lord, not union with a Brahmanistic pantheon. Spiritual favor and righteousness come from what Christ has done for us (Eph. 2:8-9), not the positions we do for him. Yoga ultimately strives for the deification of man and his spiritual enlightenment. It also promises release from the endless cycles of reincarnation, an unbiblical teaching.

Background Sources: Swami Vishnudevananda, *The Complete Illustrated Book of Yoga* (East Brunswick, N.J.: Bell, 1960); Jess Stearn, *Yoga, Youth and Reincarnation* (New York: Bantam, 1963); miscellaneous texts on yoga and Hinduism.

Address/Location: None specific. Yoga centers and teachers in most major cities.

See also Sri Chinmoy.

CULT

INFORMATION

RESOURCES

It would be impossible for any book to cover the entire scope of cultic activity. In addition, cults are proliferating, and each day brings news of another group bursting on the scene. Several organizations are dedicated to keeping watch on cult activities. These service agencies are generally very cooperative when requested to supply information regarding both newly formed and already established cults.

Answers in Action (was CARIS)
P. O. Box 2067
Costa Mesa, CA 92626

Bob Larson Ministries
P. O. Box 36480
Denver, CO 80236

Christian Apologetics: Research and Information Service
P. O. Box 1659
Milwaukee, WI 53201
(414) 771-7379

Christian Research Institute
P. O. Box 500
San Juan Capistrano, CA 92693

Cult Awareness Network
2421 Pratt Blvd.
Suite 1173
Chicago, IL 60645

Jesus People USA
4707 N. Malden
Chicago, IL 60640
(312) 989-2080

Personal Freedom Outreach
P. O. Box 26062
St. Louis, MO 63136
(314) 383-2648

Religion Analysis Service
2708 E. Lake St., Suite 231
Minneapolis, MN 55406
(612) 722-4463

Spiritual Counterfeits Project
P. O. Box 4308
Berkeley, CA 94704

Watchman Fellowship
P. O. Box 7681
Columbus, GA 31908
(404) 576-4321

RECOMMENDED READING

The books listed below represent sources of information concerning cults for the reader who wishes to investigate more thoroughly a particular group or teaching. Not all are written from an evangelical perspective.

Adair, James R., and Ted Miller, eds. *We Found Our Way Out.* Grand Rapids: Baker Book House, 1964. A Christian book containing testimonies of people who have come out of cults such as Mormonism, Jehovah's Witnesses, Christian Science, Armstrongism, Rosicrucianism, Humanism, Theosophy, Agnosticism, and Communism.

The Agency for Cultural Affairs. *Japanese Religions: A Survey.* Tokyo: Kodansha International, 1972 and 1981. A non-Christian book distributed by The Agency for Cultural Affairs in Japan discussing all of the major religions popular in Japan today. Included are the different sects of Buddhism, Hinduism, and Shintoism, as well as Christian groups that have followings in Japan. An excellent secular resource reference book.

Amano, J. Yutaka, and Norman L. Geisler. *The Infiltration of the New Age.* Wheaton, Ill.: Tyndale House, 1989. An insightful look at New Age thought and how it has permeated our society.

Anderson, Einar. *The Inside Story of Mormonism.* Grand Rapids: Kregel, 1973. A Christian approach to Mormonism. The author shares his own testimony of how he left the Mormon Church and became a Christian. Mormon history and Mormon doctrine are discussed from a Christian perspective with biblical answers.

Anderson, J. N. D. *Christianity and Comparative Religions.* Downers Grove, Ill.: Intervarsity, 1970. A Christian book discussing comparative religions and Christianity. It does not deal with specific religions.

——. *The World's Religions.* Grand Rapids: Eerdmans, 1975. Anderson has edited this compilation of articles on the major world religions: Judaism, Islam, Hinduism, Buddhism, Shintoism, and Confucianism. It includes religions of pre-literary society and concludes with a Christian approach to comparative religions.

Benware, Paul N. *Ambassadors of Armstrongism.* Nutley, N.J.: Presbyterian and Reformed, 1977. A Christian approach to Armstrongism, including a brief history of the World-wide Church of God and a summary of the teachings of the Worldwide Church of God on Scripture, God, the Holy Spirit, Christ, angels, man, sin, salvation, the church, and eschataology.

Berry, Gerald L. *Religions of the World.* New York: Barnes and Noble, 1956.

Bjornstad, James. *Counterfeits at Your Door.* Ventura, Calif.: Gospel Light, 1979. From a Christian perspective, cult expert Jim Bjornstad examines the teachings and proselytizing efforts of the Jehovah's Witnesses and the Mormons.

————. *The Moon Is Not the Sun.* Minneapolis: Bethany Fellowship, 1976. A Christian treatment of the Unification Church of Sun Myung Moon. It contains good documentation on the major teachings of the Unification Church and some advice on how to witness to a Moonie.

Boa, Kenneth. *Cults, World Religions, and You.* Wheaton, Ill.: Scripture Press, 1977. A short introduction to all the major religions and cults from a Christian perspective. Discusses non-Christian religions of the East, pseudo-Christian religions of the West, occult religious systems, and new religions and cults. A brief but adequate introduction to cults and religions.

Breese, David. *Know the Mark of the Cults.* Wheaton, Ill.: Victor, 1980.

Burks, Thompson. *Religions of the World.* Cincinnati: Standard, 1972. This book is good to use in an adult education, or Sunday school class situation. It is divided into thirteen chapters which can be combined for a ten-week session of lessons. Includes good study outlines and discusses Judaism, Islam, Hinduism, Buddhism, and primitive religions.

Chang, Lit-sen. *Zen-Existentialism: The Spiritual Decline of the West.* Nutley, N.J.: Presbyterian and Reformed, 1969. An extensive, in-depth treatment of Zen Buddhism and Christianity from a biblical perspective.

Conway, Flo and Jim Siegelman. *Snapping.* Philadelphia: J. B. Lippincott, 1978.

Cowan, Marvin W. *Mormon Claims Answered.* Salt Lake City: Published by the author, 1975. A good technical treatment of the origin and history of Mormonism, its doctrines concerning God and the Bible, and a very careful study of the Book of Mormon. It also has an extensive section on salvation from the orthodox Christian point of view.

Dencher, Ted. *Why I Left Jehovah's Witnesses.* Fort Washington, Penn.: Christian Literature Crusade, 1966. An excellent book on the doctrines of Jehovah's Witnesses and the internal workings of the organization, including the testimony of Dencher, who used to be a Jehovah's Witness. This is a good book for a Christian to study, but since its tone is somewhat sarcastic, it would not be wise to share it with a Jehovah's Witness.

Drummond, Richard H. *Gautama the Buddha: An Essay in Religious Understanding.* Grand Rapids: Eerdmans, 1974. A lengthy treatment of the life and teachings of Buddha from a Christian perspective. It also deals with the general concepts of Eastern thought.

Edwards, Christopher. *Crazy for God: The Nightmare of Cult Life.* Englewood Cliffs, N.J.: Prentice-Hall, 1979. The testimony and life history of a young man who joined the Unification Church. He explores the time he spent as a Moonie, the deprogramming he went through, and his final release from the cult, although not necessarily from a Christian point of view.

Elkins, Chris. *Heavenly Deception.* Wheaton, Ill.: Tyndale House, 1980. The testimony of a man who was raised a Christian but joined the Unification Church. After being a Moonie for some time he was freed from the bondage he had experienced in this cult.

Enroth, Ronald. *The Lure of the Cults.* Chappaqua, N.Y.: Christian Herald Books, 1979. An extension of Enroth's other book, *Youth, Brainwashing and the Extremist Cults.* Instead of dealing systematically with individual cults, he explores the sociological and psychological characteristics of cults and explains how to help someone who is in a cult.

————. *Youth, Brainwashing, and the Extremist Cults.* Grand Rapids: Zondervan, 1977. An introduction to a sociologist's view of the cults. Case histories are presented along with a discussion of characteristics of cultic activity from a Christian perspective.

Evans, Christopher. *Cults of Unreason.* New York: Dell, 1973. A non-Christian book which deals with some of the more mystical and pseudo-scientific cults. Most of the book is devoted to a study of Scientology, and is considered to be the best current treatment of this cult from a non-Christian perspective.

Fraser, Gordon H. *Is Mormonism Christian?* Chicago: Moody, 1977. An old book that has been consistently updated. It treats all the major doctrines of Mormonism from a Christian point of view, including the restoration of the church, the Mormon genealogy, Mormons and God, Mormons and Jesus Christ, Mormons and the Holy Spirit, Mormon doctrine of man, the priesthood, Mormons and baptism, Mormons and baptism for the dead, salvation, the lost tribes of Israel, and the sects of Mormonism.

————. *The Sects of the Latter-day Saints.* Eugene, Ore.: Industrial Litho, 1978. From a Christian perspective, this book deals with the major sects of the Latter-day Saints, especially the Reorganized Church of Jesus Christ of Latter Day Saints. It also analyzes the different polygamous sects of Mormonism.

Garabedian, John H., and Orde Coombs. *Eastern Religions in the Electric Age.* New York: Grosset and Dunlap, Workman, 1969.

Geisler, Norman. *False Gods of Our Time.* Eugene, Ore.: Harvest House Publishers, 1985. Excellent analysis of atheism, pantheism, polytheism, and other anti-Christian philosophies that provide the theological background for most cults.

Great Religions of the World. Washington: National Geographic, 1971.

Gruss, Edmond Charles. *Apostles of Denial: An Examination and Exposé of the History, Doctrines, and Claims of the Jehovah's Witnesses.* Grand Rapids: Baker Book House, 1978. The best-documented treatment of the Jehovah's Witnesses from a Christian point of view. Gruss, who was a Jehovah's Witness himself, includes his own testimony at the end of the book.

————. *Cults and the Occult.* Phillipsburg, N.J.: Presbyterian and Reformed, 1980. A brief study meant to be used in an adult education or Bible class situation. It deals with Jehovah's Witnesses, Mormons, Christian Scientists, Unity, Armstrongism, Spiritualism, Astrology, Bahaism, Rosicrucianism, Ouija boards, Edgar Cayce, the Unification Church, and concludes with a Christian perspective on the cults and the occult.

————. *The Jehovah's Witnesses and Prophetic Speculation.* Nutley, N.J.: Presbyterian and Reformed, 1972. This thoroughly documented book deals specifically with the Jehovah's Witnesses' propagation of false prophecies regarding the end of the world.

————. *We Left the Jehovah's Witnesses—A Non-Prophet Organization.* Nutley, N.J.: Presbyterian and Reformed Co., 1974. Testimonies of ex-Jehovah's Witnesses showing how to leave the Watch Tower Society and truly be born again.

Hefley, James C. *The Youth-Nappers.* Wheaton, Ill.: Scripture Press, 1977. A brief Christian review of some new cults such as Unification Church, Hare Krishna, Divine Light Mission, TM, Children of God, and others.

Hesselgrave, David J., ed. *Dynamic Religious Movements*. Grand Rapids: Baker Book House, 1978. An excellent Christian book, discussing cultic religions in other countries. The first section is on Africa, the second on Europe, the third on the Far East, the fourth on the Mideast, the fifth on North America, the sixth on South America, and the seventh on Southeast Asia.

Heydt, Henry J. *A Comparison of World Religions*. Fort Washington, Penn.: Christian Literature Crusade, 1967. A historical survey dealing with Judaism, Christianity, Hinduism, Zoroastrianism, Shintoism, Taoism, Jainism, Buddhism, Confucianism, Islam and Sikhism. Chapter three gives a topical comparison of all these groups, and chapter four shows the distinctive superiority of Christianity.

Hoekema, Anthony A. *The Four Major Cults*. Grand Rapids: Eerdmans, 1963. A classic work on the major cults such as Jehovah's Witnesses, Mormonism, and Christian Science.

————. *Christian Science*. Grand Rapids: Eerdmans, 1974. Taken from *The Four Major Cults* and extensively updated.

————. *Jehovah's Witnesses*. Grand Rapids: Eerdmans, 1974. Taken from *The Four Major Cults* and extensively updated.

————. *Mormonism*. Grand Rapids: Eerdmans, 1974. Taken from *The Four Major Cults* and extensively updated.

Hopkins, Joseph. *The Armstrong Empire*. Grand Rapids: Eerdmans, 1974. A Christian perspective on Herbert W. Armstrong and the Worldwide Church of God. It deals extensively with the background of Armstrong and the Church and includes a brief survey of WCG doctrines.

Hunt, Dave. *The Cult Explosion*. Eugene, Oreg.: Harvest House, 1980. A thoroughly scriptural, psychological, and sociological perspective on the rise of the cults. Some of the topics covered are: altered states of consciousness, the ultimate lie, beyond morality, authoritarianism and responsibility, spirit communication and the battle for the mind. This book does not deal with cults individually or in a systematic way.

Kemperman, Steve. *Lord of the Second Advent: A Rare Look Inside the Terrifying World of the Moonies*. Ventura, Calif.: Regal, 1981. An excellent testimony of a young man who joined the Moonies. He describes his experiences of being deprogrammed twice, and how he finally came to be released from the cult, finding peace with Christ.

Larson, Bob. *Straight Answers on the New Age*. Nashville, Tenn.: Thomas Nelson, Inc., Publishers, 1989. Everything you need to know about the New Age Movement is documented in this comprehensive volume written by one of the world's foremost experts on New Age thought.

Lewis, Gordon R. *Confronting the Cults*. Grand Rapids: Baker Book House, 1966. A standard reference work on the major cults, including Jehovah's Witnesses, Mormonism, Christian Science, Unity, and Spiritualism. From a Christian perspective, Lewis provides theological answers to cultic claims.

————. *What Everyone Should Know about Transcendental Meditation*. Ventura, Calif.: Regal Books, 1975. A brief treatment of Transcendental Meditation from a Christian perspective.

Marsh, C. R. *Share Your Faith with a Muslim*. Chicago: Moody, 1975. A perspective on Islam, giving its history, doctrines, and explaining how to share Christ with a Muslim.

Martin, Walter, ed. *Walter Martin's Cults Reference Bible*. Santa Ana, Calif.: Vision House, 1981. A unique volume, explaining the texts of the Old and New Testaments (King James Version) used by the major cults in support of their own teachings. Martin gives the cultic misinterpretation and the biblical Christian response to each passage. Also included are essays on all of the major cults, charts comparing the teachings of the major cults, a dictionary of terms used by the cults, a brief essay on interpreting the Bible, and biblical helps for those witnessing to the cults.

———. *Jehovah of the Watchtower.* Minneapolis: Bethany House, 1982. A re-release of Martin's classic on the Jehovah's Witnesses, originally published by Moody. Martin deals with the history and doctrines of Jehovah's Witnesses and provides biblical responses to each of its major doctrines.

———. *The Kingdom of the Cults.* Minneapolis: Bethany House, 1975. This is the classic Christian volume on the major traditional cults. A 1982 edition is completely updated with current documentation.

———. *The Maze of Mormonism.* Santa Ana, Calif.: Vision House Publishers, 1978. An expansive revision of Martin's 1962 classic by the same title is perhaps the best Christian treatment of the major teachings of Mormonism.

———. *The New Cults.* Santa Ana, Calif.: Vision House, 1980. An excellent treatment of some newer cults. The history of each cult and its leader is discussed along with each individual belief in the areas of God, Jesus Christ, man, salvation, and Scripture. Cults covered include: The Way International, Hinduism, est, the Children of God, The Ascended Masters, Silva Mind Control, Church of the Living Word, and Foundation of Human Understanding.

———. *The Rise of the Cults.* Santa Ana, Calif.: Vision House, 1980. A revision and update of the 1955 classic. Condensed from *The Kingdom of the Cults.*

McElveen, Floyd C. *The Mormon Illusion.* Ventura, Calif.: Regal, 1977. A traditional Christian treatment of Mormonism, discussing Mormon history, sacred scriptures, and major doctrines.

Means, Pat. *The Mystical Maze.* San Bernardino, Calif.: Campus Crusade for Christ, 1976 (out of print).

Melton, J. Gordon. *The Encyclopedia of American Religions.* 2 Vols. Wilmington, N.C.: McGrath, 1978.

Miller, Calvin. *Transcendental Hesitation.* Grand Rapids: Zondervan, 1977. An in-depth treatment of Transcendental Meditation, with discussion of Eastern mysticism compared to a biblical worldview.

Miller, Elliot. *Crash Course on the New Age Movement.* Grand Rapids, Mich.: Baker Book House, 1989. Penetrates New Age vocabulary, discusses crystals, channeling, claims of the New Age Movement, New Age science, examines *The Aquarian Conspiracy,* looks at holism versus reductionism, and provides Christian answers.

Miller, William McElwee. *The Bahai Faith: Its History and Teaching.* South Pasadena, Calif.: William Carey Library, 1974. The best book in the English language from a Christian perspective on the Bahai faith.

———. *Ten Muslims Meet Christ.* Grand Rapids: Eerdmans, 1969. Testimonies of Muslims who have accepted Christ, and a description of the persecution they have suffered in their native Muslim lands.

Milmine, George E. *The Life of Mary Baker G. Eddy and the History of Christian Science.* Grand Rapids: Baker Book House, 1909 and 1937. A classic biography of Mary Baker Eddy, explaining how she developed her cult by taking the teachings of Christian Science from previous writers and thinkers.

Morey, Robert. *How to Answer a Jehovah's Witness.* Minneapolis: Bethany Fellowship, 1980.

———. *Reincarnation and Christianity.* Minneapolis: Bethany House, 1980. An excellent treatment of reincarnation with biblical answers. Written for Morey's doctrinal treatise, it displays good scholarship and documentation.

Needleman, Jacob. *The New Religion.* New York: E. P. Dutton, 1970. A non-Christian review of the main teachings of major religions as well as some of the new cults. The section of Zen Buddhism is particularly good.

Palmer, Bernard. *Understanding the Islamic Explosion.* Beaverlodge, Alberta: Horizon

House, 1980. A Christian perspective on Islam, the Middle East problems (e.g. oil embargo), and how they relate to the Christian.

Passantino, Robert and Gretchen. *Answers to the Cultists at Your Door.* Eugene, Ore.: Harvest House, 1981. An excellent treatment of the five major cults Christians may encounter at the door of their homes or in public places. It deals with Jehovah's Witnesses, Mormons, Moonies, Hare Krishna, and The Way International. In addition, the book discusses the reasons for cults, characteristics of cultists and cult leaders, how to protect loved ones from the cults, and biblical responses to the major claims of each of these cults.

Petersen, William J. *Those Curious New Cults.* New Canaan, Conn.: Keats, 1975. An evangelical treatment of some major new cults, as well as Spiritualism, Witchcraft, Satanism, and Astrology. A brief section on Scientology is included.

Rawlings, Maurice S. *Life Wish (Reincarnation: Reality or Hoax?).* Nashville: Thomas Nelson, 1981. A Christian perspective on the major teachings of reincarnation contrasted with biblical truth.

Reisser, Paul C. and Teri K., and John Weldon. *New Age Medicine.* Downers Grove, Ill.: InterVarsity Press, 1987. Originally published as *The Holistic Healer.* A Christian perspective on New Age medicine: Holistic health, reflexology, acupuncture, popular theories in New Age medicine. A checklist of what to watch for in a neighborhood healer.

Richardson, Don. *Eternity in Their Hearts.* Ventura, Calif.: Regal, 1981. A good perspective on the biblical view of the origin of religion, including folk religions from preliterate societies.

Ridenour, Fritz. *So What's the Difference?* Ventura, Calif.: Regal, 1967 and 1979. A brief introduction to some of the major religions and cults, including Buddhism, Mormonism, Unitarianism, Roman Catholicism, Christian Science, Protestantism, Jehovah's Witnesses, Islam, Hinduism, and Judaism. This book is especially compiled to work well in adult education.

Rosten, Leo. *Religions in America.* New York: Simon and Schuster, 1963. A standard non-Christian review of the major cults and religions in the United States; however, since the articles were contributed by each group, religion, or cult concerned, the teachings represented are not necessarily objective.

Rudin, James and Marcia. *Prison or Paradise?* Philadelphia: Fortress, 1980.

Shah, Douglas. *The Meditators.* Plainfield, N.J.: Logos, 1975. A popular Christian treatment of Transcendental Meditation, mysticism, Zen, yoga, and other Eastern movements and religions.

Smith, Houston. *The Religions of Man.* New York: Harper and Row, 1958. A classic, brief treatment of the major world religions from a non-Christian point of view.

Sparks, Jack. *The Mind Benders.* Nashville: Thomas Nelson, 1979. A church historian's point of view of the Unification Church, The Way, Children of God, Transcendental Meditation, Divine Light Mission, Hare Krishna, and The People's Temple. Sparks is a conservative evangelical Christian who uses the writings of the early church and the creeds of the church councils (along with the Old and New Testaments) to refute the major teachings of these cults.

Spittler, Russell P. *Cults and Isms.* Grand Rapids: Baker Book House, 1962. An old but still useful book on some of the major cults, including Mormonism, Spiritualism, Christian Science, Jehovah's Witnesses, Unity, Theosophy, Bahaism, Zen Buddhism, Anglo-Israelism, Astrology, Father Divine, Rosicrucianism, Swedenborgianism, Modernism, Humanism, Unitarianism, Universalism, liberalism, and neo-orthodoxy.

Stoner, Carroll, and Jo Anne Parke. *All God's Children.* Radnor, Penn.: Chilton, 1977. Written by two journalists, this book is a non-Christian observation of people involved in some of the new cults. It explains the teachings of new cults and why they may be dangerous for young people.

Strohmer, Charles. *What Your Horoscope Doesn't Tell You.* Wheaton, Ill.: Tyndale House, 1988. A biblical response to the confused world of astrology.

Sumrall, Lester. *Where Was God When Pagan Religions Began?* Nashville: Thomas Nelson, 1980. A discussion of the biblical texts related to the rise of world religions, with biblical responses to the major tenets of these faiths.

Tanenbaum, Marc H., Marvin R. Wilson, and A. James Rudin., eds. *Evangelicals and Jews in Conversation on Scripture, Theology, and History.* Grand Rapids: Baker Book House, 1978. An objective portrayal of the differences between Judaism and Christianity, especially between modern Judaism and evangelical Christianity. This is a very good resource book, using the format of a conversational interchange.

Tucker, Ruth A. *Another Gospel.* Grand Rapids, Mich.: Zondervan Publishing House, 1989. Evangelical perspective on fifteen of the largest and most dangerous cults, plus twenty-one smaller but equally critical cults.

Weldon, John. *The Transcendental Explosion.* Irvine, Calif.: Harvest House, 1976. An excellent, in-depth research treatment on the history and teachings of Transcendental Meditation.

Weldon, John, and Clifford Wilson. *Occult Shock and Psychic Forces.* San Diego: Master Books, 1980.

White, Mel. *Deceived.* Old Tappan, N.J.: Fleming H. Revell, 1979. A Christian analysis of The People's Temple in Guyana, explaining how such a tragedy could happen and how to watch out for other groups that may be similar.

Williams, J. L. *Victor Paul Wierwille and The Way International.* Chicago: Moody, 1979. The best single volume treatment of the history and teachings of The Way International, with a biblical response.

Yamamoto, J. Isamu. *The Puppet Master.* Downers Grove, Ill.: Intervarsity, 1977. An appraisal of the teachings of the Unification Church with a biblical response. Yamamoto especially emphasizes a sociological perspective.

INDEX

489

INDEX

491

497